THE FEMINIST BOOKSTORE MOVEMENT

THE FEMINIST BOOKSTORE MOVEMENT

LESBIAN ANTIRACISM AND FEMINIST ACCOUNTABILITY

KRISTEN HOGAN

DUKE UNIVERSITY PRESS / DURHAM AND LONDON / 2016

Library of Congress Cataloging-in-Publication Data
Names: Hogan, Kristen, [date] author.
Title: The feminist bookstore movement : lesbian antiracism and
feminist accountability / Kristen Hogan.
Description: Durham : Duke University Press, 2016. | Includes
bibliographical references and index.
Identifiers: LCCN 2015033350|
ISBN 9780822361107 (hardcover : alk. paper) |
ISBN 9780822361299 (pbk. : alk. paper) |
ISBN 9780822374336 (e-book)
Subjects: LCSH: Lesbian feminism—United States—History—
20th century. Women's bookstores—United States—History—
20th century. | Feminist literature—United States—History—20th
century. | Anti-racism—United States—History—20th century.
Classification: LCC GQ75.6. U5 H64 2016 | DDC
381/.450020820973—dc23
LC record available at http://lccn.loc.gov/2015033350

Cover art: Darlene Pagano, Elizabeth Summers, Keiko Kubo,
and Jesse Meredith at ICI: A Woman's Place (Oakland, CA), 1982.
Image courtesy Lesbian Herstory Archives.

To Mill, every moment.

CONTENTS

A photo gallery appears after page 106

ACKNOWLEDGMENTS

This book, and my research and writing of it, has been a practice of relationship building and feminist love. In these nearly ten years of research, conversations, and writing, I have been learning in dialogue with colleagues and loved ones how to read this work, these relationships, ethically, with feminist accountability and love. These interconnections have enacted this telling of how feminist bookwomen's histories do shape our feminist futures and provide a framework for understanding and creating ethical relationships today.

A network of supporters have advocated for, encouraged, and challenged me in this work. For sustaining visits, food, conversation, and love, I am grateful to Ruthann Lee and Anne-Marie Estrada, Alison Kafer and Dana Newlove, Rachael Wilder, Lynn Hoare, Kevin Lamb and Shane Seger, Jennifer Suchland and Shannon Winnubst, Wura Ogunji, Janet Romero, Jee Davis, Kathy and Becky Liddle, and Megan Alrutz and Daniel Armendariz. For all of this and helping think through the title, thank you to Linc Allen and Jennifer Watts. Zahra Jacobs, incomparable friend, bookwoman, and activist, has generously revisited our time together at the Toronto Women's Bookstore, and how we are shaped by a larger history of bookwomen, in countless conversations over oceans, pizza slices, and holidays; and to you I am grateful, as always, for important perspective (and for reminding me that if I don't let this book go I'll just keep rewriting it). My writing sister and dear friend Megan Alrutz has seen this book through with our nourishing ritual of food and writing and with a book of her own; your invitation back into embodied feminist practice changed my every day for the better, and this writing would not have survived without your love and our sister books. Thank you to Kevin Lamb for impeccably timed savvy and loving strategy support, around this book and throughout our lives. I am grateful to Lisa C. Moore for our energetic and nourishing conversations about the book industry and her vital work running RedBone Press. Abe Louise Young and her women's writing workshop made space for me to explore the writer I wanted to become. In 2006 I defended my dissertation; in these past nearly ten years, Ann Cvetkovich, codirector of my dissertation, has believed in this book. Her unwavering faith and generous encouragement made it possible to take the dissertation apart, conduct new research, and make this book. The book no longer resembles the dissertation except in my debt and gratitude to her. Though this book is no longer the dissertation, I am grateful to my dissertation committee for supporting the beginnings of this work. My committee members were codirectors Ann Cvetkovich and Joanna Brooks, Carol MacKay, Dana Cloud, Lisa L. Moore, and Michael Winship. I am grateful to Joanna Brooks for being the first person to say yes to this project. For patiently asking after the book all this time, and for all of the love and work of these years, I appreciate my parents, Eileen and Michael Hogan.

Throughout these ten years, I have benefited from public opportunities to think through this work. My thanks to the bookwomen who gathered at the 2006 National Women's Studies Association and to the Ford Foundation and the Astraea Foundation for Lesbian Justice for funding that Feminist Bookstore Network gathering, to the Ontario Institute for Studies in Education Center for Women's Studies in Education for inviting Anjula Gogia and me to talk together about our work in and analysis of feminist bookstores as part of their popular feminism lectures, to Janet Romero for inviting me to read from this work as part of an event at the 2009 Toronto Women's Bookstore (TWB) Annual Customer Appreciation Day BBQ and Book Sale and to facilitate an engaged workshop with TWB staff on the bookstore and feminist bookpeople's literary activism, and to the Center for Lesbian and Gay Studies 2010 conference "In Amerika They Call Us Dykes: Lesbian Lives in the 70s" for inviting me to present about this work and for supporting me with a travel grant.

I owe a deep gratitude to Courtney Berger for her generous reading and incisive suggestions throughout the writing of this book; her collaboration made this writing and revision a transformative and often pleasurable journey. Two anonymous reviewers took the time to read and reread the manuscript and to offer thorough comments that made the book better. I am grateful for their careful attention to feminist histories. So many people at Duke University Press have collaborated to make this book possible and are continuing to work on connecting it with readers; I appreciate all of you. Thanks especially to Christine Riggio, Jessica Ryan, Martha Ramsey, Chris Robinson, and Chad Royal.

This book remains in conversation with bookwomen, publishers, and authors who agreed to talk with me, on the record, about their lives and work. Carol Seajay, talking with you still feels like talking with a rock star—who shares her glory: your work did change my life. To Susan Post, thank you for giving me my start as a bookwoman and for sharing your stories, your humor, your wisdom, and yourself. Included in these pages are small pieces of wonderful and brave remembrances shared with me by Anjula Gogia, Barbara Smith, Carol Seajay, Dawn Lundy Martin, Eleanor Olds Batchelder, Esther Vise, Gilda Bruckman, Janet Romero, Johanna Brenner, Joni Seager, Karyn London, Kate Rushin, Kay Turner, Kit Quan, Laura Zimmerman, Lynn McClory, Matt Richardson, May Lui, Nina Wouk, Patti Kirk, Pell, Rita Arditti, Sharon Bridgforth, Sharon Fernandez, Susan Post, and Zahra Jacobs. Interviews with bookwomen, publishers, and authors not included in this version of the book have informed my understandings of this history and include: Andrea Dworkin, Catherine Sameh, Els Debbaut, Johncy Mundo, Karen Umminger, Kronda Adair, Michelle Sewell, Minnie Bruce Pratt, Myrna Goldware, Paul Lauter, Paulette Rose, Sally Eck, Sarah Dougher, Sue Burns, Susan Brownmiller, and Wendy Cutler. In the epilogue I share some of my memories in relationship with Toronto bookfolks, including Zahra Jacobs, Ruthann Lee, Anne-Marie Estrada, Janet Romero, T———, Rose Kazi, OmiSoore Dryden, Alex MacFadyen, and Reena Katz. To all of these bookfolks, I hope that my version of this shared story honors your work and words.

Photographs of the bookwomen, bookstores, and movement moments make these histories more vivid. For photographing or archiving photographs of the movement, for digging through boxes in basements and closets, and for granting me permission to use the photographs in this book, I appreciate Anne Marie Menta at the Beinecke Rare Book and Manuscript Library, Carol Seajay, Diana Carey at the Schlesinger Library, Donna Gottschalk, Gilda Bruckman, JEB (Joan E. Biren), Jonathan Sillin, Kay Keys, May Lui, Saskia Scheffer and the Lesbian Herstory Archives, and Susan Post. I am grateful to former Toronto Women's Bookstore bookfolks for generously, and with good wishes, granting me permission to include May Lui's photo of the Bowlathon: Alex MacFadyen, Anjula Gogia, Jin Huh, Lorraine Hewitt, and Reena Katz. By including this photograph we also honor the memory of Clara Ho, her kind sprit, and her activist ethics. For granting permission to use film stills from their magical short *On the Shelf*, I appreciate Naomi Skoglund and Sara Zia Ebrahimi.

Archives and reference holdings of materials from the bookwomen, bookstores, and the movement make this history possible. I researched this history with the support of collections and archivists including the amazing and spiritually sustaining Lesbian Herstory Archives, with help from Archives coordinators Deborah Edel, Desiree Yael Vester, Rachel Corbman, and Saskia Scheffer; the San Francisco Public Library James C. Hormel Center Archives, where Tim Wilson made it possible to research the then uncataloged archives of the Feminist Bookstore Network; and the Schlesinger Library, with support from Anne Engelhart for research in the then uncataloged archives of New Words. Staff at the InterLibrary Services Department at the University of Texas Libraries generously fulfilled my requests to borrow volumes of the *Feminist Bookstore News*. And bookwomen invited me to visit precious archives in their storage rooms and file cabinets at bookstores that included BookWoman, with special thanks to Susan Post; In Other Words, with gratitude to Sue Burns; and the Toronto Women's Bookstore.

Essential expenses for this research were covered in part by the Center for Women's and Gender Studies at the University of Texas at Austin, where Susan Sage Heinzelman granted me research funds, and by the University of Texas Libraries, where Catherine Hamer and Jenifer Flaxbart granted me photograph permissions and scanning funds.

I met Milly Gleckler at the BookWoman book group in 1999, and, my love, we've lived almost all of our sixteen years (of never enough but as many years as I can possibly have, please) with this book-in-process. Thank you for reading, rereading, talking past midnight, and telling the truth. You make everyday life extraordinary. Steele Barile, this book has grown up with you; I have been lucky to get to live these years with your generous kindness and humor. I'm grateful to be family together. Our animal family members have made this work possible, too; for much-needed walks, sitting, and mental health, thank you to Vamp and Cosmos.

PREFACE
READING THE MAP
OF OUR BODIES

Warm in our Roxton Road flat, despite the snow outside, my partner and I lit candles, ate walnut cakes from Bloor Street, made collage visions of our futures, and tried to imagine how a faraway life could be possible. By that January of 2007, I had been comanager and book buyer at the Toronto Women's Bookstore for nine months. The previous manager of ten years, Anjula Gogia, had taken a fourteen-month leave of absence to consider a different life, so I had been preparing for the end of my contract by applying for faculty teaching positions. Jarring us out of our imaginings, my phone rang with an invitation for an on-site interview with the English Department of a state university in the US Deep South. My lover saw the danger in the southern city, in breathing in a geography so deeply steeped in systems of slavery and segregation that time folds in on itself in the grocery store, the hospital exam room, the classroom. Still, I agreed to deliver a job talk on my concept of the feminist shelf and how feminist bookstores had changed antiracist feminist alliance practices. I splashed feminist archival treasures onto the document camera: issues of the *Feminist Bookstore News*, Joni Seager's map of New Words book sections, and the typed script of Donna Fernandez's talk on behalf of Streelekha at the 1988 International Feminist Book Fair. To me, these moments wove together into a complex web of emotional-political alliances; this electric web wielded critical influence in both feminism and publishing. A faculty member's knitting clicked a soundtrack. As I ended the talk, one excited white woman professor in her fifties asked, "Would you consider starting a feminist bookstore here?" This is a question I have heard often during my years of writing this history. This woman, like the others who have asked, eager though she knew my answer would be no, was nostalgic; she wanted a feminist bookstore in her own city. This question, are you going to start a feminist bookstore, is only possible without holding the history I have learned and share in *The Feminist Bookstore Movement: Lesbian Antiracism and Feminist Accountability*. Bookwomen, primarily lesbians and including an important series of cohorts of women of color, in more than one hundred feminist bookstores in the 1970s, 1980s, and 1990s used the *Feminist Bookstore News* (FBN) to connect with each other locally and transnationally to attempt to hold each other accountable to lesbian antiracism as well as to ethical representation and relationships. Collective accountability on this scale is not possible within a single bookstore or even with a handful of feminist bookstores open in North America. With this book I hope to redefine feminist bookstores in public memory, to remember feminist bookwomen's difficult work grappling with and participating in defining lesbian antiracism and feminist accountability. This history offers us a legacy, vocabulary, and strategy for today's feminisms.

It had taken me years to get to an interview with bookwoman, activist, and author Kit Quan. In 2004 I read her memorial remembrance of Gloria Anzaldúa. She wrote, "I met Gloria in 1978. I was a sixteen-year-old runaway working at Old Wives' Tales Bookstore on Valencia at 16th Street in San Francisco. She was attending a Feminist Writer's Guild meeting in the back of the store and came up to the counter to thank me for keeping the store open."[1] Sitting in Old Wives' Tales and FBN founder Carol Seajay's kitchen in 2003 for my first interview with a bookwoman, I had asked, "How many women were in the collective?" Definitely a first-interview kind of question. Seajay listed the women, counted on her fingers Paula Wallace, Jill Limerick, then Sherry Thomas after Wallace left: "And then we also had this young woman who was the best friend of my foster daughter. Who, actually, from the first summer the store was open, came in and started volunteering, and then we started paying her. . . . She was an immigrant from Hong Kong, and was having a hard time, wanted to get a job. . . . What do you do with this fifteen-year-old little dykelet? Well, of course."[2] I didn't know then that the best friend was Kit Quan, and I hadn't asked. It was only when I showed up at an allgo: texas statewide queer people of color organization memorial for Gloria Anzaldúa and picked up the remembrance booklet that I recognized this story. If you count from the time I heard about her without asking for more in Seajay's interview, it took me three years to make it to that interview with Quan. The wait counts out a history of distance between white bookwomen and bookwomen of color, a history of distance among bookwomen who each risked everything to imagine a nonhierarchical lesbian feminist antiracist organization and lived to tell the tale. The wait counts out my years of white privilege, even though my lesbian self identity offers (but does not guarantee) an understanding of oppression.[3] During the wait, I worked toward (and am still working toward) learning white antiracism. By respecting, listening to, and honoring the lives and stories of women of color, I learned different versions of this feminist bookstore history. The story in my dissertation was much more white. The four years it took me to write the dissertation were not enough for me to learn how to read for and with women of color in the movement, to build trust with women of color in the movement, to learn to ask good questions, to listen well. This book is an entirely new document, a new story from the bookwomen. The wait taught me, should teach us, that this story is still partial. And lives are at stake.

With 130 feminist bookstores at the height of their transnational movement, bookwomen were learning with and accountable to each other.[4] With over thirty years of a core of active feminist bookstores connected for most of those years through the *Feminist Bookstore News* (1976–2000), bookwomen attempted to sustain feminist dialogue during significant changes in capitalism and feminism. *The Feminist Bookstore Movement* is a history of feminist relational practices and how feminist movements develop new vocabularies; it contributes to contemporary activist and academic feminist thought and practice both by inviting readers to reconsider the role of lesbian antiracist thought and participation in 1970s through 2000s feminism and by sharing feminist bookwomen's vocabularies and histories for building lesbian antiracist feminist alliances. When bookwomen gathered in 1976 to record their vision for the movement, they included their intention to become both "revolutionaries . . . in a capitalist system" and "accountable to our communities and to each other."[5] The title of this book identifies what I see as the key theoretical interventions of feminist bookwomen. Bookwomen's unique attention to and relationships with questions of representation, voice, and appropriation in literature, combined with their own heavily documented work at relationships among local collectives and bookwomen in a transnational network, generate a complex theory and history of lesbian antiracism and feminist accountability.

This book provides a vital historical thread that supports the work of today's feminists toward reading and relating with each other more ethically. Accountability remains at the core of feminist negotiations, from social media conversations, including #SolidarityIsForWhiteWomen, which emphasizes the double standard of mainstream feminism with a focus on feminist media that reifies white women and scrutinizes women of color; to ongoing conversations among women of color and Indigenous women, including Bonita Lawrence and Enakshi Dua, on the relationships between diaspora and settler colonialism; to #BlackLivesMatter, created by Alicia Garza, Patrisse Cullors, and Opal Tometi, and consistent public erasure of the hashtag's foundation in Black queer feminism. Discussions of hashtag feminism focus on how feminists talk about and hold each other accountable to antiracism and queer justice. #SolidarityIsForWhiteWomen author Mikki Kendall recognizes that ending these systems of oppression requires "true solidarity and community building." Her hashtag addresses "how White the narrative around feminism is, and how that Whiteness lends itself to the erasure of the problems specifically facing women of color." "True solidarity" would, she says, "make it impossible for these same conversations to be happening 10 years from now, much less 100. In order for feminism to truly represent all women, it has to expand to include the concerns of a global population."[6] Susana Loza, writing in the open access journal *ada: A Journal of Gender, New Media, & Technology*, sees the work of social media feminists of color as drawing on a legacy from previous generations of activists of color working toward accountability: "Like their feminist predecessors of color, hashtag feminists have found common ground and are beginning to build coalitions across profound cultural, racial, class, sex, gender, and power differences. The work is not easy but they realize the only way to make feminism less toxic is to 'actually end white supremacy, settler colonialism, capitalism and patriarchy.'"[7] This work of feminism, to build toward "true solidarity" through sometimes painful accountability, has a vibrant history visible through the action and dialogue at feminist bookstores.

Today's feminist frameworks for antiracism include calls that resonate with discussions among feminist bookwomen, including calls to interrupt settler colonialism and to ethically build dialogue with each other by accurately naming and witnessing history and present oppressions and visions for justice. Feminist theorists Bonita Lawrence and Enakshi Dua participate in this dialogue of feminist accountability as alliance building with attention to the exclusion of Indigenous people from antiracism.[8] Antiracist work that "ignores the ongoing colonization of Aboriginal peoples in the Americas," they argue, "participates in colonial agendas" by advocating for changes in the state without understanding Canada (Lawrence and Dua speak specifically to Canada, and this also applies to the United States) as a "colonialist state."[9] Addressing resistance to this argument, Ruthann Lee emphasizes the ethics of representation and dialogue when she points out that "struggles for Indigenous sovereignty must be recognized and respected as a practice of solidarity by antiracist scholars and activists."[10] Kendall similarly argues for dialogue and alliance building (in place of appropriation) by pointing out that feminist media must advocate for funding for "WOC [women of color] writing about the issues that impact them."[11] The movement-based reception of #BlackLivesMatter signals feminists' ongoing difficulties listening with each other and recognizing our complex identities. Alicia Garza observes that movement artists and activists have homogenized her and her coauthors' call to versions of "all lives matter." Describing the pain of this erasure, Garza writes, "We completely expect those who benefit directly and improperly from White supremacy to try and erase our existence. We fight that every day. But when it happens amongst our allies, we are baffled, we are saddened, and we are enraged. And it's time to have the political conversation about why that's not okay." The depth of #BlackLivesMatter calls for a recognition of its authorship by Black queer women and an articulation of the full reach of its meaning: "Black Lives Matter affirms the lives of Black queer and trans folks, disabled folks, Black-undocumented folks, folks with records, women and all Black lives along the gender spectrum. It centers those that have been marginalized within Black liberation movements. It is a tactic to (re)build the Black liberation movement."[12] These contemporary conversations among or with feminists signal the importance of continuing to reimagine what solidarity looks like for feminist futures; new understandings of feminist pasts support this reimagining. With this book I attempt to build dialogue with Lawrence and Dua, Lee, Kendall, and Garza along with works like M. Jacqui Alexander's *Pedagogies of Crossing* and Aimee Carillo Rowe's *Power Lines: On the Subject of Feminist Alliances* to contribute to a vocabulary and history toward more nuanced feminist alliances acknowledging how differences of race, sexuality, and geopolitical as well as socioeconomic status affect how we talk with each other, how we think about our selves and our futures.[13]

This connected history of the feminist bookstores redefines them not simply as places to find books but as organizations in which bookwomen worked together to develop ethical feminist reading practices that, in turn, informed relational practices. In 1976, the first two issues of the *Feminist Bookstores Newsletter* (which became the *Feminist Bookstore News*) included book lists of Spanish-language feminist books, books by and about Native American women, Black women, and young women.[14] By 1993, bookwomen were immersed in transnational discussions with Indigenous feminists about literary appropriation as cultural genocide. Along the way, feminist bookwomen circulated cassette tapes of Bernice Johnson Reagon's iconic talk about feminist coalition politics, shared books they were reading, and talked about incidents at their bookstore desks to raise difficult conversations within their collectives or staff and with their communities about how power operated within the bookstores and whether they could disrupt institutionalized oppressions including racism. Of course these conversations sometimes ended disastrously, painfully. Yet the process of having the conversations, sharing them through the FBN, and having them again was part of the commitment bookwomen had made to attempt feminist accountability to their communities and each other.

At the same time, feminist bookwomen faced a quickly changing book industry between 1970 through the late 1990s. Knowing the importance of feminist literacies to the movement, bookwomen strategized to get and keep feminist literature in print. In the United States, bookwomen led the national movement of independent bookstores to expose illegal and damaging practices of chain bookstores in connection with big publishing. The daily and movement-based conversations bookwomen had around feminist accountability prepared them for these interventions in the book and bookstore industries. Then in the 1990s, faced with economic pressures and independent bookstore closures, bookwomen changed how they talked about the bookstores: in what seemed a misplaced hope to save the bookstores, bookwomen began to frame the bookstores as feminist businesses more often than as movement-based sites of accountability. As remaining bookstores struggled for survival, the move from accountability to support gave rise to the Feminist Bookstore Network slogan "Support Your Local Feminist Bookstore, She Supports You."[15] The *Feminist Bookstore News* ceased publication in 2000; with the loss of this sustaining vehicle of accountability, and as the majority of feminist bookstores closed around that time, bookwomen continued to sound out this local call to support a bookstore, a feminist business. This image, frozen in time, seemed to erase from public memory the complex and necessary movement innovations of feminist bookwomen in their previous years.

Recent articles mourning the loss of feminist bookstores or encouraging readers to sustain the few remaining feminist bookstores rely on the once-vital and now anachronistic lists of feminist bookstores generated by the *Feminist Bookstore News*. At the height of the movement, these lists served as vital tools to leverage the power of more than one hundred feminist bookstores for bargaining with publishers and other industry institutions. Recent articles, rather than updating the definition of a feminist bookstore (as FBN did over its nearly three decades in print), list bookstores that were on the last of the FBN lists and include new bookstores only when they identify solely with the feminist movement. For example, movement bookstores like Resistencia Bookstore in Austin, Texas, considered a feminist, LGBTQ, Chican@, and Indigenous space by its caretakers, are not on these lists.[16] These articles also prioritize the bookstore rather than the activism of feminist bookwomen. While article authors claim that Internet sales make it "easier to buy feminist materials elsewhere," they remind readers that feminist bookstores stocked feminist literature and provided space for feminist organizing.[17] The real history of the work of the bookwomen, as feminist organizers in their own right, is much more radical. The FBN chronicles feminist bookwomen advocating for the publishing of feminist literature and working to keep books in print, not just carrying what publishers thought would sell but working to make feminist literature available. Feminist bookwomen did not stop there but worked together to build feminist literacy to make sense of feminist literature and of each other in conversation. Throughout all of this work, feminist bookstores have been not simply spaces to gather but sites of complex conversations among staff and collectives and, in turn, with readers, about feminist accountability. I offer a description of how the economic and movement pressures of the 1990s changed feminist bookwomen's self-definition and obscured a more radical history of this movement. The authors of these recent articles are writing what they know and are working to pay homage to feminist bookstores; however, their limited access to feminist bookstore history leaves readers without a movement-based understanding of bookwomen's work. Through this book I offer a glimpse of the complex history these intervening years have blurred or erased. The vital work of bookwomen mapping out practices of lesbian antiracism and feminist accountability sees a continued life in social media campaigns and other sites of coalitional dialogue. I identify bookwomen's activism as part of a movement legacy and model we need.

Along the way, this book participates in the ongoing work of more accurately documenting the 1970s feminist movement, still too often described as a straight white movement. Maylei Blackwell's *¡Chicana Power! Contested*

Histories of Feminism in the Chicano Movement and Kimberly Springer's *Living for the Revolution: Black Feminist Organizations, 1968–1980* both interrupt the feminist waves analogy to point out that feminists of color in the 1970s drew on and participated in movement histories not visible from the perspective of feminist waves (first wave, suffrage feminism; second wave, 1970s feminism; third wave, 1990s feminism). Instead, to fully describe feminism we must recognize feminist activism within the Abolitionist Movement, the Black Power Movement, the Chicano Movement, the Civil Rights Movement, Indigenous peoples' movements, and other identity-based and social justice movements.[18] Feminist bookstore histories also document the involvement of women of color across movements, women who came to feminist bookstores from and left feminist bookstores for work in other social justice movements. White-focused historians, Chela Sandoval has pointed out, often read this mobility of women of color between movements as absence.[19] In this book I look to the decades-long feminist bookstore movement as a significantly long-running case study in part to examine some of the motivations for women of color mobility and histories of attempted transracial alliances within feminism. This book also records the feminist bookstores as usually lesbian-run and lesbian-identified spaces. In conversation with works including Springer's *Living for the Revolution* and Lillian Faderman's *To Believe in Women: What Lesbians Have Done for America, A History*, *The Feminist Bookstore Movement* documents 1970s feminism as already lesbian and multiracial.

In this book I enact a writing style that uses story as theory. Throughout the book, as in this preface, I share stories of my own research and learning process as well as stories of bookwomen's histories together. This storytelling maps out bookwomen's and my relational practices of lesbian antiracism and feminist accountability. Informed by Anzaldúa's recognition of multiple ways of theorizing, with her emphasis on theories by and for women of color, I look to story with attention to race, class, gender, and sexuality as a way of knowing, a pattern, a usable theoretical framework.[20] I write this way here for three reasons. First, bookwomen showed how knowledge creation happens in relationship. The work of feminist bookwomen was in large part to teach themselves, each other, and their communities to read feminist literature and each other differently. Through organizing books into sections in the bookstore, gathering transformative book lists in newsletters and in the *Feminist Bookstore News*, creating events, reflecting on this practice through collective meetings, and trying new formations, bookwomen created a new reading and relational practice I call the feminist shelf. Story in this book demonstrates relationships in the making, including relationships that shaped my research. This book matters because it feeds our future vocabularies for relationship building and because I hope it will strengthen our feminist alliances across difference. Second, there is accountability in sharing some of my own story. This sharing requires me to describe how I as a lesbian feminist white antiracist ally shape and understand this work. I intend this sharing as another model for researching in alliance across difference. Aimee Carillo Rowe describes how narrative reflects and shapes relationships: "Ideas and experiences, values and interpretations always take place within the context of our relational lives. Whom we love becomes vital to the theory we produce and how it might be received. The text is neither produced nor received in isolation. Others are involved."[21] Through interviews, correspondence, and bookstore work I have been in dialogue with feminist bookwomen throughout the long writing of this book, and I share that dialogue here while making my research and reading process more visible by writing some of my own life along with the stories of bookwomen. Third, this accountability to the relational practice of story as theory making also depends on an ethic of feminist love. Through story I enact my own accountability while I describe bookwomen's successes and analyze their failures by their own standards. Through sharing my own story I also make myself vulnerable as my narrators have in sharing their stories. Only by including myself in dialogue can this accountability also read as love.

In *Two or Three Things I Know for Sure*, both a memoir and theory of memoir, Dorothy Allison reminds readers, "Two or three things I know for sure and one of them is that telling the story all the way through is an act of love."[22] Here I work to tell the story all the way through. One of the challenging joys of feminist writing is being in conversation with feminist theorists about how we practice accountability to each other in writing and analyzing history. This work is learning to love each other, and this is also the work of feminist bookwomen in dialogue with the literature they advocated to keep in print and with each other, the collective members to whom they answered. "There is nothing universal or timeless about this love business," Sydney, one of novelist Dionne Brand's characters, shares as the closing words of the novel *Love Enough*. "It is hard if you really want to do it right."[23] I offer story here not as simple truth but as an act of accountability and love because, as bookwomen knew in their practice of the feminist shelf, we create the knowledge we need for feminist futures in relationship with each other.

The work of analyzing, organizing, and making literature available has been core to feminism in no small part because it involves an ethics of voice and relationships. We not only need "diverse books," we need the tools to read them and put them in conversation.[24] Rooting this use of story in bookwomen's practice of the feminist shelf, I am also in dialogue with feminist literary analysis as activist work. Feminist fiction has long been integral to and functioned as feminist theory; scholars including Matt Richardson and Katherine McKittrick have significantly used collections of Black lesbian and Black women's literature, respectively, to theorize experience.[25] This collecting and redefining our understandings of history, present, and future is a project feminist bookwomen furthered and evolved together for decades. Looking to women who used literature in this way, I seek to place this book in conversation with Maylei Blackwell's attention to the Chicana feminist publishing activists of *Las Hijas de Cuauhtémoc* and with Elizabeth McHenry's history of turn-of-the-twentieth-century Black women's literary societies and their feminist literary activism.[26] Feminist bookwomen, and their transnational network, enacted a reflexive practice of creating, sharing, and rethinking new reading and relational practices for feminist accountability; in this reflexive practice, bookwomen created a theoretical framework useful to contemporary feminisms.

I enact this reflexive practice, learned from the bookstores, throughout the book in a series of creative narratives about my own research process. These narratives resist a disembodied telling by emphasizing my relationship with and my embodied understanding of these histories. I put my body, my story, in conversation with this history in order to model one way the reader might do so as well. The work of building lesbian antiracism and feminist accountability is embodied work both because our differences are located in stories about our bodies—stories about race, gender identity, gender expression, sexuality, dis/ability—and because this work lives in our bodies, energizes us, makes us tired, and requires physical self-care and attention. With the framework of "reading the map of our bodies," I invite readers to recognize this history in our bodies and to use this history to embody antiracist and accountable feminist alliances.

Taken together, the chapters of *The Feminist Bookstore Movement* offer a history of how feminist bookwomen both documented and influenced feminist thinking and relationship practices starting in 1970. Rather than wax nostalgic for a time when there were more feminist bookstores, I suggest attention to this history to understand how our current conversations have been informed by feminist bookwomen. Bookwomen sustained decades-long conversations about feminist accountability, and their advocacy for feminist literature provided a unique context for these conversations because discussions about who controlled feminist literature, publishing, and distribution required difficult conversations about voice and agency: who gets to write and publish their own stories, how we talk with rather than about each other, and how we read and move toward understanding each other's stories. Too often overlooked in feminist movement histories, feminist bookstores served as tools bookwomen used to develop feminist literacy and alliance practices, which required grappling with and, in turn, shaping some of the most complex conversations in feminism.

In chapter 1, "Dykes with a Vision, 1970–1976," I document feminist bookstore beginnings as movement spaces in major and dispersed cities: Oakland, New York, Toronto, Cambridge (Massachusetts), Austin (my own hometown), and San Francisco. These stories carry the energy building with the opening of each new bookstore toward what would become the Feminist Bookstore Network. The bookstores provided context for each other; none operated alone. These origin stories also describe how the specific identity of each bookstore brought new issues and vocabulary to deepen the sustained transnational conversation bookwomen shared for more than three decades. As bookwomen staked out their values in founding documents, they defined their bookstores in relationship to feminist issues that included collectivity, economic justice, racial justice, allyship, socioeconomic class, and academic feminisms. The resulting variety of ethical frameworks illustrates the differences between the cities as well as their bookstores and suggests how the collective force of the bookstores put these differences in conversation to generate movement, learning, and new feminist futures.

The second chapter begins where the first leaves off, at the gathering that formalizes these interwoven beginnings into a network. Chapter 2, "Revolutionaries in a Capitalist System, 1976–1980," sees the start of the *Feminist Bookstores Newsletter* at the first Women in Print gathering at a Girl Scout campground in Nevada. In these first years of the network created by the FBN, feminist bookwomen fulfilled their vow to be revolutionaries interrupting "a capitalist system." On a national scale, they taught each other how to influence the publishing industry and their communities, in a practice informed by movement-based accountability to addressing racism in feminist movements. As the bookwomen began to recognize their substantial feminist literary activist skills, they got books onto publishers' lists, returned books to print, and actively distributed a feminist literature. The chain bookstores began their sweep in the late 1970s, and bookwomen defined their bookstores, against capitalism, as movement spaces sustaining feminist knowledge.

Dialogues in the *Feminist Bookstores Newsletter* defined key issues feminist bookwomen would take up, including their intention, one of several outlined in Nevada, to "develop ways of working together that make us more accountable to our communities and to each other."[27] Chapter 3, "Accountable to Each Other, 1980–1983," begins in the mountains of the West Coast Women's Music Festival, where feminist bookwomen are in the crowd at Bernice Johnson Reagon's pivotal speech about transracial alliance building. This talk became a tool for difficult conversations about white women giving up power and recognizing leadership of women of color in the bookstores. Such conversations generated what the chapter calls lesbian antiracism, antiracist practice with attention to heterosexism and sexism. Work toward lesbian antiracist feminism at two core bookstores, and reports about their processes in the widely read *Feminist Bookstores Newsletter*, emphasize bookwomen's contributions to feminist vocabularies and relationship-building practices. Lesbian antiracism was one ethic of the bookwomen's practice of feminist accountability, building feminist dialogue to define, grapple with, and evolve a shared set of ethics and ideas about how to live by those ethics.

In chapter 4, "The Feminist Shelf, A Transnational Project, 1984–1993," I name the practice of the feminist shelf, a new term to describe how bookwomen created new reading and relational practices through naming shelf sections, narrating book lists, contextualizing events, and using this reading practice to differently understand each other and hold each other accountable. In this chapter I trace conversations around shared documents that focused significant moments in this work, including a bookstore map of New Words in Cambridge and the *Women of Colour Bibliography* at the Toronto Women's Bookstore. The interconnections of this practice also demonstrate how bookwomen used transnational relationships and the newly renamed *Feminist Bookstore News* to hone their ethics for the feminist shelf around core issues that included relationships between feminists in the global South and global North, as well as the cultural genocide at stake when white women authors appropriate Indigenous women's voices and stories. Literature was a staging ground for developing this vital antiracist feminist relational practice. New bibliographies and shelf sections created by women of color at major feminist bookstores generated transformations inside and outside the bookstores that demonstrate how significantly bookwomen shaped feminist reading and alliance practices to create an ethic of feminist love.

Chapter 5, "Economics and Antiracist Alliances, 1993–2003," focuses in on the US context to describe the culmination of tensions within both feminism and the book industry. In the mid- to late 1990s the Feminist Bookstore Network was a leading force in independent booksellers' advocacy to transform the American Booksellers Association. Faced with chain bookstores and big publishers making illegal deals that would put independent bookstores out of business, feminist bookwomen put their substantial feminist literary activist skills to work for independent bookstores at large. They effected an astounding, though temporary, success in the industry. Along the way, individual feminist bookstore staff continued to grapple with articulating lesbian antiracist feminist accountability. However, as the Feminist Bookstore Network turned toward the national conversation around independent bookselling and saving the bookstore structure, white bookwomen in leadership turned away from vocabularies of lesbian antiracist accountability. The devastating cost was a simplified public identity for feminist bookwomen and the loss of the vital difficult conversations about race and feminism that the transnational conversation among bookwomen had required over the previous two decades. I suggest that the bookstore narrative demonstrates that in the face of economic disaster, feminists must continue to prioritize antiracist alliances over traditional economic survival. I read a legacy of grappling with accountability and alliance building, rather than the continued life of a few feminist bookstores, as the success of the feminist bookstore movement.

My stories of researching and living with reverberations of these histories culminate in the epilogue: a reflection on why this book matters as a map of a still-necessary lesbian antiracist practice of feminist accountability. Through a telling of my own last days at the Toronto Women's Bookstore, I imagine what a feminist practice informed by feminist bookstore histories might look like. Throughout the book I have also used feminist bookwomen's ethics of feminist accountability as a guide for discussing difficult breaks in and connections through the movement. In the epilogue I name this historical practice as one of feminist remembering, a practice that requires us to hold close both the painful breaks and the powerful connections of feminist bookwomen's history. This is the practice of the feminist shelf that feminist bookwomen created and pass on: using a context of feminist histories to understand the significance of these breaks and connections, to understand them in dialogue with each other, to use this history, this feminist work, to build toward a common language for queer antiracist feminist accountability.[28]

I accepted the faculty job in that southern city. In the midst of unpacking in a house on a street shaded by ominously historic gothic oaks, I sat in the echo of the empty living room and dialed Kit Quan's number. We had agreed that instead of me asking questions she would tell me a version of her story. "As part of a collective, even though I was younger, I was invested in the store because I was pouring my labor into the store. I was beginning to have a political vision of the role of a women's bookstore. I was probably pretty articulate at the time, even though now I would be able to say it much better." Quan remembered her teenaged self working in a movement in English while still often thinking in Chinese and eager for her feminist vision to be realized: "One of the ways that there was tension was that, for me, at my age, and at the place where I was in life, the bookstore was about politics. It was about wanting a women's movement or wanting a Women in Print Movement that would be very inclusive: race, class, age, etc. Where someone like me, who was actually having trouble reading, could actually be a part of it."[29] Feminist bookstores were sites of this struggle, different each time, toward a feminist present and future, and bookwomen shared these hopes in tension with each other at collective meetings and through writings, including Quan's important contribution to Gloria Anzaldúa's edited collection *Making Face, Making Soul / Haciendo Caras*.[30]

Nearly a year after moving to the Deep South, in the thick humidity that seemed to make time stand still, I continued the search for a feminist future and felt frustrated navigating the city's too-hidden spaces for queer transracial organizing, in church pews dimmed by stained glass–filtered light. My partner and I had decided to head back to Austin, and we were boxing up our belongings for the third time in three years. Relieved that I still remembered where I had packed the phone recorder, I settled in with the echo in that empty living room one more time and called Pell. Pell is her last name and the only one she uses. She worked at Old Wives' Tales, too, and Seajay connected me with her. As I continued this research, I was learning how to read with and connect with women of color in the movement. Pell, an African American woman from the Northeast, felt transformed "exchanging information" with Quan, she says, "because she came from a different background than I did."[31] Like Quan, Pell used the bookstore to imagine new realities, and she honed her visionary skills both in conversation with other bookwomen and in reading the bookstore shelves. She remembers "being awakened to the different writers, the styles, and discussing books more thoroughly. That was a change for me. Also, to listen to a lot of the discussions that went on, the political discussions, opened me up to a lot of the different branches of feminist thought, different women and feminists who were well-known, even in history, women that I hadn't heard of before. . . . It was a full education, practically, working there." Quan's and Pell's feminist visions, like those of so many bookwomen, happened not just through a local bookstore but were possible only as part of an interconnected movement. The transnational conversation of feminist bookwomen through the *Feminist Bookstore News* and the connections across and within bookstores among bookwomen made this full education possible. These bookwomen teach me, too, through these interviews and their archives.

Lifting a decorated box of interview tapes into the U-Haul, I wondered, how do we prepare ourselves to listen for the complex histories I did not know how to hear when I started this research? This history, redefining bookwomen's successes and failures on their own terms, offers an embodied feminist theory for our futures. Moving through these cities, this writing, I am learning how to read the map of my own body, of our bodies, and of a feminist accountability I can't live without.

ONE
DYKES WITH A VISION
1970–1976

In the second-floor kitchen of Carol Seajay's rowhouse walkup, I set up the video camera as a backup for the tape recorder while she washed up from the day. Seajay, book industry maven and founder of the Feminist Bookstore Network, reemerged in shorts and a black ribbed tank top; an affectionate cling of cat fur matched the longhaired calico she let out the kitchen door. Seajay's gray-black hair fell almost to her waist. She sat down; I adjusted the camera. "Make sure *you're* in the frame," she reminded me, "that's more feminist than having me talking to some disembodied voice." At the time, I couldn't manage to tell a story with me in it. My interviews with Seajay and my work at the bookstores have taught me a thing or two since then. The video is of her and what seems like a view of all of San Francisco behind her through her window on the hill.

In the 1970s, Seajay was working as an abortion counselor and reading feminist newspapers like *The Furies* (Washington, DC) and *Ain't I a Woman* (Iowa City) that arrived on exchange subscription to her lover's publication, the *Kalamazoo Women's Newspaper*. In those pages she read about the feminist bookstores starting to open across the United States and about the West Coast Lesbian Conference coming up in 1973. Feeling the pull of the coast (*The Lesbian Tide*, after all, was published in Los Angeles), Seajay headed west to the conference. There, she immersed herself in an ethnically diverse and lesbian feminist movement connected by the transformative power of feminist books collected together.

Organized by a multiracial group of lesbians, including Jeanne Córdova, Latina founder and editor of *The Lesbian Tide* (1971–1980) and president of the LA Chapter of Daughters of Bilitis,[1] the West Coast Lesbian Conference gathered the lesbian feminist communities along the Pacific. The conference was fraught with disagreements around the exclusion of trans folks and lesbian mothers, which simultaneously marked devastating limits to the early movement and the vital involvement of trans folks and lesbian mothers in it.[2] The event was part of attempts at justice flawed and learning, even while it generated new futures for a young lesbian like Seajay. From amid the buzzing conference of "almost 2,000 women from twenty-six states and several countries,"[3] Seajay returned to Kalamazoo with a book from Diana Press and *Sleeping Beauty: A Lesbian Fairy Tale* published by Sojourner Truth Press in Atlanta. She also returned with the memory of other books, like *Edward the Dyke* from the Oakland Women's Press Collective, that she had seen but didn't have the budget to buy. Seajay remembers the promise of change she read in these pages:

> I brought those books back and said to friends of mine, "These are the lesbian books with *good* endings. These are going to change our lives." And they all looked at me, like, "Yeah, yeah, Carol. All about books, Carol, again. Yeah, yeah, yeah." "No, these are going to change our lives. No, you have to *read* this. *Songs to a Handsome Woman*, you have to read these!" They did read them. And it changed some of their lives and not some of them. But I do think that there being lesbian books changed even the lives of the women who didn't read. Because it changed the lives around them.[4]

Seajay was keen to the transformative work that collections of texts created. Not only the existence of "lesbian books with *good* endings" but the collection of them together prompted Seajay's promise that these books, books published by feminist presses, books by and about lesbians thriving, would "change our lives," and that the conversations made possible by these books would change the lives of even those who didn't read them.

Returning home to Kalamazoo for less than a year after the life-changing West Coast Lesbian Conference, Seajay headed back toward the Pacific with all her belongings, including not a few books published by lesbian feminist presses, stacked on her motorcycle. She wended her way through the Midwest to stop at Amazon Bookstore in Minneapolis; she had to see the feminist bookstores she had read about in the feminist papers. Social movements in the 1960s and 1970s staged multiple migrations and pilgrimages; Seajay was one of a sea of women who found wheels and set out to connect with feminist activism. In the 1970s, 1980s, and 1990s, women used feminist bookstores as resource centers for finding out what was happening in each city, who had a place to stay to offer to travelers, and where to find a job when they found a city that felt like home.

Motoring into San Francisco, Seajay pulled off of I-80W and into the city; the breath that waited for her by the Bay might have smelled of fresh ink on paperback pages. A friend of hers named Forest (then known as Gretchen Milne) lived in San Francisco and had cofounded the Oakland feminist bookstore ICI: A Woman's Place. Forest brought Seajay on the long bus ride from the Bay to the Oakland bookstore, where Seajay soon began volunteering, and then working as a member of the collective. Thinking back to her first collective meetings, Seajay describes the collective as representative of its ethnically and socioeconomically diverse community: "There was my friend Forest who taught philosophy at State, and there were the women in high school . . . [and] several women that hadn't finished any kind of formal schooling. There were Asian, Filipina, Black, white [women], it was a real mix. The only thing that wasn't strongly represented were straight women; there were a few straight women and a few kind of asexual women, and mostly a bunch of dykes that had this vision and were going to make it happen."[5] Identity differences within the collective reflected the complex reality of 1970s feminism, and Seajay's rememberings document the origins of feminist institutions, including bookstores, in collaborative work across racialized difference. Seajay's demography also documents the spectacularly lesbian beginnings of feminist bookstores, often lesbian-run spaces.[6]

Seajay's iconic journey sketches a sense of the energy and excitement building around feminist bookstores as destinations on a lesbian feminist map, as places to reliably find the books that would "change our lives," and as what would become public sites of (often heated) feminist dialogue over thirty years of an active movement. Even in the early years of the feminist bookstore movement, with the large size of bookstore collectives and high staff turnover, the number of women moving through the bookstores as workers suggests that bookstores served as a training ground both for the women working in the bookstores and for those visiting them. Seajay would become a central voice in the feminist bookstore movement: by the late 1970s she had cofounded and was editor of the *Feminist Bookstores Newsletter* (later the *Feminist Bookstore News*), the journal that fostered a transnational network until 2000 and that widely circulated local conversations about becoming accountable to each other and to the ideal of lesbian antiracist feminist practice.

In these beginnings, I trace the common and different stakes of bookwomen in feminist bookstore projects in Oakland, New York, Toronto,

Cambridge, and Austin. In Oakland and New York, women of color participated in founding these early feminist bookstores, and lesbians of color or white lesbians participated in founding each bookstore. These founding narratives, then, contradict remembrances of 1970s feminism as straight and white. Instead, the work of these dykes with a vision adds to valuable narratives of a more vibrant movement history and establishes feminist bookstores as sites that, at their beginnings, drew together lesbians and their allies from across racialized difference to attempt to enact feminist futures. In the early and mid-1970s, bookwomen began conversations that became central to the growing feminist bookstore movement. In Oakland and Toronto the bookstores began as part of feminist and lesbian movement projects, mapping the bookstores as part of a larger feminist movement. Academic institutions in New York, Toronto, and Cambridge looked to their feminist bookstores as supporters and shapers of women's studies as an academic and community project. The Oakland bookwomen's influence on bookwomen in New York and Austin, as well as the New York bookwomen's support of the bookwomen in Toronto, suggests that the interrelationships between multiple bookstores make these spaces sites of a national movement as well as accountable to each other in conversation. Immigrant and diasporic communities and institutions in Oakland, New York, and Toronto allowed bookwomen in those cities to make the bookstores part of transnational conversations. Along the way, bookwomen staked out different approaches to what became the defining tension between a capitalist business format and movement accountability: while feminist bookwomen in Oakland, Cambridge, and Austin began their work with large collectives focused on movement and community support, smaller groups of bookwomen in New York and Toronto already articulated friction between a feminist business model and a grassroots organizing model. At every bookstore, feminist literature provided a basis for the theoretical practice the bookwomen began to develop. Bookwomen, steeped in contemporary movement conversations, used the bookstores as experimental sites of the movement.

"When Action Grows Unprofitable, Gather Information": ICI: A Woman's Place, Oakland 1970

Days after my interview with Carol Seajay, I landed in New York. A morning bus ride brought me early to the Park Slope brownstone where the brass plaque under the buzzer reads "Lesbian Herstory Educational Foundation."

On this, my first visit to the Lesbian Herstory Archives, Deborah Edel, co-founder with Joan Nestle of the Archives in 1975, met me at the front door to welcome me into the building full of light and lined from basement to attic with shelves, filing cabinets, and boxes.[7] On the second floor, in a small corner room, amid a stack of archival boxes, we found one marked ICI: A Woman's Place, almost three thousand miles from Oakland. There were other documents from the Oakland bookstore among the papers of the several New York feminist bookstores: the New York bookwomen had collected mail order lists, newsletters, and letters from the Oakland bookstore. Finding these Oakland documents here in New York was evidence of a network of feminist bookwomen sharing strategies. In these early documents, I see the influence of ICI as bookwomen created and shared a theory of what it would mean to be a feminist bookstore.

One of the two first feminist bookstores (Amazon in Minneapolis also opened in 1970), ICI clearly reflected the influences of Bay Area lesbian feminist organizing and of the racialized histories of the West Coast. The bookstore grew out of the Bay Area Gay Women's Liberation, an organization whose members and theories influenced the nation not only through their published writings but also through the public letters and newsletters of ICI. As Seajay observed of her first meeting, the ICI collective was large and diverse in representation of race, socioeconomic status, and sexual orientation. An ongoing history of Asian immigration to the West Coast made this region one visible national site of Asian American feminism, and Gay Women's Liberation was intentionally racially diverse. While in other parts of the country racially diverse meant Black women and white women or Latina women and white women, the Bay Area bookstores sustained long-term conversations among Asian, Black, Latina, and white women. As a result of the careful work of organizers attempting alliances across difference, ICI offers a history of and a vocabulary for working toward transracial feminist belonging.

Strengthened by their movement roots in late 1960s organizing, bookwomen offered in the public letter announcing the bookstore opening a swaggering manifesto. Here they claimed feminist writing as educational tools for activists. They created a reading practice. This letter sparked a growing movement and survived because other bookwomen saved it. Had the letter been handed out across the city at activist meetings? Taped to the window of the triangular-shaped building at the corner of Broadway and College Ave.? In one photograph of ICI, a woman reads the flyers posted in the bookstore windows. The letter begins not with a salutation but with an imperative from a feminist author: "When action grows unprofitable, gather information from The Left Hand of Darkness by Ursula K. LeGuin."[8] Bookwomen would soon initiate a campaign to keep Left Hand in print. That feminist science fiction would inform the theory of feminist bookstore practice emphasizes the work of the bookwomen gathering feminist writing to build the movement. Feminist bookwomen intended from their beginnings to show readers how women's writing could be read, interpreted, and used to foster action.

From its circular sign forming the top part of a painted women's symbol, the first feminist bookstore in the United States declared with its name the intention of the burgeoning feminist bookstore movement: ICI, Information Center Incorporate: A Woman's Place. With this serious name, ICI claimed feminist bookstores as resource centers. An extension of books gathered at conferences like the West Coast Lesbian Conference, where Seajay found a force in a stack of "lesbian books with *good* endings" that would change even the lives of those who didn't read them, feminist bookstores created permanent and public collections of resources for decades. Inside, visitors found shelves of theory, history, novels, and activist pamphlets by and for women; bulletin boards with flyers announcing community happenings, housing projects, meetings, performances, and signings; bibliographies on subject lists ranging from coming out to divorce; and knowledgeable bookwomen who connected seekers with information about abortion, single motherhood, care for lesbians with cancer, and getting published. This gathering of information supported women in community and fed the dialogues of collective members huddled together among the shelves, talking with each other.

Members of the ICI collective explained how this sense of place made feminist bookstores not just another bookstore but distinctly different in structure and vision both from other feminist formations and from other independent and chain bookstores of the time. "This bookstore is different from other bookstores," the collective explained. "It has tables and chairs to sit and relax at, and coffee and tea and nibbles. There are bulletin boards that women can use to get in touch with other women. And of course, a bookstore run by feminists is different from a bookstore with a feminist section in it. The store is a pretty good size, so we can have rap groups, poetry readings, movies, etc."[9] The difference was not just in content (the whole bookstore was "a feminist section") but also in structure and purpose ("we can have rap groups, poetry readings").[10] This sense of place as strategy caught on. Tellingly, bookwomen in other cities named their bookstores A Woman's Place, too, including in Phoenix; Portland, Oregon; Toronto; and Vancouver, British Columbia. The Oakland bookwomen explained in their letter why staking out square footage in bookstores across North America was integral to building and sharing feminist knowledge. The bookwomen pointed out that to "gather information" meant gathering not only texts but also women as sources of information: "As women came together in the growth of the women's movement, as women got interested in mingling with other women, it became clear that there was no place that we could go and not be interfered with by men. No place to socialize in, no place to hang out." This yearning for "place" constituted simultaneously on ground and on paper a feminist literary counterpublic, a movement-based site where collective members and visitors would learn together, from each other and from feminist writings, the relational and advocacy skills they would use to create change in society at large.[11] In sharp contrast to the billboard claiming something is "good for the bottom line" hovering just above ICI: A Woman's Place in the photograph, the core of the purpose of feminist bookstores formed not around profit but around this practice of feminist education.

In comparison with the stodgy reputation of bookstores at the time, feminist bookstores were clearly movement institutions by design. While in the 1960s and 1970s independent bookstores outnumbered chain bookstores,[12] bookstore historian Laura Miller explains that the traditional independent bookstore had "a reputation for being either patrician and clubby or dark and musty, and often stereotyped as a place of narrow aisles and a confusing jumble of books whose logic was known only to the bookseller."[13] In contrast, the 1960s bookstore chains B. Dalton and Waldenbooks established a nearly clinical order with their move into shopping malls, a new site for bookstores.[14] These outlets developed an "emphasis on self-service," with "bright colors, contemporary materials for shelving and counters, bold signage, and, above all, good lighting. Aisles were wide and shelves were low to create an open, uncluttered feel."[15] Feminist bookstores, different from both independents and chains, uniquely served as welcoming spaces, brimming with feminist information, supporting networks of women.[16]

ICI bookwomen also explained that they were not stocking a bookstore with texts they thought would sell; instead, they considered first what materials they thought women should see together in one place. As they described their selection process, the bookwomen enacted what would become a core role for bookwomen, building a reading and teaching practice, work I explore further in chapters 3 and 4. The collective members described in the letter their commitment to curate and analyze the collection: "We are acquiring books, magazines, and newspapers in a discriminating manner, and plan to have our booklist available, with our thumbnail description of each book. It will indicate what we think of a book, why we feel it is important. If we like a book for certain reasons, but dislike it for others, we'll indicate that." Here, the bookwomen commit to justifying each piece of the collection; by thoughtfully putting texts together, bookwomen developed a new theory, a way of understanding the world, through the space. The ICI collective offered a framework based on self-identification with 1960s political counterculture: "Mainly we look at things through a feminist anarchist, lesbian, paranoid-schizophrenic, dope-fiend perspective, what ever that means." The collective members wanted to describe and define their reading process (feminist anarchist, lesbian, etc.) while simultaneously marking a distrust of definitions ("what ever that means").

While in other cities the feminist bookstores were closely connected with feminists working in universities to build the new field of women's studies, ICI bookwomen distanced themselves from academia. Inviting women to donate "books, magazines, xeroxed copies of good stuff, and money," the bookwomen asked specifically for "professional journals" since "the average person (us) never gets to see stuff like that, and it's very informative, especially if stoned." By this time, KNOW, Inc. in Pittsburgh had published two issues of *Female Studies*, a collection of women's studies syllabi and resources from the nation's growing women's studies movement.[17] The bookstore's explicit request for "professional journals" records the already present perceived distance between "academic" and "community" women's studies.

ICI collective members shaped the bookstore as a site of education and information access that shared the grassroots theoretical framework of a range of other projects from Oakland Gay Women's Liberation. The Oakland bookstore shared this connection to grassroots lesbian feminist organizing with bookstores in other cities, including Common Woman Bookstore in Austin, Texas, which grew in part out of the Austin Lesbian Organization, and the Toronto Women's Bookstore (TWB), which started out as a project of The Women's Place center. The Oakland collective, however, distinguished itself with its origins in a strategically multiracial organization. Judy Grahn, white lesbian feminist poet, describes the energy of Gay Women's Liberation:

> From the meetings grew all-women's households, institutions in and of themselves, that gave rise to others, to newspapers, to the first all-women's bookstore (A Woman's Place in Oakland, CA), to the first all-women's press (The Women's Press Collective). Meetings of all kinds took place in the house, such as the first meeting of what became the Lesbian Mothers Union, called by Black Lesbian organizer Pat Norman, and dozens of other meetings ranging from prison organizing, to working for welfare rights, to anti-rape campaigns, to the editing of books and the promotion of artwork and literature.[18]

This shared beginning gestures toward the significance of both publishing and distribution as activism for marginalized histories.

The partnership between ICI and the Women's Press Collective embodied the relationship of feminist presses and bookstores; both relied on each other. The bookstores became spaces not only to find this work but also to put this work in conversation and build a feminist theory in dialogue. Shortly after the bookstore opened, the press moved into the other half of the same space. Carol Seajay's description of this shared geography maps the vital connection between feminist bookstores and presses: "We got books from every place that had them. From the women's presses, which of course had the best books. The Women's Press Collective was, literally, through that door from A Woman's Place; it was in the space."[19] The publishers of Judy Grahn's *Edward the Dyke, and Other Poems* (1971), Pat Parker's *Child of Myself* (1974), and other formative texts were in the next room with their weighty Gestetner press rolling out pamphlets, books, and album covers. "They'd come in at night and print, and we'd come in in the morning and see what they'd printed," Seajay remembers. "And the first time they did four color it was so exciting, because it was like, 'Oh, they put down the green! Oh, they put down the red!' You know, and you'd just watch it grow." This spatial connection maps out the relationship within the movement between organizational structures. The bookstores and presses, interdependent, were both necessary. While the presses worked to publish, reprint, and distribute women's work, the bookstores gathered this physical evidence for the energy of women's authorship and artwork.

In Oakland, this productivity, this attempt to reshape feminist knowledge, was fueled by the relational practices within organizations. Judy Grahn and her then-lover Wendy Cadden intentionally committed the Women's Press to transracial collaboration. Grahn explained:

> Both Wendy and I really believe in multi-cultural society—so we made sure that the press was multi-cultural and expanded our membership strategically. We worked very closely with Pat Parker, who of course was Black, and we had a multi-racial group by 1974 solidly, that included Anita Oñang, who is Filipino American and Willyce Kim who is Korean American and Martha Shelly who is Jewish American and Wendy, who is also. And two or three white working class lesbians were involved, including Anne Leonard, Sharon Isabell, Paula Wallace and myself, working class white WASP people and then Joanne Garrett, who is Black, and there were young middle class white women, Karen Garrison and Jane Lawhon, fresh out of college and very supportive.[20]

An early picture documents this multiracial collaboration around the press that thrived for eight years before merging with the lesbian feminist Diana Press in 1977.[21] The Women's Press Collective published Willyce Kim's *Eating Artichokes*, and in 1975 Kim took the iconic photograph of Cadden at the collective's Gestetner press; the picture appeared in the first issue of *Dyke Quarterly*. These women, next door to the bookstore and involved in the organization that started the bookstore, were part of and created a relational model for the ICI project.

Grahn's poetics distributed through the press and the bookstore influenced the movement and provided a theory for the relationship building of feminist bookstores. Seajay saw this theory building in action: "The store sold books by day and the Women's Press Collective churned them out at night. Thinkers and writers and activists were always hanging around, reinventing the world we knew and inventing new worlds on a daily basis."[22] In 1969, the Women's Press Collective published "The Common Woman," Grahn's chapbook of eight portrait poems.[23] The collection influenced the language of lesbian feminism on a national scale. Ntozake Shange claimed "The Common Woman" as an influence on her work in *For Colored Girls Who Considered Suicide When the Rainbow Is Enuf* (Shameless Hussy Press, 1975),[24] and feminists in Austin named their bookstore the Common Woman Bookstore. In her writings about her use of the name "common woman," Grahn develops a theory that rejects a single universal "woman." She explains that claims to a universal womanhood disserve women because "universal, 'one-world' implies everyone having to fit into one standard (and of course that one, that 'uni' is going to turn out to be a white, male, heterosexual, young, educated, middle class, etc. model)." Instead of pointing to a fantasy of a common experience, Grahn clarified: "Common means many-centered, many overlapping islands of groups each of which maintains its own center and each of which is central to society for what it gives to society."[25] She conceived these "overlapping islands" through her portraits of individual women characters in "The Common Woman" poems, and in her activism she strived to connect the interrelated work of racial, socioeconomic, lesbian, and feminist justice.

ICI found its roots not only in feminism but also in the racial justice movements of the 1960s and 1970s, perhaps in a different way from later feminist bookstores that opened within an established feminist bookstore movement. Grahn remembers that her own outsider status allowed her to identify particularly with activists in the Black Power movement "because we came from poor and immigrant backgrounds in our own families, and because we ourselves, as Lesbians and as single women, were defined and treated as marginal, displaced and oppressed."[26] Mourning the assassination of Malcolm X, Grahn "experienced his death as an understanding of the price of radical leadership, and that what we were—and are—involved in is a low-level ongoing war." By providing a space for women to gather, ICI followed what Grahn learned from Malcolm X "about the essential importance of autonomy, self-determination, and community. I could tell that separatism and the centrality of a group of people to themselves were powerful social tools." Later lesbian separatist moments focused on white women and were criticized for their racial homogeneity. Grahn's experience of separatism, however, was deeply connected, through her collaborators, with racial justice:

> I joined with seven or eight other young women, several of whom had also experienced in one way or another the teachings of Malcolm X, and who also, like me, had been strongly influenced by the Lesbian underground network of bars, cliques and a magazine, *The Ladder*. Several of our number were Jewish radical Lesbians, including my lover at the time, Wendy Cadden. Some were from the European folk "marginal culture" known variously as lower class, working class, white trash, or even middle class in sociological jargon. Some were Black, including poet Pat

Parker and an outspoken woman who changed her Anglo-Saxon name to Ama. The organizations we proceeded to define and develop [including ICI] were Lesbian separatist, with a feminist and radical underbase.[27]

This version of antiracist feminist separatism, learned from Black Nationalism, was a political strategy that fed transracial alliances. This separatism made space to examine how feminists are accountable to each other. This strategy also enacted contemporary feminist theorists' descriptions of using context-specific strategies to work toward both connection and, as a result, change: Chela Sandoval's "differential consciousness," Jasbir Puar's "assemblages," and Aimee Carillo Rowe's "differential be-longing" suggest that queer antiracist feminists', and particularly feminists of color's, strategic articulations of identity change by environment, develop alliances to learn from each other and strengthen each other, and change through these alliances.[28] At ICI the racial and class diversity among the staff also provided an opportunity for productive contention. Literature, writing, was central to this becoming, Grahn emphasizes: "We had a voice of our own, and when it spoke the first words were through the poets."[29]

Even while the books on the shelves documented and enacted key transracial conversations within and around feminism, most feminist bookstore collectives did not, over time, consist of an ethnically diverse group of women. The ICI collective thus offers an important opportunity to understand how the books on the shelves made possible conversations across racial difference within the collective. Seajay and other feminist bookwomen I talked with repeatedly described to me their work to build collections of texts by feminists of color and lesbians (and both); these collections challenged a hegemonic women's movement. Feminist bookstores as productive sites of sometimes troubled community acknowledged difference and made possible shared conversation around the common interests of their lesbian feminist politics and simultaneously attempted to broaden the scope of that common interest. Seajay explains how bookwomen advocated for a collection of texts. That advocacy and the texts themselves informed this feminist accountability. Seajay remembers:

It was while we were in [ICI: A Woman's Place] that Maxine Hong Kingston's *Woman Warrior* came out (Random House, 1976), and we had Jade Snow Wong's biography (*Fifth Chinese Daughter*, Harper and Row, 1950/1965) that we would order from her in case lots out of her basement because it had gone out of print, and that was the only way they were available anymore. We went to those kinds of lengths to get what existed; we started having those books, and, as soon as they would exist, we would hear about them, and grab them.[30]

Here Seajay emphasizes bookwomen's support for feminist books; feminist bookwomen were able to get "what existed" and wanted to "grab" feminist books as soon as they were available. She also describes the bookwomen's prioritization of texts by women of color. Because even in their earliest days feminist bookstores functioned as distributors of both in- and out-of-print texts, they became a unique site of literary activism, maintaining a feminist history and dialogue not visible in records like catalogs or *Books In Print* or the inventories of mainstream bookstores.

National Women's Studies and Commitment to the Neighborhood: Womanbooks, New York 1972

By 1976, New York City feminists were holding a fundraiser to try to save Labyris, the first of several feminist bookstores in the city. Three lesbian feminists had opened the bookstore in 1972 in a small space in Greenwich Village. The name Labyris identified the bookstore as a specifically lesbian space marked by a lesbian claiming of the double-sided axe carried by the Amazon women warriors. In an early article the founders gave their names as Marizel, Deborah, and Patricia, and built on the ICI collective's definition of feminist bookstores as sites not primarily of sales but of movement conversation: "Other bookstores," the women observed of non-movement stores, "don't discuss racism or lesbianism with you."[31] Despite their stated commitment to creating Labyris as a "place where women can go" to talk, have lunch, and exchange ideas,[32] the bookstore developed a reputation of being exclusive. Carol Seajay had visited the year that it opened; she described it as a "ring the doorbell, and they decide if they'd let you in or not place."[33] The environment at each individual feminist bookstore was shaped by the personalities and commitments of its bookwomen. Even this early in the history of feminist bookstores, feminists understood that a number of bookstores together offered important leverage for supporting literature to further the feminist movement. The 1976 Labyris fundraiser documents the fact that bookstores early on were seen not as businesses but rather as spaces that relied on community to sustain them in exchange for the movement activism of the bookwomen. Nostalgia for an easy lesbian feminist community is fueled by dreams of a time when the bookstores didn't need to hold fundraisers; that time never existed. The poetry reading fundraiser, like other events at the bookstores, brought together an impressive list of feminist and lesbian authors who valued the bookstore: Ellen Marie Bissert, Leah Fritz, Judy Greenspan, Audre Lorde, Robin Morgan, Fran Winant, and Phyllis Witte. The flyer called on readers: "Labyris Books, New York's first feminist bookstore, is in urgent need of funds. We cannot develop and maintain a feminist community without serious feminist support."[34] Despite the reputation Labyris earned for their closed-door policy and perhaps because of the bookstore's experimentation with lesbian separatism, the big-name readers at the fundraiser indicate that this space was a significant one. Even in the face of exclusion, having a space to contest was valuable.

Three women who had visited Labyris in the Village imagined starting a different kind of bookstore. Karyn London, a self-described socialist feminist just out of college, and Eleanor Olds Batchelder, a linguistics scholar interested in supporting feminist business, met in a consciousness raising group and became lovers. Fabi Romero had joined New York Radical Feminists and was part of the consciousness raising group organized by Anne Koedt and Shulamith Firestone.[35] She met Batchelder when they collaborated on the New York Radical Feminists' Motherhood Conference and Speakout. London, Batchelder, and Romero wanted a bookstore more broadly inclusive of other women, in part because of their own identities. London explains, "We came from different political backgrounds, and that was a strength, because we weren't all of one persuasion: sexual orientation, race, politics, feminism."[36] Batchelder and London were lovers at the time, Romero was married to a man; both Batchelder and Romero have children; Romero is Latina, Batchelder and London are white; London identifies as a socialist feminist, Romero was committed to New York Radical Feminists, and Batchelder was interested in a business practice. Though I attempted multiple times to contact Romero, I was unsuccessful; this missed connection is perhaps a sign of the alignment of research along racial lines, my white identity more easily trusted by the white cofounders who are less at risk given the consistent hegemonic prioritization of white stories. Surely adding to this distance were the breaks in relationships between the three bookwomen, breaks still painful and difficult for them to talk about. Feminist bookstores began with personal and movement relationships; these relationships made difficult conversations and steep learning curves possible, but when learning failed, bookstore breaches caused heartbreak.[37]

London, Batchelder, and Romero found the feminist bookstore movement, different from their experiences at Labyris, in the pages of *The New Woman's Survival Catalog*, published by a contract publisher in 1973 and available by mail order from ICI: A Woman's Place. In the oversized book with the blazing red cover, the women found pictures of feminist bookstores across the nation. When I visited her in 2003, Batchelder found her copy of the book, still on her shelf, and flipped through the large browned pages: "Here is the section on feminist bookstores. And they had all these ones, you see, with the nice couches, and the chairs, and it was all so inspiring." In 1975, London and Romero, with Batchelder as a silent partner at the beginning, opened Womanbooks in the storefront of a leaky single-room-occupancy hotel, north of Labyris, on the Upper West Side of Manhattan, at 255 West 92nd Street. A flyer announcing the opening week, March 1–8, culminating in International Women's Day, concluded with a quote from poet Carolyn Kizer: "We are the custodians of the world's best-kept secret: Merely the private lives of one-half of humanity."[38] Womanbooks proved immediately popular both as a space and as an international feminist destination. During the opening week, London remembers, "somebody came in from Australia. It was like our second day open, and she bought hundreds of dollars of books to take home." "Somehow," Batchelder explains, "we got put into a lot of guidebooks, and, so, people knew to stop."

Each feminist bookstore had its own personality and made its own contributions to a growing conversation about organizational strategies, literary representation, and feminist accountability. New York was eventually home to multiple feminist bookstores, creating distinct sites of community within the often-insulated neighborhoods of the city. The feminist bookstores of New York, then, were also neighborhood bookstores, as well as specifically New York bookstores. Feminist publishing flourished in New York, long the center of the national publishing industry. Home to the headquarters of the United Nations as well as a central immigration port, New York is a transnational and multiethnic hub, sometimes legislated into separate neighborhoods. As a result of this interwoven identity, the city was home to one site of a transnational feminist movement connected with the United Nations; these networks shaped a reputation for Womanbooks that brought to the bookstore international visitors, among them Simone de Beauvoir.

While ICI focused on bookstores as information centers, the struggle between academic and community-based feminisms, between business and collective economies, lived inside Womanbooks in disagreements between cofounders. The bookstore was unmistakably feminist in design: "We had a big banner hanging up" outside, Batchelder remembers, "and, as you came into the store, we had a huge woman symbol painted on the wall, a red woman symbol. We had feminist music playing, we had coffee going in the back room." The cofounders, however, disagreed about the values of that feminism. The founding charter implied that book sales were a business side of the bookstore, while the library, events, and bulletin board were services: "The business of ordering and selling books in an efficient and profitable manner supports us and thus makes possible all our other services."[39] This framework seems emphatically different from ICI, where the information, the texts available, was central to the service of the bookstore. Karyn London seemed to share the ICI framework of information as activism, while Eleanor Batchelder valued a business model that could separate the two. By the time I interviewed London and Batchelder in the summer of 2003, the two seemed worlds apart though still in the same city.

On a rainy morning in 2003, I found my way up 95th Street from Central Park to the ninth-floor apartment Batchelder shared with Fumiko Ohno, her lover, before moving to Toronto to secure Ohno's immigration status when Canada gave state sanction to lesbian marriages in 2005. The two had worked together on translations for the feminist press.[40] Their damp, gray apartment tower was three blocks from the first location of Womanbooks. In the midst of last-minute packing on their way to a gay square dance convention in Canada, Batchelder talked with me on tape at her kitchen table and on the bus to La Guardia. She described how the bookstore had informed feminism's influence on university curricula through women's studies. Batchelder explains that Womanbooks, for academic women, "was better than a book table at the conferences—that was the other place where you could go and leaf through books and take a look and see what you were getting. But, because we had almost everything on our shelves, 'My god,' they would say, 'look, you have everything here. I can look and see.' And, also, people would come, like they do now to the [Lesbian Herstory] Archives, to do research at Womanbooks, because we didn't mind if they used the books there. We had a big table."[41] Word spread quickly about the stock and the community of women, and soon the annual Modern Language Association (MLA) Convention, a sizable gathering of scholars of literature and languages, at the end of December, brought the biggest revenue of the year for Womanbooks. During the life of Womanbooks (1975–1987), the MLA met in New York five times (1976, 1978, 1981, 1983, 1986), the most often in any one city. Batchelder describes the throng: "All the women's studies women would come in, and they would all make this pilgrimage up to 92nd Street to basically spend their book budget. They'd spend hundreds of dollars each at the store. They'd just make these huge piles of books, and ship them home." Ellen Messer-Davidow diagrams the close involvement of these MLA women in founding a humanities-based women's studies: "The names of the *Female Studies* editors and contributors show that an academic network radiating outward from the MLA Commission on the Status of Women boosted its development as a national field."[42] If these central women were informed by what they found at Womanbooks, Womanbooks was able to support the growth of women's studies. Womanbooks provided women's studies founders with resources unavailable (or unreadable) elsewhere.[43]

In a red brick apartment building not far from where Womanbooks had been, I met with Karyn London on a cloudy December day in 2003. London shared her different intentions for the bookstore. We sat on her couch accompanied by shelves crowded with feminist books, some of them remaindered titles (remaining copies of books the publisher has let go out of print) that she was still connecting with readers. She offers an explanation of her current work as a way to understand what she did at Womanbooks in the 1970s and 1980s. Now, London is a physician assistant practicing holistic health care and sharing preventative health education: "I provide HIV primary care to people living in welfare hotels around the corner, two blocks away from Womanbooks. So I'm still right there, next door to Womanbooks, the same neighborhood, seeing the same women." London's focus is responding to systems of oppression and working for universally accessible resources that, in turn, end oppression against women; the health care practice, then, continues the work of connecting women with each other and with literature that matters. She explains, "It's still very much the idea of networking, of . . . creating solutions to the problems that exist." She sees "about 45 percent women" and "especially people of color, African American women." She now addresses through health care the effects of the oppression she previously fought through the bookstore: "Most of the women have a history of abuse. Many of the men, too, but, for most of the women, that's how they came to HIV. That's how they got to drugs, and how they got HIV. And, so it [moving from Womanbooks into this health care work] seems like the most natural thing in the world. And, once again, they're my neighbors." London, living in the same neighborhood, is still serving a systemic need. Though she saw the influence Womanbooks had on academic women's studies, she saw this work as a side effect of the bookstore's purpose, to provide vital information to women: "We were more comfortable with someone asking for books about rape or abortion, and they weren't researching a paper. That was their experience. . . . They wanted a connection, where to go and who to talk to, and who's in a similar situation. One couldn't find that kind of information and support in just any bookstore or a library." Feminist bookstores shared a goal with and occupied more accessible spaces than university-based women's studies programs. Batchelder and London pulled at different sides of this connection. In combining their visions, they provided services to both the women's community and women's studies teachers, and Womanbooks became a space where the academic and community projects would remain, as they began, linked.

Tired of the leaks and outgrowing the hotel, in 1976 Womanbooks moved up 92nd Street to 201 West 92nd Street.[44] For Batchelder and London, the new space offered different advantages. The site was just a few doors down from where Joan Nestle housed the Lesbian Herstory Archives in her apartment at 215 West 92nd Street from 1974 until 1992, when the Archives moved to its current home in a brownstone in Brooklyn. Batchelder explains this proximity to the Archives in terms of power: "With both of those heavy-duty institutions on 92nd Street, nobody could afford not to go up there." Womanbooks, then, was geographically connected to other community institutions of lesbian history and culture as well as to academic sites, including Columbia University, just a mile and a half up Broadway. For London, the space offered more visibility to connect with and accessibility for neighborhood women: "It was one large room, that was a thousand square feet and rectangular. We tried to divide it up a little bit, to make cozier corners. There was the poetry corner and the children's book area, and a reading area. All before Barnes & Noble."[45] All of this was clearly visible from the street in a way that made the second location distinctly different from and more accessible than the first. The three women wrote in the first newsletter from the new space, "The large expansive corner windows flood the store with sunlight and make us more visible within the community. Women living nearby or passing on their way to work and school who would not have sought out a women's bookstore, lured inside out of curiosity, are surprised to find out how comfortable they feel being in a woman-defined space."[46]

Tension between Business and Movement:
Toronto Women's Bookstore, Toronto 1973

The year after women created Labyris in New York, the feminist bookstore movement went international. In Toronto, planning meetings began in the winter cold of 1972 to open a feminist bookstore the next year as part of the existing Women's Place, home to Interval House Shelter for Battered Women, Times Change Women's Employment Service, and the Women's Counseling Referral and Education Centre.[47] Two early geographies of the bookstore describe the environment that would, in the late 1980s and early 1990s, transform what had started as a bookstore run by white women into an antiracist feminist bookstore prioritizing alliances among the work and words of women of color. At 31 Dupont Street, the Women's Place was north of downtown and above Bloor Street, which divides the city along one of Toronto's main subway lines. When the bookstore outgrew the Women's Space, the collective looked south to Kensington Market, a central outdoor marketplace over several blocks that serves as a site for political activism, immigrant communities, and community-based shops.[48] With a new name, the Toronto Women's Bookstore reopened in the shared space available in a building called the Amazon Workshop occupied by a women's printing press and the Amazon Women's Self Defense Collective.[49]

The Toronto bookwomen had been in touch with the women of Womanbooks, and, perhaps as a result, they shared some of the same tensions around the structure of the bookstore in their early years. Patti Kirk remembers that she learned how to run a bookstore from Womanbooks: "I loved Womanbooks in New York . . . , and I actually went early on and talked to them several times about what worked for them, what didn't work. It was interesting, because when we first got started, I knew that it would be great to find out something about running a bookstore. There was no place to do that at the time." Under Kirk's leadership, the Toronto bookstore transitioned (against resistance) from a grassroots organization to a business; later it would return to a more collective model. These organizational changes made the conversation about the power and economics of feminist relationship building more explicit at the Toronto bookstore, and the movement and labor union ethics of the city's social movements ultimately held the bookstore accountable to build an antiracist feminist vocabulary and structure.

One afternoon in 2007 I met with Patti Kirk in the backyard patio garden of TWB, the bookstore she had helped to move to Harbord Street. As a result of a break over power structures and feminist approaches, Kirk hadn't been to the bookstore in years. Before this visit, few of the bookstore staff knew that Kirk, who co-owns the bookstore Parentbooks up the street, once worked at the Women's Bookstore. In the early 1970s, Kirk, then a young teacher, found out about the bookstore through word of mouth; a friend of hers was volunteering there and brought her around.

Only the last person out could lock the shared space on Kensington, so the evening sessions at the Amazon Women's Self Defense Collective meant that the bookstore, unstaffed, was open, too. By this time, Kirk was deeply involved with the bookstore and wanted to see some changes. She wanted more space, a lock on the doors, and some monetary recognition of her involvement. Her business-centric framework conflicted with the collective's original vision for the bookstore: "The climate of the day was antibusiness, that was really too bourgeois." By 1975 or 1976, though the bookstore was still a collective, Kirk and her like-minded collective member Marie Prins were "starting to draw a tiny salary." Kirk explains, "I know we worked a year or two pretty much full time for no pay or ridiculous pay, because that's what you do." For Kirk, the bookstore was a business, her life's vocation, and she did not support the collective model.

In 1975 tensions in the collective reached a boiling point. It turns out that the reason Kirk and Prins started to draw a salary that year was that they, together with "Joy, the Saturday person," took over the bookstore that they saw "running really inefficiently with the collective model." Kirk remembers that there "were a lot of bad feelings about that," though she thinks it was good for the bookstore. This could be a space of attempted or missed negotiation, and I have not found the other collective members from this time. Kirk was easier to find at her bookstore just up Harbord Street.

Negotiations between the business and nonprofit models involved complex tensions around income, energy, and shape of commitment to the movement. Kirk and Prins left the Women's Bookstore together, on bad terms, when their business-based goals failed to nourish the collective. Kirk recalls, "We had run it as though it was our own store for eleven years and ended up with nothing, basically, when we left. That was also a very painful part for me." A desire for ownership and recognition at the bookstores lives in tension with the anticapitalist goal of the bookstores as sites of resistance, socialist feminism, lesbian separatism, or other theoretical experiments. The bookstores were, even when owned by a single woman, community spaces. The narrative of sacrifice to the bookstore emphasizes the work that individual women put into the bookstore even while the work of many women (like the other early collective members) goes unrecognized, erased from the record.

Part of the difference between the Toronto bookstore and US feminist bookstores stemmed from its context within Canada's democratic socialism, which claimed at least a nominal state commitment to multiculturalism. As a result, the bookstore received funding early on through International Women's Year (1975) and later for projects that included building an accessibility ramp. The 1975 funding, ironically, contributed to Kirk and Prins beginning to draw a salary. Following the work of feminist activists, the UN designation of International Women's Year included the first World Conference on Women, held in Mexico City that July. The transnational feminist movement had put into motion a demand for materials on women, and feminist bookstores served as distributors as well as educators for the cause. Because it was International Women's Year, Kirk remembers,

> All of a sudden, there was money for women's materials, primarily for the regular libraries to get some women's materials. At the same time OISE [Ontario Institute for Studies in Education] had a fabulous women's center which had a library. They weren't doing courses; it was more research. They had a wonderful library, and they came to us for all of their stuff. And the Y had a women's resource center, the Y on Birch Street, and they came to us and bought all their purchases. I mean, this might have been $1,000, $1,500, but we were hysterical when it happened; it was so incredible. There was no question that they would come and buy the books from us.[50]

The women at TWB already knew where to find materials on women and were ready to provide for this transnational call. In addition to the women's resource centers, women's studies programs, and public libraries, the Women's Bookstore filled orders from the Toronto District School Board as the bookstore quickly built "credibility and financial stability." For Kirk, it was "a thrill": "The librarians were coming, the textbooks were being ordered, the dykes from Boston were coming, and it was so exciting."

In 1974, "dykes from Boston" had a bookstore of their own on a different model. New Words grew directly out of the national feminist (and, specifically, feminist theological) academic conversations anchored at central universities of Boston and Cambridge. Four women connected by interwoven academic and grassroots feminist conversations in the city founded the bookstore not as "a big money-making venture" or even as an investment, cofounder Gilda Bruckman remembers: "It was seen as a living, and it was seen as a way to be creating something significant in the community."[51] Demonstrating this community accountability with annual birthday statements to their public, the bookwomen developed a theory of feminist bookstore practice more closely related to ICI: A Woman's Place, yet distinct in its close relationship with feminism's influence on the academy.

The spaces of my interviews as late as the early 2000s indicate the ongoing work of New Words influencing academic feminisms while also in conversation with grassroots feminist practice. The 2004 NWSA Conference in Milwaukee featured Rita Arditti, a cofounder of New Words, as one of the keynote speakers on a panel called "Feminist Uses of Science and Technology." After the keynote, we met at a hotel coffee table, one floor up from most of the conference proceedings. She was a bit shorter than me, aged seventy that year, with cropped stone-gray hair. She unraveled the double-stranded history of New Words' beginnings. Born in Argentina, where she grew up part of a Sephardic Jewish community, she earned her degree at the University of Rome and then came to the United States to research genetics and to continue her political practice of science. By 1973, these combined interests had led Arditti to a teaching position at the alternative Union Institute and University while living in Cambridge. There, she began to imagine a feminist bookstore:

> I was thinking about the need to have a feminist bookstore, a place for women to buy books about women. Because in those days, if you would go to a regular bookstore and ask about books for women, one, they would have almost nothing, two, they wouldn't pay attention, or they would look at you like you were a weird person. And if there was something, it was difficult to find, so. And the idea of a whole space devoted to women seemed to me very important. I had lived in Italy, and I used to

go to a left-wing bookstore near Rome, and I thought, "How come there isn't a bookstore for women?"[52]

Arditti began making plans with Barbara Starrett to develop "a whole space devoted to women." Starrett, a women's studies PhD student in her last year at Union Institute and University and working on her dissertation, "Women, Art, and Evolution," mentioned their idea to Mary Daly, the feminist philosopher and theologian. Daly had heard about two other women, Jean MacRae and Mary Lowry, who wanted to open a feminist bookstore; she connected the women, and the four decided to collaborate and to fund the bookstore startup themselves. Here, Arditti recalls, "Barbara dropped out. She thought that she couldn't do it," and the remaining three sought a fourth woman. Emily Culpepper, another Cambridge-based feminist theologian, hosted feminist discussions on a public access television show. One show featured Mary Daly and several of her students, and they mentioned the incipient feminist bookstore. Watching from home, Gilda Bruckman had just graduated with her master's degree and was working in a bookstore. She called and offered her help. Here in Cambridge, grassroots and academic feminism seemed essential to each other, each feeding the other; this was a different environment from the Bay Area described by the ICI bookwomen. Gilda Bruckman, Jean MacRae, Mary Lowry, and Rita Arditti opened New Words at 419 Washington Street in Somerville, Massachusetts, in the spring of 1974.

New Words' collection of a large body of women's literature in one place contributed to the national feminist bookstore project of making visible and readable a women's literature. The first order that New Words placed to local wholesaler Paperback Booksmith, on March 12, 1974, included around two hundred titles on a handwritten list. A quick run through the alphabetical list offers a sense of the collective force of the New Words shelves: Hannah Arendt's *On Revolution*, Gwendolyn Brooks's *Selected Poems*, Toni Cade Bambara's *Black Woman*, Dorothy Day's *On Pilgrimage*, George Eliot's *Mill on the Floss*, Nikki Giovanni's *Gemini*, Lillian Hellman's *Unfinished Woman*, Elizabeth Janeway's *Man's World, Woman's Place*, Helen Keller's *Helen Keller: Her Socialist Years*, Billie Jean King's *Tennis to Win*, Denise Levertov's *Poet in the World*, Margaret Mead's *Coming of Age in Samoa*, Anaïs Nin's *Spy in the House of Love*, Joyce Carol Oates's *Expensive People*, Marge Piercy's *Dance the Eagle to Sleep*, Jean Rhys's *Wide Sargasso Sea*, Gertrude Stein's *Three Lives*, St. Teresa of Avila's *Interior Castle*, and Mary Wollstonecraft's *Vindication of the Rights of*

Woman.[53] The list makes a limited but strong claim to a transnational feminist context, diverse in racial and socioeconomic class identities, both contemporary and historical. New Words became a familiar emblem of reading as vital feminist work with Ellen Shub's 1976 black-and-white photo of a young girl reading a Wonder Woman book underneath a "Women Working" sign at the end of a set of shelves in New Words.[54]

The dual history of the bookstore's name suggests the complexity of feminist histories rooted in Boston and Cambridge, and one already fraught by the productive disagreements, here particularly about racial justice and feminism, both within and supported by the feminist literature on the shelves. Just a year before the bookstore opened, Beacon Press had published Mary Daly's *Beyond God the Father*, in which she writes, "Women are really *hearing ourselves* and each other, and out of this supportive hearing emerge *new* words."[55] Daly's narration of the feminist movement articulates the way that "supportive hearing" produces new kinds of writing and reading, "new words." Though Arditti, MacRae, and Lowry had already chosen the name when Bruckman signed on, Bruckman prefers not to draw exclusively on Daly's legacy. Bruckman concedes that Daly was an inspiration for the name: "I have to say, in all honesty, the first source was a quote in Mary Daly's *Beyond God the Father*."[56] Another source, she remembers, is an earlier feminist ancestor: "There was a Virginia Woolf [quote], not so dissimilar, in *Three Guineas*. We used to fudge it when people actually said, 'Which?'"[57] In 1938, thirty-six years before Daly's book, Virginia and Leonard Woolf's Hogarth Press came out with Virginia Woolf's *Three Guineas*. In one of Woolf's footnotes, she writes, "In a transitional age when many qualities are changing their value, new words to express new values are much to be desired."[58]

The public break between Mary Daly and Audre Lorde offers context for New Words bookwomen's reluctance to trace heritage back to Daly. In 1978 Beacon Press published Daly's *Gyn/Ecology: The Metaethics of Radical Feminism*, and she sent a copy to Audre Lorde. Lorde had appreciated *Beyond God the Father*; she wrote to Daly, "Many of your analyses are strengthening and helpful to me."[59] In *Gyn/Ecology*, Daly set out to resist the sacrificing and silencing of women by tracing feminist spiritual ecologies in contrast to major religions in which "the fundamental sacrifices of sadospiritual religion are female."[60] Paging through the book, Lorde observed with some pain that the feminist goddesses Daly offered readers were "only white, western-european, judeo-christian." Taking a breath, Lorde wrote a letter to Daly to ask, "Where was Afrekete, Yemanje, Oyo and Mawulisa? Where are the warrior-goddesses of the Vodun, the Dohemeian Amazons and the warrior-women of Dan?" Having sent the letter privately and receiving no satisfactory response,[61] Lorde submitted the essay for publication in Gloria Anzaldúa and Cherríe Moraga's collection *This Bridge Called My Back* (Persephone Press, 1981). Listening in on this no-longer-private correspondence, readers encounter Lorde offering both support for Daly's struggles with her employer, Boston University, and an engaged critical response to *Gyn/Ecology* calling for Daly's recognition of images of female power from histories and spiritual traditions of women of color. In the letter, Lorde reflects on her own reluctance to initiate a discussion of racism with a white woman who might take refuge in her privilege and refuse to dialogue: "The history of white women who are unable to hear Black women's words, or to maintain a dialogue with us, is long and discouraging."[62] Rather, Lorde hopes, "we, as women shaping our future, are in the process of shattering and passing beyond" this "old pattern of relating." Though Lorde and Daly did not develop a dialogue, their exchange offers a model of feminist accountability practiced through literature, a model in dialogue with bookwomen's own vocabularies and strategies for feminist accountability.[63]

In the bookstore's birthday statements the New Words bookwomen offered another option for feminist economies.[64] Rather than a collective or a business model, the New Words women created a feminist ethic of service. The "Statement from New Words on Our Fourth Birthday, April, 1978," tells again the story of the bookstore's beginnings, explains the wages ($5 per hour as well as insurance and paid vacation) and hours (twelve to forty weekly) of the collective workers, the choice of the "for-profit" business structure ("gives us more autonomy in relation to the government and the IRS"), and emphasizes the connections of New Words to a community of women's work: "Although we have not yet realized any significant profit, we have made contributions in the form of small donations ($15–$100) or items from the bookstore to a variety of local groups on an ad hoc basis. Among the groups we have supported in this way are Women's Community Health, Women, Inc., Transitions House, Respond, the United Mine Workers, Rosie's Place, Vocations for Social Change and the Women's Center in Cambridge."[65] This outside community also shaped the physical space inside the store: "When we moved we hired a crew of women to paint the store. We are also proud of our bookcases and furniture which have been made over the last four years by six different women carpenters.

Our lawyer and accountant are women. We occasionally ask other women to work at the store and pay them at the same rate we pay ourselves." These commitments and exchanges followed the "policy of not accepting volunteers" (broken once, they note, when twenty women helped the store move "from Washington Street to Hampshire Street in less than two hours"), and indicated that the women's space of the bookstore gave women jobs and participated in interrupting capitalist efficiencies by prioritizing lesbian feminist relationships.

"A Store Could Help Overcome Isolation and Create a New Culture": Common Woman Bookstore, Austin 1975

The existence of a few feminist bookstores incited the creation of others across the United States. This building energy suggests both the significance of feminists visiting and learning from feminist bookstores as well as the value of the bookstores to widely varied and geographically dispersed feminist communities. In the early 1970s, the exchange of knowledge between bookwomen and potential bookwomen took place through pilgrimage.[66] Even early on, the force of the physical space of these collections of books and resources inspired women to create maps of feminist bookstore sites and embark on road trips, resulting in a recurring oral and written history trope of the feminist bookstore pilgrimage. For women in Austin, just such a pilgrimage incited the beginnings of the Common Woman Bookstore, now known as BookWoman, that distinguished itself as a site of women's music, feminist crafting, and feminist spirituality.

Sitting together with me in her living room on a Sunday, tired from the morning's gardening but with excitement for the tale, Susan Post recalls: "The story I know is, Nancy Lee [Marquis] and Cynthia [Roberts] went on a road trip the summer of '74 I guess, or '75. . . . They visited women's bookstores in other parts of the country, and they said we should have one, so they had a call for a meeting to start a bookstore."[67] A grainy image of the original collective members appeared in the Austin *Rag* in a section called "Women Acting on Austin." Common Woman collective member Nancy Lee told the *Rag* reporter, "We visited Oakland and other women's centers and saw that a store could help overcome isolation and create a new culture. So we decided to create collectively the most complete woman's book store in Austin." As a public site and a collection of feminist thought, the bookstore format allowed women to connect with each other and to read the context of feminist movements.[68] The bookstore started, as in other cities, amid and in connection with a range of grassroots feminist organizations. Flyers for musical events created by the Common Woman Bookstore (and its later incarnation, BookWoman) were produced by WomenSpace, the consciousness raising space that would become the Austin YWCA, printed by the Red River Women's Press, and in connection with the women's recording label Olivia Records. These flyers both document the significance of feminist bookstores as sites of distribution of women's music and emphasize the contributions of the Common Woman Bookstore to the lesbian feminist music life of Austin, the self-named live music capital of the world. The bookstore began with what would turn out to be the annual Common Woman Bookstore Halloween dance, a fundraiser for the bookstore and an extension of the bookstore space: "The bookstore, said Cynthia Roberts, has already begun input into Austin culture: a festive Halloween Ball, guaranteed to be the women-only event of the season, is on the way. The for-female fest will be a circus of activity, including dancing to disco music, special food treats, punch of 'various complexions and effects,' & free and supervised activities for children. Costumes are required for the gala, open only to women, which will unfold at 4700 Grover, the Unitarian Church. The ball-benefit will have a $2.50 donation for entry to all activities."[69] Collective member Cynthia Roberts emphasized the bookstore's early effect on "Austin culture" and the "gala, open only to women," publicly identified the bookstore as a space for women. In addition to the gala, Post reports that the collective "sold stock that was redeemable a year later, so people bought certificates in $25 or $50 increments. . . . We started with $500, that's what we raised."[70] Some people donated money by never redeeming their certificates, others donated lumber, and the building owner donated the space in exchange for the women's renovation. The space had been firebombed in a drug raid, and Dede Spontak, then an apprentice carpenter, headed up the women-run rebuild.

Above the first location, Post describes, hung a "big, red, nylon banner with grommets and yellow letters that Dede and I made. She sewed it, she knew how to sew. That was a big project. And we chose those colors because they were revolutionary, red and yellow." Women at feminist bookstores across the nation made their own shelves, desks, signs, and other fixtures for the bookstores. In Austin, the bookwomen began a long-standing tradition of feminist crafting through the bookstore.[71] Nina Wouk, then a young Jewish lesbian who eagerly wrote to *Lesbian Tide* to announce the new "lesbian feminist bookstore,"[72] worked with Spontak to paint the inside of the bookstore violet and crimson. Feminist bookstores as learning spaces served as sites of women's building projects. Feminist bookwomen supported the expansion of this apprenticeship in the feminist movement. In 1977, two years after Spontak guided Post, Wouk, and the rest of the collective through the Guadalupe Street rebuild, the Iowa City Women's Press published Dale McCormick's *Against the Grain: A Carpentry Manual for Women*. The women of the Iowa City Women's Press pledged on the first page of the spiral-bound book, "written and illustrated" by McCormick, "We have given a free copy of this book to all women's bookstores who want to use this book without buying it." I found this book more than twenty years later in the used book section of BookWoman (formerly Common Woman). As information centers, the bookwomen and feminist publishers worked together to apprentice women in building together.

The bookstores' building projects were literary as well, reading a work in common. Sitting down with Susan and Nina in the bookstore, I asked who chose the name. Nina answered with a laugh, "Judy Grahn."[73] Variations on the name Common Woman, like those on A Woman's Place, were, purposefully, common during the 1970s. The Common Woman Bookstore collective included a few lines of Grahn's "The Common Woman Poems" in their first brochure:

> For all the world we didn't know we held in common
> All along
> A common woman is as common as the best of bread
> And will rise
> And will become strong–
> I swear it to you
> I swear it to you on my own head
> I swear it to you on my common woman's head![74]

Through her poetry, and later her essays, Grahn had offered her understanding of "common women" as overlapping islands who use separatism to deeply engage with difference. In Austin, separatism brought the collective to an early historic split.

The bookstore's first location was part of the Feminist Mission de Guadalupe, a building owned by Margaret Ann Nunley. Here Guadalupe named both the address, 2004 Guadalupe Street, and feminist interpretations of La Virgen de Guadalupe. The bookwomen were evicted within the year.

Nunley's Haircut Store below the bookstore supported "women's teams in soccer and baseball" in connection with Nunley's feminist commitments,[75] and when a hairdresser, a man, tried to go upstairs to the bookstore during a break and was turned away, Nunley ended their lease.[76] With the split over separatism, half of the collective left the bookstore. Six women remained and helped to move the bookstore to its new space on San Antonio Street, then five of the remaining women left. Susan Post, a shy library worker who had reluctantly joined in, kept the bookstore alive in the room adjacent to her apartment. During the long, boisterous collective meetings at Les Amis, an outdoor café and site of the progressive community in Austin until it was replaced with a Starbucks in the 1990s, Post voted against separatism in the bookstore: "I felt that the vision couldn't go forward if men were asked to leave, because women wouldn't come." Judy Turner, who managed the accounts, practiced income-sharing with Post so that Post could pay rent and keep the bookstore alive on her part-time salary from the University of Texas Perry-Castañeda Library. Post remembers, "I worked at the library from eight until noon, four hours every day at the library, and then I would ride my bike back to 15th and San Antonio and open the store." In the evenings, Post studied the book business: "I had all the records and the catalogs, and I just learned it on the job. There was a communal bathroom for the apartments that became the bookstore, and just walking from my room to the bathroom, I'd just pick something up and start reading it or studying it, and just kind of figured it out that way." The life of the bookstore would become a center for music and feminist crafting, including an altar making collective; Post draws on this feminist spirituality to emphasize the bookstore as her calling. Post stayed with the bookstore, she explains, because "She made me. The Virgin, the Goddess, She, the big She in the sky. It had to be done, someone had to do it, so I learned how to do it."

Making a Movement, 1976

There were five women standing for Austin where Texas was drawn out in the sand and gravel of the former Girl Scout campground outside Omaha, Nebraska. Someone had the idea to map out the movement, to take a picture of everyone at the Women in Print Conference standing where their city was; this was a national network. June Arnold and Parke Bowman, lovers and founders of the lesbian feminist publisher Daughters Press, organized the Women in Print gathering, and here the feminist bookstore movement changed from being a collection of individual feminist bookstores shaped by their cities and the inflections of their local feminisms to an intentional network of bookwomen who drafted a shared manifesta of feminist bookwomen ethics and visions.

This conversation among the bookwomen grew into a feminist literary advocacy network that would change both the vocabularies of feminism and reading and publishing in the United States. Fed by the feminist energy of the 1970s and 1980s, the number of US feminist bookstores open at one time would only reach its peak in the mid-1990s; this long life of the feminist bookstore as institution allowed the bookwomen to influence feminism and the literary industry over decades. Feminist bookstores continued to open nationally and internationally throughout the 1970s, 1980s, and 1990s. Each collective, owner and staff configuration, and business partnership struggled with their own negotiation of the tension between business practice and reimagining the bookstore structure with feminist values. Referenced so frequently by bookwomen, the description of the feminist bookstore as a "women's resource center disguised as a bookstore" signaled that the bookwomen were attempting to imagine a new kind of exchange.[77]

Susan Post was one of those standing on the map for Austin, though she said she would rather have been walking along the railroad tracks alone; she was "scared, intimidated, and very shy" after arriving by hitchhike because her girlfriend's car broke down on the way to Nebraska from the Michigan Womyn's Music Festival. From her designated spot, Post could see that not everyone was on the map; "some people didn't want to be in the picture, because maybe the FBI was after them. . . . These are radical feminists who thought they had FBI files. I don't know that there were any bank robbers or bombing perpetrators, but there was stuff going on, you know."[78] The conference was steeped in the overlapping movements of the 1960s and 1970s. Author Bertha Harris remembers the sweaty summer camp being fraught with concern about FBI infiltrators;[79] Arnold and Bowman seemed to be constantly looking over their shoulders. Despite the distraction of looming federal intervention, feminist publishers, printers, illustrators like Daughters designer Loretta Li, and booksellers formalized an information sharing structure for the feminist movement.

The energy of the Women in Print gathering made opening new feminist bookstores, including one in San Francisco, seem possible. By 1976, the two- or three-hour bus ride from San Francisco to Oakland motivated Carol Seajay to start thinking about opening a feminist bookstore closer to home.

She and her partner, Paula Wallace, applied for a loan at the Feminist Federal Credit Union,[80] and that summer Seajay headed out to Omaha. The first night of the Women in Print Conference, bookwomen formally exchanged resources for the first time. This dialogue enacted a counterpublic focused on sharing women's words and built the foundation for a growing national network. Each bookwoman shared one question they had and one area of knowledge with which they could help others. Seajay asked, could she start a feminist bookstore with $6,000–$8,000 and live on the bookstore?

"The next day this woman, in the swimming pool, where everyone's naked—this naked woman came up to me in the swimming pool and said, 'Yes, you can.' And I had no idea what she was talking about!" Trying to stay "cool," Seajay listened to the woman's advice, "'You can, you know, we had about eight-thousand dollars, and it's supporting me half time.' That was Karyn London, who'd started Womanbooks. Later in the day, Gilda Bruckman came up to me, with clothes on, and told me what they had done at New Words." The force of the collective feminist bookstore movement inspired Seajay. "Just the fact that they had done it made it so much easier. Clearly, we were all inventing the same thing in our different parts of the world. And I'm sure it would've worked if I hadn't known that, but for them to say, 'Yes. You go do it, girl,' was great." On her return to San Francisco, Seajay, with Wallace, left ICI: A Woman's Place and opened Old Wives' Tales on Valencia Street.[81]

Almost immediately Old Wives' Tales bookwomen began publishing an annual (and sometimes semiannual) "Birthday Statement." Like the New Words bookwomen, the Old Wives' Tales bookwomen indicated with their birthday statements that the bookstore was accountable to the community. The first birthday statement documents the attempts of Old Wives' Tales bookwomen to articulate and crystallize the challenges and vision of the feminist bookstore movement. Seajay and Wallace emphasized the importance of the bookstore both as a source of income for the two women and as a movement space interrupting capitalism. The bookstore opened, in part, because Seajay began to think "about what she was going to do when her unemployment ended (this time)," and largely because of Seajay's experiences with homophobia (and compulsory white, middle-class heterosexuality) on the job.[82] Seajay expressed her "hatred for the compartmentalized life that has always gone with my past jobs (the total separation of my lesbian self and my relationships with my lovers from those 40 hours on-the-job) and not being able to change it or me this month."[83] As lesbian feminist workspaces and movement places, feminist bookstores created space for analyzing and resisting institutionalized heterosexism.

Simultaneous to imagining a new lesbian feminist workspace, Seajay and Wallace also grappled with the role of lesbian feminist bookselling. Seajay and Wallace articulated their struggle to build community accountability within a profit-driven model: "In trying to provide a service to the community and support ourselves, we are forced into a legal and political structure that defines us as owners, profit-making and capitalists, which is the opposite of our intentions. We are in a position to make decisions that affect our community as well as ourselves. How to deal best with such contradictions and the criteria for decision making is not always clear. We want and need discussion in these areas."[84] Imagining how to redefine ownership while recognizing labor remained a central and productive challenge in the bookstores. Feminist bookwomen saw the bookstores as movement spaces: "Should there come a time when a woman's bookstore is not needed (or no one has the time or energy to keep it open), the store's assets will go back into the community in the manner that seems best to the women then running the store."[85] The end these women imagined at the beginning proved different from the actual struggles that closed the hundreds of feminist bookstores that would become part of this industry-changing landmark movement.

These are some of the feminist bookstores that were open in 1976, with their founding dates:

ICI: A Woman's Place, Oakland (1970)
Amazon, Minneapolis (1970)
Labyris, New York (1972)
New Words, Cambridge, MA (1973)
Toronto Women's Bookstore (1973)
Charis, Atlanta (1974)
Xantippe, Amsterdam (1974)
The Feminist Bookshop, Sydney, Australia (1974)
Womanbooks, New York (1975)
Common Woman Bookstore, Austin (1975)
Savannah Bay, Utrecht, Netherlands (1975)
Djuna Books, New York (1976)
Old Wives' Tales, San Francisco (1976)

TWO

REVOLUTIONARIES IN
A CAPITALIST SYSTEM
1976–1980

At the 1976 Women in Print gathering in Omaha, bookwomen began to forge a movement and public identity as feminist bookwomen; they began to imagine what change they could create with this new collective self. Amid the gathering of publishers, printers, illustrators, and booksellers, women from eighteen feminist bookstores talked with each other almost nonstop, hungry for this unprecedented connection. Bookwomen were already practiced at sharing and connecting women with each other and with information. Staying up into the early mornings at the Women in Print meeting, bookwomen realized they could pool their skills and information to improve access to transformative feminist materials. In the process of sharing with each other an impressive array of books, pamphlets, magazines, and publisher information, bookwomen together wove new feminist theories for, or ways of understanding, a movement-based information economy. This history is necessary to repairing recent misunderstandings of feminist bookwomen's roles in feminism. Understanding these early bookwomen's frameworks for using their bookstores to interrupt systems of capital allows us to recognize the deep work of the bookstores as movement institutions from which bookwomen shaped lesbian antiracism and feminist accountability at large. This information economy was based not on supply and demand but on building feminist vocabularies.

At the Omaha campground, feminist bookwomen began to circulate, for example, hard-to-find works about violence against women. "It was so exciting to talk to each other and just ask these questions," remembers Carol Seajay, then a volunteer at Oakland's ICI: A Woman's Place and planning to start Old Wives' Tales in San Francisco. "Like, 'What's a book for a little girl who needs this?' and 'Do you know of anything about incest?' There was one pamphlet that you could order from this woman in Sacramento, California, and it was such an incredible resource."[1] Bookwomen were uniquely positioned to amplify the reach of these resources. To keep this vital conversation alive, bookwomen envisioned combining their strengths to create a "Feminist Bookstore Alliance."[2] Amid the sparking glow of shared energy, bookwomen sat in a circle at a session they called "Future Plans: What Do We Want." Here bookwomen drafted what they would circulate as the guiding values of the feminist bookstore movement. These collective values, in some cases, pushed up against what individual bookwomen believed. Having a joint focus meant that bookwomen were now accountable not only to their communities but also to their national (and, soon, transnational) peers.

In their own bookstores, many bookwomen had practiced transparency with their communities, committing the bookstores as movement institutions, through newsletters, letters, and annual birthday statements that included financial, staffing, and movement literature news. Now bookwomen put that strategy to work with each other: they started a national newsletter to maintain their connection with and accountability to each other. The first issue of the *Feminist Bookstores Newsletter* (FBN) reported the vision drafted in Nebraska:

1. We want a feminist bookstore newsletter (this is it!) to share information and to help create a communications network based on cooperation rather than (you guessed it) competition.
2. We envision feminist bookstores as a network of "woman's places" and information centers across the country. (feminist shelters?)
3. We are committed to developing our politics as well as our service functions.
4. We want to find ways of dealing with the inherent contradiction between being revolutionaries and being in a capitalist business system.
5. We want to develop ways of working together that make us more accountable to our communities and to each other.
6. We are committed to actively support the feminist media and to increase its effectiveness.
7. We intend to work on creating a feminist "books in print" which would include ordering information.[3]

Though the conference produced plans for three newsletters, bookwomen were the only group to create a sustained network and publication. Three bookstores put up startup money: Womanbooks in New York, New Words in Cambridge, and Amazon in Minneapolis.[4] Seajay and André (who used no last name) agreed to edit and publish the FBN. As the distribution and networking engine of the feminist bookstore movement, the FBN made it possible for bookwomen to build a vocabulary, to document and share important changes in publishing, and to wield influence in numbers to shape and sustain feminist information.

The FBN arrived to bookstores five to six times each year from 1976 to 2000. In 1976, André and Seajay stapled and folded the sheaf of legal-sized pages to share a collection of book lists, skill sharings, information about publishers, news of the book industry, notices of new feminist bookstores, and conversations about feminist practice. This movement journal combined the distinct skill sets of feminist bookstores, like those described in chapter 1, into a transnational movement. This focused and collaboratively written journal amplified local bookwomen's strategies for racial justice and literary activism; now the bookwomen were crafting a collective vocabulary and could build on each other's successes and misses. By writing for, reading, and enacting advice shared in the FBN, bookwomen intentionally shaped their influence on generations of feminists and on the book industry. On these pages, bookwomen learned from each other and held each other accountable through sustained conversations about racial justice and struggles to prioritize movement over capitalist-based information distribution. In chapter 3 I trace bookwomen's development of feminist accountability through the bookstores; this movement accountability to each other seemed particularly urgent because of the external influence bookwomen sought to exert. This chapter lays the groundwork for that history by tracing the first years of the FBN, the groundbreaking engine of the feminist bookstore movement, and its transformation of individual bookstores into a transnational feminist literary activist force to be reckoned with.[5]

Working shifts at BookWoman in Austin in the late 1990s, I propped myself up behind the heavy womanmade desk and paged through the *Feminist Bookstore News*. Susan Post, an early collective member and cofounder of the Common Woman Bookstore that had become BookWoman, combed through the issues to mark important articles and underline profiled books or sidelines. With the arrival of the journal, distinctive with a different colorful cardstock cover each time, I felt a whisper of history and context. The feminist bookstore movement was larger than the bookstore relationships, readings, and shelf titles that had made my Austin life possible. In order to describe how bookwomen had not always or only been small business owners but, rather, had been movement organizers enacting feminist literary activism, I would travel to bookwomen's homes and bookstores in San Francisco, Cambridge, New York, Portland, and Toronto. Only after leaving Austin would I learn to understand what Susan Post had showed me here at home.

Post is archivist of her own Common Woman/BookWoman Bookstore collection. She keeps almost everything. Talking together in the 2000s, I tell her how my interviews are going, that I've talked with Carol Seajay, Gilda Bruckman, Kate Rushin, Kit Quan, all women she has met, whose words she has read, with whom she has shared food. She says quickly, "You should come over and see my files." While I had seen the bookstore office lined with womyn's music LPs and stacks of flyers, foam core signs, even the door from a previous bookstore location, this was the first I had heard about Post's archival files. Excited, I jump at the chance: "Saturday morning is perfect! I'll bring the breakfast tacos." This becomes our tender routine. Stepping in from her garden, she brings me into the spare bedroom, and on the bed where her lover's mother will find refuge, where her daughter will return for sparse visits, on this thin and intimate sheet she piles treasures from her bookstore and her life in the feminist bookstore movement. She fishes out flyers from her filing cabinets, boxes from her closet. She has a story for each one; she remembers everyone's names and the kinds of books they liked to read. How to understand the historical importance of these beautiful pieces? "Wait here one minute," and she returns with a set of keys. Warm already from her hands, they clink into my palm. "Down Lamar, past 2222, just before Airport, you'll see a storage space on your right." My lover and I make the drive together, and we pull up the metal door with a clang. Amid stacks of boxes and furniture, we find Post's full collection of the *Feminist Bookstores Newsletter* and its later identity, the *Feminist Bookstore News*. We phone Post and ask to borrow them, stack them in the car. "Keep them in a safe place," she cautions. These newsletters, marked in pencil and pen by Post and other occasional staff members, are filled with articles by bookwomen offering each other advice about how to start a new bookstore, talk with each other and with publishers, call each other on racism, find children's books representing lesbians, hold letter-writing campaigns to get books back in print, and more. Weaving together the local bookstore beginnings I traced in chapter 1, these widely circulated installments called a movement into being, brought distant bookwomen together onto the same pages to share their knowledge and to imagine how they could change feminism and the book industry. Post's archive showed me that the work of feminist bookwomen has never been only to order books and arrange them on shelves (as I describe in chapter 4, a surprisingly complex practice in its own right). Fueled by the FBN, feminist bookwomen made feminist relationships and literature possible.

This feminist publishing project built a movement. Through letter-writing chains and phone calls between the bookwomen, Seajay and André compiled shared information for the *Feminist Bookstores Newsletter* and then typed it onto a "super fancy Gestetner stencil." Seajay drove a borrowed car from San Francisco to Santa Rosa, where André worked at Rising Woman Books.[6] "We would print one side of each of the pages," Seajay explains, "then I'd stay overnight while the ink dried, and then we'd get up in the morning and print the other side. Then we would staple them and address them, send them out." The giant Gestetner printing press at Rising Woman was rumored to be a press previously used by the Oakland Women's Press Collective. Seajay saw the ethics of her own working-class identity in this commitment to shared learning: "I think there's something very special about booksellers, because, you know, we're the shopkeepers. It's not, it's not like being a writer, it's not like being a publisher, you know, they're kind of genteel or glamorous, or ego-driven careers, some of them. And the booksellers are just kind of like the working-class girls. Just like, got some information, they want you to have it."[7] To distribute information, bookwomen became writers and publishers. Though they worked behind the scenes, they intentionally cultivated an active role in feminist literature and relationality as they supported and shaped new feminist bookstores. In the first FBN issue, what would become the regular new bookstores listing announced that five new groups of bookwomen had begun building their skills:

Womansplace, Tempe, AZ
Open Book, Salt Lake City
Alternative Booksellers, Reading, PA
Her Shelf, Highland Park, MI
Old Wives' Tales, San Francisco

By its second year, 1977, the FBN listed eighty-six feminist bookstores in the United States and Canada;[8] by 1978 that number was up to ninety-six in the United States, Canada, and Europe.[9] These numbers meant a substantial network training each other in feminist literary activism.

Skills to Interrupt the Literary Industrial Corporate Establishment, 1976–1977

Book lists were an early and sustained focus of the FBN. These lists were political documents sharing news of available texts, creating new ways to understand individual texts in conversation with others, and sustaining the texts with orders from the almost one hundred feminist bookstores. The focus of the feminist movement and the strengths of individual bookstores shaped the lists, which in turn shaped the titles on shelves of bookstores internationally. From Womanbooks in New York, Karyn London sent in the first list, books in Spanish accompanied by information about distributors of Spanish-language titles.[10] Bookwomen at Womanbooks in New York regularly contributed their skills in literary advocacy, honed to influence— or render unnecessary—the nearby tenants of that New York gentleman's club publishers row. Rather than promoting books to sell, these lists shared word of books as service for readers looking for information on being in the world as a woman of color, coming out, surviving and ending sexual assault, raising confident and thoughtful children, or otherwise participating in feminist movements. Book lists enabled bookwomen to connect readers with the resources they needed and, in turn, to support authors by connecting books with their readers. Fostering this connection was key to the bookwomen's agreed commitment to "our politics as well as our service functions" and to "a communications network based on cooperation rather than (you guessed it) competition."[11]

Bookwomen employed cooperation not for profit but to a feminist purpose. Like other feminists, they worked to hone and build their politics. For example, though bookwomen did not frequently explicitly write about or toward antiracist feminism in the early years of the FBN, they were immersed in feminist movement thinking about racial justice. The Women in Print session titled "Racism," held just before the bookwomen's session on "Future Plans," surely amplified commitments to accountability that they would explore more deeply (in the conversations I describe in chapter 3). The three bookwomen of Womanbooks in New York took notes at the Friday session on racism. It's not clear from the notes who wrote them, but the fact that the notes are in the Womanbooks collection at the Lesbian Herstory Archive indicates that the three brought these notes back to the bookstore and may have talked about them together. For this bookstore staff of a Latina and two white women, negotiating racism and building alliances across racial differences informed their daily work.

They wrote down short phrases from the session: "Correct feminist line: we know we're racist," and "don't feel threatened to be called racist & getting in touch with your own racism." While having a "correct feminist line" suggested that if women learned the "correct" language they could avoid difficult reflective work, the session certainly belied that fantasy. Through breaking into groups and sharing back, the workshop supported a growing antiracist feminist practice of alliance building. Women emphasized the need to understand each other, since an oppressor "can afford the luxury of misdefining" or misunderstanding through stereotypes;[12] women reminded each other of "inter-color group racism"; and at least one woman refused to be the "only black woman to work in all-white group." When some women called out that the conference had not addressed classism, other savvy organizers reminded them that people "often use class as a way of excusing our racism." Redirection would not work. At the close of the session, women imagined what it would look like to implement these lessons at their organizations: one woman suggested an "affirmative action commitment w/i our own groups," another "solicitation of ms. [manuscripts] by women of color," and another "coalition bldg."[13] Feminist bookwomen interrupted profit-driven capitalism in part by prioritizing alliances with each other; for bookwomen, these alliances sometimes looked like book lists that could transform the spaces of feminist bookstores across the nation and, in turn, conversations in many local communities.

The second FBN issue included the book lists "Native American Women," "Black Women," and "Young Women & Youth Liberation."[14] Womanbooks bookwomen had compiled and shared the "Native American Women" book list, partially, though not entirely, comprising books written by Native American women, including *Bobbie Lee: Indian Rebel: Struggles of a Native Canadian Woman*, by Lee Maracle (Liberation Support Movement Information Center, 1975). André and Seajay urged, "Everybody, please check this list against your stock, and see what you have that isn't on this list and send it in for the next newsletter. That goes for the other lists, too."[15] By starting with lists of and for Spanish-language-reading, Native American, and Black women readers, writers, and publishers, bookwomen were prioritizing the words of women of color. The book lists offered one strategy for implementing lessons learned at the "Racism" session, from the books on their shelves and from each other. These lists were also a strategy for accountability in community. The site of the new San Francisco bookstore Old Wives' Tales, for example, was "in the Latino(a) section of SF," and Seajay wrote that she and Wallace were "hot on the trails of books for Latina women in Eng and Span."[16] In the process, they shared the lists in hopes of affecting shelves and neighborhoods nationally. The lists were movement tools.

Through these lists and other collaborations, bookwomen and the FBN sustained the feminist print ecosystem. At the Women in Print gathering, the bookwomen had agreed on their commitment to "support the feminist media and to increase its effectiveness."[17] Bookwomen would achieve this goal by improving distribution: the public availability of feminist information. To do this, they ordered books from feminist authors, publishers, and distributors. For example, through the FBN, bookwomen found out they could order books like *Profile on the Mexican American Woman* from author, activist, and publisher Martha Cotera in Austin and *Female Contractions* from author Nadia Surari in Jordan.[18] Bookwomen ordered and stocked these books, in addition to supporting small presses by ordering through feminist distributors. Book distributors make it possible for bookstores to order books from multiple publishers from one place. This service saves the cost and time of ordering and shipping these books separately from each publisher. In addition to traditional and small press distributors, by 1976 there were three feminist distributors. Women in Distribution (WIND) in Washington, DC, offered "central distribution for MANY MANY women's small presses." Amazon Reality in Eugene, Oregon, though "much smaller," also carried books and posters. Old Lady Blue Jeans described itself as "an experiment in other ways of publishing and distribution by us local dykes" in Northampton, Massachusetts; they distributed to women only.[19] New bookwomen found out about feminist distributors through the FBN, and even experienced bookwomen found out about and ordered in new books profiled on the FBN pages. In this way, feminist bookwomen created circulation networks for books that mainstream distributors would not promote.

At the Common Woman Bookstore in Austin, readers experienced the validation of their representation in a well-stocked bookstore made possible by savvy bookwomen and their connection with a larger network of books, publishers, and bookwomen through the FBN. Nina Wouk served as accountant and ordered science fiction at Common Woman. In an interview on the worn pink couch in the bookstore's recent incarnation, she explained the significance of distribution through Common Woman as vital evidence of lesbian life in the 1970s. "My partner, Jessie, moved to Austin, because her friends that she was living with in San Antonio came to Austin, came to what was then the Common Woman, and brought back a bunch of proof that lesbian culture exists. They were so excited about this."[20] Like many feminist bookstores, Common Woman was a destination for lesbian feminist travelers because of bookwomen's relationships and the texts they made available.

One lesbian feminist publisher, Kay Turner, arriving in Austin from New York for graduate school, showed up at the bookstore after reading about it in FBN. Turner had been printing, publishing, and creating handmade covers for her journal, Lady Unique, Inclination of the Night, in New Jersey. Turner recalls telling her partner she was headed to check out the bookstore: "Here's this dilapidated building where the top porch is like caving in, there's the Common Woman sign, sort of pitched at an angle. It was another steaming hot day: it was well into the early hundreds. I climb up the stairs; I see these bookshelves that are all kind of at various angles to each other. Then I look down, and there's this woman on the couch in a pair of shorts and a T-shirt." The woman was Susan Post, who was on the outs with her then girlfriend. The bookstores were work and community spaces where lesbians could be out, and they were often run by women who were lovers with each other. This passion in political commitment, as in many movement efforts, resulted in an added layer of complexity in organizing. As spaces run by lovers, the bookstores were also sites of contentious break-ups and just plain bad days. "We were back within a day or two," Turner remembers, though she and her partner had vowed never to return. Soon Turner, her partner, and Post were regularly hanging out together at the bookstore, and Common Woman "became a base of operations for doing all kinds of things."[21] Bookwomen were collaborating with feminist publishers (like Post with Turner) to create and to thrive. Though Post was now the sole bookwoman at Common Woman, the bookstore was supported by a community of women. With an income supplemented by her girlfriend's day job, Post spent her nights immersed in bookstore labor. The bookstore covered its own rent but not a paycheck, so Post worked part-time at the university library. She was one among many bookwomen across the continent staying up nights to spread out catalogs, magazines, penciled notes, and the FBN to research, stock, and advocate for feminist literature. The FBN wove Common Woman and other locals into a passionate national relationship built on the energy and connection between lovers, friends, and movement colleagues in the bookstores.

FBN pushed bookwomen as a group to analyze the big-picture industry structure they were resisting, even while they were lying on their bookstores' couches. In the third issue, in 1977, Seajay wrote up the first of many FBN indictments of mainstream book industry policies. Through these readings of the industry, bookwomen—women trained in feminism, not bookselling—practiced their understandings and explanations of how a diverse feminist literature depended on active resistance to profit-making turns in the industry. Bookwomen found that FBN created a space to share these observations and ideas that before might never have made it beyond the frustrated midnight musings of women poring over mainstream publishers' terms. "Ty, at Everywoman's [San Rafael, California] gave this to me in conversation," Seajay began seemingly casually, but these conversations built in intensity and changed the course of publishing. This time, the issue was returns. Traditionally, publishing is built on a 60/40 percent split: a bookstore buys books from the publisher (or other distributor) at a 40 percent discount of the list price. Seajay observed that this split "is based on the 'return option'":[22] if the book doesn't sell, bookstores return it to the publisher. "The question is: Are we paying for a 'service' we don't use? . . . The stores I'm familiar with will literally carry a book for years without selling a copy because we believe that it is an important book."[23] Bookwomen based stock not on projected sales but on what they thought readers needed and might even use without buying, so a deeper discount without a return option would have fit their movement work better.

Here feminist bookwomen began to note the ways publishing policies controlled what and who got published. Seajay traced the inference: "Is this a way that the book industry is set up to serve profit oriented stores (that won't give ½ inch worth of shelf space to a book that doesn't sell in three months?) and hence the whole decision as to what gets into print is based on what will sell quickly. . . . and that determines what I get to read."[24] This policy requires that publishers take back what bookstores don't sell, a leverage that gives publishers incentive to publish only books that will sell in large numbers and quickly. Part of the work of the bookwomen, connected and propelled by the FBN, was to support books that mainstream bookstores and publishers did not know how to sell. Bookwomen were beginning to talk about, and to imagine how to resist, the control of "the Literary Industrial Corporate Establishment," or LICE, an acronym coined within the Women in Print movement and that Seajay used to dramatic effect, urging bookwomen to closely observe and analyze the system they were resisting. "There's the tip of the LICE-berg* and I don't know what's beneath the surface. (Which is of course the driving force behind the whole women's printing/publishing industry, but the LICE* are still with us. And crawling all over my mind, just now . . .)."[25] Not knowing then the long journey of literary activism ahead, Seajay gestured toward the future of her work at FBN building a feminist literary counterpublic, a site of discussion to prepare the bookwomen for action and to share strategies for altering a larger public.[26]

Along the way, bookwomen also used the FBN to share strategies for influencing feminist publishers. Women at New Words in Cambridge, Massachusetts, were at the center of key feminist organizing and publishing networks. After attending a meeting of Sappho's Children, a local Boston area organization of lesbian mothers, a couple of New Words bookwomen took another look at their children's section. They noticed that while feminist publishers' children's books "reflect other 'non-traditional' lifestyles such as children with single mothers, children with single fathers, children in families with non-traditional sex-roles, etc.," they offered few representations of lesbian mothers.[27] The bookwomen drafted and sent out a letter to feminist publishers. They also sent their letter on to the FBN to encourage group action and to ask other bookwomen for lists of existing children's books that included lesbians.[28] This first example of bookwomen's advocacy with publishers appeared in the same FBN issue as the returns analysis; these two efforts documented a feminist literary activist consciousness and a standard practice of sharing stories of feminist literary activism through FBN. This sharing both offered strategic models and amplified actions by generating letters from bookstores across the nation. Significantly, the bookwomen began by lobbying feminist publishers. Bookwomen worked within the movement to educate each other and to practice their advocacy through peer education, a counterpublic; once they had practiced their skills, they would take the force of this activism outside the movement.

Just a month into the life of FBN, André and Seajay asked bookwomen whether they wanted to allow subscriptions from feminist publishers, even though bookwomen might use the journal to organize actions to influence those same publishers. The conversation about who could subscribe continued for the life of the journal; it was difficult to balance a desire to generate influence through subscriptions with safe space to build effective strategy. "Our understanding is that this newsletter is for women owned feminist bookstores (and book closets)," André and Seajay wrote. "Are we correct?"[29] A slim majority of responses to a subscription questionnaire supported sharing the newsletter with publishers, like Kay Turner of *Lady Unique, Inclination of the Night*:

PUBLISHERS:
Yes—14 (should be allowed to subscribe)
Yes—3 (FBN should meet the needs of both publishers & bookstores)
No—2 (should not be allowed to subscribe)
Depends—13 (on Andre and Carol)[30]

André and Seajay then sent "sample copies and invitations to subscribe to all feminist publishers we know of which do not have men involved."[31] FBN now served the dual purpose of connecting bookwomen and providing a much-needed site for information exchange between feminist publishers and bookwomen. That Seajay and André had received requests for subscription from publishers and distributors indicates the early significance of the FBN to the Women in Print movement at large.

It was important, however, to limit the conversation to feminist and woman-owned bookstores and publishers in order to maintain the counterpublic: if bookwomen were going to share their labor and knowledge, they wanted to use those skills for their own counter-capitalist revolutionary purposes and in ethical support of their movement-based information economies. From Ms. Atlas Press & Bookstore in San Jose, California, Rosalie Nichols wrote to FBN: "We are NOT, in fact, competing against each other—we are competing against student bookstores, B. Dalton, Macy's and other traditionalist bookstores that have a feminist section; and we CAN compete successfully against them because we are SPECIALIZED and KNOWLEDGEABLE about the interests and attitudes of our feminist and lesbian customers. We also function as a source of information and contact with the feminist and lesbian movements."[32] As early as 1977 the chain bookstores were a threat to movement spaces. Bookwomen recognized that the profit-oriented goals of feminist or women's sections in chain bookstores would not serve their long-term interests in promoting feminist media and connecting readers with feminist and lesbian movements.[33]

A protected space for conversation in the FBN was modeled after the structure of the bookstores themselves. What happened inside the bookstores, in collective and staff meetings, was as important to bookstore identity as what readers saw when they visited the bookstore. Inside the bookstores, amid the shelves and bulletin boards, bookwomen were training each other as feminists and literary activists. The FBN created a space for expanding that training beyond a single bookstore as bookwomen wrote in to share strategies, failures, and possibility through collectivity. At Rising Woman in Santa Rosa, California, collective members used a revised feminist version of the Marxist tool of "criticism and self/criticism."[34] From Emma (after Emma Goldman) in Buffalo, collective members wrote that the "most important aspect of EMMA is not just our effect on the local community (ie, the women's movement, the neighborhood, the left and the general Buffalo population), but [the effect] the experience of working at EMMA and working as a Collective, has on the lives of each of us associated with the bookstore."[35] These letters to FBN refer to the hours bookstore staff and collective members spent in meetings together learning to be allies; the process was as important as the result. This movement work, including the personal work of relationship building, also defined the bookstores as counter-capitalist, inefficient by business standards while astoundingly productive for feminist movement building.

With letters like these from Rising Woman and Emma collective members, the FBN documented feminist bookstores as sites of collective process. This was another revolutionary act interrupting economic profit mechanisms. Bookwomen were, after all, spending hours of their busy days not only in collective meetings and movement discussions but also writing up their experiences and sending them in or sharing them by phone with André and Seajay to report in FBN, and then reading reports from other bookwomen as well. Vulnerable in these conversations about accountability and feminist ethics, bookwomen experienced the bookstores as both liberatory and risky. In 1977, Kit Quan was preparing to run away from home, to escape what she would later recognize as domestic violence, and to search for a place for her lesbian feminist identity. At a young lesbians' picnic in Dolores Park, she struck up a conversation with a young woman who turned out to be Seajay's foster daughter. Old Wives' Tales sounded promising, and Quan, then fifteen, said she was sixteen when she went in to ask for a job. Seajay and Wallace hired her on the spot. By 1978, Quan had run away from home. Having keys to the bookstore meant that "in a way, the bookstore was a shelter, too," where she would sometimes go at night by herself.[36] Feminist bookstore collective and staff members had unique access to these spaces. This immersion or hoped-for refuge in the bookstores intensified the personal relationships and affective learning and teaching along the way.

Alone those nights at the bookstore, Quan also felt isolated: "I left my family and my culture to live by my political beliefs, but except for the driving forces of anger and hunger, I did not have much backup for my new life. . . . I was young and vulnerable, struggling with language issues, trying to bridge the gap between my life experience and that of the people around me who were older, far more educated academically and politically, and well-versed in feminist rhetoric."[37] Quan felt the contradictions within the collective: "Even though feminist rhetoric does give me the words to describe how I'm being oppressed, it still reflects the same racist, classist standards of the dominant society and of colleges and universities."[38] Part of the work of feminist bookwomen in collective and of the FBN was to prepare bookwomen to critique—in an attempt to improve—even their own interactions and methods. This process of self-critique, an inefficiency in capitalism, was essential to the revolutionary peer education among bookwomen.

Getting Feminists (Back) into Print, 1977–1979

The line drawing first appeared in April 1977: at the top left corner of the FBN front page, a naked, curly-headed woman sat on a stack of books while reading another book she held in her hand. This new FBN masthead logo, drawn by Emily Schweber, accompanied every issue until February 1979.[39] Schweber's graphic pictured the act of reading, rather than bookselling, and imagined a reader vulnerable and strong, embracing her naked self. This image of intimate reading represents both what the bookwomen imagined for the readers they connected with books and what the bookwomen themselves experienced through FBN. In response to a regularly occurring query of what bookwomen liked about FBN, bookwomen emphasized the sense of connection that came with turning these pages. Women from Sister Moon Feminist Bookstore & Gallery, Milwaukee, wrote, "I read you front to back, then begin the 1–4 hours of work I've marked you for follow up." The women of the Oracle in Hayward, California appreciated information exchange "on ideas not just on specific books," and the Common Woman collective looked for "letters from other bookstore women." When the newsletter arrived by mail to Womanbooks, Karyn London reported, "It's a lifeline of communication and support. Much of the credit belongs to Carol and Andre for keeping it alive and to all of us for speaking and listening to each other."[40] From 1977 to 1979, feminist bookwomen solidified their counterpublic by talking and reading with each other.

As more feminist bookstores opened internationally, FBN editors recruited them to subscribe and thus built up their strength in numbers to influence publishing and feminism. In 1977 Seajay declared, "Women's bookstores are in an era of mushrooming. Think about that for a while and enjoy it."[41] The FBN made it possible to imagine feminist bookstores as a collective force of sites of demand for feminist literature. In April, the FBN published its first accounting of the movement: "The List of Feminist Bookstores and Distributors in the U.S. and Canada" documented eighty-six bookstores.[42] A year later, a second iteration of the list included ninety-six feminist bookstores in the United States and Canada, as well as Lilith Frauenbuchladen in Berlin.[43] As bookwomen traveled or received travelers, they would let Seajay know about new bookstores, and Seajay would add them to the mailing list. Like many bookwomen, those at Women's Works in Brooklyn found out about FBN when they received it in their mailbox: "We were amazed & excited to find FBN appearing at our store a couple of weeks after we opened! It was wonderful to know that our venture was known of, and that there was so much of a precedent & tradition already, and that there was a NEWSLETTER."[44] Or bookwomen would tell newcomers to the Women in Print movement about FBN and urge them to get in touch; publishers of the Editora Das Mulheres collective in Lisbon, Portugal, did just that in November.[45]

When André left both Rising Woman and the FBN, Seajay took on sole editorship. Just a year into the publication, Seajay tested the waters of her leadership: "Most of the time I've enjoyed doing the newsletter, and I'd like to keep on doing it, IF it's OK to do it every 6 weeks, and IF there's money to Pay me for my labor again. If someone else wants to do it, I'd be open to passing FBN on. Write and let me know."[46] No one took her up on her offer, and her defining vision of a literary activist enterprise would shape the life of the publication. When a collective member at the Common Woman Bookstore wrote in to promise, if "we ever get tax exempt status from IRS I'll be glad to write an article on how," Seajay used this as a teaching moment to the bookwomen readers she considered contributors: "Dear Common Woman, I'm glad you brought up the 'guest article' idea. . . . This newsletter is supposed to be a collection of articles, comments, questions, etc., from all the bookstores. EVERYONE is expected to write up anything they think is important, and send it in. Don't wait to be asked, or invited. DO IT!—Carol, the compiler."[47] Women did write in from the bookstores, and Seajay, far from being simply a compiler, offered her substantial framing narrative in introductions to, parenthetical remarks within, and articles for the issues.

Seajay used her guiding editorship to hone feminist bookwomen's awareness of and strategies to interrupt the machinations of LICE. Feminist bookwomen used FBN to collect the mounting evidence that the profit-driven book industry would not support feminist literature without bookwomen's advocacy. In 1977, Random House refused to distribute the fall list of Berkeley-based Moon Books because, they said, "'the market for women's books is over.'"[48] Random House had previously distributed the Moon Books titles, including *A Woman's History*, by Anica Vesel Mander; *The New Lesbians: Interviews with Women across the U.S. and Canada*, by Laurel Galanda and Gina Covina; Dorothy Bryant's widely popular *The Kin of Ata Are Waiting for You*; and Eva Forest's *From a Spanish Prison*. A year after Random House declared the market over, they had to acknowledge that "there really does continue to be a market (profits, to them) for feminist books," irrefutable since they saw "THE WOMAN'S ROOM bobbing around on the bestsellers lists." To explain the contradiction, the "straight press" called this "the third wave of feminist publishing." Seajay credited feminist literary agent Elizabeth Lay with "this insight as to what's going on in the hearts and minds of LICE."[49] A true publishing industry maven, Seajay was regularly in conversation with a range of well-placed feminist informants from the "straight press." Seajay reported, "They no longer want the books that identify the problems, however, now they want books that portray solutions." LICE, that is, was already willing the "third wave" to recede. The mainstream, or "straight," press, had to be continually reassured that feminist books would sell; feminist bookstores, in their era of mushrooming, were a central and vocal part of that proof.[50]

After a strategy session with feminist literary lawyer and agent Carol Murray, Seajay reported to FBN that if mainstream presses "felt they had direct access to outlets (stores) for the feminist books they publish they would publish more feminist writers/authors." Murray explained that the prospect of eighty feminist bookstores in the United States each selling fifty copies of a new book would mean four thousand copies sold for mainstream publishers, "or ½ of the 8000 copies they think they need to sell to make a profit." Seajay assured bookwomen that it would not be necessary to actually sell fifty copies of the book: "I don't expect (even as wonderful as all the feminist bookstores are) that we're going to sell 4000 copies of every book

New York thinks is feminist. But they don't know that. The problem is not getting feminist books sold, but getting them published. If the NY Publishers will just publish the books, they WILL sell, even in the numbers needed for LICE to make their damned profits."[51] Seajay here guides feminist bookwomen to envision their own influence, and to manipulate the perceptions of the "straight" press for feminist gain. A couple of issues later, Murray and Seajay together put this plan into action.

As agent for the feminist author Susan Griffin, Murray had closed the deal with Harper and Row to publish Griffin's formidable feminist title *Woman and Nature: The Roaring inside Her* (1978). Part of the deal included placing an advertisement in FBN for advance orders. This "advertisement," though, was in itself a strategy workshop: it appeared along with a note from Murray and an interpretation from Seajay. Murray explained that if Harper and Row received a lot of advance orders, they would increase the publicity budget for the book. Seajay encouraged bookwomen to "order as large quantities as you can," even if it meant "doing returns when the bill is due." This collective action would interrupt the common pattern Seajay observed: "LICE publisher published book. Doesn't publicize it, no one knows it exists, it doesn't sell. Publisher decides there's no market and OP [out of print] it goes."[52] Bookwomen understood that the books they needed for their communities and movements were often not available; they knew that getting them on the shelves was the central challenge. In order to do so, they would have to convince "straight" publishers that there was a readership for these books. The bookwomen were realizing and teaching each other that publishers do not use the market to guide their publishing; rather, they publish to their limited perceptions of readers as a market. Movement bookwomen interrupted this propped-up fantasy of supply and demand with advocacy for themselves, their authors, and their readers.

By 1977, the year-old FBN was regularly coordinating feminist bookstores' literary advocacy. A handwritten title in the December issue announced, "Strategy Session: Getting books re-issued." The "strategy session," introduced by Carol Seajay, explained to feminist bookwomen how their letters could support women's literature: "Sometimes writing letters to publishers and editors can get books re-issued or issued in paperback."[53] And in our 2003 interview, Seajay pointed out that feminist bookstores were uniquely positioned to take action: "We're the bookseller, we sell it, so we order some more, and, as soon as it's not available, we know. And, being the troublesome, rowdy women we are, we don't take 'No' for an answer."[54]

FBN generated a "coordinated effort" by a national network of "rowdy women" by educating readers and serving as a literary activist toolkit.

Feminist literary activists in training could track some of the success stories across FBN issues, where bookwomen could get involved or get inspired to share ideas for the next action. By 1977, Bantam had allowed Joanna Russ's feminist science fiction classic *The Female Man* to go out of print. Paula Wallace of Old Wives' Tales decided to take action. When Bantam representative George Sullivan responded dismissively to Wallace's letter to him, she used the FBN to ask other bookwomen to help. In one issue of the FBN, Wallace offered the text of her letter as an example and the negative response from Bantam to energize bookwomen.[55] In his response to Wallace, the Bantam representative described the book as a "very unique science fiction title" that had "not performed well enough to be kept in print."[56] Sullivan's description identified the different stakes for him and for Wallace in its publication. The context of the feminist bookstore (and, indeed, Wallace's letter) claimed *The Female Man* as a *feminist* science fiction title, and one whose project was not entirely unique since it was shared by a range of feminist authors. Wallace was especially aware of the vibrant work of Russ and her contemporaries because, as Seajay remembers of Old Wives' Tales, "Paula was committed to having every science fiction novel by women, and we had every science fiction novel by women."[57]

A note in handwriting rather than type at the bottom of the page added a breaking news item, marking the FBN as a successful activist tool and as an information center for news of books coming back into print: "Last minute info: ICI-A Woman's Place's Bantam rep said that *Female Man* will be re-released in April!"[58] Within the context of the "strategy session," this note in the margins also positioned *The Female Man* reprint as (at least in part) the outcome of a successful letter-writing campaign. A later issue copied directly onto the page a February 1978 letter to Wallace from the Bantam representative announcing the book's reprinting:

> Enclosed you will find a sample cover of our reprint of THE FEMALE MAN by Joanna Russ. If you will recall, back in November of last year I had advised you that we had no plans to reprint this title, despite your evaluation of its potential in the feminist and science fiction markets.
>
> Since then, we have had numerous requests and inquiries regarding THE FEMALE MAN. It is now available directly from Bantam or through your local distributor.

Let me take this opportunity to thank you for your comments. It is this type of relationship between publisher and bookseller that makes this business what it is today.[59]

Sullivan's letter revised his original assessment of the book's classification, adding "feminist" to "science fiction," and he credited the book's republication not to sales but to "numerous requests and inquiries." A handwritten comment from Carol Seajay on the letter announced, "It *works!!!*" Seajay's note and the FBN's tracking of this exchange presented the advocacy feminist bookstores could, and did, perform on behalf of feminist books. FBN reminded readers that writing and publishing women's texts does not guarantee a women's literature: maintaining this body of work required strategizing.

Bookwomen knew, too, that getting books republished once did not guarantee sustained availability. The June 1981 issue of the FBN, just three years after *The Female Man* success, announced under the heading "WRITE NOW": "THE FEMALE MAN BY JOANNA RUSS IS OUT OF PRINT. WRITE TO SYDNEY WEINBERG (♀) AN EDITOR AT BANTAM TO COMPLAIN."[60] In full capitals, the announcement at the bottom of the page stood out, reminding readers of the continuing work of the FBN as feminist literature lookout. Like other readers, Joanna Russ described the result of this activism on the bookstore shelves: "Feminist bookstores helped me by carrying books I wanted to buy, which I couldn't find elsewhere, and by carrying my books."[61] Behind the scenes, FBN made clear that carrying the books and letting publishers know that feminist bookstores would shelve and talk about the books helped not only with visibility but also with availability. At this writing, *The Female Man* is in print with the Beacon Press Bluestreak imprint, "a paperback series of innovative literary writing by women of all colors."[62]

By 1979, bookwomen knew they had a populous network of activists prepared through the feminist literary counterpublic organized by and reachable through the FBN. Calls to action, as those bookwomen who wrote to or phoned Seajay with news to print knew, would bring results.

BLITZ ＊＊＊＊URGENT＊＊＊＊＊DO IT NOW＊＊＊＊BLITZ＊＊＊＊URGENT＊＊＊＊

Write to WW Norton & ask them to put May Sarton's AS WE ARE NOW in paperback. Tell them you're getting requests for it from teachers who would like to use it in classes but can't ask students to buy the hardcover.

Tell them that customers keep asking when it will be out in paperback. Tell them you want to give it to your grandmother. . . . If we all blitz them, they will probably respond. They put THE SMALL ROOM in paperback on the request of ONE women's studies teacher in Colorado, or so I've heard.[63]

* * * * * * * * * * * ** * * * * * * * * * * * * * * * * ** * * * * * * * ** * * * *

This news alert went out in a 1979 FBN as one of an energetic series of calls to action. Seajay, as author of this "blitz" call, identified her inside line to the corporate literary establishment with her closing "or so I've heard." These connections, built carefully through and for her identity as FBN editor, author, and bookwoman, contributed to the established conversation in FBN pages between authors, publishers, and bookwomen, to provide feminist bookwomen with early information about book endangerment or availability. As a result of such intricate systems of information, the FBN functioned as a vehicle for coordinating letter-writing campaigns calling for the reprinting of books like Del Martin and Phyllis Lyon's *Lesbian/Woman* (Glide Publications, 1972; Bantam Books, 1977) and Merlin Stone's *When God Was a Woman* (Harcourt Brace Jovanovich, 1978). At E. M. (Esther) Broner's request, Seajay ran a letter-writing campaign to bring Broner's *Her Mothers* back into print. After hearing from another author about the good work of the FBN, Broner wrote to Seajay: "*Her Mothers* (Berkeley Publishing Corp.) has gone out-of-print. Shebar Windstone, that great nooge and scholar, has insisted that I write to you about it. She said that you were insistent enough to get a reprint of Joanna Russ's book. . . . I wanted to urge you/your newsletter to pressure for reissue of *Her Mothers*."[64] Harper reissued *Her Mothers* in 1983. E. M. Broner's letter joins an archive of letters documenting the substantial and effective literary advocacy work of the FBN to construct and preserve a feminist literature.

Feminist bookwomen cultivated a growing reputation for their influence on mainstream publishers. Darlene Pagano enjoyed talking up feminist authors with mainstream publishers at the American Booksellers Association (ABA) convention, the major annual meeting for the US book industry. She urged other women to join in: "I would like to see women's bookstores have their presence felt." Soon feminist bookwomen were meeting up at the ABA to "have a good time" and to influence publishers.[65] Wallace had talked with Bantam representatives at an ABA meeting, and Susan Post remembers Seajay orchestrating group action: "If we were on the show floor, and Carol [Seajay] or someone would say, 'Go talk to someone and do this,'

I would usually do that."[66] Bookwomen talked with their regional publisher's representatives at their bookstores as well, if the bookstores were large enough to attract an in-person visit from the publishers. Gilda Bruckman at New Words remembers she suggested to a Harper representative that they should bring back into print Ella Leffland's *Rumors of Peace*, and they did.[67] Bruckman sees this as a time "when savvy book reps were asking feminist booksellers, what's happening? what should we know about? and passing it on to their presses because this was the place where things happened first. . . . This was the place where the voices of women began to be heard and made it into the mainstream."[68] That is, women's writing went mainstream in part because feminist bookwomen proved (and proved again) to an interminably skeptical mainstream press that readers were looking for it.

Even when feminist books did go out of print, bookwomen, through the FBN, found ways to support them and their authors. This literary community building operated beyond the reach of capital (out-of-print books are no longer operating in the standard market economy) and within a revolutionary economy of information and accountability. To teach other feminist bookwomen how to keep books alive, Karyn London, the socialist feminist at Womanbooks and a prolific contributor to FBN, wrote a special FBN guide to "Doing Remainders." London explained, "Our involvement with remainders [at Womanbooks] first began when individual authors whose books we carried would tell us that their book was being remaindered." When a publisher declares a title out of print (no longer promoted or sold through the publisher), the remaining copies in existence are remaindered. One exception to this rule, London offered, is when a publisher decides "that a backlist title is not 'moving' quickly enough" and they dump only some of the copies of the title to reduce storage costs while keeping the title technically in print. London explained that the publisher might contact the author and give "her first option to buy," or might sell the books in a lot "to the highest bidder."[69] For London, selling remainders was one way bookwomen could "give new life to titles that we feel good about but which the publisher had little confidence in and didn't promote enough, allowing them to die." That is, remainders were physical proof of mainstream publishers' inability to promote feminist books. Feminist bookwomen, on the other hand, could effectively connect remaindered titles with their readers.

Feminist accountability made feminist bookwomen's remainder sales different from those at other bookstores. If distributing remainders could support feminist literature, it could also endanger feminist authors: while the books were more affordable and thus more accessible to readers, London pointed out, the authors did not receive royalties. Here London's location amid New York feminist author networks allowed a solution: "when we know the author personally or how to reach her," she explained, the bookwomen would "price the remainder to include the author's (approximately 10%) royalties and send this amount to her."[70] After this strategy session, the practice spread. Four years later, bookwomen at Old Wives' Tales reminded FBN readers about their relationships with and responsibilities to authors: "When we find ourselves selling 150–200 copies of [remaindered] hardcover books like [Adrienne Rich's] ON LIES SECRETS AND SILENCES, and [Mary Daly's] GYN/ECOLOGY, we see that we then sell noticeably fewer paperbacks, and that DOES hurt the authors. And these are women whose work matters passionately to us." The Old Wives' Tales women, too, sent off a portion of sales to the authors.[71] Through distribution of remainders, feminist bookwomen made feminist books available while they were out of print and otherwise unavailable. London explains that by sharing them through the feminist bookstore network, "they could still be everywhere for somebody to find."[72] The FBN here reminded readers of the connection between bookstores, books, and authors, modeling bookwomen's responsibility to a complete cycle.[73]

Womanbooks' "thousand-square-foot store, plus basement," allowed London to "buy a thousand or so copies of something" and share them over a period of years through the bookstore and with other feminist bookwomen who would place phone orders or come by to fill their car with books. Some of the titles they sustained this way included *Stage V: A Journal through Illness* by London's friend Sonny Wainwright, Audre Lorde's *Zami*, Gloria Anzaldúa and Cherríe Moraga's *This Bridge Called My Back*, several books by Joan Nestle,[74] and Isabel Miller's *Patience and Sarah*.[75] At both ICI: A Woman's Place and Old Wives' Tales, Seajay remembered, they ordered Jade Snow Wong's out-of-print autobiography, *Fifth Chinese Daughter*, directly from her.[76] London and Seajay, as white bookwomen, here acted as allies with authors, including women of color, to actively support the distribution of books by feminists and lesbians. Learning from women of color literary activists, bookwomen here partially interrupted the institutional racism of a publishing industry that refused to understand a "market" for feminist books by and for women of color.[77] Women of color received more support inside the bookstores as collective members learned to describe the importance of a racially diverse feminist literature.

Soon feminist bookwomen were energetically trying out and sharing new strategies for distribution. Responding to a request about how to find the British book *Scream Quietly or the Neighbors Will Hear*, by Erin Pizzey, Patti Kirk of the Toronto Women's Bookstore wrote in to volunteer to serve as a North American distributor because the Canadian bookstore could easily order copies.[78] Another heading offered news from an author: "MARION ZIMMER BRADLEY'S science fiction books go out of print super-fast. Sometimes w/in 2–3 months. She says that science fiction bookstores buy a year's supply as soon as the books come out. She suggested that we do the same."[79] In the Common Woman Bookstore's copy of this FBN, the reader marked the Marion Zimmer Bradley announcement with a penciled check mark. Such notations, along with the international reach of the FBN, indicate that these announcements were widely used as part of the ordering strategies of feminist bookstores. If bookwomen had not paid attention, many of these books might not have been available, as Batchelder explained: "For us, this was like treasure. For every other bookstore it probably would've been nothing."[80]

Interrupting Systems of Capital with Lesbian Antiracism, 1977–1979

Increasing numbers of new requests from literary agents, librarians, and ex-bookwomen for subscriptions to the FBN indicated the movement-based success of the bookwomen and offered an expanded audience for the influence of feminist bookwomen on movement strategies of lesbian antiracism and feminist accountability. Feminist bookwomen's activism was increasingly influencing and empowering feminists in a larger public. Would opening up subscriptions close down dialogue that thrived in the protected pages? Or would more subscribers mean the capacity to educate more feminist literary activists and offer financial stability for FBN? Seajay put the question to her readers: "Should individuals, book-crazies (OK, Bibliophiles), feminist literary agencies, feminist writers, feminist literary lawyers and other women be allowed to subscribe to FBN? Would this affect the freedom we have to discuss issues?"[81] On the other hand, an expanded readership could itself be a literary activist practice, since it could support the broader distribution of feminist authors. Feminist literary lawyer Elizabeth Lay pointed out that FBN served as an "excellent source of invaluable information on women in publishing, from writers to presses, publishers, and agents—almost equivalent to Publisher's Weekly."[82] Librarian activist and feminist publisher Celeste West and Seajay saw such a close link between their work that Seajay printed and distributed West's new short book-azine ("an issue of a magazine but published as a book"),[83] published by her Booklegger Press, *The Passionate Perils of Publishing*, as a "'special' double issue" of FBN.[84] In her introduction to the double issue, Seajay emphasized that the value of *Passionate Perils* was a reminder that feminist bookwomen were involved not simply in advocacy in publishing but also in ensuring and facilitating the distribution, accessibility, and understanding of feminist information: "The only way we can be assured of a continuing feminist literature is to be aware of how the information-system in America works so as not to get stamped out in the shuffle of twinkies, pantyhose and military hardware profits. 'We' being not only the bookstore workers and publishing women, but the entire feminist community."[85] The decision about subscriptions would further define the role that feminist bookwomen would play in shaping feminist information.

Expanding subscriptions was one way to prepare "the entire feminist community" to take action within the increasingly monopolized information system; by running FBN and focusing on feminist bookstores, feminist bookwomen began to educate the feminist movement about their vital role in creating and sustaining feminist information. Only bookwomen could vote on permitting FBN subscription requests from individual women, librarians, and literary agencies. One bookwoman wrote in to explain, "You never know when an 'individual woman' will become inspired and turn into a bookstore woman." Seajay admitted the subscriptions would bring in necessary money: "It's more income, or no newsletter."[86] Bookwomen decided that individual women, including literary agents and librarians, could subscribe, but movement stores that were not women-owned could not. In order to protect the important space for sharing strategies, FBN would print two versions; bookwomen's internal discussions would be for feminist bookstores only.[87] This knowledge-sharing strategy prioritized the skill building of women working together.

By 1978, bookwomen, as intimate readers of FBN, trusted their publication enough to begin to share news of internal conflict and the difficulty of movement-based organizing. Through this vulnerable sharing, bookwomen acknowledged this risk and challenge as a necessary part of feminist bookwomen's work. Bookwomen of A Woman's Place Book Center in Portland, Oregon, published a series of articles in FBN as the collective grappled with collective documents and antiracist feminism. The conversation in FBN made the Portland women's experience accountable to and an educational tool for a transnational feminist audience. Here bookwomen themselves become authors of feminist theories and practices of alliance.

"I like to think that I like struggle," Seajay typed, listening to Meg Christian sing out from her new album: *"Woman you know you've got to face the music."*[88] "I like to make communication happen on these pages. . . . Struggle is harder."[89] As FBN editor, Seajay followed the lives of feminist bookstores internationally; this could be an emotional roller coaster. After more than a year of growth and challenge in Portland, Seajay read with relief notes about collective meetings and internal shift: "Good, I thought, they have crises and survive. Gives me faith that we'll survive our crises, too." Seajay and the Portland women offered their story as a reminder of the productive feminist work of "crises." The FBN shared news of the vital feminist work of crisis when the Portland bookwomen began working on a Basis of Unity or coalition policy, a document that bookstore collectives across the nation were also drafting.[90] The Basis of Unity document would articulate the vision and commitment of the bookstore, what brought the collective members together in collaborative work. While Portland bookwoman Rebecca Gordon related to difficult FBN discussions around political commitment, sexuality, and class, the resulting change in bookstore leadership and community accountability reveals that the core issue at stake was defining antiracist feminism. Feminist bookstores, the articles suggest, offered unique tools for moving toward antiracist feminism; this account from Seajay and the Portland bookwomen invited FBN readers to make this move. The bookstores mattered not because of sales but because of movement commitments.

The Portland bookwomen defined themselves not primarily as bookstore staff but as crafters of theories of alliance: "The Woman's Place Book Center is a tool in this fight providing books, resources, educational activities and a place for the practice of non-oppressive behavior."[91] This was the promise underlying the ability of bookwomen to be successful feminist literary advocates: in order to sustain and distribute feminist literature, bookwomen would need to be able to work together to define their goals, to learn from each other, and to commit to a lesbian antiracist feminism. Creating lasting movement relationships requires reflection and accountability. In daily life at feminist bookstores, this process could look like arguments between bookwomen. The Portland story offered a bigger picture to demonstrate that such "arguments" are part of a larger process of relational shift. According to Gordon, the rift building at A Woman's Place pitted socialists against separatists. Were the socialists "driven to the wall by separatist members"? Were the separatists ousted because of homophobia? Gordon suspected "homophobia WAS part of the problem," based on a comment she heard during a meeting.[92] Pushing through these disputes, A Woman's Place published their final Basis of Unity in November 1977 in FBN. At its core, the document codified the bookwomen's commitment to work "within the collective on struggles around race, class, age, sexuality, ethnic background, nationality, life-style, politics and heterosexism."[93] A practice of alliance building within the bookstore prepared bookwomen to engage in lesbian antiracist feminist coalitions outside the bookstore as well. This was intentionally part of the Basis of Unity document, which also outlined the types of organization a bookstore would build coalition with.[94] A Woman's Place collective members explained that in "Portland there currently seems to be a growing movement towards coalitions as a means for political action."[95]

By the next FBN issue, the Woman's Place collective had attempted to put their theoretical commitments into practice. Gordon proclaimed, "We at A Woman's Place have been, along with the rest of the women's community here, through a crisis about racism, and emerged whole on the other side." Portland's Black Women's Rap Group had identified racism in the service and treatment from other customers at Rising Moon, "Portland's only women's bar." In collaboration with the Black Women's Rap Group, white women at the bookstore created a campaign to educate other white women about the need for change. The bookwomen began within the collective and then moved into the community:

> By working first among ourselves, we discovered there was a two and a half hour average discussion that could take a woman from saying "I don't want the bar to be a 'political' place" to saying, "I see that there really is a problem, and that something has to be done." By going through this process ourselves, we were able to give strong support to the Black Women's Rap Group on an issue that they had chosen. We were able to close the store down for sales and spend an entire week talking to women about the bar, and the larger problem of racism in the women's community here. We took turns staffing and talking to customers, and all of us learned a lot about collectivity—when to speak for one's self, when to speak for the group, and when to shut up. It's unfortunate, but

true, that, had many white women in the community not approached the bar owners and told them we were concerned, they probably wouldn't have listened to the demand of Black Women.[96]

On behalf of the collective, Gordon describes the process of white women learning to be antiracist allies with women of color. Significantly, white women here took leadership from women of color ("give strong support to the Black Women's Rap Group on an issue that they had chosen") and utilized white privilege for antiracist change ("they probably wouldn't have listened to the demand of Black Women").

This reflective alliance process also emphasized structural racism in the collective. White women educated each other within the bookstore: they started out by "working first among ourselves" and shaped what they came to recognize as the "two and a half hour average discussion" necessary for recognizing structural racism. Once their consciousnesses were raised around racism, they looked again to the collective: "We're also spending energy now on questions we should have dealt with months ago: Why are there no women of color in the collective? Why do so few women of color come into the store? Why don't we listen when women of color tell us they feel uncomfortable here, instead of trying to defend ourselves?"[97] Answering the first three questions with their last, the bookwomen needed to account for their own role in the bookstore's exclusion. They began with a "mini-conference on racism," which they created in collaboration with "third world women," though the conference created space primarily for "white women to examine our own racism."[98] The process successfully shifted the bookstore from one committed to discussing antiracist feminism to one committed to supporting a multiracial staff.

A year later, Niobe Erebor sent in a letter to FBN; in addition to her participation in the women's music scene as part of the group Baba Yaga, she was now comanager of the bookstore. That year, the bookstore conducted "monthly meetings to deal with the problem of Racism in the bookstore and our responsibility to the community in combating racism wherever we find it—and we do find it in *every* community of women as well as society in general." In the tradition of literary activism, the collective turned to the rich visual work of the women in print movement. Erebor emphasized, "As a woman of color, I get mighty tired of seeing poster after poster, calendar after calendar page full of white women. One would guess that we are not considered beautiful enough or strong enough to merit being seen. In nearly every feminist bookstore on the continent there aren't enough materials by/about women and peoples of color."[99] Erebor here invited FBN readers to look around at their shelves, and then, in case white bookwomen were asking the same questions Gordon had proffered from the all-white collective, Erebor explained, "the invisibility of women of color in the items in the store does absolutely nothing to encourage peoples of color to use the store as a resource." Under Erebor's leadership, the bookstore collective announced they would create a poster to distribute nationally through feminist bookstores; the poster would have an image of and a quote by a woman of color. In addition to carrying this poster, Erebor engaged readers in advocacy: advocate with "women who make posters and calendars to make it a priority to print items (and solicit new material) with Black, Hispanic, Asian, and Native American women on them." It was not enough to add the materials to the existing space: "When the materials come into your store, contact local communities of color and let them know that books, posters, calendars, and other items of specific interest to those communities are available in your store. Start building bridges between yourselves and communities of color—and therefore women of color in your town." The letters from A Woman's Place modeled the move of an all-white collective to self-reflection, addressing racism within the collective, building effective alliances with women of color, supporting women of color leadership within the bookstore, and seeking to change the information and visual representations available in feminist bookstores around the nation. In order to "have crises and survive," bookwomen would need not only savvy book industry advocacy skills but also a willingness to be held accountable to each other.

Sustaining Feminist Publishing against the Chains, 1979–1980

In a special *Emergency* FBN, titled in large hand-drawn block letters, Seajay announced the portents of change: "WIND ended. Such a dark day the day I heard the news."[100] When Women in Distribution (WIND) closed in 1979, feminist bookwomen faced substantial increased costs and work time to continue to stock the small press titles WIND had distributed with a single order form. This substantial change for feminist publishing endangered publishers whose work might not be as visible without WIND's catalogs. The longevity of the FBN—and Seajay's commitment to the life of the publication—made it a unique tool for sharing word of and responding to book industry challenges to feminist literature. By taking on some of the work of WIND, feminist bookwomen began to take on more movement work and attempted to wield influence against the further mainstreaming of the book industry. As these changes in the book industry increased the amount of time bookwomen spent on ordering and on literary activism in the book industry, it became more difficult to balance the industry infrastructure work with the also time-intensive movement and relational infrastructure work.

This FBN issue arrived printed on letter-sized paper rather than the legal-sized paper of its beginnings. This layout visually marked the changing role of the publication. With the coverage of WIND's closing, FBN began regularly documenting changes in the book industry with attention to their effect on feminist bookstores and feminist publishing. WIND had made it possible for feminist bookstores to order a range of small press titles, with a specialty in feminist press titles, from a single place. Seajay, as the FBN, reiterated the importance of distribution to feminist publishing: "If we can't publish and distribute our own words, we certainly can't expect anyone else to do it!" That fact had been proven time and again during mainstream publishers' representative visits (or lack of visits) to feminist bookstores and many a tête-a-tête between a bookwoman and a publisher at the ABA convention. At the first Women in Print meeting, bookwomen had "committed to actively support the feminist media,"[101] and this support now involved reporting on changes in the book industry and attempting to maintain institutional ballasts for the feminist press.

Seajay and the FBN were also committed to economic survival of the bookstores in order to maintain spaces for relational feminist literary activism. With the end of WIND, supporting feminist authors would mean an increased cost for feminist bookwomen "continuing to carry just as much feminist and small press work as we possibly can." Ordering individually from all of the small publishers WIND had carried meant "one stamp for the order, one for the invoice, whatever your check charges are times the number of orders you will now do a month PLUS the increase in postage costs that will come from having to pay that *@#*! 58c for the first pound of each order rather than just paying it once on a distributer order."[102] Seajay, through the FBN, urged bookwomen to figure out where that money would come from and to revise their budgets if necessary "rather than letting the costs sneak up on us and sink us later." The new cost would be "$26.60 per month for 30 additional orders. . . . A lot or not a lot depending on your store size and how many orders you actually will do each month after the first flurry of orders. Figure it out for the number of orders your store will write."[103] This was a crisis not only of how to distribute small press publications but of how to keep bookstores alive in order to do so.

Against this signal of the Women in Print movement's undoing, Seajay applied the salve of Judy Grahn's lesbian feminist poetry, which had shaped the movement from the beginning. For Seajay, this newsletter was

> my form of a love letter to each of us in feminist publishing—from the writers to the publishers to the printers to the distributors to the bookstores who will take on the workload WIND's absence leaves us and will continue to go on as Judy Grahn writes in *Vera* (The Common Woman Poems):

> > . . . the common woman is as common
> > as good bread
> > as common as when you couldnt go on
> > but did.
> > For all the world we didn't know we had in common
> > all along
> > The common woman is as common as the best of bread
> > and will rise
> > and become strong—[104]

Reprinting part of this popular lesbian feminist anthem emphasized both the magnitude of the absence left by WIND and the vigilance of the feminist bookwomen.

For the national and transnational feminist bookstore network, mailing lists quickly became a pivotal behind-the-scenes tool for the long-term preservation of feminist literature and resources. Bookwomen carefully curated a feminist communication network by sharing with each other and selling to those outside the network. FBN continued to distribute their list of feminist bookstores, eighty-two in 1979, with seven in Canada.[105] Now FBN would also print and distribute the WIND list of publishers' addresses. Old Wives' Tales women Seajay and Wallace stayed up two nights going through their files to gather the ordering and returns terms for "all the publishers OWT had ever ordered from direct."[106] For those not receiving the FBN, or not receiving the feminist bookwomen's news inside FBN, the feminist bookstores list sold for $2–5, sliding scale, and the WIND list of publishers and their terms went for $5–10. WIND's mailing list cost $14. Serving as keeper of the lists further identified the network of feminist bookstores as sustaining feminist media: "Getting those lists to the feminist publishers will probably have a significant impact on keeping feminist publishing healthy."[107] In August that year, Minnie Bruce Pratt for the *Feminary* collective wrote in: "Dear Carol Seajay—Enclosed is a check for $4—please send us your list of Feminist Bookstores. Many thanks, MB Pratt."[108]

The lists simultaneously documented and built connections among feminist bookstores at a time when the ABA declared that booksellers were "facing their greatest financial crisis since the depression of the thirties." FBN urged feminist bookwomen to "continue," commiserating, "No, Sister, you're not crazy if you're having a hard time making the books balance." The ABA warned, "Escalating minimum wages, energy costs that have doubled in five years, inflationary costs of store supplies, and book postage rates which have increased 350% since 1970—all of these are making the results of running a bookstore marginally profitable at best."[109] Feminist bookstores were community centers committed to supporting feminist media and interrupting capitalism, though they were still sometimes vulnerable to the vagaries of the economic system. "Moral of the story, I guess," offered FBN, "is to take special care in figuring out how to continue."[110]

With economic and political challenges ahead, Seajay wanted bookwomen to take precautions to survive; feminist literature—and, thus, feminist vocabularies—hung in the balance. In order to survive, feminist bookstores would need community members to understand how bookwomen's advocacy made the literature on the shelves possible. This advocacy work made feminist bookstores different from chain bookstores and other independents. While FBN was the publication for people in the know, local bookwomen used their bookstore newsletters and birthday statements to attempt to educate a general feminist counterpublic about the bookwomen's activism beyond the shelves. In her dual role as FBN editor and Old Wives' Tales cofounder and longest-running collective member, Seajay brought her voice and the skills from FBN to the Old Wives' Tales birthday statements.

The 1979 Old Wives' Tales birthday statement emphasized with its very title the existence of a feminist book world and Old Wives' Tales' central role in it: "Fourth Annual Old Wives' Tales State of the (feminist publishing) World and Third Birthday Statement." The statement explained the role of feminist bookstores in building the written conversations feminists wanted to read. That year, distributors WIND and Amazon Reality closed, Diana Press folded, and Daughters Press announced there would be "no new fall list." "But," the good news began, "the Feminist Press and Naiad seem to be going strong. New publishers (ie Spinsters Ink and New Sybilling Press) have opened up. Persephone will go 'big time' with a list of at least eight books a year where before they did one."[111] Feminist publishing faced challenges but was also thriving, and the loss of distributors meant that feminist bookstores would become full-fledged distribution networks in order to keep feminist publishing alive. Old Wives' Tales bookwomen explained their service to the community: without central distributors, feminist bookstores had to "write more orders, process more paperwork." The statement emphasized that bookwomen were not only ordering books to have on the shelves this month but also working to ensure long-term survival for feminist literature: "When you *do* support us, you can fully expect to have access to feminist books 20–30 years from now and *not* lose it all in a repression or recession."

The birthday statements attempted to teach readers to understand this added ordering work as integral to the bookstore's essential support for feminist authors and literature. "Our commitment to individual women writers and small press publications," explained the collective in 1980, "means that we ordered over 6,000 titles from 2,000 different suppliers this year—where the average bookstore doesn't order from more than 200." The sheer numbers here indicate the bookwomen's work staking out a visible space for feminist literature. "Steadily increasing sales (about which we are *not* complaining) mean that we never get used to any level of ordering before it changes again (how can we predict that women will want 5 *Woman Warrior* last month and 17 this month?)."[112] Old Wives' Tales bookwomen were committed to keeping books like Maxine Hong Kingston's then five-year-old feminist memoir on the shelves.

The same birthday statement announced two new bookwomen joining the Old Wives' Tales staff. With this announcement, Old Wives' Tales bookwomen continued their accountability to their communities and reiterated their role as a movement organization. Of the sixty applicants, the collective reported that they "chose to interview women who were disabled, third world and/or who had bookstore experience." They hired Pell (who went by only her last name) and Jesse Miller. Pell, an African American crafter from the Northeast, ran a women's crafts store for nine years before driving with her poodle to San Francisco in search of a lesbian antiracist feminist community. She worked at the Bay Area Federal Feminist Credit Union and then found her way to Old Wives' Tales. Jesse Miller had worked with

Mothertongue Feminist Theatre Collective as well as with the San Francisco Women's Switchboard sharing information across the lines.[113] As the experience of these new hires suggested, Old Wives' Tales was now in the company of an array of feminist organizations, including Good Vibrations, the Women's Building, Garbo's, Osento, and others. Old Wives' Tales bookwomen, like other feminist bookwomen, saw their identity as a dual role: both in the feminist movement, "working to create more and more spaces for women in the world," and sharing and using knowledge specific to supporting feminist literature. They saw themselves as "closely connected to the growth and strengthening of the whole women-in-print movement."[114]

Over time, breaks in bookstore staff indicated the intense and exhausting affective work at feminist bookstores. Bookwomen struggled to maintain revolutionary processes within a capitalist system. At Womanbooks, the tension between Eleanor Olds Batchelder's business model and Karyn London's socialist feminism reached a fever pitch. From her new home in New Mexico, Fabi Romero Oak traveled again to New York in an attempt to save the bookstore. She stayed with her friend Deborah Edel, cofounder of the Lesbian Herstory Archives. Batchelder had been taking her turn running the bookstore while Romero Oak and London served as silent partners. Though Romero Oak and London had each spent their own years running the bookstore on their own, Batchelder now argued that she should receive more of the bookstore profits. Business ethics and feminist relationships clashed. Romero Oak suggested that Batchelder forfeit her staff position. After rounds of written negotiations about hours worked, vacations taken, money owed, and value secured, the two bookwomen transferred ownership of Womanbooks to Karyn London on a cold January day in 1981.[115] This ebb and flow of relationships within the bookstores, recorded in bookwomen's archives and memories, documents the dual focus of the bookwomen on their relational practice within the bookstores and their communities and their feminist literary advocacy in the book industry. Each sustained the other, and these moments of crisis, though painful, interrupted efficient capital in productive ways: these moments required deep process and reflection on feminist practice. This affective work kept feminist bookwomen's values distinctly different from those of the newly looming chain bookstore menace.

Writers for FBN, including Carol Seajay, the journal's driving force and most prolific author, had honed their skills documenting the injustices that endangered feminist literature. Bookwomen had become feminist watchdogs of the industry, with a sophisticated understanding of how they could work to make feminist media more effective. In the 1979 Old Wives' Tales birthday statement, bookwomen shared the first hint that unfair trade practices benefiting chains would endanger the movement bookstores and their advocacy for feminist literature: "The president of the American Booksellers Association says that he expects small bookstores to be eliminated in twenty years due to the government's postage policies (that have tripled the cost of shipping books in the last 10 years), inflation and the (straight) publishing industry's discount policy which favors chain stores."[116] By 1980 feminist bookwomen were feeling the encroachment of new chain bookstores B. Dalton and Waldenbooks. The Tampa, Florida, women's center sprouted a feminist bookstore that closed almost as soon as it opened. "Competitive Bookstores—Waldens, Daltons, etc," they explained, "sell most books we could obtain. . . . Women still need to have their consciousness raised regarding supporting with our monies other women's groups and stores."[117] Now that feminist publishers, distributors, and bookstores had proved there were readers for feminist books, mainstream attention introduced unwelcome competition against bookwomen's collaboration to support authors.

Feminist bookwomen used FBN to practice with each other how to explain that the danger was more than just "competition" now that feminist books were more widely available. The chain bookstores were receiving favorable discounts from "straight" publishers, and LICE was transforming bookselling into commodity retail, while bookwomen had created information centers fostered by relationships and the possibility of lesbian antiracist feminist education. On chain bookstore shelves, authors received not increased visibility on a shelf in every city but intensified competition for shelf space painfully decontextualized from the movement accountability of the feminist bookstore shelves. This danger to authors was a major concern for feminist bookwomen, who were becoming industry analysts: "Authors continue to panic as shelf life gets shorter at B. DALTON, leader of the chain gang (10 days)," reported FBN. While feminist bookwomen were imagining a higher discount for those central feminist books they would never return, chain bookstores allowed less and less time for readers to find books they might need. In the rhetoric of chain bookstores, books became widgets rather than the vital resources bookwomen traded news of in the pages of FBN: "JOHN POPE, B.D. [B. Dalton] Advertising Director, who formerly promoted WHEATIES and TORO LAWNMOWERS, says he's taking the 'awesomeness' out of bookstores, which have been 'stuffy places with parquet floors, heavy fixtures, and a little old lady who has been there for 30 years.'" This was an empty stereotype, FBN noted with a sinister humor: "Well, good for her, since women own only 7% of small businesses (earning 1% of business receipts) and only 2% of media properties."[118] Feminist bookwomen had their work cut out for them: they continued to advocate for feminist relationships, accountability, and literature while an increasingly monopolized industry painted the "little old lady" as the sign of a bygone era. Feminist bookwomen imagined a new life for this "little old lady" as they, and their lovers and friends, gathered on the pages of the FBN to "demystify" and remake the book industry.

THREE

ACCOUNTABLE
TO EACH OTHER
1980–1983

In the summer of 1981, hundreds of women gathered in the Yosemite National Forest for the first West Coast Women's Music Festival. A group of Old Wives' Tales bookstore collective members were there from San Francisco among the crowd listening to the music and turmoil amid the trees. Over the weekend, festival participants met repeatedly to process the lack of representation across race and class at the event. A group of women decided to march to continue the discussion while occupying the main performance area.[1] Taking the stage, musician and activist Bernice Johnson Reagon of Sweet Honey in the Rock famously delivered the speech that became her essay "Coalition Politics: Turning the Century." Bookwomen heard connections between her talk and their collective work as they listened that weekend to Reagon and, later, to the cassette tape of Reagon's talk that bookwomen shared at ICI: A Woman's Place as a tool for articulating their practice of lesbian antiracist feminism.

In the festival atmosphere, Reagon observed, it was hard to breathe, in more ways than one. While some women were accustomed to breathing easily at Yosemite, for others, the air at this altitude was poison: "There is a lesson in bringing people together where they can't get enough oxygen, then having them try to figure out what they're going to do when they can't think properly."[2] An assumed entitlement to breath put some women in danger, in pain. From this embodied experience, Reagon explained that unearned privilege, specifically whiteness, can appear as invisible as altitude and affect us as painfully.[3] Instead of assuming everyone could breathe, assuming "women" are all similar, Reagon called on listeners to recognize vast differences among "women." "Women," she warned, is "a code word, and it traps, and the people that use the word are not prepared to deal with the fact that if you put it out, everybody that thinks they're a woman may one day want to seek refuge."[4] That is, women with privilege who narrowly define "woman" by their own identities "are not prepared to deal" with the important differences among women's experiences of oppression. Feminists of color had for years been analyzing how gender is also constructed by racialized identities.[5] Reagon explained, "It does not matter at all that . . . we have being women in common. . . . We are not from our base acculturated to be women people, capable of crossing our first people boundaries—Black, White, Indian, etc."[6] To successfully organize "women" would necessarily require working against racism. The social movements of the 1960s were at a turning point of alliance in the 1980s: "The reason we are stumbling," Reagon advised, "is that we are at the point where in order to take the next step we've got to do it with some folk we don't care too much about. And we got to vomit over that for a little while. We must just keep going."[7] That idea of working together even when it was difficult, in order for everyone to live, sparked recognition for women at the Bay Area feminist bookstores. In the midst of arguments and splits within these central bookstore collectives, Reagon's talk informed a dialogue toward antiracist feminism that shaped the bookwomen's influence on feminist literature, reading, and relationship practices.

With her claim that coalition space is always dangerous, Reagon challenged the framing narratives of feminist bookstores that claimed to be "woman's places."[8] It had been exciting and important to imagine the bookstores as sites staked out for women; bookwomen in more than a few cities called their bookstore A Woman's Place.[9] But, Reagon asked, which women? Women of color working in feminist bookstores already knew that building coalition with white women was risky.[10] The Old Wives' Tales collective had been talking about their racialized and classed differences, and they heard possibility in Reagon's call. If they could unite around an antiracist feminist project, perhaps they could strengthen their alliances with each other and imagine a new feminist future. In 1982, the Old Wives' Tales collective included Tiana Arruda, a Latina woman; Pell, a Black woman; and Sherry Thomas and bookstore founder Carol Seajay, two white women. The bookwomen created and circulated a flyer claiming that the 1982 West Coast Women's Music Festival looked like it would repeat the same mistakes: "The Festival remains unaccountable to the community."[11] The collective declared they would not attend the festival.

So strong was the force of the Old Wives' Tales flyer, backed by their community reputation, that the festival organizers wrote an extensive article and announced a meeting at the Women's Building to which they invited "everyone concerned with the issue and allegations around the West Coast Women's Music Festival—especially the women of Old Wives' Tales."[12] Women of color festival organizers, now making up a quarter of the organizing crew, expressed outrage at their "invisibility in the Old Wives' Tales flyer": "We insist on being heard, as women willing to struggle in the painful and inspiring process of coalition-building that Bernice Reagon articulated so eloquently last year. We cannot be afraid of our differences in the fight for unity." The Old Wives' Tales bookwomen perhaps recognized themselves in this struggle: having women of color on staff was part of but did not wholly enact an antiracist feminist practice. With their flyer, the Old Wives' Tales collective attempted to build a new strategy for accountability and a language of lesbian feminist antiracism.

These related moments in Yosemite and San Francisco indicate feminist bookstores' location as important sites of feminist antiracism. In this chapter I describe how bookwomen's literary activism was, in this period, interconnected with and strengthened by feminist accountability around race and sexuality. In the late 1970s bookwomen had established their advocacy skills and their collective education as literary activists by sharing strategies through the *Feminist Bookstores Newsletter* (FBN) as well as in person. The reach of this literary activism, including the transnational readership of the FBN, meant that each local bookstore conversation about lesbian feminist antiracism had the potential for national and transnational resonance. Bookwomen had outlined the interrelationship of this work in the first issue of FBN, where they committed to use their network to support feminist media, to act as "revolutionaries" within the "capitalist system" of the book industry, and "to develop ways of working together that make us more accountable to our communities and to each other."[13] I use feminist accountability to name the defining framework created by feminist bookwomen, where accountability ensures a feminist dialogue to define, grapple with, and evolve a shared set of ethics and ideas about how to live by those ethics. While this dialogue happened locally within individual collectives, the FBN formalized this framework by calling for feminist accountability in the first issue and then by critically holding space for codifying and contesting feminist ethics.[14] In the 1980s bookwomen honed a practice of feminist accountability that could inform and sustain today's feminisms.

The success of feminist literary activism in the 1970s demonstrated the capacity of feminist bookwomen to share education and act as a network: bookwomen's influence had contributed to mainstream publisher, distributor, and bookseller interest in feminist titles, as I described in chapter 2. By the 1980s, it seemed like feminist literature was here to stay, and this illusion threatened feminism in two ways. First, while chain bookstores did stock some feminist literature, they focused on immediate big sellers and fast turnaround, not the promotion and support feminist bookstores provided to sustain a literature. The growth of chain bookstores would homogenize literature, with a focus on best sellers. Second, sustaining feminist literature depended on lesbian antiracist feminism built through feminist accountability not available in chain stores.

Threats to independent bookstores also endangered the less obvious but perhaps more significant work of the feminist bookstores as movement spaces where bookwomen created lesbian antiracist feminist practice. In this book I use the term "lesbian antiracism" to describe not strictly lesbians practicing antiracism together but a particular practice of antiracism developed in multiracial conversation that includes lesbians. As lesbian feminists articulate their critique of and resist heteropatriarchy, they are already understanding systems of power as interconnected; the systems of sexism and heterosexism are also rooted in racism, and all three of these systems must be taken apart in order for any one of them to be dismantled. Lesbian antiracism thus requires analyzing and mobilizing against these violently interlocking oppressions to envision a just future.[15] Central feminist bookstore histories map out approaches to lesbian antiracism; these histories offer necessary tools for current practice.

In this period, the two Bay Area feminist bookstore collectives' difficult conversations around lesbian feminist antiracism circulated widely and influenced feminist vocabularies. These struggles and the public dialogue around them mapped out a cycle for feminist accountability within the bookstores: feminist literary activism sustained the bookstores and feminist literature, which in turn created the bookstores as space for lesbian antiracist feminism, which kept literary activism accountable to the movement and informed new feminist literature, reading, and relationships. In chapter 5 I suggest that the tension between these two feminist bookstore roles—feminist literary activism and feminist accountability—caused a fissure in the 1990s when bookwomen faced the increasing marketization of bookselling that threatened independents and feminist movements. In this chapter the interrelationship between feminist literary activism and lesbian antiracist vocabulary and relationship building models for contemporary feminists the importance of and strategies for enacting feminist accountability within any feminist project.

Decades later, at the Toronto Women's Bookstore, I saw firsthand how a queer antiracist feminist commitment could inform bookwomen's feminist literary activism to shape vocabularies and literatures. In April 2006, I accepted a position at the bookstore. Anjula Gogia, the previous manager and book buyer, had built the nonprofit bookstore up to a $1.6 million budget over the course of her ten-year leadership. The staff and board hired me to fill in while she was on a leave of absence. The bookstore staff and shelves embodied the bookstore's commitment to queer antiracist feminism. When I started, I was one of three white people on the ten-person staff. Like other feminist bookwomen internationally, the Toronto bookstore staff had learned that in order to supply texts for an antiracist feminist present and future, they would need to advocate not only through ordering but also by supporting feminist authors of color to get published. In her regular meetings with authors who came to the bookstore for advice on getting published, Gogia "realized that a lot of the services for writers out there were not geared for writers of color." Publishing, she observed when I interviewed her in 2007, "still remains a very white-dominated industry, as does bookselling."[16] When I arrived in Toronto, bookwomen Janet Romero and Edite Pine were supporting queer and queer-allied feminists of color in authorship and publishing with the bookstore's second annual Written in Colour symposium. Marking a spatial network of coalitions, the symposium took place just a few blocks away from the bookstore at the University of Toronto Centre for Women and Trans People. The who's who of Canadian people of color and Indigenous authors and publishers at the conference, as on the bookstore shelves, documented an antiracist feminist present and possible futures. Publishers set up in the nearby auditorium: Kegedonce Press (First Nations owned and operated) and TSAR Publications (Toronto South Asian Review) each had a table. Kateri Akiwenzie-Damm, poet and publisher of Kegedonce Press, conducted an advanced manuscript review. Hiromi Goto led the beginners' manuscript review. Anar Ali held a workshop on how to approach a literary agent, and other sessions addressed grantwriting; writing nonfiction, poetry, fiction, or autobiography; and creating graphic novels. In the full auditorium for the Saturday morning plenary, legendary feminist Sto:Loh Nation author and teacher Lee Maracle shared her experience. In this gathering, I worked as an ally, helping to hold space to interrupt, as the program described, "the often inaccessible world of publishing."[17] Written in Colour built infrastructure for people of color and Indigenous people to become published writers as well as to create publishing houses to publicize and distribute their work, the work we all need. It was no accident that this event was happening through a feminist bookstore. This event was rooted in bookwomen's practice of feminist accountability forged in the early 1980s, a legacy of feminist bookstores as sites of lesbian antiracist feminist vocabulary building as part of advocacy to create new reading and relational practices.

Lesbian and Racial Justice Foundations for Feminist Literary Activism

As collectives struggled with movement vocabulary, mainstream publishers attempted to deny the movement altogether. It had seemed like feminist bookstores, through their numbers, their sales, and their stock, had proved without a doubt that feminist literature existed and had a readership; however, book sales alone did not convince publishers. It was the pressure exerted by bookwomen on publishers that kept feminist and lesbian books on each season's lists of new releases. In San Francisco, a publisher's representative arrived at Old Wives' Tales for what Carol Seajay thought was a regular sales appointment to page through catalogs of new books and place orders for the bookstore. The rep made the trip over, but without the catalog, Seajay recalls. He sat down to explain, "I really don't have anything for you because, you know, the women's thing is kind of, over. . . . We don't think there's a market anymore." Seajay looked at him for a moment before replying, "My sales have doubled in the last eight months." The sales reports from the bookwomen to the reps, she says, achieved results: "The next season, they'd have books for us." Emphasizing the importance of the sheer numbers of bookwomen's participation, Seajay describes the effect: "We would prove that market, and every time they said there's no more interest, we would laugh at them. . . . So, either our laughter embarrassed them . . . our numbers convinced them, or they just saw they were missing sales and didn't want to. So they kept publishing year after year."[18] The reps brought news from the bookstores back to the publishers, and the nearly one hundred feminist bookstores made a difference. On the pages of FBN, Old Wives' Tales bookwoman Sherry Thomas reported on this effect and urged feminist bookwomen to keep up their lobbying: "Norton is bringing out 2 more May Sarton paperbacks and the new Adrienne Rich in paperback because of sales representatives' pressure. Beacon is bringing out *Sunday's Women*[: *A Report on Lesbian Life Today*] at $4.95 because sales reps said lesbian stores said to keep it at that. So keep pushing those sales reps (those that do condescend to visit)."[19] The books were more available and more affordable because of bookwomen's intervention with publishers.

Bookwomen's advocacy for feminist literature relied on collective action and on space to call each other to account to the movement-based ethics that informed their literary activism. The June 1980 issue of FBN announced that the journal's cofounder, André, had returned to coedit it and that Oakland bookwoman Jesse Meredith of ICI: A Woman's Place had also joined the crew.[20] This confluence of energy signaled a new action phase for bookwomen. As they geared up for activism, the editors again raised the perennial inquiry about how to balance their external influence with their internal accountability: "To whom should the Feminist Bookstores' Newsletter go?"[21] The FBN already filled subscriptions from librarians, authors, publishers, and individual women. Now the question was whether to allow subscriptions from "straight stores," general independent stores, or chain stores. Meredith summarized why the editors favored allowing any subscriptions: "No straight store is going to order so many [feminist] titles that it will seriously undercut a feminist bookstore," and, she insisted, "we can be just as controversial and too bad if someone's nose is put out of joint (we can always hold a bake sale if we get sued, right?)"[22] The clash of the market-based business with feminist process is evident in Meredith's gesture to bookwomen's concerns that "straight stores" with feminist stock would outsell feminist bookstores or that FTC regulations against sharing discount and pricing information would shut down the FBN. Ultimately the editors agreed that, based on responses to this discussion, no decision could yet be made. In the next issue, the editors acknowledged the essential role of feminist bookwomen and the FBN in sustaining feminist publishing: "Our primary purpose is to put out a newsletter for and about feminist bookstores; our secondary purpose, to promote and facilitate feminist publishing."[23]

Feminist publishing was one central strategy for building women of color feminism amidst ongoing systemic racism both inside and outside feminist movements. At the Blackstone School in the Boston neighborhood of Roxbury, on a wintry evening in 1980, the room thrilled with the purposeful energy of feminist authors gathered for the prepublication reading of *This Bridge Called My Back: Writings by Radical Women of Color*. The Combahee River Collective and the Bessie Smith Memorial Collective had together organized the event as a benefit for their protest against the Boston Police Department's apathetic investigation of the murders of twelve Black women and one white woman in Boston. A few days before the reading, poet Kate Rushin received a call from Barbara Smith, then an organizer with the Combahee River Collective. Smith was recruiting local feminist authors of color to read the work of contributors to the collection and to share their own work as well. Hearing Smith talk with her sister about the title of the anthology, Rushin thought back to a draft of a poem she had started, "The Bridge Poem." Fahamisha Patricia Brown, Audre Lorde, Adrienne Rich, and others gathered for the reading, and Rushin read her poem. "That was the first big reading I'd given in Boston," she remembers, "and at the end of the reading, Cherríe Moraga came up and asked me if she could publish 'The Bridge Poem' in *This Bridge Called My Back*, and of course I was thrilled."[24]

In "The Bridge Poem," Rushin described the challenges of coalition building and used writing as a path to resistance:

I've had enough
I'm sick of seeing and touching
Both sides of things
Sick of being the damn bridge for everybody. . . .

I explain my mother to my father my father to my little sister
My little sister to my brother my brother to the white feminists
The white feminists to the Black church folks the Black church folks
To the ex-hippies the ex-hippies to the Black separatists the
Black separatists to the artists the artists to my friends' parents . . .
Then
I've got to explain myself
To everybody.[25]

Through her writing, Rushin built alliances with the lesbian feminists of color who together created *This Bridge Called My Back*. She formed a friendship with the women of Persephone Press, the first publishers of the anthology, and with the bookwomen of New Words, the feminist bookstore in Cambridge.

The New Words collective asked Rushin to start a Thursday evening shift at the bookstore. As she wove an identity around her writing practice, Rushin sensed she was connecting with a community. News of this Black lesbian poet traveled. Rushin had moved from the Cape to Boston, she recalls, just after "the horrible days of the violence against busing in '76." Buses had carried Black children from areas like Roxbury, where the *Bridge* event took place, into white-dominated South Boston. White mobs had rocked and stoned the buses; they had attacked Black people on board and nearby. When Rushin accepted what became a three-year residency as a poet in the schools, she imagines, "people were probably more interested that a Black woman poet was at South Boston High than I realized." Though the principal advised her not to ride the city bus into the nearly all-white neighborhood, the maze of transportation seemed unnecessary to Rushin: she would take "the Orange Line to Park Street, change to the Green Line, change to the Red Line, go out to what was then called Columbia Point, . . . and then they would come with a van and then drive me over." Even when each of these pieces ran on time, the arduous process frustrated Rushin. Taking one city bus and walking two blocks from the stop to the school would be so much easier, so she tried it. The bus driver was the only other Black person on the bus, "and everybody stopped talking; it was the tensest bus ride I ever had." Walking up the hill and almost to the school, Rushin spotted a group of kids who had cut class to hang out at the candy store: "They started yelling names," Rushin remembers, "and I kept walking." Just before she stepped through the gate and onto school grounds, three young men leaving school against regulations exited the gate. Rushin describes what happened next:

> Basically, they wouldn't have said a word to me in school, but I was outside the gates, so I was on their territory. They started yelling names, and one kid started, doing an ape imitation, "Ooh, ooh, ooh," and yelling the names. And I walked up the steps, I just kept going. I put my hand, just like this, put my hand on the door to go into the school; a bottle shattered next to me, right in the corner, and then I went in. And I went right to class, because I had my workshop to teach. On my way to class I saw the headmaster, and I told him what had happened, and his response was, "Well, you know, we can't be responsible for you outside of the school." Basically, what he was saying was: "I told you all not to take public transportation."[26]

This violence informed Rushin's activism within the bookstore. She used her Thursday shift at New Words to create feminist literary space, proof of a movement, by and for women of color. Rushin's bookstore shift became an anchor for feminists of color as she created a space she needed:

> The bridge I must be
> Is the bridge to my own power
> I must translate
> My own fears
> Mediate
> My own weaknesses
> I must be the bridge to nowhere
> But my true self
> And then
> I will be useful.[27]

Rushin's work at New Words influenced the shelves and transnational activism I discuss in chapter 4, and her poem in *This Bridge Called My Back* traveled on many networks, including feminist bookstores.

Pell had moved from Massachusetts to San Francisco before she found *This Bridge Called My Back* while working at Old Wives' Tales. The staff and shelves at Old Wives' Tales were informed by San Francisco itself, a coastal site of diasporic and neocolonial histories, and home to ethnically diverse lesbian feminist organizations. Working at the bookstore, Pell for the first time found a substantial number of books by other Black women: "it opened up a whole new wonderful world to me, because I didn't grow up knowing a lot of Black women writers. I never had that information, and I didn't know anyone else who did." As she was growing up, she knew of some Black women authors, like midcentury educator and organizer Mary McLeod Bethune, but the bookstore offered "more information that gave me a chance to *really* go from one book to the other. It was wonderful." She had been a reader, she says, "but never like that."[28] The shelves and her relationships at the bookstore not only introduced her to a history and vibrant present of Black women authors; the bookstore also provided a site for women of color connecting with each other. On the shelves, books by women of color directly reflected Pell's experiences in the bookstore. Working with women of color was a big shift for Pell, who, she says, "had never worked around an Asian woman before, or a Latina woman before. I'm from Massachusetts. I come from a black and white world."

For Pell, as for other bookwomen, her bookstore, Old Wives' Tales, was the place where she began to learn, from other bookwomen as well as from the books on the shelves, to read and collaborate across racial difference. Missed communications in these exchanges indicate the vital importance of understanding how to make these alliances work. Pell liked working with Kit Quan, "talking with her and having lunch and just hanging out, exchanging information."[29] Quan felt this kind of connection in general in the bookstore: "I think they were supportive of me in terms of my being a young dyke, someone who had left home. I think they had a generally supportive attitude, because sisterhood was a real value then." But the general connection, Quan sensed, did not extend to personal support: "I was pretty invisible as an individual. I was a worker."[30] Pell's memory of Quan as "a young person that came in, I think after school" suggests some of that distance created by age and racial difference, even as Pell appreciated working with Quan "because she came from a different background than I did."[31] Pell remembers that in the bookstore, women "talked about black and white, although we were in a Latino community," and although Quan's identity as an Asian lesbian would not fit in this dichotomy either. Even with these sites of disconnect, both Pell and Quan emphasize that the bookstores were a unique site for expanding this conversation.

Dialogue happened among staff, amid the shelves, and at bookstore events. While Quan wanted more "constructive discussions" about race and class at Old Wives' Tales, she points out, "On the other hand, it's true that all those landmark publications like *This Bridge Called My Back*, and all those writings that were coming out, were events at the store. There was a lot of history at the store." Pell remembers feeling, "It was just a fantastic time." Pell saw that feminist bookstores "opened doors for women and opened their minds with all the dialogue, in talking about the books, discussing the books. Whether racism or health issues, it was something that was going on that wasn't going on anywhere else. I don't mean it wasn't going on in other bookstores, but it wasn't going on in a lot of places outside of the bookstores." Even when imperfect, the bookstores provided vital sites for attempting alliances across racialized and class difference.

At the Common Woman bookstore in Austin, public rejection and misunderstandings of feminism emphasized that feminist bookstores had developed and sustained a particular feminist literacy, a necessary way of reading that made a feminist present possible. In 1980 the bookstore moved from the second story of an old house on San Antonio Street to a retail strip of brick buildings on Sixth Street with giant plate glass windows facing the sidewalk. This was "a radical move," Susan Post explains; at the time, the city and landlords were in the midst of a devastating project to gentrify Sixth Street from Black-owned to white-owned businesses, including a few owned by white lesbians.[32] In a few short years, tenants of the street would almost exclusively be bars, as part of the Austin city council's attempt at an Austin Bourbon Street; but in the 1980s Sixth Street was still a retail center. New white landlords who invested in displacing Black communities were also no allies to white lesbians. When Post crossed the street to meet with the white, straight landlord who ran a shop across the street, he balked at the bookstore name. "This is offensive to me," Post remembers him saying. "I don't want just any old common, *you know*." Post was sure "he was thinking: 'Lesbian. Lesbian. Lesbian! . . . He was not going to rent to a bunch of *common women*."[33] The landlord would only agree to the lease on the condition that the bookwomen change the Common Woman name.[34] By now Post was corunning the bookstore with her new lover, Karen Umminger. The two changed the name to BookWomen, Everywoman's Bookshop, but the name didn't last. When BookWomen consulted a linguist (a woman) to devise a logo for the store, the linguist explained that BookWomen, plural, might sound threatening to some, reminiscent of a horde of women, dangerous in their numbers. BookWoman, singular, the linguist insisted, was "much stronger."[35] While the name conformed to societal pressures, the bookwomen themselves did not.

On a sunny day on Sixth Street, folks in the line of people outside Book-Woman clutched Beatles albums, copies of Yoko Ono's *Grapefruit: A Book of Instructions + Drawings*, and flyers announcing the bookstore's first Yoko Ono Day. Picturing that day thirty years ago as we sit on a park bench in Brooklyn, Kay Turner leans forward in her seat; the flyers she and Post had crafted promised that Yoko Ono would be there, "but really," Turner explains, "it was in spirit that she was going to make her appearance, because we were doing all the stuff from *Grapefruit*." The fans with their Beatles albums refused to understand—Turner remembers an angry letter to the editor in the local paper about the false claim—but the performance pieces lasted all day for the faithful. In *Grapefruit*, Ono guided readers through exercises like this one:

LINE PIECE I
Draw a line.

Erase the line.
LINE PIECE II
Erase lines.
LINE PIECE III
Draw a line with yourself.
Go on drawing until you disappear.[36]

Women stood shoulder to shoulder in the bookstore, drawing lines with themselves until they disappeared. This performance might have been a metaphor for coalition, how to connect with people different from yourself and allow your own power to "disappear" into the collective. This near-spiritual ethos of interconnectedness informed the bookwomen's claim that Ono would be there. Turner points out, "I guess it was a little bit of false information, for those who just couldn't read into it in the BookWoman way, in the lezzie-feminist way."[37] The Austin feminist bookstore created space for creative imagining, and supported arts-based performances like these, music series curated by local lesbian musician Nancy Scott, and sacred crafting with the altar making collective. Reading in the lezzie-feminist way offered an understanding of how collective gathering and performance could change systems of power. As Ono invited, "let everybody in the city think of the word 'yes' at the same time for 30 seconds. Do it often."[38] Inside the FBN and at local bookstores like New Words, Old Wives' Tales, and Book-Woman, bookwomen developed and tried out strategies for building connections with each other, lezzie-feminist ways of reading each other in resistance to systemic oppressions including racism, misogyny, and lesbophobia.

Survival Means Creating, Challenging, and Re-creating Movement Practice

In order to sustain this vital reading practice and the feminist literature on which it thrived, bookwomen would need to work together against the coming chain bookstore menace and publishers' collusion. At the same time, in order to continue to be accountable to and to grow feminist movements, bookwomen would need to continue to call each other on their practice of (or failure to practice) lesbian antiracism. The survival of feminist bookstores depended on bookwomen's ability to sustain their dual work challenging both the feminist movement and a larger public. Feminist bookstores showed distinct local strengths in different pieces of an interrelated feminist vocabulary, including antiracist feminism, transnational feminism, feminist crafting, and resisting violence against women. These differences between the feminist bookstores meant that the full collective of feminist bookstores, almost one hundred bookstores by 1980,[39] were required to hold each other accountable for feminist literature, relationships, and futures.

By the early 1980s, chain bookstores were threatening feminist bookstores. In San Francisco, a B. Dalton opened up the street from Old Wives' Tales and started selling similar books for less. At Old Wives' Tales, Pell "started talking with women, letting them know they had to support the women's bookstores." In short order, "the big bookstores started getting *our* writers in to talk about their books."[40] This struggle with the mainstream bookstores paralleled the discussions about subscriptions to FBN. Widespread access to feminist literature was the ideal, so having feminist books everywhere seemed beneficial. Since pressure from the Women in Print movement had initially compelled general bookstores to carry these writers, however, what would keep these books in the bookstores once the mainstream put feminist bookstores out of business? And, as conversations about antiracism in this chapter and about the feminist shelf in chapter 4 demonstrate, finding a book at a feminist bookstore generated a different understanding of that book than finding the same book at a chain. Feminist bookstores were more than just places to find books; they were movement training grounds.

In October 1980, Jesse Meredith visited a heated meeting of the Northern California Booksellers Association (NCBA) and wrote up a report for FBN. She called the report "Organizing for Survival."[41] The NCBA was a group of independent booksellers, including feminist bookwomen like Meredith of ICI: A Woman's Place. For this meeting, they had invited the ABA's assistant executive director and staff attorney to ask them why the ABA was doing nothing about "independent booksellers being discriminated [against] by publishers in favor of chains." At that point, the ABA still purported to serve all bookstores, chain and independent alike. People at the NCBA meeting argued that chains were angling to put independents out of business. Independent booksellers had discovered that the chains had more going for them than just a seemingly savvy business model. Meredith reported, "Some publishers are at times giving chain stores and gift stores better discounts for fewer items than they give to independents."[42] That is, even when chain bookstores did not order in bulk, they still got a better price than independent bookstores. This discrimination in discounting made it more expensive for feminist bookstores to stay open. This meeting was an early articulation of the brewing independent bookstore challenges to the illegal monopoly created by the chains in cooperation with big publishing.

Having already developed a core group of feminist literary activists and a savvy group of editors committed to influencing the book industry, the FBN was strategically positioned to take a lead in this organizing. Meredith left the NCBA meeting with a plan to create an official organization of feminist bookstores. "I think that the lure of 99 feminist bookstores around the world must be fairly attractive to publishers," she ventured, emphasizing a transnational network. "Our organization could say to the boys, 'publish feminist books; let us know about them; do cooperative advertising with us. We are a big, enthusiastic market; we keep our titles in stock until they go out of print; and we push them!' How can they resist?"[43] The organization Meredith articulated sounded much like action already informally under way through the FBN; the difference was in the delivery. Meredith pointed out, "Writing publishers as the F.B.N. may not be very impressive," but a named network of ninety-nine feminist bookstores could be. Meredith asked bookwomen to respond: "So women; what do you think? Yes, it sounds like a lot of hassle. But it could also bring us a lot of rewards; maybe more financial solvency and more feminist books; and maybe, a chance to cause some change in the literary-industrial complex, instead of functioning as passive middlewomen. Please, please, PLEASE; fill out the form on the last page now and let us know what you think!!!"[44] Meredith hyperbolizes here for emphasis; while feminist bookwomen had been anything but "passive middlewomen," they would now begin to discuss how they would participate in the book industry in a more organized way in order to sustain the literature their readers, and they themselves, needed.

Meredith's call to create an advocacy organization seemed urgent but not yet timely. Women at Sonya Wetstone Books & Cheese in Hartford, Connecticut, worried about violating federal antitrust laws. Wetstone cautioned, "Neither the A.B.A. nor any regional booksellers' group can even talk to each other as an organization or group about discounts, pricing, freight, etc. without running the risk of being slapped with a lawsuit."[45] At New Earth in Kansas City, Missouri, women complained that the good idea might be "unrealistic" in expected results.[46] Informally, then, the majority of the feminist bookstores would provide numbers for the lobbying conducted by the larger and more active stores as well as by the FBN editors, who lamented the lack of interest. For those who were interested, Meredith offered an interim strategy: "I still heartily encourage anyone who is moved to protest unfair publisher policies to write them and send the F.B.N. copies of the correspondence."[47]

Soon after this exchange, Carol Seajay finally realized "a long time fantasy": *Publishers Weekly* (PW) profiled Old Wives' Tales. Seajay had conspired with Dorothy Bryant (author of *The Kin of Ata Are Waiting for You*, Moon Books/ Random House, 1976) to get PW author Patricia Holt to an Old Wives' Tales book reading where Seajay convinced her to write the piece. Ever a savvy advocate for feminist bookstores, Seajay ensured that they made it onto the pages that would document and influence the publishing industry. The article began Seajay's long and storied relationship with the industry publication: as I document in chapter 5, by the 1990s, Seajay and the FBN were appearing regularly in PW as influential players in the major bookstore industry changes. When this first article appeared, Seajay sent a copy of it to the bookwomen, along with an FBN report explaining her strategy. "One of our main goals," Seajay says of her and Sherry Thomas's interviews with Holt, "was to talk about the publishing of feminist books, and to point out graphically and literally that there is a marketing network for GOOD feminist books." Distinctly different from mainstream women's literature, "GOOD feminist books" are those not watered down because of publishers' assumptions about readers' tastes. Seajay's and Thomas's mentions of books in their interviews offered a new definition of feminist literature by example.

Publishers who published "good feminist books," the article promised, would be rewarded with a network of bookwomen dedicated to stocking the books and connecting them with readers. Seajay and Thomas provided evidence that feminist bookwomen could order and sustain sales of good feminist books over time. They were committed to "finding those hundreds of specialty suppliers whose books are never listed in traditional publishing/bookselling directories." The additional work of ordering from such specialty suppliers, as Seajay and Old Wives' Tales had already explained in FBN and in the bookstore's birthday statements, was necessary: "It takes much more effort to find and purchase such titles as 'Feminist Japan,' 'The Changing Role of Women in Asia,' or 'The Legal Rights of Battered Women in California,' but to our audience it's absolutely crucial that we stock these titles here."[48] With these titles, the bookwomen prioritized movement over business.

The article shared strategies of the bookwomen's practice of both using and interrupting circuits of capital. Bookwomen both established that feminist books do sell and refused to return the books that did not. The book-women realized that ordering a breadth of literature, of necessity in small batches so that feminist bookstores could afford the number of titles, might imply that publishers would see fewer sales of each title. The bookstore's numbers showed that these books could not only sell big but continue to sell over time to dedicated feminist audiences. Bookwomen at Old Wives' Tales had sold "to date" 400 copies of the Pocket Books edition of Maxine Hong Kingston's *Woman Warrior* over three years in 40 orders, 286 copies of the Bantam edition of Toni Morrison's *Sula* in 50 orders, 347 copies of the Norton edition of Adrienne Rich's *Dream of a Common Language* in 41 orders, and 400 copies of the Random House and Ata Books editions of Dorothy Bryant's *The Kin of Ata Are Waiting for You*.[49] If sales mattered to publishers, returns could indicate a failure of capitalism—if not for the movement. Bookwomen would not allow a book that did not sell (which, for the movement, did not mean it was not needed) to support publishers' claims that the "women's thing is over." A picture accompanying the article showed a table full of books surrounding a handwritten sign announcing "O.W.T.'s first overstock sale": "These are books that normally we would return to the publishers. But we think that returning these books would discourage N.Y. publishers from bringing out new Feminist books, or in some cases from bringing these books out in paperback. So we are experimenting instead with selling limited quantities of books we care about at 1/3 off. This is a one-time only sale. Enjoy!"[50] Holt wrote that the sign "reveals a great deal about the bookstore's political and professional commitment."

While feminist bookwomen advocated for more—and more complex—representations of feminism in literature, this first article in PW brought with it the specter of the divisive costs of mainstream representation. In the FBN, Seajay shared her frustration that the mainstream media continued to resist representing the shared political commitments of feminists and lesbians. "What didn't come through," Seajay cautions bookwomen reading the essay, "is Lesbianism, either our own or the marketing and selling and publishing of good LESBIAN books. We think we said 'lesbian' about every other word in the interviews." The mainstream press, like many feminist histories, erased lesbians from feminism, while most bookwomen were lesbian feminists. In a related erasure, Seajay and Thomas represented the bookstore alone, two white women. The version of the collective that had attempted to hold the West Coast Women's Music Festival accountable to race and feminism did not make it onto the pages. Representation was a reading practice for validation; no one knew this better than feminist book-women. "A lot of the books featured are lesbian," Seajay emphasized, "but if you don't already know that WANDERGROUND, ON STRIKE AGAINST GOD, Mary Daly, Susan Griffin, Adrienne Rich, et al are lesbian, you could read the whole article and miss it. So the article speaks clearly to feminist publishing. Lesbian publishing will have to try again."[51] Those looking for lesbian books—and books by and for all feminists of color—and not already knowing which ones those are would find them through feminist book-stores but, it would seem, not through press coverage of the bookstores.

A strategic mention of the FBN did make it through to the final version of the PW article. Literature was booming at Old Wives' Tales and other femi-nist bookstores, while general independents, faced with the new chains, were beginning a downward trend. A carefully placed and detailed mention of the FBN let publishers know that this strength was due to similar actions tak-ing place in feminist stores (and, though unremarked, at lesbians' hands) throughout the nation. "Obviously something very dramatic is happening with that audience in San Francisco," Holt acknowledged. "Thomas and Seajay suspect it is spreading throughout the country as well. This is per-haps the reason why Seajay, backed by owners of other feminist bookstores, has launched the *Feminist Bookstores Newsletter*, an idea-packed, highly-informative and often entertaining periodical that is mailed out every two months to 130 feminist bookstores in the U.S. and Canada."[52] Even though Holt made it sound like Seajay started FBN on her own and just last week, this description of FBN and its impressive circulation numbers documented a movement gaining speed. This national publicity was itself a tool of femi-nist literary advocacy. That same year Sherry Thomas wrote to Macmillan to bring Blanche Boyd's 1977 *Mourning the Death of Magic* out in paper and urged other bookwomen to write letters too. This letter-writing campaign had an additional kick: "The PW article about Old Wives' Tales helped,"[53] Thomas mentions, indicating that the article opened a door at Macmillan. Feminist bookwomen had trained each other, and now they were taking part of their work public for full effect. The counterpublic was on the move.

After a decade of feminist literary activism, bookwomen prepared for the second Women in Print Conference, this one in 1981 in Washington, DC. Mary Farmer at Lammas, the DC feminist bookstore, volunteered to coordinate a two-day gathering of bookwomen, and bookstore collectives began discussions about who from the bookstores would attend. Within collectives, discussions about who would travel to DC provided a visible site of power dynamics and, in some bookstores, opened lasting fissures. In the Bay Area bookstores, these discussions provided a view into what attempts at antiracist feminist organizing looked like in multiracial organizations. At Old Wives' Tales, Seajay asserted they were working to bring everyone: "[We] think it is vital for as many of us as possible to connect, talk, pool ideas and information, see where we can work together to solve common problems, present a united proposal, whatall."[54] Indeed, all five members of the Old Wives' Tales collective made the flight from San Francisco to DC for the second national Women in Print Conference (WIP) in early October. Though struggling internally with defining an antiracist feminist practice, the bookstore's public narrative imagined a smooth whole. The 1981 Old Wives' Tales birthday statement announced, "We now range in age from 19 to 46, come from four different racial and cultural backgrounds; we include a broad class spectrum, are born on three different continents, and speak five languages."[55]

Across the bridge in Oakland, collective members at ICI: A Woman's Place argued that negotiating a practice of antiracist feminism within the bookstore was as central to organizing for survival as the bookwomen's related feminist literary advocacy. The survival of bookwomen, of literature, and of the bookstores depended on it. In a reflective letter to the ICI collective, collective member Keiko Kubo urged the other bookwomen not to require her, as an Asian woman, and Elizabeth Summers, as a Black woman, "to take sole responsibility for our differentness." Kubo sought antiracist feminist accountability from the white members of the collective: "I am beginning to read more clearly the lights going off in my head during the meeting while we discussed whether or not we should give the 'privilege' of going to WIP to a coloured woman."[56] Attending the mostly white conference would, for women of color representatives, exact emotional and physical tolls. Kubo pointed out, "White people do not want to confront directly how much work it is for coloured people to work with them."[57] Ultimately, Kubo believed that the collective wanted her or Summers to attend the conference only because the white collective members "did not want to go to Washington and have to explain and to take responsibility for [the fact that] no coloured woman from ICI had come." When Seajay and Thomas visited from Old Wives' Tales to urge Jesse Meredith (then a coeditor at FBN) and Darlene Pagano, two white women ICI collective members, to attend Women in Print, Kubo wanted to know, why had Meredith and Pagano not put this discussion about representation on the ICI collective meeting agenda? Doing so would "have been a good example of non-coloured women raising an issue involving racism, something that needs to happen in our collective not to mention the larger world." Kubo closed her letter by offering an agenda item for the next meeting: she requested that the bookstore pay for more of the Women in Print expenses to recognize the travel as work. Meredith and Pagano were, it turned out, listening to Kubo's invitation to an antiracist feminist practice and put that practice into action when they returned from Women in Print.

At the summer Women in Print Conference, Old Wives' Tales bookwomen drew clear connections between feminist literary activism and lesbian antiracism. This Women in Print Conference, Seajay described in the FBN, gathered "a solidly rich and diverse group of women in terms of age, race, class, cultures, able-bodied and challenged. We challenged each other. It felt like the heart and the best of the women's movement."[58] Pell was struck by "all the stars, all the women talking not only during the convention itself but at the socializing after."[59] She remembers spotting and listening to Black lesbian authors Barbara Smith, Ann Allen Shockley, Audre Lorde, and Hattie Gossett. Feminist women of color used the conference to announce new reading and relational projects, now movement institutions: Kitchen Table Women of Color press was just beginning and would start accepting submissions in January; the Third World Women's Archives had begun shaping history in New York; and two publishers announced the transformative new titles *This Bridge Called My Back: Writings by Radical Women of Color*, edited by Cherríe Moraga and Gloria Anzaldúa (Persephone Press, 1981), and *Ain't I a Woman* by bell hooks (South End Press, 1981).[60] Over the next four months, Old Wives' Tales sold three hundred copies of *This Bridge*.[61]

While Pell found validation in Black lesbian feminists at the conference, Kit Quan ached for a complex Asian American lesbian feminism. She felt like an outsider: "I was young and it was before I had a chance to grow stronger in my own identity as an Asian American. There's actually a photograph of the Women of Color Caucus at this conference, and it has people like Cherríe [Moraga] and Barbara Smith, all the people that were involved in the movement then who attended that conference. And there I was. But I really can't say I was in my body. . . . All my issues were being triggered."[62] Quan's and Pell's different experiences of the conference speak to their different socioeconomic, national, and age identities: Quan, born in China, had started working at the bookstore as a young teenager, while Pell was older and had come to the bookstore after closing her own business in the Northeast. By bringing these women together, Old Wives' Tales provided a public site of extended exchange and learning across difference. Feminist authors and texts in the bookstores mapped this dialogue and set the stage for this ongoing work. Pell remembers using Women in Print as an opportunity to line up authors to read at Old Wives' Tales and to find out about new authors and their books.

Among the Women in Print tradeswomen, the bookwomen were in the strongest position to network and generate influence to keep these books— and these conversations—alive. "It was exciting to see how much bookstore skills and directions had grown," Seajay proudly proclaimed. "We didn't talk as much about how and when to use a S.T.O.P. [Single Title Order Plan] form as we did about controlling cash flow, about how to get 'X'-book into paperback, about how to influence cover design and quality."[63] This conference provided another site of organizing for survival. Here, Pell remembers, the Old Wives' Tales collective strategized with other bookwomen about "how we were going to keep the bookstores open" to continue this influence. The conference emphasized that collaboration across difference would strengthen bookwomen's influence on literature, vocabularies, and the larger public. Discussions about interlocking oppressions threaded through the conference in workshop sessions, including "Racism & Classism in Periodicals, Bookstores, and Publishing Organizations," "Creating an Inclusive Lesbian Literature," "The Politics of Reviewing," "Increasing the Availability of Writing That Has Traditionally Been Suppressed," "Skills Sharing on Cultural Ethnicity in Copy Editing," and "Making the Literature Available to Print-Handicapped Women." Seajay promised FBN readers, "You will be feeling and seeing the effects of these conversations over the years to come."[64]

The buzz of energy at the Women in Print Conference had renewed FBN connections with bookwomen, publishers, and authors. Now circulated among a broad movement audience, the journal was a site for building lesbian antiracist vocabularies for the larger feminist movement. This energized readership meant more accountability for FBN writers. This feminist ethic demanded that bookwomen simultaneously advocate outward and reflect inward. Directly after the DC conference, a dialogue on the pages of FBN modeled the publication's work building bookwomen's antioppression skills and supporting their necessary engagement in difficult conversations. Two comments judged by readers to be anti-Semitic appeared in the same FBN issue; the responses of readers indicated both the energy of their connection with FBN and their commitment to lesbian antiracist skill building that includes working against anti-Semitism.

Coming off the high of the conference and being surrounded by women in print feminists, Seajay arrived home to reports of community criticism of Old Wives' Tales. Some Jewish feminist books they had carried were being allowed to go out of print by their publishers; the bookwomen would not be able to reorder them. Readers finding these books gone missing called the bookwomen "uncaring of women" and anti-Semitic.[65] Seajay shared this story briefly in the FBN, blowing off steam at having big publishers' silencing read as bookwomen's failure. This offhand remark might not have been met by voluminous response had it not been amplified by another article later in the same issue. Celeste West, feminist librarian and publisher of Booklegger Press, used the pen name Medea Media to write a literary commentary column for FBN. Her insider report on the antioppression workshop that closed the Women in Print Conference jabbed, "I learned that feminist publishing is controlled by JEWISH-WORKING-CLASS-LESBIANS and the 4-H."[66] West's satire could not both inhabit and reject the ever-present stereotype of Jewish control over the media. Her attempt at humor through hyperbole seemed to many readers to diminish Jewish, working-class, and lesbian women.

These two comments in the FBN generated letters from a veritable who's who of feminist bookwomen and publishers. As editor, Seajay modeled for readers the ongoing learning process of antiracist feminist practice by publishing a substantial twelve pages of these letters. The letters indicated both the vibrancy of the publication and the substantial investment readers had in those pages practicing (and, in turn, helping readers practice) antioppression work. In these responses, feminist bookwomen and publishers exercised the skills they had honed in collective meetings at their bookstores and publishing houses as well as through reading and contributing to the pages of FBN. Simone Wallace of Sisterhood Bookstore in Los Angeles and Mary Farmer with Susanna Sturgis of Lammas Women's Shop in DC wrote in from the bookstores. Farmer and Sturgis contrasted the FBN comments with their experience of the conference as "particularly remarkable for its persistent efforts to grapple with the issues of race/class privilege and oppression in feminist print media."[67] Michelle Cliff and Adrienne Rich wrote in separately in their roles as editors at the journal *Sinister Wisdom*; Pat McGloin for Persephone Press, and Maureen Brady for Spinsters Ink publishers. Elaine Gill and Nancy K. Bereano each wrote in from the Feminist Series at the Crossing Press. These letters, along with responses from Seajay and West (where she came out as herself), appeared on salmon-colored pages in a special response section in the following FBN. This supplement of responses, delivered as an insert only for feminist bookwomen subscribers, documents a national network willing to engage in self-education about lesbian antiracism that includes resisting anti-Semitism;[68] the FBN provided a forum for this discussion, as for other skill-building columns.

For women who had missed the conference, Adrienne Rich invoked the salient power of the final session: "Jewish women presented a statement on the difficulty of engaging with anti-Semitism at the conference, and Mab Segrest of FEMINARY also spoke of the need for non-Jewish women to recognize and point out anti-Semitism where it arises, just as white women need to identify and respond to racism."[69] Rich and Maureen Brady each sent FBN a copy of "Anti-Semitism in the Lesbian Feminist Movement," a recent article by Irene Klepfisz that had appeared in *Womanews* in 1982. The FBN editors included Klepfisz's essay in full in the response section.[70] Both Rich's narrative and Klepfisz's essay reminded readers to listen and to make space for dialogue. The women of Lammas urged readers to remember that "humor" serves as a tool for oppression: "Most of us have at one time or another been accused of having no sense of humor because we don't laugh at misogynist, homophobic, racist, or other unfunny remarks. Let's be especially sensitive to how *we* use humor."[71] There, within each letter, was the call to the feminist counterpublic, to challenge and revise how we talk with each other, including through the literature we produce, in order to strengthen our relationships and more effectively advocate for alternative narratives within larger publics.

Responses from West and Seajay offered two distinct approaches to the conversation. West offered a brief exculpatory note in which she explained her intended strategy in the offending sentence: "Its irony was intended in part to parody the offensive remark that 'the Jews control publishing,' as in the NYC–NYRB Random House–etx. constellation conspiracy. Which is anti-Semitic." She clarified her understanding that "Jews do not control publishing" but that "WASP, homophobic corporate men with no loyalty to religion, nation, or morality" do. Finally, she reassured readers that her "aim is to use humor to unite rather than to isolate us" and signed off, "Trying harder, Celeste West."[72] As the central editor and founder of FBN, Seajay's significant investment in its role and reputation merited a lengthy two-and-a-half-page response. While Seajay, for her part, referred to her "immense personal trauma," "time pressures," and exhaustion,[73] she framed her letter with a responsive understanding of the role of the FBN: "It is vital that anti-racist work be a part of the newsletter and I appreciate the many women who have contributed that work to this issue. . . . It is essential that we take the time to call each other on these issues, to struggle through with each other, to care for each other, to raise one another's consciousnesses, to learn, and to grow, in order to make the changes to which we, the women's movement, and the women in print movement, are committed."[74] This conversation was, for Seajay, an example of organizing for survival. The conversation provided its readers and participants with strategies for alliance building. The word spread; Susanna Sturgis in DC made copies of the issue and passed them on to friends.[75]

"What It Meant to Be a Feminist Bookstore"

That readers consistently sent in letters indicated their understanding that FBN readers had an ethic of action; readers of the FBN expected to be challenged by lesbian antiracism, to find out how to support the literature they needed, and to learn about the systems that attempted to silence that literature. In 1980 a letter from Spinsters Ink, a small feminist publisher in Argyle, New York, asked for help funding the publication of their next two books, Audre Lorde's *The Cancer Journals* and Lynn Strongin's *Bones & Kim*.[76] The call, published in FBN, worked. Maureen Brady of Spinsters Ink reported back, "I remember one day in particular when over $200 came in and the effect on the spirit of a couple of worn down Spinsters was one of ebullient ecstasy, unparalleled since. So we'd like to thank the bookstores."[77] Even such seemingly small support from bookwomen demonstrated the work of the FBN and bookwomen together with publishers in supporting women's literature. This was the first publication of Lorde's now well-known collection. The feminist press supported Lorde, a Black lesbian feminist author and poet, and Strongin, a Jewish author and poet.

The influence peddling of the FBN also made bookwomen important middlewomen between authors and feminist publishers. In 1983, coeditors and authors Gloria T. Hull, Patricia Bell Scott, and Barbara Smith wrote in to alert bookwomen that their book, *But Some of Us Are Brave: Black Women's*

Studies, published by the Feminist Press in 1982, had been out of stock but was available again. "So that this does not happen again," the editors urged bookwomen to keep ordering the title and to write to admonish "the Feminist Press that many sales were lost when the book was unavailable."[78] Barbara Smith, Black feminist author and Kitchen Table: Women of Color Press cofounder and publisher, knew that when bookwomen ordered books they circulated and stayed in print longer. She repeatedly wrote in to share new publications by and about Black feminists. In March 1980, Smith wrote to "recommend that you assign for review" *Between a Rock and a Hard Place* "by the Black Lesbian feminist writer, Joan Gibbs"; *Lorraine Hansberry: Art of Thunder, Vision of Light*, "a special issue of the Black quarterly *Freedomways*"; and *In the Memory and Spirit of Frances, Zora and Lorraine: Essays and Interviews on Black Women and Writing*, edited by Juliette Bowles. As a result of her letter, these books made it onto feminist bookshelves: BookWoman bookstore collective members in Austin penciled stars beside the books on this list.

The influence of FBN grew in the early 1980s as feminist bookstore growth accelerated transnationally. The use of the feminist bookstore format signaled the vitality of bookwomen's role in a transnational feminist movement. Seajay, sustaining the networks as the constant keeper of FBN, continued her practice of outreach, tenderly folding new bookstores into the information network and the movement shaped by FBN. New feminist bookstores SisterWrite in London and Lavender Menace, a "Lesbian & Gay Community Bookshop," in Edinburgh received welcome issues of the FBN in their mailboxes; they subscribed immediately, grateful for the book lists and the community.[79] SisterWrite women pinned above their desk an FBN column on avoiding burnout, and they volunteered to "act as British correspondent"[80] by sending lists of new books and a copy of their own catalog. FBN created a transnational resource for book discovery.

This transnational reach of the FBN was built on alliances of bookwomen. Perhaps because of their cofounders and their location on the East Coast, women at New Words in particular built and sustained transnational bookstore relationships. Rita Arditti, a Sephardic Jewish woman from Argentina, had helped found the bookstore after moving to Boston, and she brought with her a transnational consciousness. As a scientist she was a researcher for and ally with the Argentinian Madres de la Plaza de Mayo and an activist for cancer prevention against industrial pollution. In 1979 she discovered that her breast cancer had spread to her lungs, and she left the daily work of the bookstore to undergo treatment. Her commitment to transnational networks of information influenced the life of the bookstore. In Argentina in 1984 Laura Memurry sent this letter to the New Words collective, evidence of their sustained relationship with Arditti's former city, Buenos Aires: "I was at the demonstration for International Women's Day here in Buenos Aires when the letters of support were read. What a surprise out of the blue to hear the name of New Words Bookstore, Cambridge (although as 'Nuevas Palabras' it took a few seconds to sink in)."[81] New Words was one nexus of transnational activity: a group of Brazilian women wrote the Cambridge bookwomen to ask for resources for their plan to "create a women's center, library, bookstore, a place to gather, talk, discuss between ourselves, a women's publishing house, a place where women could find information on our history, our struggles, our memory."[82] New Words collective members penciled on the letter their plans to send the women the address of both the Lesbian Herstory Archives and Womanbooks, to share a copy of the letter with a group called Latina Woman, and to send the women flyers from the bookstore.

These relationships between bookstores also identified US-based bookstores as resources for women readers and researchers transnationally. A letter to New Words bookwomen from Vivienne Crawford at King Saud University began, "I am marooned in a city in which there are no bookstores like yours (women professors here are still fighting, so far in vain, for access to the university library, that's the level things are at) so asked a friend to pick up some material from you for a poetry reading I was helping organize."[83] Gilda Bruckman remembers, "There was someone in Japan who was an academic of some standing, and she was ordering books from us pretty regularly. There were also women who would come from Europe, and South America, and come in and visit, and then ask us to send books. So we did that."[84] The women at New Words, in connection with the network of feminist bookwomen through the FBN, certainly had the tools to share back not only works by Western feminist authors but also works by authors in the regions from which these women were writing: as early as the second issue of FBN in 1976, the journal had circulated news of books by women in the Middle East; the 1980 PW article on Old Wives' Tales included at least one title edited by a Japanese feminist author; and New Words cofounder Rita Arditti maintained connections with feminists in South America. Feminist accountability required such a recognition of transnational feminisms. New Words consistently built a transnational presence, and the relationships this work made possible gestured toward the possibility of a transnational feminist bookstore movement that affected the ways feminist literature was distributed outside of mainstream and border-constricted pathways.

When FBN carried news of a bookstore fire in Toronto, the word reached a wide-ranging transnational community of bookwomen. By 1983 the Toronto Women's Bookstore had moved out of the Amazon Workshop and into 85 Harbord Street, just down the block from where Sharon Fernandez worked in lesbian mystery novelist Eve Zaremba's secondhand bookstore. At first the bookwomen did not know the Morgantaler Clinic was moving in above their new bookstore location. Henry Morgantaler, a physician widely known for performing safe illegal abortions, would receive the Order of Canada in 2008. Just after comanagers Patti Kirk and Marie Prins returned from the Women and Words conference in Vancouver, the Canadian equivalent of the Women in Print Conference, they got a call in the middle of the night. A friend walking down Harbord Street had seen the store in flames. While the clinic upstairs had a reinforced steel door and an alarm system, the bookstore was unprotected. Unable to infiltrate the clinic, a protestor had settled for the space just below and firebombed the bookstore. Kirk and Prins looked at their gutted, smoky store, now sopping wet from the firehoses, and they wept. The FBN article urged bookwomen to send support: "If each of the 80 women's stores could raise $100 to $200, that . . . would put them very close to reaching their goal. And I think it would really open our eyes to what we are capable of doing."[85] Here, Seajay as FBN editor pointed out that internal accountability within the movement prepared bookwomen for external action.

As now experienced organizers, feminist bookwomen were ready to become leaders in the struggle against chain bookstores and publishers. Seajay, through the FBN and through Old Wives' Tales birthday statements, urged bookwomen and readers to understand that the very future of feminist literature was at stake in the brewing storm in the book industry. Two years after Jesse Meredith reported on the October 1980 meeting of the Northern California Booksellers Association, the NCBA filed a suit against Avon Books. This was the beginning of two decades of lawsuits on behalf of independent bookstores, and Seajay, along with Old Wives' Tales and the FBN, was at the scene. In her literary watchdog role, Seajay described the suit to FBN readers: "What has been going on is that most of the mass market houses are giving an extra 4–5% discount to chain stores EVEN WHEN THEY ORDER IN QUANTITIES LOWER THAN WE DO. Which is blatantly illegal. (Violates the Robinson-Patman act.)" Seajay pointed out that publishers make these illegal deals "because chain stores are such a big % of the trade book market (about 40% now, will probably control 75% of the retail business by 1987. . . . . . don't much expect that they'll carry a lot of feminist titles in 1987, either . . .)."[86] She and the Old Wives' Tales Collective in their sixth birthday statement sounded the alarm for feminist readers: "Chain bookstores control 40% of all booksales and . . . they virtually dictate to publishers which books will get advertising campaigns and which books will get buried." If readers understood these lawsuits, bookwomen seem to have hoped, they would realize that chain bookstores operated not on supply and demand but on profit by market fixing at the cost of feminist movement literature and relationships.

A Crown Books had opened on Castro Street in an attempt to capitalize on the "gay market," and Old Wives' Tales women reminded readers that this availability was temporary, not a signal of acceptance. At Old Wives' Tales, the year's best seller was *The Color Purple* (which sold five hundred copies in four months); the previous year's best seller was *This Bridge Called My Back*. At bookstore events Alice Walker and Ntozake Shange read to overflow crowds in the bookstore's "sixth year of readings, performances, and slide shows every Thursday night." Without the bookstores, the bookwomen declared, "none of the women's presses would survive,"[87] and this narrative suggested that the books readers needed would not survive without the bookstores either. What remained to be seen was whether readers would take note and resist the lure of the discounted prices on the shelves of profit-making bookstores.

To those who might argue that the chain bookstores earned a wholesale price, Seajay spelled out: "There is a similar practice in which all the stores in a chain order on a single order, then the books are drop-shipped to each store." While the chain received the "large-quantity discount of 48–50%," "the publisher ends up doing just about the same amount of work as if 300 stores had ordered individually, except for there's one (long & complicated) order and only one bill." Even though publishers recognized the "large-quantity" discount as an unreasonable deal when spread over multiple stores, the chains were setting the terms: "Two publishers tried to refuse this deal with the chains and were boycotted until they submitted." If publishers wanted their books in the chains, they would be held to these untenable discounts. Ideally, the NCBA lawsuit would support publishers to "refuse the coercion of the chains." In what might have been a plea to publishers reading the FBN, Seajay cajoled: "My belief is that there are a lot of publishers of integrity out there who don't want to be giving this kind of edge and advantage to the chains. And they, too, know what is likely to happen to their publishing lines when chains control 75% of the market: basically there won't be a lot of point to publishing what the chains won't buy. Makes my blood run cold." Seajay underscored the gravity of this moment by inviting feminist bookwomen to donate to the lawsuit.[88]

With a chilling history of chain bookstores' insatiable hunger, Seajay illustrated how the profit motive that drove the chain bookstores posed a near immediate danger to feminist bookstores. In 1972, she began, looking back ten years, "the 4 largest retail bookstores controlled 11% of the retail book business. Only one company had more than 100 stores."[89] Throughout the 1970s, chain bookstores expanded but seemed to self-isolate in suburban malls and areas without bookstores; they specialized in "'non-book' books . . . cookbooks, auto-repair, coffeetable books . . . and sold them to people who ordinarily wouldn't buy books." By the 1980s the book industry seemed to have maximized the market, but the ravenous capital machine would not be satisfied. The chains began to feed on the independents. "In 1981, Dalton & Waldenbooks together had 1300 stores, did 250 million dollars in business and accounted for 25–30% of the retail bookstore market." Over the next five years, B. Dalton planned to open 556 stores, and Waldenbooks planned 400–450 new stores. These bookstores would move out of malls and into urban areas, where they were already "drowning out independent stores like mad." Seajay cautioned, synthesizing book industry predictions, that by 1987, 75 percent of the book business would belong to chains, leaving 25 percent to independents, "down from 89% in 1972." The "mass merchandising principles" of the chains would "emphasize best-sellers" and "pay scant attention to local interests." The chains would leverage their numbers to influence publishers' choices, as the editors of FBN had done, but this time the driving force would be capitalism rather than feminism.

Even with the specter of chain bookstores undeniably altering the book industry, feminist bookstores' business was still on the rise: "In 1981, feminist bookstores sold $4 million in books." A year later FBN announced the opening of eleven new feminist bookstores.[90] As the general independent bookstore market shrank, Seajay predicted that the feminist bookstores' share of that market would increase. As the chains homogenized literature, she ventured, feminist readers who might not have valued feminist bookstores before would seek them out to find the books they needed. Feminist bookstores would be more likely to see these new feminist readers, Seajay urged, if feminist bookwomen figured out how to "do outreach to these women." There was power to be had, Seajay called, "if we can find and make use of the connections." This change in feminist bookstore status, if bookwomen used it correctly, could influence mainstream publishers to publish more feminist work. "Think about it," Seajay wrote, issuing a call to action.[91]

Bookwomen's capacity to connect with women readers also depended on their accountability to their communities, including racially diverse collectives and a working practice of antiracist feminism. Not far from Seajay's bookstore in San Francisco, collective members at Oakland's ICI: A Woman's Place were developing a new vocabulary together through a traumatic break. On September 12, 1982, a group of collective members showed up to the bookstore to find that their keys no longer worked. The locks had been changed and a letter posted on the bookstore's glass door. "This collective is not a collective," the letter read. "It is a collection of women completely at odds with each other."[92] Alice Molloy, a former member of the collective, had joined with Carol Wilson to change the locks in frustration with challenging conversations about accountability to racial justice. Natalie Lando, initially one of those locked out, ultimately reunited with Molloy and Wilson. Over the previous year, Keiko Kubo and Elizabeth Summers had been sharing strategies for lesbian antiracist feminism and interrupting patterns of racism they experienced and witnessed; transformed by Kubo and Summers's analyses, Jesse Meredith and Darlene Pagano worked toward becoming white antiracist allies. The "Locked Out Four," Kubo, Summers, Meredith, and Pagano, had been on a journey together learning about alliances among women of color and between women of color and white women. In an open letter they defined their struggle within the bookstore as one for antiracist feminisms and against "hegemonic feminism."[93] Dialogues like this one accentuated the difference between chains and feminist bookstores. At chain bookstores, feminist books would only ever be part of a stock meant to sell; feminist bookwomen organized in dialogue with each other and with their books. Events that appeared to be breaks, like this one at ICI, in fact introduced new strategies for feminist accountability and documented the racial diversity of women working on the feminist bookstore project.

The larger feminist movement watched this story closely; feminist press coverage of the lockout, from the Berkeley-based *Plexus* to the Washington, DC–based *Off Our Backs*,[94] evidenced both bookwomen's savvy use of media and the role of the bookstores as sustained public sites of feminist organizing and, at their best, places of new language and strategies. Bookwomen wrote in to ask Seajay to use the FBN to "provide some context" about the conflict.[95] Readers' desire to see the coverage in the FBN indicates that the break at A Woman's Place was more than simply a collective's dysfunction. The FBN editors had established the journal as a site to learn from other bookwomen, and readers would settle for nothing less. That winter Seajay reprinted in the FBN "the most complete statements I could find from each side," followed by the arbitrator's decision. The statements document a women-in-print perspective on building feminist coalitions across racial difference.

The FBN coverage began with the statement from the two who locked the door, Carol Wilson and Alice Molloy, along with Natalie Lando. Wilson and Molloy had originally locked out Lando as well, but welcomed her back when she refused to join the Locked Out Four in filing a complaint. The statement from Wilson, Molloy, and Lando shaped an argument based on history. They claimed their place at the beginnings of ICI: A Woman's Place and anchored their movement credibility in transformative lesbian feminist organizations. The three identified as "dykes since the 1950's," and all three had been members of Daughters of Bilitis. They used quotation marks to qualify their acknowledgment that all three are "white," Natalie Lando identified as Jewish, and the three emphasized their socioeconomic class identities by pointing out that none of them were college graduates. They were involved with Gay Women's Liberation and published the newspaper It Ain't Me Babe, among other organizing projects, including starting an antirape group, teaching a women's auto repair course, and starting Free Women's Distribution, a magazine distributor. In 1970 they had founded ICI: A Woman's Place with Rosalie, Starr, and Forest.[96]

By 1981 Molloy had left the bookstore, and Keiko Kubo, Jesse Meredith, Elizabeth Summers, and Darlene Pagano had joined the collective. In collective meetings, this group of women working at the oldest feminist bookstore in the nation were taking up issues that they knew affected the distribution and racial diversity of feminist literature. The expanded group talked about representation of women of color at the 1981 Women in Print Conference, about "dealing with customers' racist behavior in the store," and about issuing "statements of support for anti-imperialist and anti-racist political groups." Kubo, Meredith, Summers, and Pagano noticed that in these discussions and even in everyday interactions the collective "became divided along color lines."[97] Kubo and Summers, who identified as women of color, saw that when the collective discussed racism, the "white women would refuse to acknowledge" what they had to say. When Kubo responded with anger and Summers by withdrawing, the collective would discuss Kubo's and Summers's reactions rather than racism or the group dynamics around discussing racism. As the four emphasized, "This repeated dynamic kept the collective from working on racism, and made Kubo and Summers into 'the problem.'"[98] In an attempt to "raise consciousness about racism within the collective," Kubo and Summers wrote letters to the collective, issued written statements, and initiated discussions. In the fall of 1981, the collective brought in a facilitator to run a workshop on "Unlearning Racism and Unlearning Anti-Semitism." Throughout their more than a year at the bookstore before the lockout, Kubo and Summers worked together to foster antiracist feminism within the organization.

These visionary refusals to allow the erasure of racialized difference or the denial of responsibility for white privilege within the collective succeeded in raising the consciousnesses of Meredith and Pagano. The two white women wrote in 1983 that they "began to understand the concept of white women acting as allies to women of color in the fight against racism," and they were determined to become white antiracist allies within the collective. Through letters, meetings, and discussions, they urged Lando and Wilson to become allies as well.[99] Meredith brought in a tape of Bernice Reagon's talk on coalition building, the talk that she had delivered at the West Coast Women's Music Festival earlier that year. Reagon's talk was not yet available in print but was circulating on cassette. Her recorded voice filled the bookstore, and Meredith asked each collective member to listen and prepare to discuss the talk at the next bookstore meeting. Kubo, Summers, Meredith, and Pagano emphasized the importance of Reagon's talk: "It gave us a name for our understanding of feminism as a coalition." The four modeled antiracist feminism as a learning practice. While Wilson and Lando created the "barred room" Reagon warned against (the four remember Wilson and Lando telling them "that we were not feminists when we disagreed with Carol [Wilson] and Natalie [Lando]"),[100] Kubo, Summers, Meredith, and Pagano worked to allow for a difference that required change.

The Locked Out Four saw feminist bookstores as potentially unique models of coalitional feminism. They described the high stakes of this conversation as "our differing *visions of feminism*, and thus, of what it meant to be a feminist bookstore." This conversation was not only about what it meant to be a feminist, but in particular what it meant to form a feminist bookstore. The Locked Out Four interpreted Wilson's and Lando's feminism as the idea that "sexism is the primary problem in all women's lives." Alternatively, Kubo, Summers, Meredith, and Pagano asserted their belief that "A Woman's Place as an institution should understand feminism as a *coalition* of women who oppose sexism and are struggling against sexism in many different ways. For example, for the four of us, the oppressions we've experienced due to sexism, class, racism, anti-semitism, and homophobia are all central in our lives."[101] In their open letter following the lockout, Keiko Kubo, Elizabeth Summers, Jesse Meredith, and Darlene Pagano self-identified, respectively, as Asian, Black, Jewish, and Italian. Transformed by Reagon's language of coalition, the four described bookwomen's work as building coalitions of feminists experiencing different oppressions and working as allies with each other, what I call lesbian antiracism.

While feminist bookwomen struggled to keep the work of feminists, including women of color and lesbians, in print, Kubo, Summers, Meredith, and Pagano emphasized that how they did so mattered. The next chapter describes how feminist bookwomen shaped shelf sections to foster feminist accountability in reading and relationship practices; here the Locked Out Four were enacting that transformation using their shelves. The traveling, portable words in books and on tapes and in other formats could inform and challenge women to build coalitions across differences of race and class. Three mutually appointed arbitrators declared that the bookstore was "a political business formed for the benefit of the women's community, the essence of which is decision making by unanimous agreement, ie consensus." Because the lockout broke consensus, the arbitrators removed Molloy, Lando, and Wilson from the bookstore. The Locked Out Four would act as interim managers; within two years they would have to "rotate out" of the bookstore.[102] The bookstore closed two years later, in 1985. Molloy, Lando, and Wilson went on to start Mama Bears feminist bookstore, also in Oakland. Pagano later went on to work at Old Wives' Tales.

Kit Quan of Old Wives' Tales observes that, though feminists often talk about how necessary alliances between white women and women of color are within the feminist movement, "there is little said of how that process actually happens." The narrative of the Locked Out Four offers us a glimpse of this vital process. Quan asks readers to remember, to imagine, "what happens when these alliances break down and the people who've worked hard together towards a political vision feel that they have failed themselves and each other?"[103] These breaks are always also stories of attempts at alliance.[104] Feminists can learn from these moments how to build something new. In this history I emphasize the foundational work and leadership of women of color in the feminist bookstore movement. This history contradicts mainstream narratives of a solely white feminist movement in the 1970s. Quan emphasizes an important difference, though, between presence and power: "Although women of color have always worked within the feminist movement, we do not hold the power in most feminist structures. . . . Where there are more than one of us within an organization, white women feel threatened when we take our power seriously and actively seek alliances with each other."[105] In Oakland in the early 1980s, Kubo and Summers, along with their white lesbian antiracist allies in Meredith and Pagano, gathered power enough to articulate a new, brief vision of "what it meant to be a feminist bookstore."

"A Proper Trade Magazine"

Other feminist bookstore collectives were attempting new lesbian antiracist feminist alliances in the early 1980s as well; these simultaneous efforts in multiple places mark this period as one of transition. Feminist bookwomen were balancing the strain and possibility of feminist accountability against pressure to organize a unified external profile that could stave off the threats of a changing book industry. The FBN had become witness, report, and advocate for bookwomen within the movement, and this energy fed the brewing resistance against chain publishers and bookstores homogenizing literature and endangering feminist futures. As Carol Seajay contemplated leaving Old Wives' Tales, the bookstore she and Paula Wallace had founded, she envisioned a new life as full-time editor of a more powerful FBN. The first change would be the name. "Somehow," she eased readers into the idea, "'newsletter' doesn't quite describe this 40 page magazine." A new name could emphasize the importance of feminist bookstores with even her friends who wondered why she spent all her time "on what they conceive of as a 4 page mimeograph." A name change would more accurately represent FBN as a force to be reckoned with. Which name was another question. For Seajay, *The Feminist Bookstore* seemed "a bit grandiose," while *The Feminist Bookseller* (a play on *The American Bookseller*) "omits about 75% of what we do & trivializes that." In standard FBN practice, she requested feedback from the readers.[106]

A change in the identity of the publication turned the force of the movement outward with a focus on keeping feminist literature and bookstores alive. The *Feminist Bookstore News* emerged as the final title in the winter 1983 double issue.[107] FBN style changed as well. Previous issues had arrived on letter-sized paper stapled at the top left corner. The first issue carrying the title *Feminist Bookstore News* arrived booklet style, with a blue cardstock cover.[108] Having a different cover color for each issue was a trademark look of the publication over its remaining nearly twenty years. As the page count grew, the journal still came out bimonthly, and an outward-looking description of the publication appeared as front matter: "THE FEMINIST BOOKSTORE NEWS is a communications vehicle for the informal network of feminist bookstores. It reaches 110 stores in the US and Canada, as well as a number of libraries, women's studies departments, and feminist bookstores in Great Britain, Europe, Australia, and New Zealand. Combined annual sales of the US and Canadian stores is $4 million annually."[109] The number, 110 stores, emphasized the importance of the network in lobbying efforts and sold page space, as indicated by the addition of standard advertising rates. The same issue announced a new list of feminist bookstores; as with previous lists, readers could write in to purchase copies of the list.[110] The bookstores amplified each other.

While the public identity of feminist bookwomen became more unified through FBN, the tension and growth that honed the bookwomen's ethics and alliances continued. Feminist accountability in practice meant that the bookstores, if effective, would not be comfortable places; this discomfort signaled the bookstores as sites of Reagon's framework for coalition building. As part of her commitment to lesbian antiracist feminism, Seajay had succeeded in hiring women of color to lead the Old Wives' Tales bookstore collective. Struggles around power tore at the seams. At a collective meeting in November 1982, Old Wives' Tales bookwomen sat in a circle processing what seemed not to be working in the collective. It had been two months since they had posted the flyers calling for accountability to racial justice at the second West Coast Women's Music Festival. Tiana Arruda reflected that the action "was not the answer to the problem."[111] Outside the bookstore, the collective had hoped the flyer would offer witness and alliance with other organizers of color. Arruda's comment suggests that the collective's flyer action was also an internal attempt to heal collective discord by working together on a joint action in antiracist feminism. Unable to resolve the ongoing discord, the bookwomen's collective dissolved, as both Carol Seajay and Kit Quan began to imagine new strategies for their involvement in feminist literary activism.

Breakups at the bookstores always marked new beginnings. As Seajay made plans to leave Old Wives' Tales, Kit Quan left the bookstore as well. Both continued to significantly shape what feminist literary activism and feminist accountability look like. Their paths documented feminist bookstores' roles as training grounds, even through difficulty, for feminist activists. Quan had built alliances at the bookstore that shaped her next work. She and Gloria Anzaldúa had become friends after meeting one evening at the bookstore. On her way in to a Feminist Writers Guild meeting, Anzaldúa "came up to the counter to thank me for keeping the store open," Quan remembers. "I thought she was from another planet—she stood out, she noticed me when I was invisible to most people."[112] Creating more of these connections, Quan took a class from feminist poets and activists Merle Woo and Nellie Wong called "Revolutionary Feminism and the Leadership of Women of Color," where she sought to describe "exactly what I was doing 'politically' at OWT."[113] Quan worked to enact the attention to language, class, and transnational feminist literacies she had hungered for and worked to raise awareness of at Old Wives' Tales. She built vital feminist literacies by learning Japanese "from Sarhie, a Japanese feminist who lives here now. She worked in a feminist printing collective and in the feminist movement in Japan for 10 years. She has lots to say," she told Anzaldúa, "but she can't say most of it in English."[114] A year later, Quan and Sarhie made a slide show about Asian American women in the Bay Area and toured it during July in Japan.[115] Quan here created the new networks and frameworks for feminist literacy and transnational information sharing that she and other feminists needed. Her work gestures toward the connections bookwomen built within a transnational women in print movement and their collective work to articulate a lesbian antiracist feminism using their skills developed as bookwomen.

By 1983, Seajay had decided to leave the bookstore as well. She had finally publicly acknowledged her essential work keeping the FBN alive for the movement: "FBN is my work and my responsibility. It's an after hours job that I do with love and passion (and sometimes burnout). At this point and for about half of FBN's 5+ year history, I do it primarily alone. It isn't the work of my lovers, my co-workers, or my collective. They aren't responsible for it nor do they (bless them) get credit for it."[116] Recognizing the journal as her own allowed her to shape the vision for the publication as her own next work. On Old Wives' Tales collective meeting notes marked "Wed. 11th,

C, T, P, L," the note taker wrote: "Carol resigns."[117] Tiana Arruda, Pell, and Lydia Bigsby-Hermida were there for the announcement. When Seajay left, she wanted to sign the store over to Arruda and Pell, but Pell had plans to resign as well.[118] Ultimately, Seajay, legally named as Old Wives' Tales owner but participating as collective member, transferred the store to the non-profit corporation newly incorporated by Lydia Bigsby-Hermida and Tiana Arruda. Seajay remembers there were "huge collective battles going on, as happened."[119] While this shift was painful for Seajay, it came at an ideal time for the FBN. Seajay started working on the FBN full time to bolster book-women's influence in the book industry. In the address of her public letter, Seajay acknowledged the multiple audiences for FBN:

Dear Feminist Publisher, Small Press, Corporation, Sisters, Friends, and Co-workers in the book world,

Rather than leaving the bookworld, I seem to be diving in even deeper. My previous "spare-time" project, THE FEMINIST BOOKSTORE NEWS will become a full time job as I turn the periodical into a proper trade magazine serving feminist bookstores in much the same way that PUBLISH-ERS WEEKLY serves the more traditional bookselling community.[120]

The status of Seajay and the FBN (and Seajay's eye to publicity) made this transformation news: the *Media Report to Women* published the letter to an even wider audience.[121] As the *Publishers Weekly* for feminist bookstores, the *Feminist Bookstore News* in the 1990s became a megaphone for independent bookstores while navigating the unsteady balance between movement ethics and an increasingly monetized industry vocabulary.

[top] ICI: A Woman's Place (Oakland, CA) in the 1970s. Image courtesy Lesbian Herstory Archives.

[bottom] The Oakland Women's Press Collective (left to right): Wendy Cadden, Anita (Taylor) Oñang, Judy Grahn, Martha Shelley, Felicia Daywoman, and Willyce Kim in the mid-1970s. Photograph by and permission granted by Donna Gottschalk.

I.C.I.* - A WOMAN'S PLACE BOOKSTORE
525I BROADWAY at COLLEGE   OAKLAND CA.

Open Every Day of the Year   —— REALLY

HOURS: 10 - 6 Daily and til 10 Tuesday and Friday nights. 1 - 5 on Sundays. Sometimes we are open late evenings . . . give us a call - 415 - 547 - 9920

CHILDREN ARE WELCOME

LENDING LIBRARY

Bulletin board space with rides, housing, events classes, therapy groups, study groups, services offered, information on political organization and action

DONATE YOUR USED BOOKS : We sell them, and use the money to buy books for women in prison and prison libraries.

"When action grows unprofitable, gather information." from THE LEFT HAND OF DARKNESS by Ursula LeGuin.

Books by, about and for women . . . Books from the women's presses . . . Lesbians . . . Third World women . . . On being young and growing old . . . Women in socialist countries . . . Books and posters from China . . . Politics/economics . . . Working class women . . . Women's liberation movement theory and analysis . . . Herstory . . . Women and work . . . Wife and child abuse . . . Women in prison . . . Parenting . . . Anti-sexist, anti-racist children's books . . . Women and psyche-logic . . . Changing consciousness . . . Women and health . . . Herbal Healing . . . Novels and plays . . . Science fiction and mysteries by women . . . Poetry by women . . . Art and photography books by and about women . . . Posters and cards by women . . . Survival resource books . . . Women's newspapers and magazines . . . Pamphlets . . . Records, tapes and songbooks of women's music . . . Pins and buttons . . . T-shirts . . . Bumper stickers . . . Coffee and tea always - free .

*INFORMATION CENTER INCORPORATE

[*above*] Inside ICI: A Woman's Place (Oakland, CA), 1982. Image courtesy Lesbian Herstory Archives.

[*opposite*] Announcement of ICI: A Woman's Place (Oakland, CA), 1970. Image courtesy Lesbian Herstory Archives.

[*above*] Womanbooks (New York), early 1980s. Photograph by JEB. © 2015 JEB (Joan E. Biren).

[*opposite, top*] Darlene Pagano, Elizabeth Summers, Keiko Kubo, and Jesse Meredith at ICI: A Woman's Place (Oakland, CA), 1982. Image courtesy Lesbian Herstory Archives.

[*opposite, bottom*] Womanbooks (New York) cofounders Fabi Romero Oak, Karyn London, and Eleanor Olds Batchelder, 1975. Image courtesy Lesbian Herstory Archives.

[*above*] Toronto Women's Bookstore staff and family in 2005 at the annual Women's Rape Crisis Center Toronto Multicultural Women against Rape Bowlathon Fundraiser: (seated, left to right) Nicole Ysabet, Alex MacFadyen, Reena Katz, Anjula Gogia; (standing, left to right) Lorraine Hewitt, Clara Ho, Jin Huh, May Lui. From May Lui's collection.

[*opposite, top*] Toronto Women's Bookstore, 1981. Photograph by JEB. © 2015 JEB (Joan E. Biren).

[*opposite, bottom*] Toronto Women's Bookstore, 2005. From the author's collection.

[*above*] Kristen Hogan, Janet Romero, and Zahra Jacobs at the Toronto Women's Bookstore, 2007. From the author's collection.

[*opposite*] Map of New Words (Cambridge, MA) shelf sections by Joni Seager, 1986. Schlesinger Library, Radcliffe Institute, Harvard University.

New Words Directory

[top] The four founders of New Words on opening day, 6 April 1974, on Washington Street in Somerville, MA (left to right): Jean MacRae, Gilda Bruckman, Mary Lowry, and Rita Arditti. Photograph courtesy of Gilda Bruckman.

[*top*] Common Woman Bookstore, later known as BookWoman (Austin), late 1970s. Photograph by Robin Birdfeather. From Susan Post's collection.

[*bottom*] Streelekha (Bangalore) brochure, 1988–1989. Schlesinger Library, Radcliffe Institute, Harvard University.

[*opposite, bottom*] New Words (Cambridge, MA) Collective in April 1987 at their 13th Birthday Sale: (seated, left to right) Joni Seager, Laura Zimmerman, Mary Lowry; (standing, left to right) Doris Reisig, Gilda Bruckman, Kate Rushin, Madge Kaplan. Photograph courtesy of Gilda Bruckman.

[top] Display window at BookWomen: Every Woman's Bookshop, later known as BookWoman (Austin), 1980. Photograph by Susan Post. From Susan Post's collection.

[bottom] Susan Post in front of BookWoman bookstore (Austin); window display is celebrating the twenty-fifth anniversary of the Feminist Press; gathering inside is celebrating BookWoman's twenty-fifth anniversary. 1995. Photograph by Kay Keys. From Susan Post's collection.

[*above*] Judy Grahn reading at BookWoman (Austin) at 6th and Trinity Streets, 17 February 1985. Photograph by Kay Keys. From Susan Post's collection.

[*above*]   Inside Old Wives' Tales (San Francisco), 1982. Photograph by JEB. © 2015 JEB (Joan E. Biren).

[*opposite*]   Old Wives' Tales Collective, Carol Seajay (bookstore co-founder), Pell, Tiana Arruda, Kit Quan, and Sherry Thomas, at old wives' Tales (San Franciso, CA), 1982. Photogragh by JEB. © 2015 (Joan E. Biren)

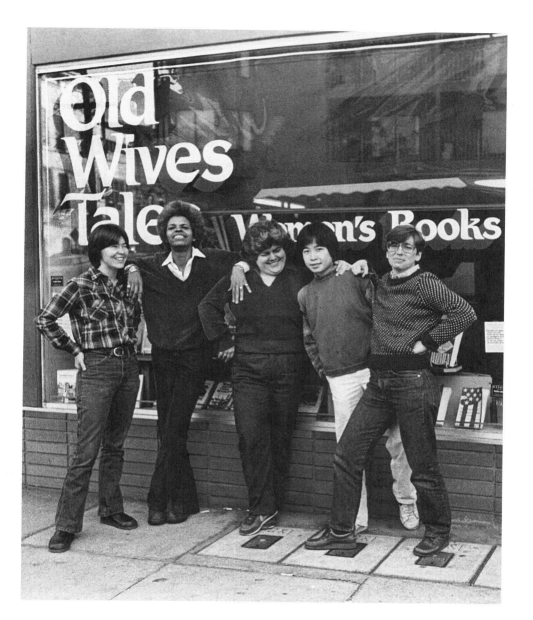

[*above*] Carol Seajay, editor and publisher of the *Feminist Bookstores Newsletter* and *Feminist Bookstore News*, reading an issue at her home in front of her shelf of FBN issues, 1992. Permission granted by Carol Seajay.

[*opposite, top*] Kit Quan at Old Wives' Tales (San Francisco), 1982. Photograph by JEB. © 2015 JEB (Joan E. Biren).

[*opposite, bottom*] Carol Seajay at the Feminist Bookstore Network booth at Book-Expo America, Chicago, 1995. Permission granted by Carol Seajay, FBN editor and publisher.

Feminist

Bookstores

Newsletter

Volume 2 *No.* 2

TABLE OF CONTENTS

GOING TO THE ABA CONVENTION?

The first thing is, what are we going to do/say/demand around the fact that the ABA is being held in a state that refuses to ratify the ERA? And following that--what do we want to do around the ABA decision to hold the 1980 vonvention in Chicago, Illinois, being another non-ERA state. (1979 is scheduled for Los Angeles.)

I, for one, already planned to go to the ABA Conf. long before it even dawned on me about that twist. I still do plan to go. Maybe we can ask the ABA to make some kind of $ retribution to pro-ERA forces to make up for their blunder? (Assuming as I am that it wan in no way deliberate.) I know that's a pretty mild gesture, but I can think of few other little-time-to work-On-it tactics. What does anyone else think?

Now, with that all said (and Meant) I want to say that I am going to the conf, and am eager to make my time there VERY worthwhile. Could people drop me a line, if you're going, with some of the reasons you're going to the ABA. (I'll do the same for you). Does anyone see a need/reason for a meeting of feminist bookstores. I do. Maybe we could plan a meetint to swap info, ideas, questions, complaints and just plain meet each other and have a good time. I'm willing to try and do some co-ordination around that.

I went last year and it was just wonderful. (But then I'm the sort of person who schedules her vacations just so, to go to this thing. Which I did. So you may want to take my enthusiasm advisedly.) For some reason, I expect t that being on the east coast more small and women's presses will be there. D Does that sound logical?

In any case, the messageis that I'm going to the conference and I would like to see women's bookstores have their presence felt and am willing to do as much work as I can to that end.

Darlene
A woman's Place
5251 Broadway
Oakland, Ca 94618

EMERGENCY FBN.

Volume 3 Number 3

WIND ended. Such a dark day the day I heard the news.
(More on that later.)

This issue of FBN is dedicated to Cynthia Gair and Helaine Harris in appreciation for their vision in seeing the necessity of a solid feminist distribution service and all their work in trying to reach that end. And is also dedicated to all the rest of us bookstore and publishing women who are picking up the pieces and going on. Continueing to be committed to supporting the feminist press. (If we can't publish and distribute our own words, we certainly can't expect anyone else to do it!) Continueing to carry just as much feminist and small press work as we possibly can. Figuring out our new work loads, ordering from all those small publishers rather than just whipping out a single order to WIND. Listening to the financial impact of ordering from individual publishers rather than one distributer--one stamp for the order, one for the invoice, whatever your check charges are times the number of orders you will now do a month PLUS the increase in postage costs that will come from having to pay that *@#*! 58¢ for the first pound of each order rather than just paying it once on a distributer order. Then figuring out where that money is going to come from and re-budgeting if necessary to cover these expenses rather than letting the costs sneak up on us and sink us later.*

When I heard that WIND was closing I wrote to Cynthia & Helaine to say that I'd publish a list of their publishers' addresses in FBN if they'd send them to me. My letter crossed in the mail with theirs asking me if I could do just that. Paula Sperry from Woman to Woman in Denver phoned a day later offering to type up the list & did so. Sherry Thomas (once of Country Women magazine, now working at Old Wives Tales) and I worked until 11 pm two nights going through our files to get the terms for all the publishers OWT had ever ordered from direct. Then I worked until 11 another night typing them onto the addresses list that Paula had typed. And here I am now, beginning to type this at 11pm on another night. And so this emergency issue of FBN came together in the midst of her editor (lover or mother might be better terms) looking for & moving to her new home. The terms listed in this issue are only as up to date as OWT's last order from each publisher. They may well

---

*That's $26.60 per month for 30 additonal orders. 30 x (15¢+15¢+58¢+10¢ check charge). A lot or not a lot depending on your store size and how many orders you actually will do each month after the first flurry of orders. Figure it out for the number of orders your store will write.

Extra Copies of this pub. [unclear] to out stores or 10¢ if you can afford it. Also avail. to straight stores for $1[unclear]

[above] *Feminist Bookstores Newsletter* 3.3 (1979). Permission granted by Carol Seajay, FBN editor and publisher.

[opposite] *Feminist Bookstores Newsletter* 2.2 (1978), with sketch by Emily Schweber. Permission granted by Carol Seajay, FBN editor and publisher.

[*above*] 5th International Feminist Book Fair, Amstradam 1992, participants on the feminist bookstores panel "Strategies for the Future": (left to right) Traudel Sattler (Italy), Yvette Ellis, Sisterwrite (England), Pamela Pattynama (Netherlands), Farida Akhter (Bangladesh), Elisabeth Maderdo Amaral Gurgel (Brazil), Lariane Fonesca and Colleen Lynoner (Australia). *Feminist Bookstore News* 15.2 (1992): 29. Permission granted by Carol Seajay, FBN editor and publisher.

[*opposite*] *Feminist Bookstore News* staff Susan Buie, Carol Seajay (editor and publisher), and Dawn Lundy Martin in June 1994. Photograph by Robert Giard. Permission granted by Jonathan Sillin. Yale Collection of American Literature, Beinecke Rare Book and Manuscript Library, Yale University.

[top] *Feminist Bookstore News* 18.1 (1995). Permission granted by Carol Seajay, FBN editor and publisher.

[bottom] *Feminist Bookstore News* 21.1 (1998). Permission granted by Carol Seajay, FBN editor and publisher.

FOUR

THE FEMINIST SHELF,
A TRANSNATIONAL PROJECT
1984–1993

A conversational array of screenprinted, letterpress, and photocopied flyers hung in the Toronto Women's Bookstore entryway, where I stood on a
bright spring morning in 2006 awaiting my job interview. It had been just
a week since they'd called and said the letter I'd sent on a long shot looked
good; could I get on a plane? There was hardly room for me and the six-
member hiring committee teetering on folding chairs between the rows of
textbook storage shelves. A year before, I had met and interviewed Janet
Romero, events coordinator and queer artist of language and its complic-
ity in colonization. This time, she ran her fingers over a piece of carefully
ironed hair and asked me a question: "We're making hanging signs for the
bookstore and we've had long discussions about what to call the area that includes the Caribbean, First Nations, Pacific Asian, Southeast Asian, and other
identity sections. We're deciding between 'Identity and Beyond' and 'Indigenous and Diasporic Voices.' Which would you choose?" I was enticed by a
map of the bookstore's political geography, where shelves guided readers
to see and account for our specific histories and presents of oppression and
resistance, and, through these vocabularies, to together weave new futures.
The next day, pulling my shoes on before my flight out, I answered my cell
phone, nervous that I might actually get what I wanted. Alissa Trotz, bookstore board member and director of Caribbean Studies at the University of
Toronto, offered me the fourteen-month position. "We're choosing 'Indigenous and Diasporic Voices' in part since you picked it, though I wish I'd
pressed you to be more specific." She explained, "It's important, I think,
for the histories of imperialism and colonialism to be specifically marked."
This book continues my practice toward being more specific.

The Toronto Women's Bookstore (TWB) shelf sections named literature by authors' identities and the focus of their work, including Caribbean, Mixed Race, East Asian, South Asian, African, African Canadian, First Nations, Disability Studies, Critical Race Studies, and more. It is no accident that these are not the sections you will find at your general independent bookstore, at the nearest big box store, or even at your library. Through this naming work, feminist bookwomen have explicitly defined themselves not as supplying consumers but as constructing a particular reading practice. Thinking back to her work at New Words Bookstore in Cambridge in the 1980s and early 1990s, Kate Rushin explains:

> If you don't have a Black women's section or a women of color section or a lesbian section or a lesbian mothers section or an international section, the person coming into the store has to know exactly what they want. They either have to have a name or a title to find the book, and I think that having the sections increases visibility. . . . It also means that you can come in with a vague idea and look and discover things and learn about things that you didn't know to ask for.[1]

From their beginnings, transnational networks of feminist bookwomen saw this naming as part of creating a new context for understanding feminist writings and each other.

In 1976, three feminist bookstore collectives published statements of purpose that used the same language to describe their work as collecting women's books together in one place. The shared language of these three collectives, across two continents, suggests that this intentional reading and relational practice was a feature of a transnational feminist bookstore movement. In 1975 in Italy, women of the Milan Women's Bookstore wrote, "We want to bring together, in the same place, the creative expression of some women with the will to liberate all women."[2] In 1976 in New York, a Womanbooks newsletter opened with a similar claim: "It is important to us that works by women be allowed to define their context by being brought together in one place."[3] In Austin, the Common Woman Bookstore Collective used the same words in an early brochure.[4] Finding a book amid a context of other feminist titles was distinctly different from reading it on its own. As the Milan Women's Bookstore flyer suggested, this new context sought to transform readers into activists: the "creative expression of some women" would become "the will to liberate all women." This was perhaps the most radical contribution of feminist bookwomen: they changed the way readers understood feminist literature so that reading became relational, a call to accountability that required action. I call this act of recontextualization the feminist shelf.

I create the term "feminist shelf" to describe bookwomen's complex practice of using spatial organization, programming, and reflection to map shelf sections as ways of relating to each other, as feminist love; to change reading and relational practices by creating new contexts for each text and for ourselves through the books on the shelf or the list; to build a collective accountability to new vocabularies for lesbian antiracist feminism through events, narrative signs, and newsletters; to enact a feminist ethics of dialogue, speaking with each other rather than for each other, as sections and programming required accountability for our own identities in relationship; and, throughout, to revise this knowledge building in conversation as bookwomen discussed, contested, and redefined these contexts in collective meetings, transnational gatherings, and through the *Feminist Bookstore News* (FBN). I use this definition to structure this chapter.

Documenting bookwomen's practice of the feminist shelf also makes visible the rich transnational conversations bookwomen developed in the late 1980s, when there were feminist bookstores on almost every continent. The feminist shelf could not have been practiced by bookwomen in isolation in a single bookstore but, like all feminist vocabularies, required a larger movement to evolve ethically. The feminist shelf required an ethics of dialogue and accountability that bookwomen put into practice exchanging articles, newsletters, bibliographies, and advice with each other, both locally and across continents, on the pages of the FBN, and at gatherings like the biennial International Feminist Book Fair. As Indigenous feminists contested national borders within the US and Canada, Indigenous feminist authors called the women in print movement to account around authorship and appropriation. Bookwomen's skills in transnational dialogue prepared them to engage with these vital conversations about feminist ethics of nonappropriative authorship. The feminist shelf offered a cyclical process of bookwomen shaping books into fields of knowledge that changed reading practices, then talking together and revising their understandings of their own and each other's identities—particularly across racialized and class differences, and then rearranging and revising the shelf and, thus, reading practices. This relationship-shaping work relied on the bookwomen's framework of feminist accountability, as I documented in chapter 3. In this chapter I focus on core examples of how bookwomen developed the feminist shelf as a transnational and lesbian antiracist feminist practice of relationship building;[5] I share this history as a call for accountability in contemporary feminist activism.

This chapter traces the last stages of deeply movement-based feminist bookstore activism, before some US bookwomen, recognizing the looming growth of chain bookstores and publishers as a real threat to all independent bookstores, turned to use their substantial literary advocacy skills to sustain independent bookstores at large. In this choosing, bookwomen turned away from the practice of movement accountability they had created. In chapter 5 I describe this split in the bookstores. At the same time as the feminist organizing I describe in this chapter, North American chain bookstores were strategizing for a monopoly. During the late 1980s and early 1990s, US chain bookstores like B. Dalton moved in, soon to be bought out by Barnes & Noble on its way to infamous expansion. Amazon.com, founded in 1994, would not start selling books until 1995; that same year saw the founding of the Canadian giant Chapters. Feminist bookwomen, by proving there was a market, ensured that those chain bookstores carried some feminist literature. In this chapter I document bookwomen's work honing their movement accountability through the early 1990s. Bookwomen's practice of the feminist shelf differentiates these movement bookstores from general independent or mainstream bookstores and identifies the feminist bookstores as sites of movement making.

Mapping Feminist Love

Bookwomen knew from their own experiences that a collection of books together changed how readers understood any one of those books, and they used this practice of the feminist shelf in the bookstores to change their own understandings of feminism, of what was possible. In each of my interviews with bookwomen, they talked about what finding books together meant to them, from Carol Seajay's visit to the West Coast Lesbian Conference in LA, where she found lesbian books in stacks, books that would "change our lives," to Pell finding Black women writers together on a shelf for the first time at Old Wives' Tales in San Francisco, and to May Lui building the Mixed Race section at TWB.[6] At New Words in Cambridge, a city immersed in educational institutions, collective member, biology scholar, and transnational health activist Rita Arditti used her cofounding of the bookstore as a way to build an interdisciplinary feminist practice of health activism: "My background is in biology, but I was doing biology and social issues, which is an interdisciplinary thing, and I was trying to learn about women's studies. I learned about women's studies by doing the bookstore, because I started to read literature, history, science, philosophy, you name it, and so it was clear for me from the beginning that women's studies covered all these disciplines and how they were interrelated."[7] The bookstores thus provided a visual and relational map for this interdisciplinarity that attracted others as well. Arditti remembers Ruth Hubbard, the "very well-known biologist at Harvard, who was also a feminist," coming into the bookstore and buying books there amid the new connections of feminism and science studies.[8]

Often feminist bookstores stocked books not available anywhere else, and even when the books were widely available at other bookstores, feminist bookstores made these books uniquely visible. Janet Romero, working at TWB in 2005, remembered that the shelf organization affected real availability: "I realized after I'd been here [TWB] a few times that some of those books *were* available [at other bookstores], but they're not set out in a way that's necessarily accessible."[9] She first came to TWB for course books and came back because of the Latin American section. Romero, whose family had immigrated from Chile to Canada when she was young, recalls that this was a section "I had never seen anywhere else. I'd read very little literature at that point by Latinas, and didn't even really know where to get stuff like that until I came here and saw that there was actually stuff out there. I remember having to leave because I had to go back to school. . . . It was probably within that same week I came back, and again I spent another couple of hours in the Latin American section." For both Arditti and Romero, bookstore shelves validated and expanded self-identity and community.[10]

Feminist bookwomen's prolific list-writing made visible the intellectual and relational labor behind these shelf formations. Feminist bookwomen gathered books together into lists as though they were writing manifestos, poetry, and theory—and they were. Feminist bookwomen created bibliographies for mailing lists, for newsletters, for orders, and for classes. Lists were one forum through which feminist bookwomen taught readers, including each other, to read feminist literature and, in turn, to become literary activists. With these lists, which often reflected changing shelf section titles, feminist bookwomen put books in conversation with each other, demonstrated the existence of a field of knowledge, and mapped new vocabularies for understanding feminist literature. For example, Zora Neale Hurston's

Dust Tracks on a Road might be understood as literary fiction or Harlem Renaissance fiction, depending on a reading practice. If a reader has read the other titles in ICI: A Woman's Place's "Lives" section of their 1973 Mail Order Guide, including Charlotte Perkins Gilman's *The Yellow Wallpaper* and Lorraine Hansberry's *To Be Young, Gifted and Black*, the reader might (as was the case with A Woman's Place collective members) understand *Dust Tracks* as a kind of feminist life narrative, as a feminist of color text, or even, read together with *How to Do Your Own Divorce in California*, as a feminist guide to finding your own love.[11] This change in reading practice appeared in the sections and lists feminist bookwomen made as they imagined and reimagined what these texts meant to each other, how they redefined each other.

Bookwomen also collectively developed the practice of the feminist shelf by creating and sharing lists through the FBN. Throughout the 1980s and 1990s, a bookwoman anticipated the FBN in her mailbox four times a year. The publication regularly ran around a substantial 125 pages of news, strategies, and book reviews. While they could influence publishers and readers with the FBN's regular best sellers list, bookwomen influenced each other's shelves with the regular and recurring lists of books labeled "From Our Own Presses" (the feminist presses), "Small Presses," "University Presses," "Publishers Row" (the mainstream press), "Magazines," and "Mass Markets." Other lists recurring in more than ten issues included Susanna J. Sturgis's "Science Fiction"—with special issues including "A List of Lesbians in Fantasy/Science Fiction," "Mysteries," Tee A. Corinne's "Art Books," and "Gay Men's Literature for Feminist Bookstores." Columns with shorter runs included "Women's Studies," "Selling Poetry in Feminist Bookstores," book lists for youth with titles like "Gay and Lesbian Books for Young Adults" or "AIDS Books for Young Adults," "Books in Canada," "International Women," "Addiction and Recovery," and more. The lists bookwomen sent in to FBN modeled a practice of list making, of shelf building, as a core role of feminist bookwomen and one that required critical analysis. Bookwomen created, dismantled, and re-created their shelves together because they recognized that the ways they arranged books together, titled sections, and connected events in these intentional spaces could change the meanings of these books for readers, could build readers' accountability to each other, could articulate a lesbian antiracist feminist practice of alliance across difference that could change everything.

North American feminist bookstores shared similar commitments to lesbian feminism, often explored antiracism, and sought to bring some of a transnational field of women's writing to their neighborhoods. Individual bookstores were also shaped by local influences, political commitments, and the bookwomen themselves. Cambridge was one site of the beginnings of *This Bridge Called My Back: Writings by Radical Women of Color* and was home to a bevy of exclusive and radical universities as well as alternative educational projects. These local influences manifested in the New Words staff and on the shelves with a commitment to literature by women of color and a new articulation of interdisciplinary women's studies. Readers could see these frameworks in a new way in 1986 when Joni Seager, a feminist geographer and new bookstore collective member, drew up a map of the bookstore sections. In a letter to readers, the collective made the connection between Seager's map of the store and her sociopolitical maps of the world, a move that emphasized the bookstore as a political space:

> New Words has our very own geographer, Joni Seager. A feminist geographer you ask? Yes and when you come into the store ask for your own New Words' floor plan complete with list of sections mapped out by Joni. (Bet you can find at least one section you didn't know about.) Joni is also co-author with Ann Olson of *Women in the World*, Simon and Schuster, 12.95, an informative collection of colorful, subversive and striking maps of the world with artful graphs depicting, among other topics, the incidence of women's illiteracy, infant mortality, plus noting our presence in the media and the work world. There are more than forty maps. This is great for gift giving, women's studies courses, conversation starters, and a prominent spot on your reference shelf.[12]

Seager's floor plan, with its overview of the store, offered readers a cognitive map in which to place their own reading at hand, in connection with a range of women's texts. The letter invited readers to "find at least one section you didn't know about," indicating that the section titles themselves introduced readers to new categories of information. Later in the letter the collective acknowledged the shifting sections of the store, explaining, "We have a new section on books about Adult Children of Alcoholics. The number of books on the subject has grown amazingly in the past year." That was a fifty-third book section, one too new to appear on Seager's map of the bookstore;[13] with this announcement the collective reminded readers that sections changed and shifted to reflect and contribute to feminisms. Seager's own atlas of the world, originally published in 1986, emerged at the same time as her mapping of New Words. Her issue-driven world atlas points out the political nature of geography;[14] her map of New Words recognizes feminist bookstore space as equally political.

Poet and New Words bookwoman Kate Rushin observed that having women of color sections created conversation around the meaning of "women of color": "One of the things that we were really proud of, and came around the time of the publication of *This Bridge Called My Back* and all that, is that we established a women of color section. And out of that grew an international section."[15] Amid the conversation among women of color authors and activists at the time, a burgeoning transnational consciousness prompted North American women of color to question their self-identification as "third world women" and to claim their identities as "women of color." Coeditors Cherríe Moraga and Gloria Anzaldúa, sending out their call for writings for *This Bridge Called My Back*, addressed their first draft to "Third World Women" and then revised that to "women of color."[16] This shift by women of color to naming difference between women in the global South and women of color in North America fed their transnational alliances, and at New Words this shift mapped onto the growth of an international section related to the women of color section. These sections, Rushin explained, also changed the sense of who belonged in the space: "I have the impression that many, many women came to New Words because we did have a women of color section." Collective member Laura Zimmerman pointed out that Rushin's work as a woman of color in the bookstore also marked New Words as a space of alliance; indeed, this change in space participated in educating the (largely white) collective members as antiracist allies sharing power as well as changing readers. Zimmerman wrote of Rushin in FBN, "Kate's expertise and commitment to African-American literature and the literature of other women of color has deeply influenced and informed the very nature of the store from the arrangement of our sections to our window displays to the books we read and discuss among ourselves."[17] The commitment of the collective to recruit and hire Rushin risked the very kind of request Rushin writes against in "The Bridge Poem," but this work of white antiracist allies educating themselves to build alliances across difference meant they did not rely on Rushin as an informant. Rather, Rushin initiated the feminist shelves that changed the collective's own reading practices and made the collective members, in turn, better antiracist allies.

Though feminists have not sufficiently recognized the theorizing work of feminist bookwomen, feminists have reflected on a similar practice: editing feminist anthologies.[18] Understanding bookwomen's work as a version of anthologizing emphasizes both how bookwomen's seemingly simple practice of creating new sections is a radical intervention and how this practice of the feminist shelf changes what readers expect from reading and from each other. Maori feminist sociologist Linda Tuhiwai Smith makes a distinction between anthologies that are "simply a gathering of authors or a collection of disembodied and dis-interested 'voices'" and one that "acts as a meeting place, a conversation."[19] I see the same distinction between general bookstores and feminist bookstores where bookwomen practice the feminist shelf, create and recreate sections, talk with each other about what to include or exclude, and narrate those decisions in newsletters, events programming, catalogs, and shelf section titles. When Rushin created the women of color section at New Words, she brought both books and people together in the space. This gathering created visibility and changed reading as well as relational practices.

Gloria Anzaldúa created the anthology Haciendo Caras, Making Face, Making Soul (including an essay by Old Wives' Tales bookwoman Kit Quan) because, she explains, "I had grown frustrated that the same few women-of-color were asked to read or lecture in universities and classrooms, or to submit work to anthologies and quarterlies. . . . Repeatedly tokenizing the same half dozen mujeres was stymieing our literary/political movement. . . . The urge to anthologize, to bring more voices to the foreground, grew stronger."[20] Vibrant bookstore sections, circulated in lists nationally and transnationally, resulted from a similar urge as bookwomen shared book titles through the FBN to influence each other's shelves and then read the FBN to find out about and order in other bookwomen's recommendations. At BookWoman in Austin, as in feminist bookstores across the world, bookwomen marked up their issues, leaving behind an indication of what they likely ordered in and shared news of with their communities. Among many underlined, circled, and otherwise noted books to order in, a 1984 FBN announcement of La Luz Journal, self-published by Juana Maria Paz as Paz Press, appears with a circle penned in by the Austin women; the book offered what Paz described as a "true story taken from my own journal entries at the time. La Luz describes lesbian of color land struggles from the late 1970's."[21] This visibility—local bookwomen's influence amplified by the FBN—in turn changed readers. Tuhiwai Smith reflects on her anthology reading: "As a reader I have also come to expect that the anthology is connected to something a little more dangerous and enticing, an intellectual, social, and political project that has something 'at stake.'"[22] Positioning herself "as a reader" and describing what she has "come to expect," Tuhiwai Smith indicates that anthology editors framing the "dangerous and enticing" political stakes of a conversation affect her expectations of anthologies, change her reading practice, and connect reading with activism. Seen this way, Tuhiwai Smith's statement implies the power of activist bookwomen as anthology editors in action as they curated and narrated collections of writers to incite readers to action.[23]

A reader at New Words in the 1980s, African Caribbean lesbian feminist theorist M. Jacqui Alexander experienced this call to action through the feminist shelf. Alexander, an editor of one of the anthologies Smith reviewed in her article, writes of finding Audre Lorde's self-proclaimed biomythography *Zami: A New Spelling of My Name* (Persephone Press, 1982) in the "section 'Woman of Color' at New Words Bookstore in Cambridge."[24] At this moment in the 1980s, Alexander was reflecting on her move from Trinidad to Cambridge, Massachusetts, where, she explains, "for the first time in my life, the majority of people around me were white."[25] "Not a part of the sweat and fire that birthed a woman of color politics in this country in the 1970s and 1980s" but "shaped by" that movement, Alexander writes what it means to "become women of color," to "become fluent in each others' histories" against a particular North American instantiation of colonialism.[26] "I was giving birth to myself in 1986," Alexander writes. "I navigated the passage in the waters of *Bridge, Homegirls, Cancer Journals,* and *Sister Outsider*."[27] She would also have seen this collection of books along with *Zami* at New Words in the section articulating the identity that "Women of Color" had newly claimed. At the edges of Alexander's writing, I see the anthologizing practice of feminist bookwomen collecting and naming book sections together in ways that changed how women understood themselves and their world, in ways that supported women in their own anthologizing. The two practices, anthologizing in print and in the bookstore, built on each other. The fact of the matter, Alexander advises, "is that there is no other work but the work of creating and re-creating ourselves within the context of community."[28]

Sara Zia Ebrahimi and Naomi Skoglund's short film *On the Shelf* illustrates my argument that the feminist literary map bookwomen created on their shelves engaged readers in a practice of creating and re-creating themselves in the context of community, a practice they continued amid and beyond the shelves. This self and community creation is part of the feminist shelf. *On the Shelf* visually interweaves the aesthetic, political, and affective powers of feminist books, together on a shelf, with a young Black queer person's search for the perfect lover.[29] The film's opening sequence sounds out voices reading from feminist books shown with close-ups of their covers: Elaine Brown's *A Taste of Power: A Black Woman's Story*, Anne Marie MacDonald's *Fall on Your Knees*, Shani Mootoo's *Cereus Blooms at Night*, Toni Cade Bambara's *The Salt Eaters*, Zadie Smith's *White Teeth*, and June Jordan's *Some of Us Did Not Die*. The narrative frame positions these books stacked together on a shelf, and the voice-overs invoke readers speaking out loud to enact the feminist force of this shelf. Friends in a range of gender-norm-challenging dress and attitudes, among them one who works at the local feminist bookstore, surround the central character identified in the credits as "the book lover." The film locates several scenes in feminist sites in New York, including Bluestockings, a feminist bookstore in New York founded in 1999.[30] After the opening sequence, the book lover at home picks up their wallet off of a stack of books: Nalo Hopkinson's *Brown Girl in the Ring*, Jeanette Winterson's *The Passion*, and Chinua Achebe's *Anthills of the Savannah*. Feminist books, and books claimed in context as feminist, are everywhere in the apartment.

After a first date ends in failure when the book lover discovers their date only has a few books (on a shelf on top of the television), the book lover gives their friend who works at Bluestockings a list of books with the request "If any girl comes in and picks any one of those books up off the shelf, call me immediately on my cell."[31] Soon after this agreement, the bookstore friend watches a woman come into the bookstore and pick up Edwidge Danticat's *Breath Eyes Memory*. She checks the list and calls the book lover, who arrives just as "the dream date" gets to the front desk with bell hooks's *All about Love: New Visions*. The book lover flirts earnestly with the dream date: "You know, I'd really love to hear your opinion about the book." The connection works, and the dream date replies, "Maybe I'll even read you my favorite part." This exchange sets up the interest in a set of books in contextual conversation as an indication of political conviction and even passion. The book becomes the love making in a later scene showing the two in a coffeehouse talking and the dream date reading aloud from hooks's book. The film follows the two lovers to the public library, at home making a protest sign reading "war is racist!," and walking to the dream date's apartment. The protest sign links the politics of identity with the politics of literature, noting the support structure enabled by the feminist shelf: with a woman who practices reading feminist books, the book lover could find a partner in politics and love. The shelf-full of books from the opening credits and

[Figures 4.1–4.4] Film stills from *On the Shelf*, directed by Naomi Skoglund and Sara Zia Ebrahimi, 2003. Permission granted by Naomi Skoglund and Sara Zia Ebrahimi.

sprawled across the book lover's apartment together shape a feminist love as alliance building, an understanding of feminist love as a resistance to interlocking oppressions. The closing sequence shows yet another series of books, stack upon stack, inviting pleasure in looking at the books in volume as well as emphasizing the importance of each as part of a context for each other and for our relationships.

While the film follows the lovers to the library and to women's apartments full of books, the feminist bookstore is the place where the connection happens, where love becomes legible. I argue that what makes this possible is not simply the existence of a feminist bookstore, but the history of feminist bookstores as national (and transnational) sites of practicing relationship building. The film evokes the feminist legacy of the feminist bookstore as a place where queer people (including bookstore collective members) have met lovers. With substantial numbers of feminist bookstores across the nation in the 1980s and 1990s, bookwomen's practice of the feminist shelf transformed generations of readers by creating places to find love and by gathering feminist writers (in text and in person) who were redefining feminist love. In *All about Love*, on pages the book lover and the dream date shared, bell hooks explains why we need to define love: "Had I been given a clear definition of love earlier in my life it would not have taken me so long to become a more loving person. Had I shared with others a common understanding of what it means to love it would have been easier to create love." Indeed, she points out that popular books claiming that love defies definition or arguing that "women" and "men" have essential and incompatible definitions of love intentionally defuse the political power of love: "This type of literature is popular because it does not demand a change in fixed ways of thinking about gender roles, culture, or love."[32] In conversation with hooks, feminist theorist Chela Sandoval proclaims the power of love to resist recolonization and to connect allies. Language and interpretation, she points out, are vital tools: "My contribution is to identify a hermeneutics of love that can create social change."[33] For Sandoval, this radical love is in particular a tool for women connecting with each other as women of color, where "love is understood as affinity—alliance and affection across lines of difference that intersect both in and out of the body."[34] I offer these moments in feminist thinking about love to illustrate the power of defining feminist love, the power of language and the practice of the feminist shelf. In *On the Shelf*, in relationships built in and legible through feminist bookstores, the love of lovers and friends is inseparable from a love that builds political alliances for social change. Aimee Carillo Rowe explains, "I mean 'love' not necessarily in the narrow sense of lovers, or even friends, although I mean those relations too—I mean 'love' in the more expansive sense of whose lives matter to us."[35] Feminist bookstores, as indicated by their persistence as cultural touchstones, contributed through the feminist shelf to generating a definition of feminist love. There is a deeper story here: feminist bookwomen in the mid-1980s figured out what feminist love was as they continued to learn to hold each other accountable and refine their literary activist practice.

Changing Reading and Relational Practices

Participants in the transnational movements of the 1980s, feminist bookwomen together wove a definition of feminist love as ethical relationality, being accountable to each other, in part through events that brought people into the bookstores. The changing shelves, in turn, made new meaning of the events bookwomen hosted amid the books. Just as the shelves created vital context for each other, only our relationships with each other across difference make a feminist future possible. At their best, bookwomen used events as part of the feminist shelf to enact a lesbian antiracist feminist practice of learning to see and share the connections between resistance movements. Bookwomen at Womanbooks, Old Wives' Tales, New Words, and other bookstores worked differently to build collections of what they called international women's literature. The books simultaneously shared the exciting promise of a transnational movement and emphasized the differences among women, the importance of listening closely in order to practice allyship with each other. Theorizing from her own interracial relationship to a feminist love with which she would build transnational, literature-based alliances, publisher and author Audre Lorde wrote:

> we have chosen each other
> and the edge of each other's battles
> the war is the same if we lose
> someday women's blood will congeal
> upon a dead planet
> if we win
> there is no telling.[36]

From their beginnings bookwomen created a vital network of places where women could learn to choose each other and the edge of each other's distinct and interconnected battles. A 1976 Womanbooks flyer lists events that include "Readings and Rappings on Getting Older," an event about countering stereotypes and accepting women's selves, alongside a "Poetry Reading for Assata Shakur with Jayne Cortez and June Jordan," for "Women only," about political prisoner Assata Shakur, the Black Panther Party and Black Liberation Army activist who had been brutally incarcerated in New York since 1973 and would escape in 1979 and find political asylum in Cuba in 1984; and a "Presentation by Action for Women in Chile," about women in Chile after the 1973 coup.[37] No doubt the work of Fabi Romero Oak alongside her white cobookwomen and their commitments on the shelves defined Womanbooks as another space fostering the work of feminists of color. Action for Women in Chile was founded by three white women, Sally Jeanne Guttmacher, Barbara Ehrenreich, and Helen Marieskind.[38] The shelves of the bookstore would prohibit these women, if they had been so inclined, from suggesting that women in Chile could not speak for themselves, and at the 1988 International Feminist Book Fair, US bookwomen would meet and talk with Chilean bookwomen. This context on the shelves and in conversation shaped the events as a practice of both women of color and white women antiracist allies in transnational relationship. The three Womanbooks events together emphasized the interconnectedness from a reader's individual body to her responsibility to understand difference and transnational alliances.

A similar grouping of events at ICI: A Woman's Place in the 1980s points both to lasting US activist attention to Latin American movements and to the importance of feminist bookstores as spaces for these conversations in feminism. Women could stop by the bookstore in Oakland for an update from the El Salvador Sanctuary Movement, a presentation by the East Bay Organizing Committee "on U.S. refusals to give political asylum to refugees from El Salvador"; to sustain their still-necessary "solidarity with Assata Shakur and Black prisoners of war"; a screening and discussion of *Blood of the Condor*, a film about "the Peace Corps' sterilization of Bolivian women without their consent," with the group Women Against Imperialism. The bookwomen also provided free child care and announced a wheelchair accessible bookstore.[39] Bookwomen practiced the feminist shelf to create sites of sustained engagement with transnational feminist issues and to encourage a transnational feminist literacy with each other.

During a cool mid-June in 1988, six hundred feminist writers, publishers, distributors, and bookwomen from forty-five countries gathered in Montreal for the third International Feminist Book Fair, nearly a week of workshops, events, and relationship building focused on the theme "memory, power, history."[40] The biennial event had gathered feminists in London in 1984 and Oslo in 1986, with a different team of women volunteering to organize and host it each time. Bookwomen leveraged their presence at the International Feminist Book Fair to lobby for changes in publishing and distribution that made the feminist shelf possible. Over a short lunch hour, in between talks about feminist bookstore work and gatherings with bookwomen, Carol Seajay staffed the FBN table. Seajay was a powerful presence at the conference; Laura Zimmerman and Kate Rushin suspected that Seajay "did more work behind-the-scenes than we'll ever know."[41] Part of that work involved talking with Mev Miller of Inland (Miller had formerly worked at Amazon feminist bookstore) and representatives at BookPeople; these two book distributors made commitments at the book fair to bring in more feminist press titles from India, South Africa, and England.[42] After the lunch buzz of activity, an early afternoon session titled "Bookselling and Ethics" brought together Carol Seajay; Donna Fernandez, with Streelekha, still open in Bangalore; Marian Lens, with Artemys, the feminist bookshop in Brussels; and Ximena Pizarro, with Librería Lila, still open in Santiago.[43] Artemys shared with many North American feminist bookstores an insistence on lesbian politics as integral to feminism.[44] In addition to talking about the works of Chilean feminist writers Julieta Kirkwood and Margarita Pisano, Ximena Pizarro, like other bookwomen, used the International Feminist Book Fair as an opportunity to bring back as much feminist literature as she could to distribute through her bookstore.[45] Through conversations with each other across national, ethnic, and socioeconomic differences, bookwomen changed what books were available transnationally and continued to develop their practice of the feminist shelf as relational.

This reading as relationship building in turn informed feminisms. Bookwomen's literary activism made it possible to understand feminist and transnational movements differently because of the books on their shelves. At the International Feminist Book Fair, Streelekha cofounder Donna Fernandez read from a paper she prepared with her collective, who had opened Streelekha, the feminist bookstore in Bangalore, in 1984. "By ensuring easy accessibility of feminist literature," the women of Streelekha argued, feminist bookstores provide "the necessary theoretical ballast for feminist action. To this universal role must be added, in the case of Third World countries, the desideratum of making such feminist literature affordable, so that the fledgling feminist movements in most of these countries can acquire greater momentum than they would otherwise be able to do."[46] Certainly the bookstores were one movement space of many; what they had that other spaces did not was books and the capacity to make this movement-based language accessible in terms of reading practice and affordability. Pizarro had founded Librería Lila in 1984 in an articulation of feminist literature as feminist resistance: "I wanted to open a space for women, at a time when oppression was very present. Santiago was in a state of siege, and I wanted to create a women's bookstore, for women by women. I was very strict and bound to women's issues, feminism and gender theory, and also writers or books about women's issues."[47] These texts fed women's marches and rallies; Pizarro recalls that the bookstore "was also a distribution center for the marches, gatherings for women to get together and organize."[48] This literature together in one place was at once library and education. Bookwomen's collection building both participated in and fed transnational feminisms. Fernandez, on behalf of the Streelekha bookwomen, argued that the bookstores wielded substantial influence: "We would see a special role for the feminist book shops, of endeavoring the widest possible circulation of feminist values through literature; not only through sale but by finding spaces to reach women for whom purchase of expensive books is out of reach."[49] The feminist shelf, a new movement reading practice created by bookwomen's gathering, curation, and narration of literature, articulated and shared an evolving set of feminist values.

After Fernandez delivered her rousing speech, she and Celine Segune, also of Streelekha, gathered a meeting of feminist bookwomen to build a transnational exchange. Bookwomen from Ontario pledged that the Toronto Women's Bookstore would serve as a "'sister' North American bookstore" to Streelekha, and bookwomen from Cambridge, Massachusetts, committed to remain connected through New Words Bookstore.[50] Zimmerman and Rushin of New Words reveled in the chance to "talk about the practical details of surviving as feminist bookstore workers in our own communities and as part of an international movement."[51] Feminist bookwomen's negotiations of resource sharing required a critical analysis and subversion of postcolonial global capitalism and its effects on feminist organizing. Joni Seager remembers bookwomen from Streelekha visiting Boston and coming to New Words. The bookwomen shared their experiences organizing, and Seager was struck by the gap in resources: "We were talking about the problem of getting a computer that's good enough to do a newsletter on, and they were talking about getting a typewriter. So, it became very clear to us that there was this huge resource gap between the resources that we could muster; basically we were so much richer than they were, even at the same time that we thought of ourselves as pretty marginal."[52] Having learned from their practice of the feminist shelf about appropriation and the ethics of feminist relationships, bookwomen recognized that the resource gap did not indicate a gap in knowledge or activism; rather, this information exchange built bookwomen's sense of a transnational movement.

Through this movement building, bookwomen developed a new familiarity with the globalized capitalism they were trying to interrupt and created new pathways for information sharing. Fernandez and other women at Streelekha kept up correspondence with women at New Words, the Toronto Women's Bookstore, and other feminist bookstores, sharing news of their strategies as well as materials. In Cambridge, Rushin and Zimmerman booked Casselberry-Dupree, Annette Aguilar, and Toshi Reagon, with readings by Hattie Gossett, for a fundraising concert in support of Streelekha's dream of a book van.[53] The New Words bookwomen also sent word through the FBN of books published in the US that Streelekha wanted on their shelves: the Streelekha "'wish-list' includes books that focus on Third World women in development, literature, and politics, and books by feminist theorists. They welcome books from University presses, Zed Press, Kitchen Table Press, and other progressive and Third World presses."[54] These donations helped to circumvent currency battles and the vagaries of the international neocolonial money market. Women in Toronto and Cambridge were not just sending their literatures to India, though; they also began to see, read, and purchase, in their local feminist bookstores, Indian feminist magazines distributed through Streelekha and the annual feminist daybook published by Streelekha.[55]

Sharon Fernandez of the Toronto Women's Bookstore remembers meeting with Donna Fernandez and Celine Segune at the International Feminist Book Fair in Montreal and beginning a lasting relationship that changed her own practice:

> We did feel connected to Streelekha. We did a number of things with them, and we sent them different kinds of resources. We learnt a lot from them, because they were so radical and so innovative and interesting

and smart. We learnt a lot from the way they wrote about issues, and we learnt about how the same issues that were going on in India were going on in Toronto, in terms of the women's community and the issues that women were facing: backlash against women from mainstream communities, educating women to empower them around health and sexuality, organizing in collective ways for greater strength, lesbian issues. And we learnt how with so little they could do so much.[56]

In this way, bookwomen used the feminist shelf to work against capitalism from within a seemingly profit-oriented framework of book sales: through shelf sections and related relationships, bookwomen created a separate, noncommercial value by changing the meaning of the books in the sections and their relationships to each other.

This organization of texts informed and built the knowledge bases of even readers who did not buy the books. For example, those readers in Bangalore unable to afford skyrocketing prices on books by local authors, published abroad and sold back at astronomical prices further increased by exchange rates, could read at Streelekha and check out books from the Streelekha library, Kavya for Women.[57] The Streelekha bookwomen's organization of shelf titles also informed even those readers who did not buy books by shaping a feminist theory. The section titles, reflected in their catalogs and on their shelves, embodied a feminist theory of alliance building: "Besides our focus on feminist literature, we also stock titles in green politics, development studies, questions of disarmament and peace, and caste politics, because we believe the feminist movement to be inextricably linked to all peoples' movements that fundamentally challenge the power relations between the rich and the poor, between women and men, the upper and lower castes, the blacks and the whites."[58] Exchanges with Streelekha bookwomen built North American bookwomen's capacity for making connections without appropriation, for being accountable to each other.

As bookwomen honed their skills in dialogue across racialized, class, and national differences, simultaneous productive rifts at the Montreal International Feminist Book Fair raised bookwomen's awareness of their unique role in working against voice appropriation. In her now iconic essay "On the Problem of Speaking for Others," feminist philosopher Linda Martín Alcoff identifies the Montreal International Feminist Book Fair as a central site for thinking through the question of her title: "Anne Cameron, a very gifted white Canadian author, writes several first person accounts of the lives of Native Canadian women. At the 1988 International Feminist Book Fair in Montreal, a group of Native Canadian writers ask Cameron to, in their words, 'move over' on the grounds that her writings are disempowering for Native authors. She agrees."[59] Even in this short description, Alcoff herself is influenced by mainstream pressures to support, as "gifted," white authors appropriating Indigenous voices. A dialogue between Anne Cameron, author of *Daughters of Copper Woman* (Press Gang, 1981), and Lee Maracle, member of the Sto:Loh Nation and well-known feminist First Nations author of titles including *I Am Woman* (Write-On Press, 1988) and *Bobbi Lee: Struggles of a Native Canadian Woman* (Liberation Support Movement, 1975),[60] made public how feminist bookwomen were necessarily involved with power and voice. Maracle explained to readers of the Canadian feminist magazine *Trivia*, "The other thing about Anne is that she has Native children. This is a special thing for us. These children have children, and they're Native. So she's one of our Grandmothers in another way, even though she's white. But we *asked* her just to move over, to give us some space, because you know, when I'm on the bookshelf and she's on the bookshelf, I know what the citizenship of this country is going to buy. And Anne knows. She agreed that she would move over, she would help promote our work." Taking one step further, Maracle invited Cameron to fill in an important gap in the literature: "Where in the literature of white women is the struggle against racism in their community?"[61] The dialogue was amplified by the geography of the conference, which took place on a hill in a middle-class neighborhood. Both the place and the registration fee effectively excluded local working-class women, particularly women of color.[62]

Esther Vise, Jewish lesbian white antiracist ally and bookwoman at the Toronto Women's Bookstore, remembers being at the Montreal International Feminist Book Fair and witnessing Indigenous feminists explaining, "When you actually write these books and they get published, it means ours don't get published."[63] Vise recalls "some very prominent white women, lesbians, who said, 'I hear what you're saying, and I'm going to stop writing in that vein, I'm going to stop assuming that voice.'" Vise's experience informed her work at the bookstore: "The whole discussion around voice and appropriation is huge, and the importance of carrying books written by people in their own voices, had an enormous impact that I think I then went into book buying later on with in a big way."[64] On the pages of the FBN, at other gatherings, and at subsequent International Feminist Book Fairs—in Barcelona in 1990, Amsterdam in 1992, and Melbourne in 1994—feminist bookwomen continued to collectively build their concept of how the feminist shelf shaped feminist theory and ethics and feminists' relationships with each other.

Building a Collective Accountability to New Vocabularies

The new feminist literacies generated through shelf sections and their attendant relationships and reorganizations also required accountability to power sharing within bookstores. These local bookstores, sites of feminism, influenced the now transnational movement. In 1980s Toronto, women of color and their allies were successful in calling for accountability and power sharing from white women monopolizing control over organizations. In some organizations this meant splintering: at the Toronto-based Women's Press, attention to white privilege and a need to prioritize narratives of historically marginalized women gave a group of women, including Makeda Silvera, the courage to leave the Women's Press and start Sister Vision, a Canadian feminist of color press.[65] In other organizations, like the Toronto Women's Bookstore, calls for reflection and power sharing successfully changed the organizational identity. Patti Kirk and Marie Prins had just spent a year moving and rebuilding TWB after the firebombing of the abortion clinic offices upstairs; exhausted from the effort, they were not ready to be responsive to calls for their accountability and leadership sharing, though Kirk recognized that not having any women of color on staff "was a big deal." The two left to start Parentbooks a few blocks west on Harbord Street in 1986.[66] Sharon Fernandez joined the bookstore and, along with Marilyn McCallum, Beth McCauley, Wendy Wine, and Jude Johnston, transformed the organization back into a collective.

At this point, the still majority-white staff meant that the bookstore was almost completely isolated from the activism and priorities of women of color; this identity showed on the shelves. By the time Sharon Fernandez started working at the Toronto Women's Bookstore, she had been involved in feminist of color organizing for years. Fernandez remembers her sense of TWB: "It was seen as a white woman's bookstore in terms of content, in terms of the literature that was carried." Building on the work of women of color on staff before her, Fernandez began the "incremental, slow building of networks, relationships," from shelf to community. She remembers the beginnings of conversations about prioritizing the work of women of color and Indigenous women at the bookstore: "When you go into any institution that hasn't had a track record of dealing with women of color issues, they always say they don't know where to begin. They don't realize that there's such a huge amount of content out there that's available, that it's all around you except that you haven't looked. When we decided that, yes, it was time to really be inclusive . . . , it was just a question of researching where are the books, where are the voices published."[67] The Toronto bookwomen were putting to work the practice of the feminist shelf that bookwomen were honing together transnationally.

Through a collective research process, Fernandez created the *Women of Colour Bibliography*, a central and vital document that changed the bookstore and feminism in the city. Internally, the *Bibliography* created the conditions for a sea change as it, and conversations around it, prepared the Toronto bookwomen to take responsibility for unearned privilege, to prioritize authors and bookwomen of color, and to participate in transracial alliances. Throughout this process, Fernandez used the *Bibliography* to transform the bookstore into a space of and for Toronto feminists of color and Indigenous feminists. Vise saw Fernandez take "on the brunt of the white women on staff trying to work through their own racism and assumptions around things" as well as answering to "women of color in the community, who wanted to see things happen in a different way or faster."[68] Externally, Fernandez also saw the *Bibliography*, for sale in the bookstore, as a tool for redefining feminism within the academy. Course book sales had been significant to the economic revival of the bookstore, and it was "within that network that we put out the *Bibliography* to make sure that it was a service to the professors that were looking for content. So that we were profiling the work that was available at that time."[69] Fernandez's work with the *Bibliography* enacted what bookwomen transnationally attempted: connecting levels of organizing, from internal collective relationships to larger movement relationships, to influence larger public systems.

The *Women of Colour Bibliography* had been preceded at the bookstore by the twenty-four-page *Mail-Order Catalogue* in the mid-1970s. This earlier list offers a sense of the vision and work of the store prior to 1989. The earlier *Catalogue* named a "special emphasis" on "the Canadian women's studies section," which included "books on Canadian herstory, biography, Native women, current analysis of women in Canadian society, and children's books."[70] The coverage did achieve visibility of a history of white Canadian women's literature and gestured toward transracial experiences. The lack of representation of authors of color, particularly in Canada, and the emphasis of section titles on issue areas kept this catalog from inviting or sustaining alliances across racialized difference. Most sections in the *Catalogue* organized around issues like arts, health, and religion and spirituality, while only three section titles held space specifically for addressing racialized identities: "Black Women," "Native Women," and "Women in Many Lands." Though missing the vital antiracist feminist ethic of alliance, this earlier catalog built a foundation for the later bibliography by mapping out the bookstore and claiming that part of the function of the bookstore was to reach out, to educate readers, and to shape understandings of what counted as "written materials for women."

The *Women of Colour Bibliography*, published in 1989, documents the substantial publishing of and by women of color in the 1980s, and it records the ongoing relevance of literature by women of color published in the 1970s. The *Bibliography* thus contradicts claims that women of color feminism began in the 1980s.[71] The ninety-four-page *Bibliography* refused to allow teachers, bookwomen, publishers, or readers to imagine that women of color were not writing, theorizing, and speaking with each other. In this section I offer extensive analysis of the lists in the *Women of Colour Bibliography*, in order to demonstrate how I and other readers learn from the texts and arrangements created by Fernandez and her collaborating bookwomen. While my text will always be one written by me, a white lesbian feminist antiracist ally, in this telling I seek to prioritize the voices and work of women of color. This practice of developing an ethic of transracial intertextuality in order to shift power, historical narratives, and the possibility of future alliances is one lesson I learned from bookwomen's practice of the feminist shelf.

Beginning on a steamy summer day in 1989, readers could step into the Toronto Women's Bookstore on Harbord Street and purchase a copy of the *Women of Colour Bibliography* for $3.50 at the front desk. While the cover of the earlier *Mail-Order Catalogue* had featured a sketch of a white woman reading, the cover of the *Bibliography* listed its contents, claiming the list as a meaningful representation in place of drawing:

Aboriginal Woman
African Women
Anthologies
Asian Women
Black American Women
Black British Women

Black Canadian Women
Caribbean Women
Children's Books
Cross-Cultural
Latin and Central American Women
Maori Women
Middle Eastern Women
Native Women
South African Women
South Asian Women
South Asian and Asian Canadian Women

The substantial *Bibliography* was bound with a heavy-duty staple at the top left corner, and the credits at the bottom of the page claim the work as a research project:

Toronto Women's Bookstore
July 1989
With the assistance of the
ONTARIO WOMEN'S DIRECTORATE
Compiled by SHARON FERNANDEZ
In collaboration with CINDY BEGGS
And the TWB Collective
TWB is a non-profit collectively-run women's book and cultural service[72]

In this work of "becoming fluent in each other's histories,"[73] who is creating the list is as important as who is on the list. While the *Mail-Order Catalogue* had not listed the names of its creators, the *Bibliography* claims its authors as a reminder to readers that the identities and ethics of the collectors always influence how collections of texts represent histories and futures.

This attention to authorship also made the *Bibliography* revolutionary in prioritizing writings by women of color who share the identities of or are allies with those about whom they write. This step toward ending appropriation became a well-known and valued practice of the Toronto Women's Bookstore that influenced bookstores throughout the movement. Six pages of books about "Asian Women" are all written and edited by Asian women authors representing a transnational reach, including Zhang Jie's *As Long as Nothing Happens, Nothing Will* (Virago Press, 1988), Mila D. Aguilar's *A Comrade Is as Precious as a Rice Seedling* (Kitchen Table: Women of Color Press, 1987),

Yuan-tsung Chen's *The Dragon's Village* (Women's Press, London, 1981), Mei-ling Jin's *Gifts from My Grandmother* (Sheba Feminist Publishers, 1985), Zhang Jie's *Love Must Not Be Forgotten* (China Books & Periodicals, 1986), and Merle Woo, Nellie Wong, and Mitsuye Yamada's *Three Asian American Writers Speak Out on Feminism* (Radical Women Publications, 1979).[74] Fernandez describes another of Makeda Silvera's books, *Silenced!* (Sister Vision Press, 1989), as a "non-fiction book which provides a forum for 10 women, aged 20 to 55, to discuss their experiences as immigrants to affluent countries to work as domestic workers in order to provide for their families still living in their native countries. They are from the English-Speaking Caribbean."[75] Even the "Children's Books" section prioritizes the authorship of children of color, including *Breakfast of Sjamboks*, a "collection of poems by Mozambican children ranging in age from 12 to 18 years," edited by Lukas Mkuti (Zimbabwe Publishing House, 1987), and *Children of Resistance: Statements from the Harare Conference on Children, Repression, and the Law in Apartheid South Africa*: "testimonies of the children interviewed in September, 1987 in Harare," edited by Victoria Brittain and Abdul S. Minty (International Defence and Aid Fund for Southern Africa, 1988).[76] This gathering of books by authors of color theorizing their own experiences takes further the bookwomen's concept of books creating context for each other. The result would change each other's lives: of Makeda Silvera's *Growing Up Black: A Resource Manual for Black Youths* (Sister Vision Press, 1989), Fernandez writes, "A manual for teenagers which covers issues of racism, school, sexuality, and the law."[77] The *Bibliography* sketched a model for bookwomen to both learn about differently racialized histories and to become allies for racial justice by making space for dialogue rather than speaking for others.

The short narrative descriptions in the *Bibliography* guide users in a reading practice. Read together in the *Bibliography*, these descriptive list entries emphasize the presence of a substantial body of work sharing histories and fostering transracial alliances. A reader sitting down to coffee with the eight-page "Native Women" section, for example, learned that Maria Campbell, with her still-influential autobiography *Half-Breed* (Formac, 1973), offered not simply an individual story but "an understanding of the Metis people and of the racism and hatred they face."[78] This short and pointed framework taught readers to understand *Half-Breed* not, as the earlier TWB catalog had identified the book, as part of "Canadian Studies," but as a challenge to the nation-state. This description guided readers to understand individual memoirs as critical analysis of systems of oppression. The authors of the *Women of Colour Bibliography* identified this significance of connecting movements across interlocking identities when they described *Enough Is Enough: Aboriginal Women Speak Out*, edited by Janet Silman (Women's Press, Toronto, 1987), as a "compilation of Native Canadian women's voices which adds to the history of the Canadian women's movement and of the Native peoples of this century";[79] and *April Raintree*, by Beatrice Culleton (Pemmican, 1985), as a "fictional account of the prejudice and ignorance in Canadian society of Indian and Metis culture."[80]

Esther Vise remembers staff discussions about the *Bibliography*; the document felt "absolutely new" in the face of what Vise describes as "the total lack of representation on the shelves of writings by women of color."[81] Lynn McClory, a bookstore board member who advocated for women's literature through her own Lexa Publishers Representatives firm for more than twenty years, remembers that after the *Bibliography*, "the section titles changed drastically at TWB." While it seemed to her that postmodernism had been in "every book title before that," McClory explains that at this exciting moment, postcolonialism came into public focus: "The bookstore reflected political change in the city generally, and was a major part of that change."[82] With the *Women of Colour Bibliography*, Fernandez and the TWB collective reshaped the entire bookstore and its influence on the feminist movement at large. The *Bibliography* incited this change, from the shelves to the staff, which would last until the bookstore closed.

When Vise joined TWB, Fernandez was the only woman of color on staff. Before the *Bibliography*, Vise remembers "big, painful events happening around hiring." The active bookstore board included feminists of color with a high profile in the community, including Stephanie Martin, from Sister Vision Press, and Anne-Marie Stewart, who worked in conflict mediation. With the support of the board, TWB hired Pauline Peters, who, Vise explains, "experienced racism within the collective and named it." In 1987 or 1988, Vise recalls, Peters was connected with the Black Women's Collective and with activist artists including musician Faith Nolan and author Dionne Brand. Peters left the bookstore, and the Black Women's Collective, responding to the racism in the bookstore collective, used their weekly newspaper to call for a boycott of the bookstore. The bookstore carried the newspaper, so the news arrived at the bookstore's doorstep with the weekly delivery. Fernandez was the only woman of color staff member during the boycott, and to Vise this seemed a trial for Fernandez, who was well connected to women of color feminist communities. For Fernandez, responding to the boycott was part of becoming allies. At the time, Fernandez explains, "especially the white feminists were very, very frightened of the word race, and any accusation of racism would paralyze them. It didn't happen at the Women's Bookstore," she proudly affirms. Instead, Fernandez and the Women's Bookstore used this struggle for accountability and dialogue to get to work on the *Bibliography* and the substantial changes on the shelves reflected in the collective. By 2007, the year my fourteen-month term with the bookstore ended and the year I interviewed Fernandez, her influence still strongly shaped the bookstore. Fernandez claimed the bookstore "as an amazing example of integration in terms of women of color issues." On a staff of ten queer-allied, lesbian, bisexual, and straight, trans and cis people, mostly people of color, I was one of three white people. The shelf sections made accountability in bookstore relationships possible by preparing book-women to understand and represent racial justice as feminism.

Across the phone line, as we talked about the Black Women's Collective boycott, Sharon Fernandez cautioned me not to "play up this kind of struggle, because, really, it's par for the course; if you want to touch on it, you must touch on it based in a very contextual way. You must understand why you would want to talk about it." We had exchanged only a few emails, and this would be our only phone conversation (so far); I wanted to reassure Fernandez of my motives. "Yes, definitely," I agreed. "I'm interested in how at the bookstore, in the way that you're talking about the relationship building, the response is different at the bookstore than it would have been in other places." "Absolutely," she replied. I wasn't digging for dirt. I was hungry for stories of struggle that white antiracist allies and women of color allies with each other survived together. What it took to be different, what the bookstore collective had already been working on, though imperfectly, was "strong communication loops, the ability to articulate truth in a certain way." Fernandez continued, "And not be frightened. It's your own racism that keeps you silent." This last resonated with me from the pages of feminist writings I had read in feminist bookstores; I felt the feminist shelf in action, and I had to know if Fernandez felt it, too. I asked, "In the response and in the daily work of TWB, do you think that TWB was creating a kind of feminist theory through the way that it put the space together with the relationships?" She did feel it: "The Women's Bookstore was creating a kind of feminist theory," she agreed, "and it is actually based in feminist theory: the ability to speak your truth and have the courage. Because 'your silence,' as Audre Lorde would say," referring to Lorde's line "your silence will not protect you."[83] Fernandez explained the connection between the shelves and bookwomen's activism: "Audre Lorde was a seminal person for us at the Women's Bookstore, and for me particularly. Her poetry exemplifies empathy and courage, and her articulation of the issues was how we also went about doing our work."[84] Looking to these texts from the shelves and to these conversations amid the shelves, I offer bookwomen's feminist shelf as a practice of alliance. As a lesbian feminist writer and white antiracist ally, I have a responsibility to document these histories of reckoning. I want to show that these moments of difficulty are the moments we need to learn from, because in them bookwomen committed to paper or to cassette tape or to memory how they were trying to understand each other, how they were educating themselves, how they were using the books on their shelves, the author events in the bookstores, and each other's words to change the way they related to each other to build feminist futures.

Around the time Fernandez and Toronto Women's Bookstore published the *Women of Colour Bibliography*, two young women who would later become managers of the store ventured into the space. Anjula Gogia had been to Mother Tongue/Femmes des Paroles, the feminist bookstore in Ottawa, where there were fewer books by women of color, and to the Vancouver Women's Bookstore, where there were sections on women of color and "Third World women's writing" but no women of color working there. "Once you get interested in women's bookstores," Gogia explained, "you'd look for other ones."[85] The bookstores transformed their visitors into activist readers seeking community. Gogia visited Streelekha, too, and emphasized the significance of the context the bookstore created: though she had seen some of the Kali for Women Press books at a well-stocked general bookstore in Delhi, Streelekha "was a combined bookstore and community space, too, it wasn't just a bookstore." When she made it to TWB, she saw sections that made an impression on her: "I remember that there was a South Asian women's section. . . . I remember there being a theory one, there was a lesbians of color one. There were definitely things in there that were quite extraordinary, because the issues around race were much more front and center." May Lui saw herself, too: "I was fascinated that there were these books that were focusing on me, and I think I read my first bell hooks around that time. Up until then it had just been white feminism for me, Gloria Steinem and Adrienne Rich, who pushed me in my own way. I actually only became politicized at that time. I wasn't political before then. So, it was exciting."[86] Through these shelves bookwomen engaged feminists of color in a practice of making activists of readers.

Bookwomen saw deep connections between the organization of the shelves and women's relationships with each other. In a cyclical conversation between shelf and selves, the Toronto bookwomen created a lesbian antiracist feminist accountability that they continued to develop, to share with readers, and to teach generations of bookwomen and bookfolk working at the bookstore. "I want to emphasize this," Fernandez urged, "the work that was done was based in a feminist ethos and value system, which is about building relationships and respecting difference. That ability to deal in a mutual way then creates the kind of integration that happens." She pointed out the leadership of the bookstore by women of color from the early 1990s until our interview, and until it closed in 2012. She described how the feminist shelf informs this interconnection. For example, Dionne Brand's influential collection of poetry *No Language Is Neutral*, published the year after the *Bibliography*, would have been shelved in multiple places that might have included Black Canadian Women, Caribbean Women, Lesbian Non-Fiction, and Poetry. "It was a little complex," Fernandez described bookwomen's theoretical practice. "We weren't creating little ghettos of you go here if you want this, no, we're part of the whole community." This system fostered visibility and validation and insisted on "respecting difference."

In our interview by phone from Ottawa, Fernandez reflected on how working at the bookstore, an institution becoming accountable to its communities, changed her: "A relational platform always creates voice. I grew by being able to be an actor in the issues of the day within my community." At the same time, she noted the difficulty of "negotiating and reconciling differences": "there's a certain level of accountability that is placed on you as the only woman of color in this place. People can try to dismiss you as being part of the white community." Resisting this simplification, Fernandez actively created alliances among women of color and with some white allies to change the bookstore: "When we stood up to the Black Women's Collective, that was a huge undertaking that I led through the support of many women of color. I stood my ground based on my own sense of right and wrong, but it was a very brave thing to do in that period. That in itself allows you to grow tremendously, because you are able to test yourself in relationship to the challenges that surround you." This relational practice, this collective attention to voice, became the signature work of the Toronto bookstore.

By the time Esther Vise left the bookstore, other women of color had come on staff, including author and now professor Mona Oikawa, artist Sandra Haar, and Vicki Moreno, who would return to run the bookstore from 2010 until it closed in 2012. Vise had been changed by this experience of justice on the shelves, in hiring, and in collective engagement. "I think it's made me a huge part of who I am," she gestured with her hands open. "It allowed me to integrate my understanding, from very early on, from a teenager, of sexism and racism and homophobia in a whole way that was not fractured. . . . On a personal level, it's provided me with some of my best friends. . . . It constantly challenged me to see the world in much broader terms than just my own experience." Sitting in office chairs amid the whirring of sleeping computers on the second floor of the Toronto Women's Bookstore after hours, we looked at each other. Vise paused, and then said, "I love this place." I think of my friends from the bookstore, how I love them deeply, how working with them and among the shelves made it possible for me to write with what I hope is a lesbian antiracist feminist love like this. I feel the vibrating thread of a connection between these stories and feminist literacies of alliance building today.

Enacting a Feminist Ethics of Dialogue (against Appropriation)

Local groups of feminist bookwomen had contributed to lesbian antiracist feminist vocabularies. In the early 1990s transnational gatherings of these bookwomen set the stage for a series of conversations that would define feminist ethics for the bookstore movement at large. Bookwomen's practice of the feminist shelf had brought them to this moment, had prepared them to articulate how their movement practices contributed to high-stakes feminist conversations against appropriation and toward alliances across racialized difference. Building on the energy of the 1988 International Feminist Book Fair, Carol Seajay made extended transborder relationships possible through the FBN. During the late 1980s and early 1990s, the FBN regularly featured interviews with and articles by feminist bookwomen, transnationally, writing with and about each other. This conversation stepped off the page at the 1990 International Feminist Book Fair in Barcelona when bookwomen gathered as panelists discussing "The Sale of Feminist Books in the 90's," with Heide Braun (Sal de Casa, Valencia, Spain), Renee Albrecht (Women's Bookstop, Hamilton, Canada), Donna Fernandez (Streelekha), a representative from Xantippe Bookshop (Amsterdam), Ximena Pizarro

(Librería Lila, Santiago), Nancy Vezner (Odegard Books, Minneapolis), a representative from Librería del donne (Milan), Farida Akhter (Narigrantha Prabartana Feminist Bookstore, Dhaka, Bangladesh), Sandi Torkildson (A Room of One's Own, Madison, Wisconsin), and Carol Seajay (FBN). The energy grew, Seajay explained, "and more booksellers were added at the last minute. There were so many booksellers on the panel that, even as quickly as we talked, there was only 20 minutes for discussion so we scheduled a follow-up meeting the next day."[87] This dialogue in print and in person documented bookwomen's development of and participation in their transnational movement. This connection built on earlier bookstore conversations about lesbian antiracism. Ultimately, the transnational network of feminist bookwomen transforming each other emphasizes that the significance of feminist bookwomen exists not within a single bookstore but within the context of a larger movement accountability. As Donna Fernandez remarked, "feminist bookshops cannot exist outside a movement that is dynamic."[88]

As part of this contribution to feminist accountability, bookstore profiles in FBN mapped the evolution of some bookwomen's lesbian antiracist feminist ethic of centering the voices of and building dialogue with historically marginalized women, an ethic that informed both organizing and literacy practices. In Auckland, New Zealand, the feminist bookstore Broadsheet Bookshop published a collection of Donna Awatere's *Maori Sovereignty* articles in order to support Maori people and to validate Maori women on Broadsheet's shelves.[89] Susana Sommer, of SAGA: Librería de la Mujer in Buenos Aires, explained her work to support books published in Argentina.[90] At the Japanese feminist bookstore Ms. Crayonhouse, founder and author, politician, and bookwoman Keiko Ochiai emphasized the importance of Japanese feminist literature.[91] While feminist bookwomen in North America read about Ochiai in the FBN, Ochiai visited New Words and wrote about the Cambridge feminist bookstore for the Japanese feminist bookstore's magazine, *Women's Eye*. At Fembooks, the feminist bookstore founded in 1994 in Taiwan and still open in 2014,[92] bookwomen, committed to feminism as dialogue, produced and supported Taiwanese women's literature. Beth Morgan noted in 1994: "Bestsellers at Fem Books include a history of the women's movement in Taiwan (written by founding members of [the Taiwanese feminist NGO] Awakening), feminist cultural criticism from foremost women writers in Taiwan, periodicals from various women's groups, and lesbian journals!"[93] Some of these bookstores centering historically marginalized, including globally marginalized non-Western, feminist literature originated as NGOs and through development policies. Feminist scholars have criticized international development projects that simplistically represent all women as the same in order to promote the misguided concept of economic progress through capitalist enterprise.[94] Just as feminist bookwomen in the United States claimed their intention to serve as revolutionaries in a capitalist system, feminist bookwomen operating through NGOs have enacted resistance to a harmful international development discourse. Interrupting the development narrative of economic progress at a 1990 International Feminist Book Fair panel in Barcelona, "Farida Akhter was adamant that Narigrantha Prabartana/The Feminist Bookstore in Bangladesh is viable and successful, not because it makes money, but because it contributes to The Movement both locally and internationally."[95] These profiles in FBN reminded bookwomen readers to see feminist relationality as their success.

In 1990, just after the Toronto bookwomen published the *Women of Colour Bibliography* and the Dhaka bookwomen opened Narigrantha Prabartana, Carol Seajay spent a warm June with the FBN building and documenting a crescendo in bookwomen's growing transnational conversations about women speaking and writing about themselves and against appropriation. In early June Seajay was in Las Vegas for the American Booksellers Association (ABA) Convention, in mid-June in Barcelona for the International Feminist Book Fair, and at the end of June in Akron, Ohio, for the National Women's Studies Association Conference. The hum of bookwomen's conversation at these summer meetings set a rhythm for new ethics for the feminist shelf. Feminist bookwomen were increasing their mainstream market influence even as they sought to undermine that market. At the Feminist Bookstore Day meetings, gathered by FBN at the ABA in Las Vegas, bookwomen reported that they were doing well financially; Seajay reported in the FBN, in a paragraph that would remind publishers of the potential sales at these stores, "Collectively, the sales of the 20+ stores gathered for the meeting exceeded five million dollars."[96] While publishing this number to build influence in the book industry, bookwomen interrupted mainstream economies by focusing not on what would sell but rather on articulating an ethic of collecting materials together in order to learn to be allies with each other. The explicitly antiracist feminist Toronto Women's Bookstore reported the highest sales.[97] In the early 1990s, bookwomen challenged each other to reflect on survival embodied not just in sales but in accountability to their communities.

At this point, the FBN was also working to hold other movement organizations accountable to working toward alliances across racialized difference. Another, younger, literary advocacy organization gathered at ABA was the Lambda Book Report, now the Lambda Literary Organization. The 1990 ABA saw the second annual Lamda Literary Awards, affectionately known as the Lammys. The then gay and lesbian focus of the Lammys recognized the FBN for its support of lesbian and gay literature. Seajay reported, "I was honored to be given the Lambda Book Report Publisher's Service Award for FBN. FBN is a body of good work and I'm both proud of it and pleased to see the magazine recognized."[98] The FBN, a reflection of the North American feminist bookstore movement in transnational conversation, was always clearly a lesbian feminist production. In his Lambda Literary Award comments, Deacon Maccubbin recognized the role of FBN in "enhancing the viability of the gay, lesbian, and feminist book market,"[99] thus acknowledging both the lesbian identity of feminism for FBN and the journal's influence on publishing. At the same time, Seajay commented that "the Lammys were their own contradictory selves" as the FBN documented the need for what would become the growing LGBTQ movement to learn from lesbian antiracist feminist accountability. Seajay referred readers to Ruthann Robson's "excellent analysis" in the *Gay Community News*. Robson called out the Lammys for prioritizing "palatable" writing published by "multinational corporations" and for "the overwhelming tendency towards selecting whiteness" for award recipients and ceremony attendees.[100] In her acceptance speech, Seajay emphasized that lesbian feminism must also be antiracist, and the mutual education on the pages of FBN enacted strategies and standards for this practice. Seajay remarked at the ceremony, "Our goal was to tell the truth about women's lives—lesbian lives, Black and Asian and Native women's lives, poor and working class women's lives, old women's lives—all our lives. And, to see that truth into print and then into the hands of the women whose lives would be radically changed by it."[101] In fact, the very coverage of this awards ceremony in FBN offered a further effort to change bookwomen's reading practices and, in turn, their relationships.

At the same ceremony, the Triangle Group intended to confer on Audre Lorde the Bill Whitehead Memorial Award; Lorde refused the award by sending a speech Jewelle Gomez read in her absence. Lorde allowed FBN, and, a year later, *Callaloo*, to reprint the speech. Lorde urged the Lambda Book Report to use the money of the award to work toward supporting queer writers of color: "There are Lesbian and Gay writers of Color in this country articulating in their work questions and positions which must be heard if we are to survive into the 21st century. How many of these Lesbian and Gay writers of Color are included in the Triangle Group? Supported or encouraged by its individual members?" To fully share power on the award selection committees, in publishing, in funding, Lorde pointed out, would be to build "upon the creative use of differences in all our survivals."[102] Through sharing critical analyses of the Lammys (and other literary events), bookwomen honed and shared their activist practice of the feminist shelf.

After attending the Lambda Awards celebration, feminist bookwomen at the ABA meeting in Las Vegas gathered to talk about a paper Carol Seajay had sent to each of them in advance. Seajay was scheduled to table at the National Women's Studies Association (NWSA) meeting later that summer, and the NWSA had sent out to everyone selling materials at the conference a paper titled "A Position Paper on Indian Spiritual Abuse," by activist scholar Andrea Smith, representing both the NWSA Indigenous and Native American Task Force and the NWSA Women of Color Caucus.[103] Seeing that the paper explicitly addressed feminist bookwomen, Seajay copied the document and shared it with feminist bookwomen to read and discuss in depth at the Feminist Bookstore Meeting at the ABA Convention.[104] This conversation circled back to the discussions about voice appropriation and Indigenous authorship of the 1988 Montreal International Feminist Book Fair; bookwomen were developing their vocabulary on authorship and intellectual sovereignty.[105]

Precipitated by the popularity of writings by Lynn Andrews, a white woman purporting to offer access to "Indian spirituality," Smith's call identified the "new age craze" as a "spiritual and cultural genocide for the Indian people." Because Indigenous survival through ongoing colonialism depended on what Smith called "the spiritual bonds that keep us together," white appropriation of spiritual practices results in mainstream publishers' prioritization of white authors over Indigenous authors and, thus, a diminished capacity for future generations of Indigenous peoples to draw on their own ancestors' words and works. Smith offers this account:

> Today, many white writers, such as Lynn Andrews, are continuing the practice of destroying Indian spirituality. They trivialize Native American practices so that they lose their spiritual force. They have the white privilege and power to make themselves heard at the expense of Native Americans. Consumers like what many of these writers have to tell

them and do not want to be concerned with the facts presented by Native Americans. Our voices are silenced as a result. Consequently, the younger generations of Indians who are trying to find their way back to the Old Ways become hopelessly lost in this morass of consumerist spirituality.[106]

Noting the "disturbing silence among white feminists on the issue of Indian spiritual abuse," Smith emphasized that distribution of white authors' appropriations contributed to the genocide: "Even those who do not engage in these practices, sell or promote these practices in their bookstores, record stores, or magazines. Even at the 1989 NWSA Conference, Lynn Andrews books were displayed in a prominent area." Smith spoke directly to feminist bookwomen: "Feminist book and record stores must stop selling these products. All women who call themselves feminists should denounce exploitative practices wherever they see them." This call directly addressed a tension between what is still perceived as "freedom of speech" and an ethic of making space for dialogue, rather than appropriation, across difference: "The promotion of this material," Smith explained, "is destroying the freedom of speech for Native Americans by ensuring that our voices will never be heard."[107] By emphasizing in her final sentence that "our spirituality is not for sale," Smith intended "sale" as in "selling out" and was seeking to hold space on shelves for sales of Indigenous authors.[108] This use of the term "sale" reached the heart of feminist bookwomen's practice of interrupting market goals of increasing sales with feminist ethics of sharing the word. "Sales" at feminist bookstores were part of the movement; the ethics bookwomen had been generating over decades called them to return to their commitment as both revolutionaries in a capitalist system and accountable to their communities.

While the promised NWSA conversation about Indian spiritual abuse seems to have not taken place ("The issue, FBN was told, was 'overshadowed by everything else'—'everything else' being the Women of Color Caucus walking out over the firing of the first woman of color hired in NWSA's 13+year history"), feminist bookwomen discussed the paper in depth in their meetings at the ABA.[109] The tone of the feminist bookstore meeting was one of grappling with feminist ethics, of learning together. Bookwomen shared with each other their understandings, based on their own experiences, relationships, research, and readings of Smith's position paper. Together the bookwomen understood, Seajay reported, that white appropriation of Indian spirituality, which they acknowledged was itself a term referring to a complex web of heterogeneous spiritual traditions, simplifies and depoliticizes that spirituality: "Native spirituality does not and *cannot* exist separate from community life," Seajay wrote. "But 'new-age' versions of 'Indian spirituality' offer a spirituality divorced from community."[110] This concept was perhaps not news to feminist bookwomen who sought to build vital community context for each feminist book on their shelves. This practice of feminist shelf curation evolved further through this conversation as bookwomen mapped these relationships: "We talked about the ways that commercialized spirituality takes people away from the idea of community and helps people feel comfortable with the idea that they need only 'solve' their own problems—and how this encourages isolation rather than activism—as if 'personal problems' (such as rape or incest) can be 'solved' without addressing the conditions in a society that make incest common. This idea and practice is the opposite of Indian spirituality which is community-based and includes responsibility to community." Insisting on the politics of authorship accountable to community, then, was a major lesson of and through feminist bookstores in the 1980s and early 1990s.

Bookwomen offered narratives from their bookstores of how their own lapses in supporting Indigenous spiritual and intellectual sovereignty had resulted in severe rifts. In order to build the movement and to effectively influence publishers to value Indigenous feminist authors, some feminist bookwomen recognized their responsibility to understand and respond, through action, to Smith's position paper. Much of what they shared demonstrated the obstacles white privilege posed to bookwomen's alliances with Indigenous feminists. One bookwoman reported that a previous group of staff, since gone after "significant staff changes," had created a "rift in her community" by inviting Lynn Andrews for a reading at their bookstore five years earlier, in 1985. "Native women still don't come into the store," the bookwoman acknowledged. "It isn't a resource for Native women. It's been very painful."[111] As a result of these conversations, bookwomen of Full Circle Books "removed Lynn Andrews books from their shelves" and decided to host a community discussion about Indian spiritual abuse. They wrote in to FBN to share a caution to white bookwomen attempting the same: "By the end of the evening the group realized that the conversation had been dominated by white women, despite the presence of women of color and Native American women. 'In other words,' said Full Circle coowner Mary

Morell, 'We (white women) didn't let them talk. Hopefully we've learned to keep our mouths shut and listen!'"[112] These narratives offered cautionary tales to other white bookwomen on preparing for transracial dialogues and indicated the difficulties that an entirely white staff, not having internalized this work, would have in developing dialogues on racial justice. Bookwomen reminded each other at the ABA meeting, "Your customers will look as much alike as your staff."[113] In order to support a racially diverse staff, bookwomen needed to engage in self-education.

The feminist shelf offered both motivation and tools for creating such dialogues. Choosing not to stock Lynn Andrews titles—books already banished from the shelves at Full Circle, the Toronto Women's Bookstore, and other bookstores—was not, Seajay emphasized, censorship but rather a necessary refining of bookwomen's ethical relationality: "Several booksellers spoke powerfully about the difference between censorship and buying decisions. . . . We make buying decisions every day and buy the work we want to promote and don't buy things that are in conflict with our values. All of us have limited resources and it's our responsibility to use our resources in the most useful ways possible."[114] Since feminist bookwomen, through the FBN, emphasized their ordering and sales power in order to influence what kinds of books publishers promoted, they saw that selling white appropriations of Indian spirituality in the bookstores sent a message to the publishers that they need not publish Indigenous women's own writings about spirituality. Seajay summarized: "Native people's reality gets driven out of the media which favors a sanitized version that doesn't include uncomfortable realities. Selling these books contributes to the problem."[115] Bookwomen talked about their work shaping readers' understandings of books on the shelf, of "inform[ing] their buying decisions before, rather than after, they have gone through a decision-making process." Bookwomen could, they imagined, in a continuing extension of their work with bibliographies, newsletters, shelf sections, and collection development, shift reading practices through the bookstore, thus changing how people read even when they are not at the bookstore. This education seemed vital, "especially given ready availability of many of the worst titles." Bookwomen took action to create tools for this education. One bookwoman had recently heard Chrystos read her poem on the subject, "Shame On: There Are Many Forms of Genocide & This Is One"; bookwomen asked Press Gang Publishers to print a broadside of the poem, and both the publishers and Chrystos agreed with excitement.[116] Feminist bookwomen pledged to post the broadside in their stores.[117] Other tools of the feminist shelf included buying more copies of "quality books," "giving prime space to small press books from Native-owned publishing companies," and shelving these titles face out.[118] Bookwomen at the Toronto Women's Bookstore had partnered with Native communities, including a council of elders, and conducted their own research to develop a formal collection policy on Indigenous materials.[119] Drawing on such partnerships, and indeed on conversations like this one, to shape their collections further developed feminist bookwomen's alliance and accountability practices through the feminist shelf.

Where Did You Get This Book?

These conversations should call our attention to the *where* of where we get (acquire) or *get* (understand) our reading material. How do spaces of access and distribution support or suppress vital authors and shape how we read and understand each other? At their best, feminist bookwomen in transnational dialogue created feminist bookstores as ethical literary spaces that wove a context for women's writing and a training in feminist accountability in reading and relationship-building practices. Feminist bookwomen's practice of the feminist shelf suggests that the shape of each space (physical or virtual) where we encounter literature will either limit or challenge our understandings of that text and each other. While some individual feminist bookwomen are committed to continuing an antiracist feminist ethic, the loss of the full movement and FBN has resulted in a loss of formal accountability to each other as well as of peer training on antiracism and communication across difference. Feminist bookwomen in the force of their full movement worked together to articulate on the pages of the FBN an ethic of lesbian feminist racial justice through the literacy they created on their shelves. Feminist bookwomen practicing the feminist shelf in the late 1980s and early 1990s offer a powerful example of what's possible, producing themselves and their readers as lesbian antiracist feminist readers. Where did you *get* this book?

FIVE

ECONOMICS AND
ANTIRACIST ALLIANCES
1993–2003

On another hot summer day in Austin, I was still sweating from my walk to get us iced coffees when Matt Richardson arrived at my office tucked away on the ground floor of the University of Texas main library. We sat together in stuffed chairs around a small table, as we had before in our collaborations to create the Black Queer Studies Collection. Richardson, Black LGBTQ studies scholar and a faculty member on our shared campus, had agreed to talk with me about his experiences in the 1990s book industry working at Kitchen Table: Women of Color Press. Before the mid-1990s, he pointed out, the feminist "bookstores . . . were crucial to trying to figure out what was an antiracist feminist politic."[1] In my previous chapters I have described how the bookstores functioned in this way; in this chapter I offer an explanation of how the intervening years erased this vital work from our public feminist memories.

The 1980s and 1990s saw feminist bookstore leadership by lesbian and feminist bookwomen of color, including Niobe Erebor at A Woman's Place in Portland, Oregon; Sharon Fernandez at the Toronto Women's Bookstore (TWB); and Faye Williams and Cassandra Burton at Sisterspace and Books, the women of color bookstore they founded in Washington, DC.[2] While A Woman's Place closed in 1990, by 2007, Sisterspace and Books and TWB were still defined by the leadership of women of color; both bookstores have since closed. This leadership documents a history of feminist bookwomen—lesbian women of color and white antiracist allies—using their shelves, their collectives, and the pages of the *Feminist Bookstore News* (FBN) to develop a fluency in the multiple histories of women of color in order to build alliances across racialized difference. In turn, this work toward lesbian antiracist feminism shaped reading and alliance practices in the larger feminist movement. In the mid-1990s, facing drastic market changes in publishing and bookselling, white bookwomen turned to influence the book industry and left less space for accountability around racial justice in feminist bookstores. The gains in bookstore advocacy were substantial, the losses in antiracist feminism devastating.

In this chapter I return to the US context because the focus of US bookwomen turned inward with industry threats of the 1990s. As I described in chapter 4, bookwomen had honed their skills through a transnational network. By the mid-1990s, the US context seemed unique, in that having over one hundred US feminist bookstores, the most in any single country, enabled US bookwomen to imagine leveraging their numbers for larger public advocacy in a turbulent period of national publishing and bookselling. Starting with a scintillating revolt in 1993, independent booksellers claimed the American Booksellers Association (ABA) as their own, kicked out the chains, sold the ABA Convention, and used the money to launch both a marketing campaign and years of lawsuits against bookstore chains and big publishers for trade violations that endangered independents and what they called the "diversity" of literature. This was a heroic last-ditch effort to stem the tide of capitalist claims to literature. Feminist bookwomen acted as leaders in this resistance, and they sought both to end big bookstore and megapublisher pressures on publishing and to educate their readers about how publishing industry practices affect what we get to read.

In this chapter I grapple with the cost of the strategy US bookwomen chose to use to save feminist bookstores. In the 1990s bookwomen made the future of feminist bookstores about a women's economy rather than about their own well-developed practice of dialogue about and evolution of feminist movement ethics, theories, and practices with a vital focus on lesbian antiracist feminism. Turning to influence a largely white and straight publishing and bookselling industry, white bookwomen continued to talk about but did not build structures for accountability to or alliances with women of color as they had done in the past. In chapter 3 I wrote about how feminist bookwomen strategized to hold each other accountable to lesbian antiracism; in chapter 4 I described how this accountability became the feminist shelf, work that shaped reading and relational practices toward an alliance-based feminism. This history offers a framework of feminist accountability built by bookwomen, a framework I use here to both value and question the activism of bookwomen in the mid- to late 1990s.

Tracing the work of feminist bookwomen at two major ABA conventions and the lawsuits they initiated, tracking the ongoing articulations of antiracist feminism by feminist bookwomen in this same period, and reading the growing influence of FBN, I examine how feminist bookwomen endangered their legacy as a central site of the formulation of lesbian antiracist feminism, a central site for making possible and sustaining "books that tell the truth about women's lives" (including, I hope, this one).[3] As the identity of the national movement shifted, locally bookwomen continued to draw on the feminist shelf practices of lesbian antiracism and feminist accountability developed by the feminist bookstore movement: women at Old Wives' Tales drafted principles of unity, women at the Toronto Women's Bookstore created classes for women of color only, and women at In Other Words fostered community-based women's studies education. This continuing work in a faltering movement constitutes bookwomen's own standard for movement accountability.

With this chapter, I honor feminist bookwomen. Their work requires me to offer a critique they made possible. As racial justice feminist theorist Aimee Carillo Rowe promises, "To frame a critique as a resource and a gift is to divest from zero-sum logic and invest in a more possible feminism."[4] In this chapter I both document bookwomen's substantial successes at a moment when it seemed bookwomen could save independent publishing and use bookwomen's own histories to suggest that movements measure success not in survival but in accountability and legacy.[5] Reading the vibrant struggles of the late 1990s claims our foundations for an accountable lesbian antiracist feminist future.

"Our Survival Depends upon Having an Accountability around Race and Racism"

The ABA Convention of 1993 offered a deceptively air-conditioned oasis in the steamy Miami summer. In truth, this convention floor would become the field of a battle that had been brewing for years in US bookselling, and feminist bookwomen were stirring an intentional storm. The introduction to the special convention issue of the FBN set the stage:

Greetings to all of you who are picking up FBN for the first time at the ABA. FBN is the trade magazine for the Women-In-Print movement. It's read by booksellers, publishers, and everyone who cares passionately about books that tell the truth about women's lives. . . .

Turn to page 31 for Convention Watch 93, FBN's short-course on getting around the Convention floor and all of the convention related events. Don't miss ABA's annual Membership Meeting on Sunday afternoon at 4:00. ABA's fence-sitting position vis-à-vis the war between independent bookstores and chain stores has not done anything to cheer its (largely independent) bookstore membership. Many see this year's meeting as a chance to knock ABA off that fence and into action for independent bookstores.[6]

Carol Seajay crafted this introduction to stake feminist bookwomen's claim to the publishing industry with their well-read journal and to emphasize bookwomen's use of this influence to advocate for "books that tell the truth about women's lives." This issue of FBN itself continued to wield that influence. The looming presence of chain bookstores and the changes in publishing they wrought threatened these very books. The shift between the two FBN paragraphs above shows the dual identity feminist bookwomen bore at this point, both as feminists engaging in literary activism for the movement and as independent booksellers fighting for survival in a changing industry. In 1993, feminist bookwomen and feminist publishers shared a fear that their gains over more than the past twenty years might be erased. The FBN offered readers a guide to the action, the "war between independent bookstores and chain stores," and the goal of the independents to "knock ABA off that fence and into action."

How did this sense of industry changes—as Toronto bookwoman Anjula Gogia put it, facing "this train that's going to mow you down"[7]—affect the conversation that feminist bookwomen were having about antiracism? "It shut it down," says Matt Richardson.[8] The challenge bookwomen faced was both to maintain their long-standing accountability to feminist communities and to attempt to influence the book industry in order to keep the bookstores open. Richardson, representing Kitchen Table: Women of Color Press at his first ABA Convention in 1993, remembered the conversation among feminist publishers as "let's talk about our survival, and not, our survival depends upon having an accountability around race and racism." For Kitchen Table: Women of Color Press, Richardson pointed out, "If we suddenly lost an antiracist focus, then our publishing would be in danger. Our economic survival depended upon being clear about that in ways that theirs didn't." The largely white group of feminist bookwomen attempting to shape activism at the ABA had collaborated with and learned with women of color; they had participated in and shaped conversations about lesbian antiracist feminism. In this moment, these bookwomen focused on mainstream activism, perhaps not fully realizing that without feminist accountability and lesbian antiracism, economic survival would be an empty success.

In the week leading up to the 1993 ABA Convention, feminist bookwomen met in Miami for Feminist Bookstore Days, their regular pre-ABA gathering to connect in person and strategize their advocacy at the convention and throughout the year. At this Feminist Bookstore Days gathering, the bookwomen finalized their decision to officially declare themselves the Feminist Bookstore Network, an advocacy strategy they had been considering for years. Dawn Lundy Martin, editorial assistant and then assistant editor of FBN in the mid-1990s, remembers the potential influence of the list of the more than one hundred feminist bookstore members in the Network: "You could see from the list the impact on the imagination of the folks who were running the ABA in a way that each of them individually wouldn't."[9] The Network members immediately put the name to use and changed the ABA forever. Jennie Boyd Bull, owner of the feminist 31st Street Bookstore in Baltimore, spoke out in the ABA membership meeting and made the motion, soon approved, that required the ABA to, as the FBN reported, "develop and implement, in 1993, a national promotional and advertising campaign in major media educating the American public about the necessity and importance of independent and specialty bookstores to the preservation of free speech, First Amendment rights, and diversity in the United States."[10] Recording this motion in the FBN provided a public record and additional pressure on the ABA board, whose members read the FBN. Feminist Bookstore Network members' public language at the ABA, then, had a double impact, both spoken and written. The ABA accepted Bull's motion, which ultimately resulted in the ABA selling the annual convention in part to fund the marketing campaign; this serious action indicated the ABA's new commitment to independent bookstores.[11] The still-viable ABA-funded national program, called BookSense and then IndieBound, ran national ad campaigns for independent bookstores, promoted a monthly list of books recommended by independent booksellers, hosted websites for member stores, and coordinated transferable gift certificates among member stores across the nation, thus offering independent bookstores resources and technical support previously available only to large bookstores.

This was immediately a battle of rhetoric and, thus, of political ethics. Joining forces with independent booksellers at large required bookwomen to water down the vocabularies they had so carefully built. ABA president Chuck Robinson, quoted in *Publishers Weekly* (PW), described the new ABA promotional campaign as focusing on "the First Amendment, access to information and the importance of bookstores in the community."[12] While Jennie Boyd Bull had also attempted to feed the ABA the line that independent bookstores support "diversity in the United States," already a compromise of feminist bookwomen's explicit commitment to lesbian transracial alliances, the ABA brass, such as it was, took up the even less specific First Amendment argument. As I described in chapter 4, bookwomen had grappled with the ways First Amendment arguments were at odds with supporting historically marginalized authors not valued by a straight white publishing industry and they had articulated an ethic against appropriative authorship. Feminist accountability, then, was not supported by "First Amendment" arguments that could be leveraged, for example, to support white women authors writing Indigenous people's histories at the expense of Indigenous feminist authors. The vague concepts of "diversity" and the "First Amendment" seemed a version of feminist bookwomen's commitments no longer recognizable to their former selves.

In 1993, Dawn Lundy Martin attended her first ABA Convention. She was then a graduate student in creative writing and the editorial assistant of FBN. She is now a poet activist and professor of creative writing. Martin mapped a "trajectory of disconnect" in the rhetoric from the bookstores to the ABA national campaigns. She saw a disconnect between the group of "predominantly middle-aged, or approaching middle-age, white women" and the fact that "the voices of the very women they seek to represent often weren't present": "there were very few younger women" and "very few women of color in the room."[13] Martin saw the activism of feminist bookwomen and knew, informed in part by the words and shelves of bookwomen themselves, that fulfilling feminist accountability would require substantial change: "Those moments at FBN were the first moments that planted the seeds for the question of what is the feminist future going to look like. . . . What strategies, institutions, mechanisms, outreach, possibilities do we need to have in place in order for younger women to be as invested in feminism as their foremothers? . . . Why isn't this group more racially diverse? Those kinds of questions were starting to formulate in my imagination in that moment." As a new participant in the feminist bookstore movement, and as a graduate student whose "other life was deeply invested in fairly experimental poetry," Martin could step back from the fever pitch of real economic panic in the book industry to connect to movement strategies the bookwomen themselves had developed that could create new foundations for collaboration. Martin's life of feminist and racial justice arts-based work after FBN points out that ongoing projects are taking up and remaking pieces of the feminist ethics and relationships bookwomen shaped: Martin worked at the Astraea Foundation for Lesbian Justice, which now prioritizes lesbian antiracist advocacy worldwide; she cofounded the Third Wave Foundation, an organization that supports young women in creating social justice movements; and she cocreated the Black Took Collective, an experimental Black poetry performance project that grew out of Cave Canem, the well-known center for Black poets and writers.

Widening the growing distance between bookwomen's activist foundations and accountable futures was the wave of professionalization sweeping feminist movement institutions, and bookstores and publishers were no different. Notes from a Feminist Bookstore Days gathering at the ABA Convention record a reflection by Mev Miller, literacy activist and feminist bookwoman of Amazon Bookstore, founded in 1970 in Minneapolis: "'Comm. Ctr' [Community center] doesn't come as naturally as it used to, now that we're (all) more professional."[14] Barbara Smith, cofounder with Audre Lorde and publisher of Kitchen Table: Women of Color Press, observed of feminist publishers at the 1993 ABA that "women come to these meetings now as professional publishers, not as feminist activists who see publishing as a means to inspire other women and strengthen the movement."[15] This professionalization convinced mainstream bookpeople like ABA president Mark Avin Domnitz to see bookwomen as a force to be reckoned with,[16] and it cost feminist organizers their connection with principles they had created.

All of this happened in a climate of fear. On May 29th, booksellers on the convention floor received a pamphlet reminding them not to discuss prices or discounts. Titled "ABA Guidelines for Antitrust Compliance," booksellers promptly renamed the pamphlet, printed on pink paper, the Pink Sheet. The Pink Sheet warned booksellers that "any meeting among competitors," indeed, like meetings of the Feminist Bookstore Network, "has the potential to lead to antitrust violations, whether intentional or inadvertent," and included a list of issues of which to avoid discussion. Seajay explained in the FBN, "The Pink Sheet, although *perhaps* not intended to inhibit discussion, was quoted and used to stop almost every reference to price and discount or to limit other legitimate bookseller discussion in almost every ABA event I attended."[17] While the flyer factually reported legal restrictions on a commodity trade, it is significant that the ABA chose to distribute it in 1993, the year when independent bookpeople's organizing culminated in their demand for ABA action against chain bookstore special discounts and price fixing with big publishers. The flyer indicated that the ABA was more inclined to support business than advocacy, but the independents would soon turn the tide.

Audrey May, owner of Meristem feminist bookstore in Memphis, took the floor at the ABA membership meeting, and her widely reported speech both claimed a public reputation for the Feminist Bookstore Network and set the tone for independent bookstore demands of the ABA. Both ABA *Newswire* and PW reported on May's speech. "The role of small independents is crucial," said May emotionally. "Feminist bookstores are fighting for survival. They're fighting for their lives. And now we're being told that we have to look over our shoulders and wonder if we can even talk about the issues. And yet if we don't talk about them, how do we survive?"[18] If the bookstores could not legally collaborate to circumvent and survive despite the suspect trade practices of the chains, the ABA would have to take an activist role on the independent bookstores' behalf.

At this transformative ABA Convention, Dawn Lundy Martin represented FBN alongside Carol Seajay on the convention floor. She noticed the book industry drama happening behind the scenes, not visible to broader feminist or at-large publics. Martin says of the Miami ABA: "What I remember most is getting an education and beginning to understand what the particular predicament was for independent bookstores. I had lived in towns where . . . independent bookstores to me seemed to be thriving. I think that this was the cusp where things really started to shift towards the larger chains in a way that felt potentially devastating for independent bookstores, and I was just coming into this knowledge."[19] Feminist bookwomen at the ABA were facing the oncoming train, and they had some success in redirecting it. Changes in the ABA, for example, resulted in its executive director Bernie Rath finally pointing out that best-seller status is purchased, since "major publishers pay money to obtain favorable positions in chain bookstores for their leading titles," so the best-seller lists, in turn, "perpetuate industry hyperbole." And Sandy Torkildson of A Room of One's Own, in Madison, became the first feminist bookseller to join the ABA board.[20]

By involving younger feminists like Martin in the bookstore movement, bookwomen sought to share their perspective and continue the work. As Martin points out, though, there were not enough younger people or people of color in the conversation to successfully envision a feminist future. She saw the bookwomen replicating past models while, she explains, "I was already thinking about what is the next stage of the movement going to look like." While Martin and other writers for *Aché: The Bay Area's Black Lesbian Magazine* "were engaging in this question of the historical significance of different feminist presses, like Kitchen Table Press," they were also wondering "if this was still a kind of salient and significant way of putting our work out into the world." Ultimately, Martin says of the organizing at the ABA Convention, "as radical as it was, it also felt pretty mainstream."[21] As I have described in the previous chapters, feminist bookwomen had laid the foundation for a vibrant feminist literature and transnational conversations about lesbian antiracist feminism. Faced with a marketization of literature, bookwomen's vocabularies seemed mainstream as they attempted to—and did—influence mainstream institutions. As the ABA pledged to use some proceeds from the sale of the ABA Convention to take legal action to purge the book market of illegal practices, the Feminist Bookstore Network served as a primary commentator on and public advocate for these suits. At the same time, conversations within feminist bookstores about how to advocate for lesbian antiracism and feminist accountability imagined a different pathway to feminist futures.

"The Most Progressive Women in Publishing"

The ABA had spent the year gearing up for the lawsuits they had promised in 1993. In the days before what would be the "biggest ABA convention ever,"[22] ABA 1994 in Los Angeles, publishers, including FBN, set up tables on the convention floor. St. Martin's, Houghton Mifflin, Penguin USA, Rutledge Hill, and Hugh Lauter Levin had hoisted their signs above their linoleum square footage and laid out their books. The day before the event, the ABA announced its first legal campaign on behalf of independents: the ABA was suing these five major publishers. The five were stuck: already set up on the floor of a convention that was suing them. A cartoon in PW described the publishers' position: under a welcome banner at a podium reading "ABA Los Angeles 1994," an announcer tells his audience, "And it's wonderful to greet you all—booksellers, agents, publishers, authors, defendants."[23] Outgoing ABA president Chuck Robinson quipped in response to attacks on ABA's timing, "No one gave us notice that they were engaging in illegal activity."[24] The anger of large trade publishers was balanced by independent bookpeople's appreciation during the first ever ABA Town Meeting, an informal conversation between members and board members. Jim Milliot of PW reported, "Because of the suit, the tone was so friendly and jovial that at least one observer called it a 'love-in.'"[25] As usual, the Feminist Bookstore Network positioned itself at the center of the meeting and the advocacy for independents. Theresa Corrigan of Lioness Bookstore in Sacramento, California, opened the meeting with a Feminist Bookstore Network statement, presenting the Network as an active agent and concerted group within the ABA. The FBN reported, "Feminist Bookstore Network Committee member Theresa Corrigan opened the meeting by reading the resolution FB-Net passed on Friday commending the ABA for taking this stand."[26] The statement inserts official documentation of the Feminist Bookstore Network's support for the ABA's lawsuit: "Your continued vigilance on behalf of the financial welfare of independent / specialty bookstores is greatly appreciated by our 140 bookstore member network throughout the U.S. and Canada."[27]

Representatives from twenty-five feminist bookstores attended the ABA Convention, including bookwomen from the new bookstore In Other Words, which had opened in Portland in 1993.[28] Carol Seajay had just promoted Dawn Lundy Martin to assistant editor of FBN.[29] While the energy of the previous ABA Convention, 1993 in Miami, had no doubt driven up attendance numbers at ABA 1994, Martin remembers that in Los Angeles the Network faced the challenge of how to use their growing power within the ABA:

> It's on the one hand a desire to be inside the establishment so that we could have an impact in the world of literature, and on the other hand it felt like we can in some ways be a part of the conversation, now what do we do? It was a much harder conversation in Los Angeles because it wasn't as fresh. . . . So then the hard work begins of really figuring out, strategically and as a big group of women, which is never an easy task, what do we do next.[30]

The 1990s brought a new challenge to bookwomen's intention, from their beginnings, to be revolutionaries in a capitalist system. Feminist bookwomen at the ABA Convention documented and narrated the industry advocacy under way in an attempt to educate each other and their readers about the importance of independent bookstores for feminist literature. At the bookstores, feminist bookwomen used various strategies, from professionalism to politicization, to attempt economic survival in support of feminist literature.

The July/August 1994 FBN explained that the lawsuit described, among other charges, publisher strategies intended to narrow the range of books promoted to the public: "The suit . . . alleges that the defendants routinely make payments to bookstore chains so that the chains will advertise and aggressively promote the publishers' books and place them in favorable locations in their stores, but that these payments are not proportionally available to all booksellers."[31] Not only did these publishers allegedly pay chain stores to promote specific books, the payments for this promotion may have kept chain bookstores in business, generating an artificial market that closed independent bookstores and threatened the feminist literary public sphere. The FBN continued:

> To illustrate the significance of these illegal discounts, [ABA executive director] Bernie Rath noted that Barnes and Noble had said in 1993 it had received $11 million in coop money from publishers [to prominently display publishers' books], an amount that is substantially more than the chain's profits. Many industry observers believe that the illegal discounts and other advantages that the chains are receiving are, essentially, shoring up their bottom lines and keeping them open. . . . Why would publishers want to do this?

Seajay offered an explanation: "Perhaps because the chains, collectively, owe publishers so much money that corporate publishers' survival could be jeopardized if those debts became uncollectible."[32] That is, these publishers were gambling in hopes of big profits with chain bookstores, and, in the meantime, were paying chain bookstores' bills.[33] In this system, only big publishers could afford to pay for promotion of their books, and independents, particularly movement-based bookstores, which often eschewed coop money as against their ethics of promoting meaningful writing, saw little of this money.

While major publishers bet on chain bookstores, feminist publishers and authors used the essential tools created by bookwomen to sustain feminist literature. The FBN, which was, as Seajay pointed out in the 1993 ABA issue, widely distributed, created visibility for feminist literature and independent presses in each issue with lists of books "From Our Presses," as well as from university presses and mainstream publishers. At the 1993 ABA Convention, Matt Richardson had proposed to Carol Seajay and Dawn Lundy Martin that the FBN gather a list of feminist press books "by/for and about women of color." Just before the 1994 ABA Convention, the FBN published the first installment of the "Woman of Color Booklist," which included books from Arte Público Press, Aunt Lute Books, Calyx Books, Firebrand Books, Kitchen Table Press, Press Gang Publishers, and Seal Press;[34] the next issue featured the second installment, with books from African American Images, Between the Lines, Bilingual Press, Black Angels Press, Cleis Press, Coach House Press, The Crossing Press, Eighth Mountain Press, The Feminist Press at CUNY, Gynergy Books, Harlem River Press, ISM Press, Naiad Press, Serpent's Tail/High Risk Books, South End Press, Three Continents Press, Woman in the Moon, and Women's Press, Canada.[35] In the introduction to the list, Seajay and Martin recount Richardson's request based on his travels to "otherwise excellent bookstores, with books from mainstream presses by and about women of color," where bookwomen "seemed not to know about many of the excellent books published by feminist and other independent small presses. Perhaps if we compiled a list and circulated it . . ."[36] For Richardson, this request was strategic. He meant the list both "to push them so that their antiracism was being reflected in the ways that they presented and documented the books on the pages of the *Feminist Bookstore News*" and to share news of vital books: "Having that information in the *Feminist Bookstore News* meant that we would all know what was coming out."[37] The FBN was, significantly, still a vital and well-read tool for sharing lesbian antiracist feminist thought.

The power of who was publishing the work, as feminist bookwomen discussed, is also important. Martha Ayim of the Women's Press in Toronto explained, "Even if white women's presses publish a lot of work by women of color, the fact that they don't hire women of color ignores questions of appropriation and power. We need to ask, who is evaluating and editing women of color's words?" For Ayim, women of color "having access to publishing (mostly through women of color presses and through some previously white women's presses who began to take racism seriously, as is the case with Women's Press) has played a crucial role in our becoming a force that can no longer be ignored. When the writings of women of color are shared, so many people are inspired by it and recognize themselves in it."[38] The FBN provided one site for promoting visibility of women of color in publishing. The FBN was still mostly written by white women involved in conversations about lesbian antiracist feminism. While Martin brought her perspective as a Black lesbian literary activist working with FBN, Seajay shaped and wrote most of the publication. Seajay's work was a vital service and impressive accomplishment, and Martin's involvement demonstrated the difference having feminists of color in editorial positions makes, as Ayim points out. Martin recalls thinking:

> This is a publication organized around both gender identity, a kind of political way of thinking about gender, and, in a lot of cases, sexual orientation. Identity was a really big part of this work. It was how these folks were thinking about books and about publishing and about the feminist movement. So, it was always surprising to me when this group of folks needed to be nudged towards a particular kind of racializing of that, of thinking about how race impacts that experience, how race impacts the experience of women, of queer women, and how those texts might be different from other texts and how they might need to be highlighted and conceptualized in different ways. . . . I remember there kind of being a constant sense that these were probably the most progressive women in publishing, yet, still they need to be in some ways reminded or reeducated.[39]

Martin qualified this statement by pointing out that bookwomen "were also feeling this impending doom from the threat of giant bookstore chains and the discounts they were getting. They had no idea that Amazon was coming, for instance. But they felt something." Richardson's suggestion for and Martin's commitment to the list Martin and Seajay created made it possible for the FBN to sustain, at the same time, the conversation about lesbian antiracist feminism.

While at the bookstores the struggle to maintain movement accountability could seem contingent on the higher stakes of economic survival, accountability to the movement ultimately defined the difference between chain and feminist bookstores and publishers. Bookwomen at Old Wives' Tales in the early 1990s were working with a consultant to draft a "Principles of Unity" document; many feminist bookstores followed the movement-based practice of creating principles of unity to outline bookwomen's ethical and political commitments to each other and their communities. During the six-month process of developing the document, the San Francisco bookwomen clarified how they talked about lesbian antiracist feminism. In early versions of the document, the women wrote: "We are committed to multicultural(ism?)," and "We acknowledge the needs of women of color and lesbians."[40] In the final version, these two pieces evolved into a proactive statement: "We desire a world in which all people are honored. We want this store to counter the negation of women of color and lesbians through the books we carry, resources we commit to, programs and productions we choose to engage in and the training and work we do among ourselves to build our awareness and skills." Literature was vital to a commitment to antiracist lesbian feminism, the Old Wives' Tales women argued in another principle on the list: "We believe in the printed word and the importance of books as 'packages' of values and ideas."[41] Perhaps counterintuitively, the women also "committed to running the store within the legal and business framework demanded by this capitalist society."[42] Feminist bookwomen faced this double bind in their daily bookstore work as well as on the national stage: their work focused on creating social change through supporting the writings of women, particularly lesbians and all feminist women of color, and their organizational structure was shaped by the oppressive system that had institutionalized the racism, sexism, and homophobia they resisted.

In the early 1990s at Old Wives' Tales, the resistance looked like events with Makeda Silvera, author and publisher at Sister Vision, the Black lesbian publisher in Toronto; Shani Mootoo;[43] Chrystos; Red Jordan Arobateau; and others.[44] It looked like ordering in Leslie Feinberg's out-of-print *Stone Butch Blues* from anywhere they could find it (like Avon, Kentucky),[45] like commemorating "lost lives on this 50th anniversary of Hiroshima," like cosponsoring events with the Women's Buildings.[46] At a reading by Chrystos, on an August night in 1995, Victoria Alegría Rosales bought a copy of *Fugitive Colors* and left it for Chrystos to sign. Two nights later, she read at the bookstore's Open Michelle Night, then stopped by the front desk to pick up her signed copy of Chrystos's poetry. Rosales explained in a letter to the Old Wives' Tales staff that the white woman working at the desk did not believe she had paid for it and accused her of attempting to steal the book.[47] Marieka Brown, Twyla Stark, and Tricia Lambie of Old Wives' Tales responded with a letter: "Your letter has acted as a catalyst for discussion about some of our policies. . . . Some of our policies may appear inconsistent as we struggle with walking the line between creating a space that operates on trust and the reality of running a business."[48] The relationships between women of color and white women, and among women of color in the feminist movement, were alive daily at feminist bookstores in that twilight space between movement organization and business.

The Toronto Women's Bookstore was one site where bookwomen were redefining movement accountability as central to economic survival in the changing 1990s. In 1993 the bookstore nearly went bankrupt; committed bookwoman and activist Esther Vise stepped in to run the store as a volunteer for nearly a year and to develop a new manager-led staff team with a nonprofit board.[49] Anjula Gogia remembers that it was public knowledge that the store "was coming out of a very deep crisis" in response to "a call from the community to keep it open."[50] Gogia had known "very key women of color who had really worked hard there at the end of the 1980s to make that space more accessible to women of color. I had seen women of color working there when I hadn't seen that at the other feminist bookstores in Ottawa and Vancouver." Having worked with the Toronto South Asian arts and cultural festival Desh Pardesh,[51] Gogia knew Sharon Fernandez as "a South Asian lesbian artist who had really struggled at the Women's Bookstore to make it more inclusive to women of color, so I had heard about those struggles, definitely." The public nature of the difficult process of working toward racial justice within the organization built community trust in the bookstore that reinforced community support of the bookstore. For Gogia as a reader, then staff member, and then manager, TWB "felt like this amazing space where I could have all my politics in place. Even working at Amnesty [International] I felt like there was half of me there, because the antiracist antioppression politics were not in the organization." As I describe in chapter 4, Fernandez's *Women of Colour Bibliography* provided a blueprint for bookstore sections that prioritized and made visible the voices of authors of color; the force of this vision carried out at the bookstore in turn influenced local readers through sale of the list, through the bookstore shelf section titles, and through the book titles themselves. Ultimately, the list and the work of Fernandez, Vise, and others transformed the bookstore into a space run by women of color. This leadership forged strong connections between Toronto activist communities and the bookstore and laid the foundation for alliances to face the 1995 opening of Chapters and the 1997 opening of Indigo, the two major Canadian bookstore chains that would later merge.

Increasing corporatization of the publishing industry meant less opportunity to advocate within the industry; Gogia saw this from Canada even as the ABA attempted advocacy through lawsuits in the United States. For TWB, the limits of big publishing offered the opportunity to refocus activist attention back to the movement. Both Richardson and Gogia remember big publishers becoming even bigger in the 1990s; for example, HarperCollins acquired Avon, Penguin acquired Putnam, Simon and Schuster acquired Macmillan. These growing businesses, Gogia confirms, meant that publishers' representatives could no longer influence publishers with information from the bookstores. Resisting this trend, the Toronto Women's Bookstore refocused on carrying and promoting books by women of color and lesbians. The bookwomen worked to rebuild connections with First Nations women through events, including a book launch with Patricia Monture-Angus, and recruiting community advisory members, including Sandra Laronde.[52] Through such daily work in movement accountability, bookwomen's advocacy at a few feminist bookstores created an ethical practice that would outlast the bookstores themselves, along with what proved to be the temporary— though extraordinary—success of the ABA lawsuits against the five major publishers and their collaboration with chain bookstores to mainstream and homogenize literature on an international scale.

After filing several unsuccessful motions to dismiss the lawsuit, including one memorable claim that the ABA's suit was founded on "emotional reactions to competitive changes in the marketplace,"[53] all of the publishers settled with ABA between 1995 and 1996. The ABA had added Random House to the ongoing litigation in 1996, singled out by ABA because while other big publishers outside the suit appeared to offer the same discounts to large and small bookstores, Random House showed "a four-point spread between larger and smaller customers."[54] The eventual settlement with Random House, then the largest publisher in the nation, was the most significant in providing an impetus for other publishers, not named in the suit, to reform prior to legal action. According to a PW interview with ABA executive director Bernie Rath, "since the ABA began its lawsuit against five publishers in 1994, many publishers have adopted flatter discount schedules that will benefit booksellers."[55] Jim Milliot of PW explained in 1996, "Although no publisher admitted to any wrongdoing in settling with the

ABA, the terms of the agreements, as well as the fact that the ABA received approximately $2 million in court costs, suggest that the weight of evidence favored the association."[56] Carol Seajay similarly concluded that the lawsuit's outcome "validates independent booksellers' concerns that unfair and illegal discounts have routinely been available to a wide variety of competitors."[57] The weight of this evidence, then, indicated that mainstream publishers did offer illegal deals to chain stores.

Penguin was the only publisher whose settlement included monitoring, and Penguin's violation of the settlement terms just a year later, in 1997, indicated the fleeting victory of any single legal action. For returning to favoring chain bookstores with deeper discounts, Penguin was required by the courts to pay out $25 million to independent bookstores.[58] Seajay saw and articulated on the pages of the FBN the continuing danger that backroom industry deals posed to independent bookstores: "This is the first time that *any* remuneration has been made to independent booksellers for the enormous damage done to independents nationwide by illegal and unfair trade practices that favor the chains and superchains. In just this one case, Penguin acknowledges that, over six years, it gave $77M in discounts to a handful of accounts, presumably superchains. Independents will get a $25M settlement. Superchains and independents did roughly the same amount of business during the period covered, but the chains got $77M— three times as much as the indies."[59] Penguin-watch ended in 2000, and the fragility of these agreements suggests that resisting homogenization of literature by corporate publishing requires constant vigilance of advocates, while a true advocacy for movement-based literature requires movement-based ethics of the kind attempted at the feminist bookstores working on innovative lesbian antiracist feminism. The distance between these two efforts indicates the tension between economic success and supporting the "books that tell the truth about women's lives."

"No One Else Would Have Done a Book Launch for That Book"

High on the settlements with publishers in the mid-1990s, the ABA and its team of lawyers next sued chain bookstores for their part in illegal deals. In 1998, Seajay emphasized to readers of the FBN that the suit was big news: "The really exciting news this issue is the lawsuit ABA filed against mega-chains Borders and Barnes & Noble." She explained the suit "alleges that these chains solicit and receive all kinds of preferential—and illegal—discounts and deals that are not available to independent bookstores, that the chains' market saturation strategies are fueled in significant part by these secret and illegal deals, and that driving independent stores out of business is an intentional and long-held strategy."[60] I want to convey some of the energy and excitement in the industry around this lawsuit, because the reading public seemed not to notice the roiling waters. This oversight was perhaps due in no small part to newspapers like the *New York Times* reporting, for example, the Random House and Bantam Doubleday Dell merger on the front page while covering the ABA lawsuit inside and briefly. Seajay suspected this was because "the *Times* has recently sold its Web site links to Barnes & Noble" and the chain bookstores purchased major advertising space in the *Times*. She also pointed to what she called a "class issue" in the industry: "Publishing books is Important; selling them is beneath contempt."[61] Indeed, even the feminist press perpetuated the image of booksellers as simply making visible what was already available while covering over the advocacy of feminist bookwomen.

Lesbian author and activist Karla Jay claimed publicly on the pages of *Ms.* that lesbian authors who made the mainstream owed at least part of their success to chain bookstores: "For those of us who have been mainstreamed, whether by the major publishers or by the more successful feminist presses, success can be attributed in part to integration into the large chains of bookstores that dominate the U.S. bookselling scene." "Lesbian authors," Jay explained, "are flattered or awed to see their titles on the shelves in a Waldenbooks or B. Dalton." Of course, Jay pointed out, big bookstores take on "only the more 'accessible' titles"; this emphasis on what mainstream audiences find already accessible underscores the significance of feminist bookstore events, sections, and newsletters geared toward educating readers to read, perhaps especially, what they might assume is inaccessible. Jay conceded, "Many lesbian books are exiled twice—once from mainstream publishers and then from larger stores. Should the feminist stores fail, such books would have few outlets at all. Then feminist publishers would have to change their marketing strategy or go out of business."[62] That is, chain bookstores seemed to at once allow big success for a few lesbian authors, while lesbian authors at large and the feminist publishers who supported them relied on feminist bookstores for survival. Jay's possible future where "feminist stores fail" seems a perpetuation of the fantasy of an economic marketplace where any well-run bookstore might succeed.

That a cultural critic and lesbian feminist of Jay's stature would publicly consider chain bookstores as a feminist tool in the 1990s indicates that indeed many feminist bookstore readers bought into the fantasy that a market demand for feminist and lesbian literature would ensure its availability at chain bookstores. In chapter 3 I documented the ways feminist bookwomen were instrumental from the early 1980s in proving the existence of such a market to publishers who would not otherwise believe readers existed for books by lesbians, feminists, women of color, and all of these identities at once. Now, just a decade and a half later, authors and readers still did not seem to understand feminist bookwomen's advocacy within the publishing industry or what was happening to their movement information institutions.

The ABA lawsuit against Barnes & Noble and Borders proposed to prove that not all booksellers are the same, and the plaintiffs argued for a distinction based on the purpose and advocacy of the booksellers. Ann Christophersen, cofounder of the Chicago feminist bookstore Women & Children First, served as one of twenty-six coplaintiffs with the ABA, and she explained to FBN how the suit was particularly important to feminist bookstores and to women's literature: "Feminist publishers and bookstores were starting to make a wide range of women's voices available to readers. The consolidation of retail outlets into a few major chains seriously threatens that important work. Independents are being driven out of business, buying (and consequently publishing) decisions are being made by fewer (probably not feminist) people, and publishers are being undermined by high levels of returned, unsold books. This lawsuit is about reclaiming the conditions that make a rich and diverse literature possible."[63] Christophersen pointed out how unfitting it is to use a business model for bookselling. She explained that consolidation, by definition, closes down "diverse literatures," even as she did not commit to a movement-based definition of "diverse." The ABA's fifty-page legal complaint took up this general sense of "diversity," as it laid out the danger of the impending monopoly: "Because of the large and growing volumes of books purchased by the national chains, they have considerable and steadily growing influence concerning the books that are published, those that are promoted, and those that remain on the shelves for more than a brief period. The concentration of this power in two national chains—each of which imposes a single corporate mission and philosophy on more than one thousand stores across the nation—threatens to undermine the diversity of book retailing in this country and the product choices ultimately available to customers."[64] The ABA articulated the influence of the national chains and warned against the "single corporate mission and philosophy" espoused across the nation through the chain structure, as opposed to independent bookstores, each of which has its own mission, focus, and specialty.

In Toronto, May Lui remembers the mid-1990s as a time when the major Canadian chains Chapters and Indigo came into full swing. Juggling the bills at the Toronto Women's Bookstore, Lui explains that she did not at first see the connection between the chain bookstores and TWB's money trouble. But then she realized, "If people were shopping here more then we'd have more, and no one can compete with 40% off."[65] This was a sea change in how feminist readers related to books and created a false visibility of feminist literature at chains. Lui remembers that Gogia "used to order ten, or twenty over a period of a certain number of months, of Toni Morrison's new hardcover." Chapters offered these big name sellers, by "someone who was well known enough to not simply be known as a feminist author anymore or a woman or a woman of color," at deep discounts. These major sales had kept feminist bookstores afloat, and now they were developing new strategies.

At the Toronto Women's Bookstore the survival strategy was twofold, to address both the economics and the movement ethics. Gogia realized: "We need to do something to make money; just being a feminist bookstore isn't going to cut it," so she sought out course book business with faculty at the University of Toronto, and their orders created a sustaining stream of revenue. At the same time, she knew the community reputation of the bookstore needed rebuilding, so "we definitely started to be responsive to the changing nature of feminist and antiracist politics." TWB bookwomen created new sections, including trans, antiracist, critical race theory, environmental, and disability studies sections. They hired Rachel James, an activist and artist, as well as a past coordinator of Desh Pardesh, to create an events series for the twenty-fifth anniversary of the bookstore in 1998. Gogia remembers, "She managed to organize an event with Alice Walker, which put us back on the map." Walker's publisher, Random House, decided where Walker would read, but TWB had an in with Gabrielle Schriber, a sales representative at Random House who, according to Gogia, "believed in feminist bookstores and who was a lesbian herself and . . . fought internally for the Women's Bookstore to get that event." There were over five hundred people at the event. Lui explains the contradictions feminist bookwomen were struggling with as chain bookstores and publishers redefined books as products: "There's a unique thing about books in terms of what books represent, what they are, how they teach people. . . . Books are quite powerful or have that potential, and you can't just turn them into a product. But they did."

This battle over the cultural significance and power of books is perhaps at the center of the industry wars and the feminist movement changes in the 1990s. Reporters at PW mapped the changes Lui described. Businesspeople at chain bookstores insisted, indirectly, that readers were not sophisticated enough to miss unpublished, unavailable books at the chains. They masked this argument by praising customers' taste for the books chosen for them. In 1992, Tom Simon, then Waldenbooks' vice-president of merchandising for specialty stores, told PW's Joseph Barbato, "Customers don't know the difference between a small and a big publisher. They want good books. And that's the sort of book that will do best in the superstore: a good book. I can't emphasize that enough."[66] Vincent Altruda, president of Borders stores worldwide, brought Simon's concept of the "good book" to the present-day superstore by claiming he would work "with vendors to find out what customers want."[67] That is, the "vendors" will tell us what the "good books" are, the books we "customers" want. The language here sets up a clear capitalist relationship in which the "customer" is assumed to be the homogenous, anonymous, and gullible reading public. We all want the same "good book." Nora Rawlinson, then PW's editor-in-chief, wrote an editorial that corroborated this reading of chain bookstores' threat to literature: "We think the spate of chain superstore openings could have an impact reaching all the way back to the publishing decision. The growth of large independent bookstores has supported the enormous diversity represented by American publishing. If the superstores reduce the number of independents, publishers will be forced to rely on just a few routes for getting their books to market—a potential stranglehold."[68] The beginnings of that stranglehold looked deceptively like full shelves at chain bookstores.

If chain bookstores were looking for record sales of just a few "good books," what gave Karla Jay the sense that "accessible" lesbian literature was going mainstream? She saw the books on the shelves. Seajay pointed out that the brimming shelves in the chains were the writing on the wall. These books were "wallpaper—books that are used for decoration, books that make stores look full and rich but that can't possibly sell. And then, when the books begin to get dusty, they're returned and, inevitably, replaced with newer, fresher titles that will also, in turn, get dusty and turn into returns."[69] While the publishers thus "helped to finance the super-chains' expansion with new-branch store discounts, sweetheart deals and very extended credit terms," they were the ones stuck with the price tag of chain bookstores' expansion. In his PW article about books as wallpaper, Jim Milliot quoted extensively from Seajay's analysis in FBN; Seajay was on the forefront of helping even the industry understand what was happening. Chain bookstores stocked "accessible" feminist books (certainly not the books on the "Women of Color Booklist" and other influential FBN lists) as a business strategy, not as a lasting commitment.

Meanwhile, feminist bookstores stocked their critical sections with books vital to social justice and taught readers how to read and to love them. When Shani Mootoo's *Cereus Blooms at Night* was nominated for the Canadian national Giller Prize, the mainstream McClelland and Stewart bought the book from its original publisher, the feminist, antiracist, and lesbian Press Gang Publishers. Gogia saw feminist bookstores sustaining these small and feminist press beginnings that proved the market for national prizes and big publishers: "Dionne Brand, we sold more copies of her books than probably most bookstores did, so we created a market. We promoted the works by women of color, by lesbian writers, Shani Mootoo, we sold a ton of her books because we championed and we hand-sold tons of books that the big bookstores didn't care about. [. . .] We were very committed to feminist books, to books written by women of color, and we hand-sold a lot of them." When I was working at the Toronto Women's Bookstore in 2006, just before this interview with Gogia, a woman came into the bookstore looking for Brand's new *What We All Long For* (Knopf Canada, 2005); she had gone to Chapters first, but she said the people there didn't know who Dionne Brand was. Feminist bookwomen studied and knew the field of feminist literature.

Antiracist feminist bookwomen in particular learned how to read and talk about the vital importance of books by lesbians and feminists of color. Just before my interview with Gogia, University of Toronto faculty member Patty McGillicutty had just ordered for her class twenty-four copies of a book Gogia mentioned as an example of feminist bookstore advocacy:

I remember one of the early launches we did was for a book called *There Were Times That I Thought I Was Crazy* by Vanessa Alleyne [Sister Vision, 1996], and it's a book about a Black Canadian woman and her story of surviving incest, published by SisterVision Press. That's a pretty good example of a book that probably no other bookstore sold that we have continued to sell dozens and dozens of copies of ten years after its publication, and we did the launch for it. So, yeah, you could argue that if we and other feminist bookstores weren't there, there wouldn't be a market to sell these books that are about looking at issues around violence against women, Black women's lives, stories of incest, that we were the places that would do that and create the information. No one else would have done a book launch for that book.[70]

Ten years after that launch, she pointed out, "There still aren't a lot of books for Black women dealing with issues around incest and child sexual abuse." Feminist bookwomen had spent more than two decades collectively building an understanding of the vital interconnections between racial justice, feminism, and lesbian feminism. Bookwomen mapped this understanding in their bookstores with shelf titles, events, and newsletters profiling books. A few bookwomen enacted this practice by building alliances across racialized difference in their communities and collectives in order to build multiracial staffs that shifted power within the bookstore. Chain bookstores were not interested in movement reading practices, but their prices lulled many feminists into forgetting that feminist bookstores were never just bookstores. The Feminist Bookstore Network, too, contributed to this forgetting as they began to use market-based language to urge readers to activist buying.

In 1996 the Network sought to generate an economic boost for feminist bookstores by creating the well-received *Feminist Bookstores' Catalog*, published annually each December. In addition to encouraging readers to buy books, T-shirts, and calendars at their local feminist bookstores, through the *Catalog* bookwomen attempted to educate readers about industry pressures and support feminist literature. In the first issue, the Network women reproduced the language of the ABA lawsuit:

> Even as we send this catalog off to you, the book industry is undergoing a tremendous change—from being a community-based network of independent and specialty bookstores to one that is increasingly dominated by chain bookstores and discounters.
>
> If we are to have a diversity of ideas and images available to us as readers, then we need many different kinds of bookstores, not just a few national chains, to make the widest range of books available to the reading public.

Over the next few years the book-buying public will vote with its book-dollars for the kinds of bookstores and the range of ideas that will be available in the decades to come.

We encourage you to use your shopping power to vote—as often as you can—for feminist and other independent bookstores.[71]

The language of feminist bookstore advocacy had changed significantly since the founding documents, described in chapter 1, that claimed the bookstores as community centers and women's places. The Network now seemed to assume that readers understood the struggle for survival as one of economics and marketing savvy. It was proving difficult to be "revolutionaries in a capitalist system" in the 1990s, and the *Catalog*'s commitment in its beginnings to support all independent bookstores, not just feminist bookstores, meant that editors did not emphasize the work of movement-based bookstores. The *Catalog* included thirty pages of books with twenty-seven different subheadings to guide readers and buyers. The sections, like the space of the bookstores, informed how readers understood the titles; for example, the Network continued feminist bookwomen's long-standing commitment to lesbian visibility and lesbian feminism with sections that included lesbian literature, lesbian video, and lesbian nonfiction; one section highlighted National Jewish Book Month; other sections were based either on genre (poetry, essays, art, and gift books) or on general content (making change, women's lives, women and work). Works by women of color appeared throughout the catalog, but there were no regular sections highlighting the writings of women of color.

The *Catalog* seemed an effective way to build customer allegiances to feminist bookstores. At TWB, Anjula Gogia remembered ordering and distributing "thousands" of the catalogs, and TWB bookwomen also stocked everything that was in the *Catalog*. From feminist bookstores renewing their memberships in the Feminist Bookstore Network (a requirement in order to be included in the list of feminist bookstores at the back of each *Catalog*), bookwomen responded to a questionnaire asking what they wanted from and liked best about the Network. In addition to support and information, topping the list was the *Catalog* itself. One bookwoman said she appreciated "The Catalog! + watching my customers' eyes light up when they see it. The credibility and recognition it provides us from the industry as a whole."[72] The first *Catalog* in 1996 listed one hundred feminist bookstores in the United States and fifteen in Canada. About a third of them had opened in the late 1980s or early 1990s;[73] the Network was still growing. The *Catalog* supported this movement by offering to supply "further information about promoting feminist, lesbian, and gay books" when requested by mail.[74] By the late 1990s, the Network was having trouble collecting dues to sustain its three publications: the *Catalog*, the newsletter *Hot Flashes*, which shared information among feminist bookwomen, and the larger professional project the *Feminist Bookstore News*.[75]

In 2001 the ABA lawsuit against Borders and Barnes & Noble ended in a settlement. The focus on industry practices ultimately cost the independent bookstores the different future they might have had with a focus on books as packages of values, as the Old Wives' Tales women framed it in their principles of unity. ABA had spent $18 million on the suit, and the settlement awarded them $4.7 million, enough to "keep the light on on behalf of our members," said ABA president Neal Coonerty.[76] The ABA press release claimed that the "scrutiny brought by the suit" revealed corrupt practices in the past, but that "in great degree, the industry has been reformed." While the settlement was unusual in that it did not restrict ABA's right to sue over illegal trade practices in the future, the ABA had not made back the millions it had spent on the suits thus far, so the right to file future litigation was an empty concession. The suits against the publishers and the booksellers generated exciting hope in the industry in the 1990s and redefined the central message of the Feminist Bookstore Network away from the antiracist lesbian feminist work of individual bookstores during that time. This was perhaps the risk of advocating from the inside. As Lui put it, "maybe compared to other industries, the book industry is slightly more progressive than others, but I don't think you can really go that far, because it's dominated by a white intelligentsia, and you can only go so far when that's your basis."[77] In Toronto, Lui and Gogia had joined an independent bookstore advocacy group called the Bookstore Specialists, but they took turns attending meetings: "It became not so pleasant to go," Lui explained, "because the race analysis was not so good." This insight into local organizing also offers a sense of what organizing within the ABA was like for feminist bookwomen; working on the inside of mainstream independent bookselling meant giving up a critical race consciousness. While at some individual feminist bookstores a conversation about the future of antiracist feminism and the role of feminist literature continued, this dialogue no longer carried the force of the movement.

"Promoting Lesbian Ideals in the Community"

In 1999, bookwomen at the Minneapolis feminist Amazon Bookstore sued Amazon.com for trademark infringement on their name. A close reading of coverage of this struggle reveals industry anxiety about the influence of feminist bookwomen, in the words of the Amazon.com lawyers, "promoting lesbian ideals in the community." Through advocacy in ABA suits against big publishers and chain bookstores, bookwomen had attempted to make space in the increasingly profit-oriented book industry for independent bookstores' survival. Breakthrough conversations about racial justice strategies in and through feminist bookstores documented the pull of bookwomen's movement ethics toward community accountability. Along the way, readers in the bookstore, as indicated by Karla Jay and reinforced by the language of the *Catalog*, seemed to have the impression that the battle over literature was merely about where they should spend their money. At some feminist bookstores in the late twentieth century, local bookwomen, building on decades of development of these "lesbian ideals," continued to move toward lesbian antiracist feminism. Feminist bookstore spaces had been vital because bookwomen and their communities had constantly contested and redefined "lesbian ideals," a model of difficult alliance building that was unlike the mythical easy "community" of which Amazon.com told its customers they were becoming a part.

Amazon Bookstore, one of the two first feminist bookstores, had opened in 1970 in Minneapolis. Twenty-four years later, Amazon.com opened online. "Patrons ordered books from Amazon.com, thinking they were supporting the feminist bookseller. Vendors called [Amazon Bookstore] to offer deep discounts, then lowered the discounts when they discovered they were not dealing with Amazon.com. Sales plummeted."[78] The lawsuit lasted just a year before the tactics of Amazon.com lawyers coerced Amazon feminists into a settlement. While Amazon feminists refused to answer questions on the stand about their sexual orientation, Amazon.com lawyer Paul Weller "defended this line of questioning by saying, 'I think . . . it's important for the jury to know, for example, whether the people who work in this bookstore have a particular sexual orientation [and how the bookstore represents itself].'"[79] Though Amazon.com now funds the Lambda Literary Foundation's annual Writers Retreat for Emerging LGBTQ Voices,[80] the lesbian-baiting strategy they used to shut down the Amazon Bookstore lawsuit suggests this funding is a PR effort. Even in its early days, Amazon.com used some of the tactics of independent bookstores to create a façade of a welcoming "community" that masked an underbelly of manipulating publishers in exchange for shipping status and searchability on the website.[81] The book industry still talks like a movement and behaves like a for-profit market.

Feminist bookwomen in their constant work on alliance building learned to read and to support books by women different from themselves; even when white bookwomen did not apply racial justice to their own workplaces, they sometimes successfully advocated for literature by women of color. The fact that this victory is partial points to the work in feminism that is still left undone, work necessary to imagining our futures. Lesbian antiracist feminist literature makes possible this imagining; as Gloria Anzaldúa wrote of her own literary activism, "Nothing happens in the 'real' world unless it first happens in the images in our heads."[82] Amazon.com actively worked against feminist literature, and thus feminist futures, by furthering the epidemic of what Lui described as turning books "into a product" while attempting to convince its customers it was doing the very thing it was not doing, creating community. A PW piece described Jeff Bezos starting the company with a studied approach to making profits. Bezos was a Wall Street executive in 1994 when he heard "that Web usage was growing by 2300% per year. He immediately sat down and drew up a list of the twenty best products to sell online. Books topped the list, in large part due to the vast number of titles available."[83] With the company launch in 1995, Bezos set out to "compete with traditional bookstores" by simulating what he called "a virtual community." This profit-oriented community that Bezos simulated focused on "customer-to-customer interaction" without the vital bookseller and publisher interaction that feminist bookwomen had sustained.

Instead, the relationship between Amazon.com and publishers was contentious and skewed to benefit Amazon.com's bottom line. While Bezos touted "the vast number of titles available," he used "availability" as a threat to effectively censor publishers who would not (or could not) agree to Amazon .com's terms. Amazon.com had two distinct methods of forcing publishers' hands on terms that could compromise or even shut down small publishers. In 1998, Seajay asked readers of the FBN, "Is anyone else watching Amazon.com's Advantage program?" The Advantage program requested small presses "to provide books at 55% discount, postage paid, and on consignment." Seajay noted that "every independent bookstore" would love these terms "but can't get" them because the small publishers that mattered to feminist bookstores could not afford to offer these terms or because big publishers refused to offer them. Amazon.com, however, threatened inaccessibility to ensure dream terms. If the publishers agreed to the terms, they would get a "slightly better listing in the database—'usually ships in 1–2 days' instead of the dreaded categorization 'hard to get, usually ships in 4–6 weeks' (even if the title is available at Amazon's major supplier)."[84] That is, the shipping designation depended on Amazon.com's profits rather than on the real-time accessibility of the book on order. Until 2004, Amazon.com had used major book wholesaler Ingram to fulfill its orders. In 2004, Amazon.com ended its relationship with Ingram to deal with publishers directly. By this time, the influence of Amazon.com meant the company could name its terms, and it did: the online bookseller required publishers to offer them a 52 percent discount, deeper than the industry standard of 40 percent. In addition, Amazon.com asked many publishers to "pony up a 5% co-op fee for advertising."[85] Jim Milliot reported that "publishers that decline to take part could lose their partnership status, which would subject them to such changes as Amazon not selling their books at a discount and not having their titles 'surface' in various merchandising and advertising programs. Amazon also *may turn off the search options to publishers' books*, making it possible to find a title only when the correct name of the book or the ISBN is entered."[86] Amazon.com controlled the visibility of books not only to Amazon.com shoppers but also to publishers and readers who use the site for reference. "Dennis Johnson, owner of Melville House, said Amazon's proposal isn't co-op but 'blackmail. What they are saying is pay up or disappear.' . . . [His] concern is that if Amazon limits the way his titles appear on the site, they will lose visibility in the entire marketplace. Johnson, and nearly every other publisher contacted by PW, said Amazon's database has become an important source of bibliographic information about books for the public and the industry."[87] Perhaps not surprisingly, these practices make clear that Amazon.com is motivated not by community but by profits.

The differences between Amazon.com and feminist bookwomen's literary activism should indicate to readers that the availability of, and the tools to read and talk about, literature that makes us better allies, that makes our lives possible, requires advocacy. In 2005 I sat down at Café Mundi in Austin with author Sharon Bridgforth. She described how feminist bookstores were a vital part of the production cycle of feminist literature. The survival of literature, Bridgforth explained, requires "the community, the independent artist who's noncommercial, the independent publishers, and the independent booksellers." Bridgforth, a Black lesbian activist feminist artist and author, said, "The feminist bookstore is the specific place that I fit. I also live in a lot of other communities, so those are critical, too, but when it comes down to where is the book going to be shelved? Nine times out of ten it's going to be at the feminist bookstore."[88] This emphasis on visibility, on having a place to "fit," was central to Bridgforth's early experiences as a writer and feminist bookstore reader. She grew up in Los Angeles, where the feminist bookstore, Sisterhood, was located in a largely white part of the segregated city. Despite the segregation, Bridgforth found the bookstore one day on her way to get coffee, "and it just, literally, rocked my world, changed my life. . . . I found all those great writers, . . . at that time Alice Walker was really pushing Zora Neale Hurston, I had never heard of either one of them." She also found Audre Lorde on those shelves, along with flyers for local performance poets who inspired her to her own work.

Later, living in Austin, Bridgforth started a relationship with Book-Woman. She explained, "The feminist bookseller has a lot of power, and . . . for me, I've benefited greatly. Susan [Post, owner of BookWoman] . . . was instrumental in having the Lambda Literary Foundation pay attention to me and to RedBone Press, and I ended up winning a Lammy, and she was there with her partner. And before I got published, she would tell publishers about me, she was advocating." Bridgforth's the bull-jean stories won the Lammy for Best Small Press Book in 1998. Lisa C. Moore's RedBone Press has published Black lesbian and gay authors since its first book, does your mama know? An Anthology of Black Lesbian Coming Out Stories, a collection that included Bridgforth, in 1997. Feminist bookstores provided important public space in this system of feminist literary production, keeping books like the bull-jean stories on the shelves. Sharon Bridgforth remembered, "When the bull-jean stories came out, it was featured in there [FBN], and that made a big difference for us with sales. And even just validating what it is that we were doing as something that they should pay attention to."

Esther Vise at the Toronto Women's Bookstore pointed out that buying for feminist bookstores was curating a feminist reading practice, emphasizing what readers "should pay attention to" and learn from. Her own buying decisions were informed by discussions in the 1980s around appropriation and not stocking books by white women writing as Indigenous women. She also remembered Anjula Gogia's impressive skills at antiracist feminist buying: "paying attention to what customers were asking for, paying attention to political movements, and really responding." The bookstore was a place for difficult conversation. For example, TWB stocked *Good Girls/Bad Girls: Sex Trade Workers and Feminists Face to Face*, by Laurie Bell and the Ontario Public Interest Group, Toronto Chapter (Women's Press, 1987), and Pat Califia's writings; "the bookstore was a place where those books needed to be carried, and at the same time not to carry other books that you could get elsewhere and that reinforced sexist, racist, and mainstream views." While Amazon.com's stock was limited only by the terms publishers would agree to, feminist bookstores' stock offered an argument and challenged its readers to engage in a difficult community practice.

In their defense against the feminist Amazon Bookstore suit, Amazon .com lawyers distinctly, and, likely purposefully, misunderstood "lesbian ideals" as a sinister influence in Bezos's claim to free market business. I argue that feminist bookwomen's "lesbian ideals" focused on supporting and building readership for feminist literature that would generate difficult and necessary conversations about lesbian antiracist feminist accountability within the movement; publishers, authors, and readers depended on those lesbian ideals. The language required of the lawsuit against Amazon.com further reframed bookwomen's work. For this suit to work in legal terms, the bookwomen and their lawyers had to argue publicly that Amazon.com and the feminist Amazon Bookstore were, as Seajay put it, "in the same business."[89] This framing further diminished bookwomen's activist commitments. In the 1970s, 1980s, and 1990s, feminist bookwomen had built a movement around gathering and creating new reading practices for lesbian antiracist feminist literature that, in turn, changed how feminists related to and loved each other. Here in the late 1990s, feminist bookwomen attempting to influence mainstream publishing and bookselling identified themselves as savvy independent booksellers; this new professional identity erased public memory of their vibrant history of necessary movement-based activism.

With only a handful of feminist bookstores left in North America, individual feminist bookstores today are doing localized work that is both connected to and painfully distant from the vibrant histories of a transnational feminist bookstore movement in which bookwomen worked to hold each other accountable and to evolve a feminist bookstore practice. In 1998, Melissa Kesler Gilbert taught a capstone course at Portland State University in partnership with the Portland feminist bookstore In Other Words, which had opened in 1993. In this first of many collaborations, students created an oral history of In Other Words. For Gilbert this history making engages students in thinking about feminist organizing: "Each term my students grasp onto the history of the bookstore as a place to ground themselves. . . . It also helps them to recognize how effective an individual woman can be in making a difference as well as the power of a feminist collective, of women working together."[90] This kind of education about feminist history and present was core to the founding vision of In Other Words, which, according to its mission statement, uses "education to improve and enhance the lives of women by"

★ Presenting positive images of women
★ Highlighting the historical and contemporary accomplishments of women in all spheres of social and cultural life
★ Providing a forum for dialogue and debate
★ Providing opportunities to increase awareness and understanding of the diverse experiences of women
★ Showcasing new scholarship by and about women for communities that don't have easy access to this information[91]

Founding member and Portland State University women's studies faculty member Johanna Brenner explained that feminist bookstores are spaces continuing movement theorizing and practice, "being a place for dialogue and discussion for the things that feminists are trying to figure out—complex questions."[92] The bookstore events and shelves created a kind of syllabus for feminist dialogue where, for example, local Portland contributors to *This Bridge We Call Home: Radical Visions for Transformation*, edited by Gloria Anzaldúa and AnaLouise Keating (Aunt Lute, 2002) gathered to read at a book launch at In Other Words in 2002. Brenner pointed out that feminist readers find out about the feminist canon and new books at the bookstores where "people like Dorothy Allison could get read, because some of her stuff gets distributed, *Bastard Out of Carolina* got on the bestseller list, but a lot of her essays and stuff haven't. And it's where people find out about them."

The specifically antiracist feminist educational vision at the Toronto Women's Bookstore built movement practice by teaching bookstore staff and readers about the importance of women of color-only space and supporting new writers. In 1998, Rachel James created a series of courses at the bookstore. May Lui remembers that Yvonne Bobb-Smith, a University of Toronto faculty member and feminist racial justice organizer, taught the first course, "Caribbean Women's Writing." "What happened," Lui recalled, "was we either reserved half the spots for women of color or we didn't and found that the first class was enough of a mixture that there were a few white women basically hijacking the agenda."[93] With feedback from Bobb-Smith, the bookwomen "ran another course, the exact same course with her again on a different day and made it just for women of color." This decision to create a space dedicated to peer education and conversation among women of color also required staff education about why such courses were necessary. These limited spaces prioritized women of color practicing engaging with each other across racialized difference to "become women of color."[94] Every staff member, Lui points out, needed to be able to offer the same response to complaining callers: "Not that we're all robots, but that it'll come from the place of, 'This is the reason why, and, actually, this is the reason why we would not have a course just for white women.'" This approach made it possible for women of color to learn from and with each other and to begin or hone their work as authors, while white women also learned about antiracist practice in courses like Sheila Wilmot's white antiracism course that led to her indispensable book *Taking Responsibility, Taking Direction: White Antiracism in Canada* (Arbeiter Ring, 2005). With twelve to fifteen courses a year, around a third were limited to women of color, and these courses were vital. Lui attended a course titled "Mixed Race Women's Reading" offered by Camille Hernandez-Ramdwar, now a faculty member at Ryerson University. Through the course Lui met Nila Gupta (who had coedited *The Issue Is 'Ism: Women of Colour Speak Out* (Sister Vision, 1989) and *Dykeversions: Lesbian Short Fiction* (edited by the Lesbian Writing and Publishing Collective, Women's Press, 1986)) and Claire Warner; the three continued to meet for five years as the Mixed Race Women's Writing Group. In the class and the group, Gupta wrote stories that appeared in her short story collection *The Sherpa and Other Fictions* (Sumach Press, 2008), which was shortlisted for the Commonwealth Writers Prize. According to Lui, "the store definitely facilitated that [Gupta's collection] and in many ways made me feel like I could do it."

These vital, contested spaces of feminist bookstores were unlike the "community" claimed by Amazon.com. Feminist bookwomen's legal and market-based resistance ultimately could not sustain the feminist bookstore movement. In 2000, the FBN announced a settlement of the Amazon Bookstore suit against Amazon.com. The settlement seemed to work against the feminist bookstore; it required the bookstore to always identify itself by its full, legal name, Amazon Bookstore Cooperative, and the bookstore traded its common law rights to the Amazon name to Amazon.com. Amazon.com licensed the feminist bookstore to use "Amazon Bookstore Cooperative" as its name until the bookstore's closure in 2012. All of this was accompanied by an undisclosed (and largely inconsequential) amount of money paid to the feminist bookstore by the online seller. The bookstore's Kathy Sharp explained, "People thought we made a ton of money with the settlement. . . . But we didn't. We had to settle. The lawyer's fees were killing us."[95] That lesbian feminist symbol, the Amazon warrior's double-sided axe, could not stop the corporate landslide of the 1990s.

Feminist Accountability, a Tool for Our Movements

The history in this chapter, read with a feminist literacy learned through the feminist shelf, is complex and requires holding two seemingly opposing ideas in one moment. In this history I see both a cautionary tale about attempting corporate advocacy at the cost of movement accountability and a success story about how deeply feminist bookwomen, drawing on their skills developed over twenty-five years together, did influence the mainstream book industry. Bookwomen's impressive advocacy in the mainstream book industry at the turn of the twenty-first century, by prioritizing independent bookstore survival, exacted devastating costs on the feminist bookstore movement as a force in alliance building.

This decade of contradictions saw the closure of more than a third of feminist bookstores in the United States and Canada, and the *Feminist Bookstore News* ended its run in the summer of 2000.[96] Carol Seajay had edited and published the unparalleled journal from its founding at the 1976 Women in Print gathering. The FBN shared the behind-the-scenes story of the struggle of economics with movement politics. There could be no discussion of the end of FBN in FBN, and thus in the movement, because, Seajay explained, "you have to not tell people you're closing, or the people that you're billing for ads will not pay. It's unkind. Mainstream publishing is like that a lot, and we had a lot of mainstream advertising."[97] She needed to cover as much as possible of the debt she had accrued creating this wildly successful and internationally loved activist vehicle. Mainstream publishing limited bookwomen's telling of their own stories.

Feminist bookwomen created a success more valuable than economic survival:[98] they sustained a transnational network and used that network to create a new lesbian antiracist feminist reading and relational practice that they evolved by putting it into practice every difficult day. At their best, feminist bookstores created networks that made alliances across difference possible, not only at feminist bookstores but in feminisms at large. Barbara Smith points out that "feminist bookstores have always been predominately white," though she names a few "notable exceptions like Old Wives' Tales, New Words, Charis, all of them have made a conscious effort to not be segregated."[99] At these and other feminist bookstores, like the Toronto Women's Bookstore and ICI: A Woman's Place, women of color worked together with each other and with white women; and at Sisterspace Books & More, the DC women of color worked together within a white-dominated industry. The loss of feminist bookstores as a network, Richardson points out, has "impacted what's available, especially to white women. Like, what kinds of things are available for white women to know what it means to be antiracist and how to do that. Because, right now, white queers of various kinds, people think that they are antiracist and they're not. They don't know what that means, there's no apparatus for other white people to check them on what they do."[100] Significantly, Richardson points not to the books on the shelves but to what people learned amid those shelves in feminist bookstores. He also points out that for women of color, attempting alliances with white women was costly. He saw overwhelming fatigue in feminist organizations in the 1990s: "Women of color are exhausted from that struggle. . . . Their bodies couldn't hold the anger of the experience, like this shit was off the charts frustrating and difficult and traumatizing." Bookwomen offer us models for attempting a more just, less violent feminist coalition building. It is the interconnection of lesbian ethics, racial justice work, and feminism that makes the future possible.

With this book, I hope to restore to public feminist memory the radical work of bookwomen in the 1970s, 1980s, and 1990s. From feminist bookstores I learned the methodology I have used in researching for this book, a methodology of learning and of building relationships to interrupt systems of oppression, not thinking just about my story or this moment, but thinking about the vital life of our interconnected stories and envisioning a just world. Bookwomen attempted to create (and repair, and rebuild) a cycle of a process for feminist accountability: bookwomen created an activist practice of learning, which generated and shaped a practice of relationship building, which held open space for accepting challenges and revisions, which required more learning and began the cycle again. The FBN articles about it all involved bookwomen, transnationally, in this cycle; this reach both made these difficult conversations required reading and thoroughly workshopped and honed this cycle as movement practice. This legacy of feminist accountability is the measure of success that bookwomen's history maps for themselves and for us.

EPILOGUE
FEMINIST REMEMBERING

Whole Universes Where Before I Saw Only Words

Before we left Toronto, Zahra and I both got tattoos from Pete in his house full of light and suspended glass and the sounds of his partner and children happy. Daniel Heath Justice had talked about his new tattoo at his book signing for *Our Fire Survives the Storm* at the Toronto Women's Bookstore that year; I tucked Pete Commanda's card into my copy of *Our Fire*. Wincing up at the warehouse-high ceiling, I squeezed Mill's hand and thought, if I hadn't been so committed to the design, if it wouldn't be silly to have a partial line on my leg, I might have stopped Pete, given up the bone-searing pain, and walked out into the sunlight. Instead, like the women in this book, like the writing of this book, I have the ink of that year in my skin: "Give me the woman strength of tongue." It's Audre Lorde's line from "125th Street and Abomey."[1]

Revisiting my journals and interviews from this time of leaving the Toronto Women's Bookstore, the end of my feminist bookstore years, I see in these stories, in these relationships, an enactment of the feminist accountability and feminist shelf practices of the bookwomen. I offer these final stories as a bridge, from history into activist present and future dreams. When we are immersed in movement organizations, we are in intense, loving, difficult, heartbreaking relationships; when the movement moment changes—or when we move on—what do we bring with our daily selves? After the bookstores, feminist bookwomen have gone on to, yes, other bookstore work and library work, and also to public health and AIDS/HIV care work, psychotherapy and counseling work, antioppression training work, union organizing work, LGBTQ center work, accounting work on women's land or off; they have each considered their work as a continuation of feminist bookstores. Our personal stories of leaving the bookstores and being changed by them offers a framework for understanding how the seemingly time-bound histories in these pages can inform our movement imaginings now.

Before Mill and I drove the packed U-Haul from Toronto back to Austin, there had been a string of lasts.[2] The last time I saw my Toronto friends together in one place was to sit on my bare floor, exchange handmade gifts, and weave our words back and forth stitching a soft and heavy anchor in time and place until late into the night. Zahra, Ruthann, Anne-Marie, Janet, and T——— were all there.[3] Our relationships together embodied the bookstore while we were there, and changed us as we dispersed across a continent, an ocean.

Zahra had been assistant manager for over a year when I arrived in 2006 to the queer antiracist feminist Toronto Women's Bookstore (TWB) as manager and book buyer. We soon transformed our positions to comanagers by name, since we were already living that reality. We relied on each other's perspectives at and after work, walking along Bloor Street or on treadmills at the fishbowl gym on Bathurst in the winter. An intuitive connector of people with books, Zahra finishes every book she reads. That year she read Doreen Baingana's Tropical Fish, Chimamanda Ngozi Adichie's Purple Hibiscus and Half of a Yellow Sun, Katherine McKittrick's collection Black Geographies and the Politics of Place, Dionne Brand's What We All Long For, and more. Her bookstore history feeds her work as an activist therapist and youth social worker, interconnected with her activism in Caribbean feminist organizing, as she thinks through—with the Adinkra and feminist symbols at her hip—land rights in St. Kitts and the complexity of her family's relationships to Indigenous, African diasporic, and South Asian diasporic lives in the Caribbean.

Together Ruthann and I kept up Anju's ritual of grinding and brewing dark coffee to drink, well creamed, in TWB mugs at the start of our shift. A bookstore staff member while in graduate school, Ruthann wove together communities by connecting people at her and Anne-Marie's imaginatively and beautifully designed house on Marshall Street, through her cocreation of the Korean Canadian Women's Anthology Collective, in difficult conversations at Inanna, an imprint of the Women's Press. She holds her deep past alongside our deep hope for the future in her current work as a professor documenting shared histories and alliance practices between

Indigenous peoples and Korean North Americans. Anne-Marie navigated the bookstore's ancient website framework for our monthly updates to our popular new arrivals list. She is a close and sensitive observer, conjurer of new bands to use music as conversation, graphic designer and space curator. Anne-Marie and Ruthann invited me along to spiritually nourishing food events at their house, to Nova Era Bakery for egg custards, to Queen of Sheba to scoop up savory greens with injera. They thought they might move to Hong Kong, be near Anne-Marie's mother, but find themselves now in Kelowna, BC, near her dear niece.

As the bookstore events and classes coordinator, Janet created her own events outside of Western time. She is a political artist resisting colonization and the impositions of Spanish and English languages on behalf of her younger self in Chile then Canada. Now she weaves history and future with performance and ink on cloth and oil paint on salvaged boards, her queer Latina feminism infusing her big love for her niece and nephew a long bus ride away. Mondays we were all at the bookstore together. Evenings we would meet up with T———, poet advocate for immigrant communities through media and communications strategies. She lived upstairs from Janet when I met them; they had rented apartments in the same house on Delaney Crescent before they'd gotten together. I stayed with them when I visited to look for a place and start my orientation to the bookstore. Teenah's work weaves through the city, her installations in subway stations and parks, love and love and justice, breaking silence in dialogue with her South Asian Caribbean heritage, with each of us. I mourned deeply as I let them go, curled into Mill on the futon for a fitful last sleep in the blue and green apartment that seemed magical, an in-between space.

My love, Mill, and I had met at BookWoman, the Austin feminist bookstore in 1999. We proffered each other chocolate chip cookies and cheesecake. Her son Steele, then thirteen and, as now, generous and kind as she is, carried in a bundle of sunflowers almost his own height. Bicycling around our hot Texas city Mill and I had cycled through the argument—what made feminist bookstores more than just businesses? Feeling called to create spaces of connection with lesbians, she had worked at Crazy Ladies, the feminist bookstore in Cincinnati, had volunteered at BookWoman in the 1980s. We had bodily memory of this feminist history but needed the evidence we have gathered in the years since to see, to explain why the bookstores mattered so much. While I lived in Toronto, Mill flew up as often as we could manage. We passed words back and forth using international phone cards, bridging geographies across a network of feminist bookwomen. Steeped in those almost fourteen months, I emerged from the city a different person.

Writing this epilogue my heart pounds. Through the vibrant summer, the soft lens of autumn, a mild winter, and the surprise of a fierce spring, I loved going to work at TWB, though sometimes I dreaded being there. Like the stories of the bookwomen I have, I hope, lovingly sketched on these pages, I, too, collaborated in the essential struggle of living toward queer antiracist feminist practice. In the history in this book, feminist bookwomen attempted (or hid from) antiracist feminisms; in this history, feminist bookwomen at their best held space for loving and sharp letters and conversations recorded in the *Feminist Bookstore News*, holding each other accountable. These interactions conjured visions of other futures. Our lives depended on it. I felt both powerful and vulnerable at TWB. As a white middle-class lesbian, I had the unearned privilege that would have allowed me to walk out the door, to ignore my racialized self, to not talk about socioeconomic class. Instead, I knew that my life, too, hung in the balance of this conversation, these relationships at the bookstore. This difficulty kept me feeling gifted to get to walk through the door each morning and also sometimes left me and my coworkers bruised. Staying present, talking with Zahra over lunch slices from Cora Pizza around the corner on Spadina, journaling furiously at home curled on the couch, I participated in a visceral collective remembering.

My time in Toronto changed how I understood the papers, pictures, stories I thought I knew when I wrote my dissertation. Whole universes now unfolded in a name, a transcript, a moment at a bookstore, where a year before I had seen only ink on paper, lines on a screen. This is the literacy practice of feminist bookstores. By working in them, by studying them, I learned to see and to read antiracist lesbian feminist history. I learned to see and to read toward the work of women of color in the bookstores, to see collaborations of women of color with white feminist allies. Look here, listen in, touch this paper. Again. Again, until we can read each other.

Feminist Accountability, Feminist Shelf

At TWB we held staff meetings every two weeks in the back of the bookstore, in the space between, on one side, the lesbians of color fiction and nonfiction, lesbian fiction, trans fiction and nonfiction, and, on the other side of the long narrow store space, general fiction. We circled up and sat on or against the wooden benches built into the shelves, and we started with a check-in. When I first joined the bookstore, some staff seemed restless. Anjula Gogia, part of whose job I was taking up, had been manager for ten years, had built up the course book sales that sustained the bookstore's staff and other work, had set a rhythm that now shifted. Ruthann, by then an author and editor, film producer, and in graduate school at York University, wore a faded T-shirt from Bluenotes at Dufferin Mall. She pushed a strand of short (or was it long then?) black hair behind her ear and faced each of us in turn for emphasis as she explained: it wasn't enough to listen to what the staff had to *say*. Speaking up could be overvalued if we heard voice at the cost of silence. *Silence* meant something, too. This tension between voice and silence, she pointed out, was threaded through racialized histories. Some of our ancestors could speak up, others couldn't, others didn't; some of us were caricatured as too loud, others completely without voice. For feminist dialogue, both speech and silence have to matter.

At the time I wasn't sure what this meant or how to consider or act on Ruthann's urging. I still remember this moment because I felt surprised by it and knew I needed this listening strategy. When I returned to my files of copies from the Lesbian Herstory Archives, the San Francisco Public Library, the Schlesinger Library, and feminist bookstore closet and cabinet archives, I began to see traces of the work of women of color and feminist accountability I hadn't seen before. I had been talking with and listening to the women who had been interviewed by others or had written their own pieces about their work in feminist bookstores, or women who were still involved with feminist bookstores. I was, I am, grateful for their voices. Now I knew I needed to learn to listen in the silences, too. There were women who had not been publicly interviewed about their experiences, there were women whose writings about feminist bookstores no one I had talked to had mentioned and I hadn't yet found. Here was Dawn Lundy Martin, pictured in the FBN at the American Booksellers Association Convention, here was Kit Quan, literary executor for Gloria Anzaldúa and mentioned but not by name in interviews, here were Pell, Keiko Kubo, Elizabeth Summers, Faye Williams, and many more. And here were dialogues among women of color and with white feminist allies struggling to understand each other.

This feminist bookstore history sketches in some missing pieces of feminist histories. This book contributes to ongoing documentation of women of color in the 1970s feminist movements and, in so doing, offers analyses of antiracist feminist practices in our histories. In this work I also interrupt contemporary calls to advocacy through purchasing power in two ways. First, by documenting for the first time the role of feminist bookwomen in feminist literary advocacy including the American Booksellers Association lawsuits and attempted intervention in illegal deals that sustained chain bookstores, an indication of the labor it takes to get and keep feminist literature in print. And second, by remembering bookwomen's own desire to be revolutionaries in a capitalist system, not as stores but as a transnational movement that called each other to account. By this account, this history also offers a vibrant example of how choosing mainstream advocacy over movement accountability sacrifices feminist successes. This feminist accountability calls on activists today to build a feminist shelf practice of context, vocabulary, and sister movements, to long for and dialogue with each other, and to understand success as the relationships we build.

Feminist bookstores formed my ethics and moral center with a place of (sometimes tenuous) belonging. That we could even have a conversation about voice and silence reached back to bell hooks, to Angela Davis, to Gloria Anzaldúa, to Theresa Hak Kyung Cha, to Maxine Hong Kingston, to Lee Maracle. People who grew up in feminist bookstores share this vocabulary, a language that makes friendship and love possible. I share this language with my lover: soon after we first met, she asked me to give her a tour of these bookstore shelves, knowing the transformations of shelf sections mean feminism afoot, our reading of the feminist shelf, though we didn't yet realize the history in the practice. We touched the books we had both read and loved, piled a stack of the books we carry in our bodies and use as guidebooks. This language was available to hundreds, maybe thousands of people who came up in feminist bookstores in the 1970s, 1980s, and 1990s. This book has been a history of some of these women's lives, the tensions they engaged in, their relationships between politics and heart and capitalism, believing in something and succeeding in some of those places and utterly failing in others. This feminist shelf practice of mapping a movement genealogy informs our accountability. The history, the language, is still vital.

About a month before we left Toronto, Zahra for Port-of-Spain and I for Austin, we had dinner at my apartment, and I interviewed Zahra on tape. By 2014 I hadn't listened to the tape since we recorded it in 2007. Playing it again, I expected a venting session about the small and gaping challenges of management, even or maybe especially in an antiracist feminist organization; instead, I was surprised by our optimism. *Yes*, I realized, *this is the framework*: our failures didn't mean this work, our months or years there, didn't matter. Rather, we did make a contribution, and we were ready to move on and do our work better.

"What made it so difficult?," I had asked feminist bookwomen in interviews, wanting to know from the difficulties the exciting promise of alliances they had attempted, to recognize even failures as helpful when shared. The sweet meat clings to the stone of that fruit. Looking out my kitchen window at a raven-blue Toronto evening sky, Zahra shared some perspective gained from talking with her aunt who worked in social services: "This is just what happens in women's organizations, and if you read the history of the store, it is what has happened at the bookstore for 30 years. There has been this continuous cycle of upheaval and trauma and drama, and I think that you and I are just in the middle of a very bad cycle. It will get through it; the bookstore is just so much bigger than you and me, and so much bigger than all the people who are driving me up a wall there right now."[4] Reading my journals immerses me in the swirl of emotion that buffeted me in those months. The days spent in the small and brimming full bookstore and its second floor offices teetering with course books offered me loving friendships, new knowledge and strategies for practicing queer antiracist allyship, and a visceral understanding of how daily experience in a space vibrates both in a far-reaching historical time and in a seemingly isolated now time.

Reading my journals, I trace the pencil crayon swirls that undulate next to my still-warm list of what I wanted to remember, a list I made that first week of June, feeling in between places, leaving Toronto for Austin. I might have made a list of loves, savored each word. Instead, reading my handwriting, I found I had also written into intentional memory the difficulties that had transformed me, moments I wouldn't ache for but couldn't live without either. For me this love letter from my years-ago self weaves a theory, learned from feminist bookwomen, of reading feminist history. I read the stories in the preceding chapters of disagreements, lockouts, boycotts, and closures as not discouragements but indications of relationships, however fraught, where transformative conversations were happening. At their best, feminist bookwomen were attempting to hold each other accountable to transracial alliances, to a vision of feminist racial justice. For example, a lockout by white women of white women and women of color, a disagreement about who "gets" to attend the mostly white Women in Print Conference and whether that's a "privilege," are moments when white women can choose to learn or not, moments when white women can perpetuate or interrupt scarring violence against women of color. A boycott of a mostly white bookstore by a Black feminist organization and the bookstore advocacy of one bookwoman of color may open or foreclose difficult transracial conversations among women of color. These larger, more easily documented breaks offer evidence of smaller and related daily interactions that informed bookwomen's shelf titles, ordering, advocacy with publishers, events, hiring, outreach, and feminist literacies. Because my list, my life at the bookstore, included these daily interactions, I want to share some of the list to set the stage for what a day at TWB was like, from my perspective at this moment. I want to be as true as I can be here, briefly, to the experience. TWB was difficult. TWB was a love story. Breathe in. Breathe out. These moments taught me to read differently.

In the month before my interview with Zahra, my working relationship with Rose (which had been steadily declining despite an early high of a late-night conversation on our shared walk home from an event at the Gladstone) had gotten worse. A couple of the staff thought TWB should be a collective or a worker's cooperative; other staff supported the management structure put in place in the 1990s. The high-stakes conversation about feminist organizational structure was as old as the bookstore itself. Zahra and I hoped that by meeting with a couple of staff members we could restore positive will and a sense of collaborative action. The bookstore had one room with a door; Zahra, Rose, and I watched each other across the small space. Rose, a Bangladeshi Canadian woman, offered an example of how staff and management (Zahra and I were management) were at odds: staff had repeatedly, she said, raised concerns about the academic coordinator position. OmiSoore, a Black Caribbean Canadian woman hired just before I started at the bookstore, took on another part of the job Anju had left: as the academic coordinator, she was our liaison to faculty to bring in the more than one hundred course book orders each semester that economically sustained the bookstore. OmiSoore soon left the bookstore after dealing with painfully racialized comments and a few staff members' negativity toward "academics," no matter how she explained that people of color, queer people, and working-class people (and people who are all of these) live in and do radical work at universities, too. Zahra and I exchanged a glance. I asked Rose, when did staff raise these concerns? This question, Rose insisted, was a white woman's attention to detail intended to distract. I backed down but shouldn't have, I tell myself in my journal. Zahra and I had worked with Beth Jordan, an organizational consultant, on bringing the bookstore's antioppression values back into everyday interactions between the staff of different racial, ethnic, national, class, sexuality, and gender identities. We traced a history of anti-Black racism alongside transracial feminist alliances in the bookstore's recent past. I do not intend this naming to criticize Rose's objection but rather to foster the recognition that the shelves, the relationships, the commitments of the bookstore required us to continually work toward queer antiracist feminism and, in turn, to recognize that queer antiracist feminism requires continual work. That recognition itself hard-won, we practiced our voices and our meaningful silences: Zahra and I in worn upholstered chairs at couples therapy for comanagers with Merlin Homer, the replenishing, incisive therapist recommended by OmiSoore. Ruthann naming her truth in a staff meeting dimming with evening. Janet calm and connected, Alex tired and creative, Rose and Reena and others who came and went loved the bookstore and practiced feminisms in their own way. The bookstore, shaped by three decades of feminist bookstores, of its own history, made those attempts possible.

Zahra remembers that when she first interviewed for a job at the bookstore, first read the shelves of TWB, she took in the complexities and ethics of the sections, the argument of the bookstore: "There's so much on all these shelves, and you wish you could soak it all in, because you know it's, this is where the world is right." She knew then that this was where the world is right in part because of the sections: "I remember being shocked that there was an African section, a Caribbean section, an African Canadian section, and an African American section, because I'd never seen that sort of division in any other bookstore." The divisions manifested an attention to regional relationships and histories of resistance that would stock enough feminist books in conversation to record and sustain nuanced dialogue within the African diaspora. We learned in our daily breath during those months that the sections were "right" because feminist bookstore workers— now including us—intentionally (and slowly) cultivated transracial alliances, built a queer antiracist staff, and learned to read differently, to read with each other and to share that literacy practice in the shelf titles, newsletters, bibliographies, and readings.

We were wrong about the bookstore living on, at least literally. Five and a half years after we left, in November 2012, TWB closed, and today I feel like I entered its story at the beginning of the end. I've said this book is emphatically not a call for new feminist bookstores; the movement as a whole made possible the accountability that in turn affected writing, publishing, and reading practices. And I still feel the loss of TWB resonating in my daily life. Through the relational reading practice I call the feminist shelf, bookwomen had developed a framework for feminist accountability; what if we put that framework back into practice? I suggest that this would enact a kind of feminist remembering.

Feminist Remembering

I offer this book and this epilogue as a feminist remembering, an enactment of feminist bookwomen's theoretical practice. This feminist remembering is a way of reading using the feminist shelf skill of understanding movement vocabularies in relationship with each other, and holds us accountable to those histories and our allies across difference. A practice of feminist remembering, then, acknowledges how both difficult and vital it is to work simultaneously toward racial, gender, LGBTQ, socioeconomic class, and dis/ability justice; a practice of feminist remembering serves not to punish or reify but to teach in dialogue, recognizing that social justice work means always (sometimes painfully) learning on our own and from each other. Sitting with former or current feminist bookwomen on the phone or in person, in bookstores, buses, and living rooms, I asked: how did working at the bookstore change you? Among feminist bookwomen of different generations at TWB, the same threads kept weaving through: making lasting friendships; shaping personal integrity by dealing with difficult organization and staff relationship issues; building skills that included feminist management, public speaking, and group decision making; taking responsibility as a public figure, known in one's community, to represent the values of the bookstore; understanding more deeply each day how justice depends on our interrelated struggles. These reflections inform my own and enact feminist remembering, a practice of reading history, learned from feminist bookwomen.

In my journal entry of what I wanted to remember about my Toronto life I find my own answer to the question, how did working at the bookstore change you? My bookstore friends and our readings together have changed how I understand myself and my world. Zahra and I at the movies on Bloor Street, Janet and I cutting our own hair together, Ruthann and Anne-Marie's gatherings always delicious even though I am usually uncomfortable at parties. All of us talking together about the surprise, pleasure, and difficulty of transracial friendships. How unlikely it seemed when they interviewed me, they have said, that we would become friends. It seemed less unlikely but still a challenge, as Zahra and I talked with staff members and volunteers of color over the year about not engaging in racialized stereotyping, that women of color might become allies to each other. The personal connection, our loves on the line, makes the learning essential, makes this book urgent. This history matters as an important documentation of histories of and model for futures for building queer feminist antiracist alliances and vocabularies. This history matters as a reflection on retaining movement accountability through feminist shelf relationships. May Lui, former TWB comanager, and board member at the end of my time there, remembered that her friendships at the bookstore made it possible for her to write, introduced her to her writing partner: "She came in asking about mixed race books and someone told her to come back the next day when I was on shift." This friendship is one of countless relationships woven through the bookstore reading practice. Echoing my own heart, May says her bookstore friendships "have changed me most definitely for the better."[5]

Attending to, turning toward and holding, these relationships means thinking carefully about how organizational relationships can support queer antiracist feminism. As Sharon Fernandez, transformative artist and TWB bookwoman in the 1990s, said, "any time you have an institution, you have a certain platform that has energy and power. And the moment you are situated within that, that allows you to grow and develop. A relational platform always creates voice."[6] In the last months of our time at TWB, Zahra and I tried out our city-wide relationships, tried to use our relational power for good. Janet had asked us to consider creating a TWB policy against co-sponsoring events including people we know to have committed acts of interpersonal violence and who have not publicly addressed these acts. Zahra and I agreed it was important not to stay silent but to speak out so that the survivors are not the ones silenced by the public stigma. The effort, focusing on a particular event in the city, split or strengthened relationships among board members, staff, and community as we tried to develop a shape for such a policy, not criminalizing but holding space. Wasn't this practice what TWB had meant by not stocking appropriative literature? Not allowing one person with power to use or erase the presence of a person with less power. There was no perfect answer, no exact language; strengthened by each other, even in our disagreements, we struggled into a new space and attempted together to work toward justice.

This kind of work transformed each of us. Former manager and long-time TWB activist Esther Vise explains of her time at the bookstore, "I think it's made me a huge part of who I am. It allowed me to integrate my understanding, from very early on, from a teenager, of sexism and racism and homophobia in a whole way that was not fractured. So, for me it was a place where I learnt to be who I am."[7] In these interviews I feel my growing up in feminist bookstores, my comparatively brief work as a bookwoman in two cities, and my longtime study of this history; in these interviews I feel the roots of my own self digging in, holding me up. TWB was for me, too, a place where I learnt to be who I am. When I asked Zahra this question, how has working at the bookstore changed you, she described this transformation, too: "It's so funny because my parents are here, and I've been talking to them a lot recently, and both my parents keep telling me how different I am." She sees the difference in her confident voice: "When I was in St. Kitts I was really soft spoken, I didn't really say too much, I was quiet. It's shocking for them to see me this opinionated and confident in what I say and how I say it and how I feel about it." She traces this confidence from an awareness of relationships: "I'm much more confident in knowing it's not just me feeling this way. There is a world of people behind me who feel the same way I feel, who think the same way I think. Granted, I have lots of problems with lots of those other people as they should have lots of problems with me, that's how change happens. But it's made me realize that I'm not alone. I'm really not. I'm not even close to being alone." Here Zahra points to a vital tender spot: the practice of feminist relationships, feminist rememberings, holds space for deep disagreements with the potential to at the least acknowledge difference and at most to challenge us to change. "I'm thinking more consciously about ability and how that works; again, that is not something I'd have without the bookstore. Thinking about trans issues and the way that works, and what Indigenous identity means in the Caribbean, how that's erased. I'm not sure how I would've gotten there, had the language to begin to have those conversations, those really hard conversations, those challenging conversations, with myself, and with other people, without the bookstore. This is a permanent change in me."

During our last two days at the bookstore, Zahra and I completed our training of the incoming comanagers: Lorraine Hewitt, a longtime bookstore worker, retail maven, and renowned burlesque dancer, and Corrie Sakaluk, a student union organizer and a white woman. In my journal I noted that Janet and Zahra reminded me to talk with Corrie about being a white manager in an organization committed to racial justice; within her sustained work as an antiracist ally, I could also see Corrie's white privilege, as I know the staff had been able to see mine when I started at the bookstore a year earlier. I made a list of items to communicate to Corrie: address racism, build trust, practice dismantling essentializing comments or assumptions, learn and read on your own, remain committed to the need for women of color leadership at the bookstore. The women of color focus makes TWB necessary and defines its community identity, I wrote; you must participate in that focus while being aware that there are women of color spaces in the bookstore you cannot take part in, courses, conversations, and events. I wrote this list, too, for my new self walking out of the bookstore and into my next life. What have I learned about being white from being here? How to practice queer antiracist feminist accountability. That it is my job to speak out in conversations with white people and call them on racism. To recognize my privilege and still do the work. To give up some power and to use the power I keep in revolutionary ways. Like this, feminist remembering ingrains movement histories in each breath.

Going Back Home

At the altitude of Yosemite, Bernice Johnson Reagon observed that coalition building is not like home. Sometimes, though, I and some of the bookwomen I have interviewed have observed, when we return home from the bookstore, we ache for that difficult and validating space of coalition building. Only one of the bookwomen I interviewed still works in a feminist bookstore; only two of the bookstores whose archives I read are still open today. I suggest that the success of the bookstores is not in how long they stay open but rather in the intense relationship building that changed the bookwomen themselves, who in turn went home to change friends, families, other coworkers, and movements. At the start of this book, I quoted Carol Seajay, coming home to Kalamazoo, saying of a stack of books from the West Coast Lesbian Conference, "These books are gonna change our lives." She said, "There being lesbian books changed even the lives of women who didn't read, because it changed the lives around them."[8] These bookwomen are still changing the lives of even people who have never been to a feminist bookstore. And we are still remaking home.

Working at TWB was difficult, and beautiful. We were at the center of powerful change. We could see and resist racism in literary distribution as we made space for queer antiracist feminist language weaving. Zahra remembers falling in love with *Unburnable*, getting almost all of the staff (including me) to read it, and hand-selling it to everyone she could. "When I meet her, because I will meet her," Zahra promised of author Maria Elena John, since she lives in Antigua, where Zahra's cousin lives, "I will tell her that I sold a bunch of her books. Because you were there," she motions to me, "with the publisher's rep when he flipped through the page. He didn't even mention it." I remember getting to meet authors and hear works that now I can't imagine living without. Anju had taught me that presentation matters, so we always draped over the tables the scarves she had left with the bookstore for that purpose, before we laid out the small feast of cheese, fruit, and nuts from Kensington Market that marked our celebration of an author's work: Katherine McKittrick introducing Cathie Dunsford, Indigenous feminist author and activist, here all the way from New Zealand; Bobby Noble, with a trans-feminist analysis of the feminist and labor movements; Leah Lakshmi Piepzna-Samarasinha, creator of BrownStarGirl productions and witness poet; Sarah Hussain, with her new collection on Islamic feminism; Chrystos on alliances between Indigenous peoples across neoimperial borders. Dionne Brand, M. Nourbese Phillip, M. Jacqui Alexander—I met them all when they stopped into the bookstore. As Zahra put it, "any book in 2006 that was feminist and great, I have it. It's on my bookcase. It's being shipped to Trinidad eventually. I'll carry it with me everywhere. I really feel as though I'm going to remember this history. I'll be able to say I was there, I remember that." I'm using what I learned; I'm breathing differently now.

My old cassette player is on the kitchen table in Mill's and my blue kitchen in Austin. It is 2014. Megan, my dear friend and a social justice scholar and creator of performance with youth, sits across the table finishing her book (interwoven in these words, too), while I push headphones into my ears and click "play" to transcribe Zahra's interview, finally, after all these years.[9] It sounds like she's right here, visiting again. I WhatsApp her and tell her so. Across the tape, across time, she says something I've been thinking, even this week: "Going back home is going to be different, and I hope that I can find people like me, like you, like the store people (and not a lot of the store people), but I hope that I can find that community there that gives me that grounding. I hope that I don't have to feel as though my only grounding in this sort of thought is here. And I know it must be at home, but how do I find it?" We brainstorm strategies together; we talk regularly. We keep connecting, using the relational practice and the vocabulary we learned in part at TWB. Mill, too, since our early days together, has been lovingly, urgently, bringing me back to this moment, now, saying, everyday life is life. This history of feminist bookwomen offers the opportunity to keep learning from the bookwomen, from their work toward feminist accountability. Using our feminist shelf skills, we build context and read each other with this history in our lungs.

NOTES

Preface

1. "Gloria Evangelina Anzaldúa: September 26, 1942–May 15, 2004," memorial booklet, Austin, Texas, 2004.

2. Carol Seajay, interview with author, 17 July 2003.

3. Feminist writers including Mab Segrest and Aimee Carillo Rowe have mapped how white lesbians can choose to acknowledge the ways their lesbianism troubles their "relationship to white heterosociality" in order to advocate for the necessarily interrelated work of racial, sexuality, and gender justice, which requires transracial alliances (Rowe, *Power Lines*, 107). Mab Segrest, *Memoir of a Race Traitor*.

4. Numbers are difficult to track given that many bookstores had short life spans. Bookwomen at the *Feminist Bookstore News* reported numbers of subscribers to influence publishers and to build community. In 1988, the FBN masthead announced: "FBN reaches 350 feminist and feminist-inclined bookstores in the U.S. and Canada as well as feminist booksellers in England, Europe, New Zealand, India, and Japan. Librarians, women's studies teachers, book reviewers, publishers, and feminist bibliophiles comprise the remainder of the subscribers." A few years later, Carol Seajay celebrated an increase in feminist bookstores in the U.S. and Canada from 96 in 1991 to 105 in 1992; this number offers a more accurate view separating the "feminist" from the "feminist-leaning" bookstores (Carol Seajay, "Notes from the Computer Table," *Feminist Bookstore News* 15.2 (July/August 1992): 1). Around this time there were also feminist bookstores in England, Australia, New Zealand, and Japan (Masthead, *Feminist Bookstore News* 11.2 (August 1988): 3), as well as eight feminist bookstores in Spain (Heide Braun, Sal de Casa/Valencia, interview by Carol Seajay and Rose Katz, "Past and Present: Running the Feminist Bookstores in Spain," *Feminist Bookstore News* 13.4 [November/December 1990]: 57–65), and others in Argentina, Bangladesh, the Philippines, Pakistan, India, and Peru (Carol Seajay, "IV International Feminist Bookfair Barcelona June 19–23, 1990," *Feminist Bookstore News* 13.2 [August 1990]: 19–23, 20), as well as Belgium (Marian Lens, Artemys, "Artemys: Running the Feminist Bookstore in Belgium: Presented by

Marian Lens at the Third International Feminist Bookfair," *Feminist Bookstore News* 11.5 (January 1989): 9–10), the Netherlands (Carol Seajay, "5th International Feminist Book Fair: Amsterdam," *Feminist Bookstore News* 15.2 [July/August 1992]: 27–34, 28), Taiwan (Beth Morgan, "Fem Books: The First Chinese-Language Feminist Bookstore," *Feminist Bookstore News* 18.5 [January/February 1996]: 17–22), Germany ("Bookstores," *Feminist Bookstores Newsletter* 2.2 [1978]: 3–5), and Kenya (Seajay, "Africa's First Feminist Bookstore: Binti Legacy," *Feminist Bookstore News* 19.4 [November/December 1996]: 15–17). As of this writing, bookwomen worldwide are operating at least sixteen of the feminist bookstores on *News* lists: Binti Legacy (Nairobi, Kenya), Bloodroot (Bridgeport, Connecticut), BookWoman (Austin, Texas), Charis (Atlanta), Fembooks (Taiwan), Herland Sister Resources (Oklahoma City, Oklahoma), In Other Words (Portland, Oregon), Libreria de Mujeres (Buenos Aires), Libreria delle Donne (Milan), Narigrantha Prabartana (Dhaka, Bangladesh), Northern Woman's Bookstore (Thunder Bay, Ontario), People Called Women (Toledo, Ohio), Room of One's Own (Madison, Wisconsin), Streelekha (Bangalore, Karnataka, India), Wild Iris (Gainesville, Florida), Women & Children First (Chicago), Xantippe (Amsterdam).

5. "At the 1976 Women in Print Conference," *Feminist Bookstores Newsletter* 1.1 (October 1976): 2.

6. Mikki Kendall, "On Feminist Solidarity and Community: Where Do We Go from Here?," *Ebony*, 19 August 2013, Web (accessed 15 March 2015).

7. Susana Loza, "Hashtag Feminism, #SolidarityIsForWhiteWomen, and the Other #FemFuture," *Ada: A Journal of Gender, New Media, and Technology* 5 (2014), Web (accessed 9 October 2014).

8. Bonita Lawrence and Enakshi Dua, "Decolonizing Antiracism," *Social Justice* 32.4 (2005): 120–143.

9. Ibid., 123.

10. Ruthann Lee, "The Production of Racialized Masculinities in Contemporary North American Popular Culture," Ph.D. diss., York University, 2011, 141.

11. Jia Tolentino, "A Chat with Mikki Kendall and Flavia Dzodan about #SolidarityIsForWhiteWomen," *Hairpin*, 16 August 2013, Web (accessed 10 October 2014).

12. Alicia Garza, "A Herstory of the #BlackLivesMatter Movement," *Feminist Wire*, 7 October 2014, Web (accessed 15 March 2015).

13. M. Jacqui Alexander points to a practice of solidarity required for taking apart oppression: "Because within the archaeologies of dominance resides the will to divide and separate, *Pedagogies* points to the reciprocal investments we must make to cross over into a metaphysics of interdependence" (*Pedagogies of Crossing*, 6). Part of this work for women of color, Alexander points out, requires solidarity work to "*become* women of color" (269): "How do we continue to be rooted in the particularities of our cultural homes without allegiance to the boundaries of nation-state, yet remain simultaneously committed to a collectivized politic of identification and solidarity?" (268). Imagining a version of this future, Aimee Carillo Rowe calls for a "transracial feminist imaginary" based in intimate reading and relational practices: "Shared languages arise from shared experience, so the intimacies we generate in transracial alliances provide the context

through which we cultivate such imagined communities" (174). This alliance requires turning toward critique, which I attempt to practice in this book. Rowe shifts feminist readings of critique in resonance with contemporary discussions around hashtag feminism: "Recognizing that women-of-color allies may 'tell you what you don't want to hear,' for instance, may allow white women to reframe the critiques women of color share with them—to understand them not as personal attacks, but as *alliance practices*" (*Power Lines*, 175).

14. Karyn London, "Books in Spanish," *Feminist Bookstores Newsletter* 1.1 (October 1976): 3–4; "Native American Women," *Feminist Bookstores Newsletter* 1.2 (November 1976): 5; "Black Women," *Feminist Bookstores Newsletter* 1.2 (November 1976): 5; "Young Women & Youth Liberation Booklist," *Feminist Bookstores Newsletter* 1.2 (November 1976): 6.

15. The Feminist Bookstore Network rolled out this slogan on buttons, T-shirts, bookmarks, and posters, as well as in an article in Ms. as part of the public relations campaign National Feminist Bookstore Week, 13–20 May 1995. Carol Seajay, "News from the Bookstores," *Feminist Bookstore News* 18.1 (May/June 1995): 27–29.

16. Lilia Rosas, group email, "We Are Moving para el East Side!" Thank you to Leah Lakshmi Piepzna-Samarasinha for publicly identifying Resistencia Bookstore as a feminist bookstore, during an event in Toronto.

17. Here I quote from Senti Sojwal's introduction to her profile of the seven bookstores she described as the last feminist bookstores in the United States. Rhian Sasseen's article "Unsteady Shelf: The Endangered Landscape of Feminist Bookstores" also exemplifies this trend in coverage; Sasseen identifies nine remaining feminist bookstores, not including bookstores like Resistencia Bookstore in Austin, and focuses on past experiences in a single bookstore, New Words, without a context for what the already-disappeared full landscape of feminist bookstores made possible. Senti Sojwal, "These Are the Last of America's Dying Feminist Bookstores"; Rhian Sasseen, "Unsteady Shelf," 8–9.

18. Interrupting the waves analogy, Kimberly Springer points out, is vital for recognizing transracial feminist histories: "In addition to situating black feminist organizations in relationship to the civil rights movement, an examination of black feminist organizations draws connections between black *and* white feminists as descendants of the civil rights movement" (*Living for the Revolution*, 9). Building on Springer's foundation, Maylei Blackwell draws on histories of feminism that "expand the scope of our historical understanding of where and how feminist consciousness and practice emerged in the postwar period and challenge us to think beyond the ways in which the dominant narrative of the second wave has overshadowed Other forms of feminisms" (¡Chicana Power!, 18).

19. Sandoval points out that US feminists of color's involvement with "the 1970s white women's liberation movement . . . was variously interpreted as disloyalty, betrayal, absence, or lack: 'When they *were* there, they were rarely there for long' went the usual complaint." While white middle-class women could identify fully with a feminist movement, women of color were, Sandoval points, out, compelled by multiple identity movements: "They were the mobile (yet ever-present in their 'absence') members of

this, as well as of other race, class, and sex liberation movements." Sandoval, *Methodology of the Oppressed*, 58.

20. Gloria Anzaldúa defines the work in her anthology *Making Face, Making Soul/ Haciendo Caras* as making theory, "Haciendo teorías." Feminists of color's theories are essential to fully understanding our collective pasts and futures, Anzaldúa points out: "What is considered theory in the dominant academic community is not necessarily what counts as theory for women-of-color. Theory produces effects that change people and the way they perceive the world. . . . *Necesitamos teorías* that will rewrite history using race, class, gender and ethnicity as categories of analysis, theories that cross borders, that blur boundaries—new kinds of theories with new theorizing methods. We need theories that will point out ways to maneuver between our particular experiences and the necessity of forming our own categories and theoretical models for the patterns we uncover" (xxv). Anzaldúa, "Haciendo caras, una entrada."

21. Rowe, *Power Lines*, 15.

22. Allison, *Two or Three Things I Know for Sure*, 90.

23. Brand, *Love Enough*, 180.

24. At the 2014 Book Expo of America, a trade conference run by Reed Exhibitions (see chapter 5 for a description of how the Book Expo of America changed hands from the American Booksellers Association to Reed to fund lawsuits on behalf of independent booksellers and how feminist bookwomen led the advocacy for this funding), Reed held BookCon, an attempt at creating events open to the public. The panel on young adult literature made up of four white authors drew criticism, including from those authors themselves, for lack of representation of racially and gender diverse authors. The necessary outcry developed into the We Need Diverse Books campaign and subsequent organization run by authors of young adult books calling for racial and gender identity diversity in young adult publishing. In chapter 2 I analyze feminist bookwomen's advocacy for racial and gender justice representation in authorship, and in chapter 4 I offer a history of feminist bookwomen's deep engagement with the important relationship between characters and author identities and alliances in order to end appropriation and support dialogue. Bookwomen are part of a long history that now includes the We Need Diverse Books campaign, and bookwomen argue that feminist ethics of voice and reading practices as relational practices are central to sustaining "diverse" books. Ian Chant, "Lack of Diversity at BEA BookCon Criticized," *Library Journal* 139.10 (1 June 2014): 24; We Need Diverse Books, We Need Diverse Books: Official Campaign Site, Web (accessed 10 October 2014).

25. For Matt Richardson, collections of Black lesbian fiction constitute vital archives, memorials, and maps of Black lesbian authors who "have commented upon and expanded the available known archives of slavery, migration, diaspora, revolutionary movements, and rural life by offering epistemologies for Black resistance, community building, and self-making" (*Queer Limit of Black Memory*, 159). These histories in fiction are also real and vital archives and ways of knowing. Geographer Katherine McKittrick traces "real-imagined geographies" through "theoretical, fictional, poetic, musical, or dramatic texts" to read them "as real responses to real spatial inequalities" (*Demonic*

Grounds, xxiii). For feminism, literature offers another pathway to theory, to making a way to new understandings, vocabularies, and practices.

26. Maylei Blackwell reads the publication *Hijas de Cuauhtémoc*, which became *Encuentro Femenil*, as central to "the formation of a Chicana print community across regions, social movement sectors, activist generations, and social differences. Through print-mediated exchange, new identities, regional and ideological differences, strategies, theories, and practices were debated and discussed in campus and community meetings and at local and national conferences" (*¡Chicana Power!*, 133). The print publication and its circulation created a necessary and unique space for the development and contestation of Chicana theories (134). Looking to the turn of the twentieth century, Elizabeth McHenry documents African American literary societies as vital sites of political power: "Practice as researchers, writers, and presenters of papers in the intimate setting of club meetings prepared black women for the demands of issuing their writing in more public forums and formats" (*Forgotten Readers*, 215). Along the way, Black women writers imagined the "literary woman" in practice as one who, McHenry points out, used "literature to express solidarity with those whose lives and sufferings take similar forms from similar causes" (250). Here McHenry marks the long history of feminist literary activism (her term) as a practice of solidarity.

27. "At the 1976 Women in Print Conference," *Feminist Bookstores Newsletter*, 2.

28. While bookwomen used the term "lesbian" throughout most of the movement, I see the current usage of "queer" as a direct ancestor of this lesbian feminist work. When I write about recent, current, and future feminist accountability, I shift from lesbian antiracism to queer antiracism to recognize both important challenges, rooted in part in lesbian activism, to binary gender identity and expression as well as the history of collaboration among genderqueer people building feminist practice.

29. Kit Quan, interview with author, 11 August 2007.

30. Kit Quan, "The Girl Who Wouldn't Sing."

31. Pell, interview with author, 26 March 2008.

1. Dykes with a Vision, 1970–1976

1. Lillian Faderman and Stuart Timmons, *Gay L.A.*, 136.

2. Faderman and Timmons, *Gay L.A.*, 190–191; Jeanne Córdova, *When We Were Outlaws*, 6–7.

3. Faderman and Timmons, *Gay L.A.*, 190.

4. Carol Seajay, interview with author, 17 July 2003.

5. Seajay, interview with author.

6. The founding of the bookstores as lesbian feminist spaces interrupts narratives that position lesbians as later arrivals to feminist organizations. For example, Verta Taylor and Leila J. Rupp, in an article that otherwise offers a powerfully complex view of lesbian feminist identities and alliances, assert that "the alternative institutions founded by early radical feminists—including rape crisis centers, battered women's shelters, bookstores, newspapers, publishing and recording companies, recovery groups, restaurants

and coffeehouses, and other women-owned businesses—have increasingly come to be driven by the commitment of lesbians and women in the process of coming out. Women find in this world a social context supportive of lesbian relationships and identity that was unavailable in early feminist organizations or in the predominantly male gay liberation movement" ("Women's Culture and Lesbian Feminist Activism," 38). The history Seajay, Grahn, and others offer in this chapter instead claims that lesbians organized early feminist bookstores in Oakland, Austin, New York, and other cities, as lesbian feminists. Taylor and Rupp do recognize that "the base of mobilization of the 'women's community' stems primarily from interpersonal networks and organizational ties in the lesbian world" (38).

7. Lesbian Herstory Archives, "History and Mission." For an analysis of how LHA space itself creates a home for lesbian affective histories, see Ann Cvetkovich, An Archive of Feelings.

8. Le Guin famously rejected critics who focused on gender in their interpretations of The Left Hand of Darkness (Walker, 1969) before revising her own reading of her work in "Is Gender Necessary? Redux" as early as 1976. She places her work in Left Hand alongside Betty Friedan's and Kate Millett's work, explaining, "I was not a theoretician, a political thinker or activist, or a sociologist. I was and am a fiction writer. The way I did my thinking was to write a novel. That novel, The Left Hand of Darkness, is the record of my consciousness, the process of my thinking" (Le Guin, Dancing at the Edge of the World, 8). The women of ICI: A Woman's Place read the book as Le Guin wrote it, the process of her thinking and part of the feminist movement through literature.

9. ICI: A Woman's Place, letter, 1970, ICI: A Woman's Place Papers, Lesbian Herstory Archives.

10. See Kathryn Thoms Flannery for a discussion of the role of rap groups and poetry for a feminist movement. Flannery, Feminist Literacies 1968–1975.

11. I use the term "feminist literary counterpublic" to connect the work of feminist bookwomen with feminist theorists who have used and revised Jürgen Habermas's concept of the public sphere. This connection offers another way to understand that the number of feminist bookstores in the 1980s and 1990s, over one hundred across North America and more transnationally, meant that work in individual bookstores contributed to a larger movement for change. I trace one thread of theoretical history here to map how feminist theorists have understood feminist organizing as public sphere work. Feminist bookwomen created a similar argument in their own documents. I see feminist bookwomen here as building movement theory. Feminist theorists help to explain how action at movement bookstores is different from comments online at Amazon.com. Significantly, feminist theorists Rita Felski and Nancy Fraser look to feminist literature as the framework for feminist or subaltern counterpublics. The term "counterpublic," referring to a movement space of education and training for activists to transform the larger public, helps to describe the work of feminist bookstores. Felski sees a feminist counterpublic as a network understanding and acting on connections "between literature, feminist ideology, and the broader public domain" (Beyond Feminist Aesthetics, 9). Fraser, too, sees feminist literature not as market-based

but as movement-fueling, and she claims feminist bookstores as part of this work. She identifies "journals, bookstores, and publishing companies" among the features of the influential "late-twentieth-century U.S. feminist subaltern counterpublic" ("Rethinking the Public Sphere," 13).

12. In 1972, for example, chain bookstores garnered only 11.6 percent of bookstore sales. Miller, *Reluctant Capitalists*, 45.

13. Miller, *Reluctant Capitalists*, 92.

14. Miller, *Reluctant Capitalists*, 44–45.

15. Miller, *Reluctant Capitalists*, 92–93.

16. Laura Miller acknowledges the influence of 1970s social movements in today's bookstore environments more familiar to contemporary readers (*Reluctant Capitalists*, 94).

17. Howe, *Female Studies II*.

18. Grahn, *The Highest Apple*, xviii.

19. Seajay, interview with author. The physically and politically connected press and bookstore became known as a single site for lesbians learning about printing and distribution. In 1975, Liza Cowan and Penny House flew from New York to weave a narrative map of lesbian public sites and events in California; they shared their travels as the "California Diary" in the first issue of *Dyke Quarterly*. They note that the press "shares space with the bookstore," and they witnessed Wendy Cadden "learning color separation"; Wendy "shows us a project, a cover for a 45 record" (Cowan and House, "California Diary," 70–74). During the 1973 bookstore meetings that Seajay attended, the members smelled the four-color inks wafting from next door.

20. Carol Seajay and Judy Grahn, "Some Beginnings: An Interview with Judy Grahn," *Feminist Bookstore News* 13.1 (May/June 1990): 19–25, 25.

21. Cadden describes the influence of the connected press and bookstore: "Because of the presence of the press and A Woman's Place Bookstore, says Cadden, 'Oakland became a center for other feminist institutions, including the Feminist Health Center, the Oakland Rape Crisis Center and Olivia Records'" (Love, *Feminists Who Changed America*, 67). In *Writing African American Women*, J. Shantz's description of Pat Parker's involvement places the press in a larger feminist context: "In the early 1970s she moved to Oakland, California, where she became involved in a range of political activism including participation in the Black Panther Party and the Black Women's Revolutionary Council. She also played a part in the formation of the Women's Press Collective. Between 1978 and 1987 Parker was medical coordinator of the Oakland Feminist Women's Health Center, where her tireless work made her a national leader on issues of women's health, particularly regarding domestic and sexual violence" ("Pat Parker," 692). According to Heinz Insu Fenkl and Walter K. Lew, Willyce Kim, another Women's Press Collective organizer, was the "first openly lesbian Asian American poet" (Kori: The Beacon Anthology of Korean American Fiction, 218).

22. Carol Seajay, "News from the Bookstores," *Feminist Bookstore News* 18.4 (November/December 1995): 15–19, 16.

23. The press collective published the poems as a part of other collections as well, including in *Edward the Dyke and Other Poems* in 1971. Along with drawings by artists,

including Wendy Cadden, Brenda Crider, Gail Hodgins, Sunny, and Susann (no last names listed), the Women's Press Collective's editions of "The Common Woman" poems and "The Psychoanalysis of Edward the Dyke" influenced lesbian feminist discourse because of the artistic production as well as Grahn's direct language (Enszer, "Have Fun So We Do Not Go Mad in Male Supremacist Heterosexual Amerika").

24. Shange, *For Colored Girls Who Have Considered Suicide When the Rainbow Is Enuf*, xii.

25. Grahn, *Highest Apple*, 74. For analysis of this passage as a response to accusations of essentialism, see Linda Garber, "Lesbian Identity Politics" (60).

26. Grahn, *The Highest Apple*, xvii.

27. Grahn, *The Highest Apple*, xvii–xviii.

28. Sandoval draws on Anzaldúa to formulate a framework of multiple strategies of resistance by women of color: "It is in the activity of what Anzaldúa calls weaving 'between and among' oppositional ideologies as conceived in this new topographical space, where another and the fifth mode of oppositional consciousness and activity is found. I think of this activity of consciousness as 'differential,' insofar as it enables movement 'between and among' ideological positionings (the equal-rights, revolutionary, supremacist, and separatist modes of oppositional consciousness) considered as variables, in order to disclose the distinctions among them. In this sense, the differential mode of consciousness functions like the clutch of an automobile, the mechanism that permits the driver to select, engage, and disengage gears in a system for the transmission of power" (*Methodology of the Oppressed*, 146). In conversation with Sandoval, Jasbir Puar calls for a productive tension between intersectional identities and assemblages: "intersectional identities are the byproducts of attempts to still and quell the perpetual motion of assemblages, to capture and reduce them, to harness their threatening mobility" (*Terrorist Assemblages*, 213). Aimee Carillo Rowe shifts Sandoval amid Puar's map between intersections and assemblages: "By privileging belonging over consciousness in this reinscription of a differential consciousness I seek to frame consciousness itself as a collective process" (*Power Lines*, 215).

29. Grahn, *The Highest Apple*, xvii–xviii.

30. Seajay, interview with author.

31. Bluh, "Empty Shelves at Labyris."

32. Bluh, "Empty Shelves at Labyris."

33. Seajay, interview with author.

34. Labyris, "Poetry Reading," n.d., Womanbooks Papers, Lesbian Herstory Archives.

35. Love, *Feminists Who Changed America*, 390.

36. London, interview with author, 11 December 2003.

37. Numerous feminist theorists have examined the significance of contention for producing and refining feminist thought. I draw on these theoretical histories in order to narrate conflict in the bookstores not as a way of blaming particular individuals or organizations for failures of alliance building but rather to describe the bookstores as sites where conflict both indicates the racial diversity of the movement and demonstrates how feminist theories of cross-racial alliance were attempted, even when they

failed. I refer to Barbara Johnson's claim that interrupting a homogeneous concept of "women," particularly as straight or heteronormative, builds feminist capacity for alliance building: "A feminist logic that pits women against men operates along the lines of heterosexual thinking. But conflicts among feminists require women to pay attention to each other, to take each other's reality seriously, to face each other" (*The Feminist Difference*, 194). I use Ann Pelligrini's claim that the recognition of differences among feminists is a practice of resistance (*Performance Anxieties*, 7–8), and Carolyn Dever's recovery of public dissent as public commitment: "Some have argued that public dissent within feminism plays into the hands of antifeminist factions pursuing a divide-and-conquer strategy. This is a risk, to be sure. But it's also the case that contention, dissent, and internal resistance within feminist discourses might signify the renewal of political commitment through the insistence on ever more rigorous, ever more precise analytical terms" (*Skeptical Feminism*, 16). Ultimately, I find value in this development of feminist thought in creating feminist alliances across racial and class difference. In the next chapter I engage with Aimee Carrillo Rowe's work on building feminist alliances between white women and women of color as well as among women of color. Rowe's work builds on M. Jacqui Alexander and Chandra Mohanty's and Rachel Lee's call for engagement of women of color with each other across racial and ethnic difference. After de Beauvoir, Alexander and Mohanty together assert, "We are not born women of color, but became women of color here" ("Introduction," xiv). Looking at the field of women's studies, Lee uses Alexander and Mohanty for an epigraph and urges collaborating "on points of disagreement and catalysts of disidentification, controverting overinvestments in 'women of color' as a 'new model for unity'" ("Notes from the (Non)Field," 98).

38. Womanbooks, Opening Flyer, March 1974, Womanbooks Papers, Lesbian Herstory Archives.

39. Womanbooks, Founding Charter, Womanbooks Papers, Lesbian Herstory Archives.

40. They published, for example, a translation in the lesbian magazine *Conditions*. Hitomi, "Yuriko, Da Svidanya."

41. Eleanor Olds Batchelder, interview with author, 3 July 2003.

42. Messer-Davidow, *Disciplining Feminism*, 157.

43. In an earlier article I traced a history of the bookstores' influence on women's studies. Hogan, "Women's Studies in Feminist Bookstores."

44. The actual address of the second Womanbooks location was 656 Amsterdam Avenue, but Womanbooks referred to the address as 201 West 92nd Street because it made the bookstore "easier to find." Batchelder, email to author, 15 October 2005.

45. Though not before the founding of Barnes & Noble, at this time feminist bookstores were providing on a large scale the kinds of comforts Barnes & Noble would only later find profitable to include in its chain stores. See Daniel Raff on the history of Barnes & Noble. Raff, "Superstores and the Evolution of Firm Capabilities in American Bookselling."

46. Womanbooks, Newsletter, summer 1976, Womanbooks Papers, Lesbian Herstory Archives.

47. Toronto Women's Bookstore Collective, "Toronto Women's Bookstore Celebrates 15 Years!," *Feminist Bookstore News* 11.5 (January 1989): 24.

48. Canadian feminist authors have repeatedly looked to Kensington Market for signs of complex relationships between diasporas. In her collection published in 1989 by the lesbian feminist Firebrand Books, Toronto feminist literary icon Dionne Brand describes the view "At the Lisbon Plate," the bar where her protagonist observes the ever-present vestiges of colonialism as they vibrate into present-day oppressions. "The bar has a limited view of Kensington Market. Across the street from it there's a parkette, in the centre of which there is a statue of Cristobal Colon. Columbus, the carpet-bagger" (*Sans Souci and Other Stories*, 99). The Black Caribbean narrator recognizes a history in her proximity to the Portuguese bartender, from slavery to socioeconomic class and economic violence. Margaret Atwood, too, traces this violence of colonization; in her 1993 *The Robber Bride*, she writes: "She likes the mix on the street here, the mixed skins. Chinatown has taken over mostly, though there are still some Jewish delicatessens, and, further up and off to the side, the Portuguese and West Indian shops of the Kensington Market. Rome in the second century, Constantinople in the tenth, Vienna in the nineteenth. A crossroads" (39). A layering of relationships across race, geographic origin, journeys, and gender takes place here, in Kensington Market, across the counters, over boxes of rosy mangoes or a bin of dried fruit. The bookstore found its second location in this central city hub.

49. Patti Kirk, interview with author, 28 May 2007; Zavitz, "The Toronto Women's Bookstore"; Toronto Women's Bookstore Collective, "Toronto Women's Bookstore Celebrates 15 Years!"

50. Kirk, interview with author.

51. Gilda Bruckman, interview with author, 23 July 2003.

52. Rita Arditti, interview with author, 19 June 2004.

53. New Words, Order Form for Paperback Booksmith, 12 March 1974, Schlesinger Library, Radcliffe Institute for Advanced Study, Harvard University, 2002-M173, New Words Records.

54. The photo is still distributed as a postcard through Syracuse Cultural Workers (SCW). The back of the postcard reads: "WONDER WOMAN © 1976 Ellen Shub; Photograph taken in New Words Bookstore (186 Hampshire St., Cambridge MA 02139 . . .) August, 1976. Feminist bookstores across the US carry many resources for and about girls as does SCW."

55. Daly, *Beyond God the Father*, 8.

56. Bruckman, interview with author.

57. Bruckman, interview with author.

58. Woolf, *Three Guineas*, 176 n. 11.

59. Lorde, "An Open Letter to Mary Daly," 101.

60. Daly, *Gyn/Ecology*, 18.

61. DeVeaux, *Warrior Poet*, 251–2.

62. Lorde, "An Open Letter to Mary Daly," 101.

63. Feminist rhetorician Krista Ratcliffe documents the longer history of delayed response from Daly to Lorde and a later meeting between the two. Ratcliffe emphasizes the importance of looking to this break: "Without downplaying how personally painful this debate was for both women (as [Adrienne] Rich says, such debates are meant to break our hearts), perhaps the rest of us can now benefit from the debate if we revision it, using it to imagine not who was right and who was wrong but rather how one moves from a rhetoric of dysfunctional silence to a rhetoric of listening" (*Rhetorical Listening*, 84). With this book I seek to put the work of feminist bookwomen in conversation with analyses of such significant moments in the development of lesbian antiracist feminist accountability.

64. Kathryn Thoms Flannery's book *Feminist Literacies 1968–75* offers a model of how to read documents from the late twentieth-century feminist movement and how these materials should inflect our understanding of feminism. While she does not address feminist bookstores, I find the bookstores poignant spaces for understanding such materials. In connection with her work, this book contributes bookwomen's histories to a conversation about feminist publishing and reading.

65. Rita Arditti, Gilda Bruckman, Mary Lowry, and Jean MacRae, "Statement from New Words on Our Fourth Birthday, April, 1978," Schlesinger Library, Radcliffe Institute for Advanced Study, Harvard University, 2002-M173, New Words Records.

66. These travels result in what Kayann Short has called "a 'circulatory tale' because it relies heavily upon a sense of mobility, of what Grahn and Seajay refer to as 'getting women out into the world'" (*Publishing Feminism in the Feminist Press Movement*, 6).

67. Nina Wouk and Susan Post, interview with author, 4 June 2002.

68. Kathleen Liddle describes the unique work of bookstores in lesbian community building: "the books being sold are part of a dispersed lesbian community. Enfolded within their pages are the voices of a diversity of women—real and fictional—whose words provide comfort, encouragement, and guidance." Throughout this book, I argue that this "imagined community" of the bookstores, in addition to important comfort, also challenged readers and collective members to hold them accountable to difficult formulations of feminist ethics. Liddle, "More Than a Bookstore," 150.

69. "Women Acting on Austin," *The Rag*, n.d., BookWoman Papers, Susan Post, Austin, Texas.

70. Wouk and Post, interview with author.

71. To sketch a context for the Austin bookwomen's focus on feminist crafting, I look to Ann Cvetkovich. In a reading of the work of lesbian craft artists Sheila Pepe and Allyson Mitchell, Cvetkovich explains the power of feminist craft: "Not only does their work embody a reparative response to conflicts within feminism and between art and craft, but the utopian spaces of their large-scale installations produce a reparative experience of depression by literally engaging the senses in a way that makes things feel different" (*Depression*, 177).

72. Nina Wouk, "Dear Tide Collective."

73. Wouk and Post, interview with author.

74. Common Woman Bookstore Collective, brochure, 1976, BookWoman Papers, Susan Post, Austin, Texas.

75. Elena Cablao, "Feminist Mission de Guadalupe: A Hystory of 2004 Guadalupe, Austin," *Our Lady's Mission* 3.2 (March/April 1983): 1, 14, BookWoman Papers, Susan Post, Austin, Texas, 1.

76. Wouk and Post, interview with author.

77. Womanbooks, founding charter, Womanbooks Papers, Lesbian Herstory Archives.

78. Susan Post, interview with author, 29 January 2004.

79. Bertha Harris chalks this concern about FBI infiltrators up to movement bravado: "More than one woman whose ideals and personal ambition had been disappointed by the women's movement half-hoped to achieve immortality in those days by becoming a martyr to the cause—and June [Arnold] wasn't the first" (*Lover*, lxxi). Certainly by the mid-1970s, as Marcia M. Gallo points out, "the misdeeds of J. Edgar Hoover's FBI, in concert with the CIA and various branches of the U.S. military, validated what many activists had long thought might have been going on" (*Different Daughters*, xvii–xviii). Phyllis Lyon and Del Martin, cofounders of the lesbian organization Daughters of Bilitis, learned by requisitioning their FBI file in 1981 that "the FBI had been keeping tabs on the Daughters of Bilitis from the beginning," with reports filed "throughout the late 1950s and 1960s" (xix). Reasonable suspicion of the FBI surveillance of activism extended to the Women in Print Movement in 1977 after a destructive break-in at the offices of the Baltimore feminist Diana Press (Harris, *Lover*, lxxii).

80. As late as 2009 the San Diego Feminist Federal Credit Union merged with the Women's Southwest Federal Credit Union in Dallas, which closed in 2012. The Ottawa Women's Credit Union was another feminist credit union open until the 2010s; it merged with Alterna Savings in 2013. Seajay and Wallace received full funding for the bookstore from their "loan from the Bay Area Feminist Federal Credit Union." Old Wives' Tales, "Birthday Statement," 1976, the Feminist Bookstore News Records, San Francisco Public Library.

81. Old Wives' Tales opened on Halloween in 1976 (Old Wives' Tales, "Birthday Statement," 1976) and two years later credited Jesse Meredith for its naming: "Old Wives' Tales was named by Jesse Meredith (then of Rising Woman Books in Santa Rosa) who never until this moment received due credit for her genius" (Old Wives' Tales, "Birthday Statement #2," 1978). Seajay and Wallace had both worked at ICI: A Woman's Place for at least a year: "Both of us have worked at I.C.I.—A Woman's Place in Oakland for more than a year, and our experience and energy is what we began Old Wives' Tales with" (Old Wives' Tales, "Birthday Statement," 1976). Old Wives' Tales, "Birthday Statement," 1976, the Feminist Bookstore News Records, San Francisco Public Library; Old Wives' Tales, "Birthday Statement #2," November 1978, the Feminist Bookstore News Records, San Francisco Public Library.

82. Four years after this account of Seajay's search for a workplace that recognized and supported lesbian and feminist identities, Adrienne Rich, in her essay "Compulsory Heterosexuality and Lesbian Existence," voiced what many, including Seajay, had

felt and discussed. In her claim that "lesbian existence comprises both the breaking of a taboo and the rejection of a compulsory way of life," and her urging that the destruction of evidence of lesbian existence was a tool of "keeping heterosexuality compulsory for women" (239), Rich provided an outline for resisting compulsory heterosexuality that, in conversation with Seajay's comments in the Old Wives' Tales birthday statement from 1976, positioned feminist bookstores as an important site for documenting lesbian existence on the shelves and in the workplace. In a 2003 collection of responses to Rich's 1980 essay, Matt Richardson emphasizes the ways Rich's call must also apply to examining compulsory constructions of gender and racial identities: "Rich challenged the notion that heterosexism is only an act by an individual bigot and demonstrated how it is part of a deeper, pervasive structural flaw that renders relationships between women invalid and invisible in every level of scholarship. . . . Her assessment of heterosexuality as an institution, like class and race, offered me a way to understand the compulsory component as creating lies and distortions maintained by every profession, cultural product, reference work, curriculum, and scholarship" ("No More Secrets, No More Lies," 63). While recognizing the limits of Rich's essay, Richardson uses the essay to think about African American literature as an archive of queer African American histories: "In order to study Black female subjects who are not feminine and feminine Black female subjects whose sexuality is not produced solely in relation to men . . . analyses must take into consideration the way categories of gender and desire are produced for raced subjects" (73). His call to connect compulsory heterosexuality with compulsory whiteness and classed subjecthood was shared by some feminist bookwomen who attempted to create transracial reading practices; in chapters 3 and 4 I discuss this work to develop a lesbian antiracist feminism in the bookstores.

83. Old Wives' Tales, "Birthday Statement," 1976.

84. Old Wives' Tales, "Birthday Statement," 1976.

85. Old Wives' Tales, "Birthday Statement," 1976.

2. Revolutionaries in a Capitalist System, 1976–1980

1. Carol Seajay, interview with author, 17 July 2003.

2. Womanbooks, spiral notebook (cofounders' notes), 1975–1976, Womanbooks Papers, Lesbian Herstory Archives.

3. "At the 1976 Women in Print Conference," *Feminist Bookstores Newsletter* 1.1 (October 1976): 2.

4. "At the 1976 Women in Print Conference," 2.

5. Here I connect with Elizabeth McHenry's formulation of literary activism in her history of African American literary societies in the nineteenth and twentieth centuries. By formulating the term "literary activists," McHenry turns readers' attention to the literary as a significant site of political change. McHenry herself roots this term in the work of Victoria Earle Matthews, and, in particular, in Matthews's 30 July 1895 address to the First Congress of Colored Women in Boston. "What was at stake, should black clubwomen not become literary activists, Matthews suggested, was nothing

less than the future of the race. She closed her address with the following words of warning: 'Unless earnest and systematic effort be made to procure and preserve for the transmission to our successors, the records, books and various publications already produced by us, not only will the sturdy pioneers who paved the way and laid the foundation for our Race Literature, be robbed of their just due, but an irretrievable wrong will be inflicted upon the generations that shall come after us'" (*Forgotten Readers*, 197). Rather than a by-product of a social movement, historically marginalized literature requires an intricate support system in order to be written, published, distributed, read, and understood. Social movements often create these support systems, and literary activists establish the necessary system to chronicle the movement and its literatures.

6. Carol Seajay, "Dear Sisters," *Feminist Bookstores Newsletter* 1.1 (October 1976): 1.

7. Seajay, interview with author.

8. "The List of Feminist Bookstores and Distributors in the U.S. and Canada," *Feminist Bookstores Newsletter* 1.5 (April 1977): 4–5.

9. "Bookstores," *Feminist Bookstores Newsletter* 2.2 (1978): 3–5.

10. Karyn London, "Books in Spanish," *Feminist Bookstores Newsletter* 1.1 (October 1976): 3–4.

11. "At the 1976 Women in Print Conference," *Feminist Bookstores Newsletter*, 2.

12. Feminist bookstores offered the tools women needed to prepare to be allies with each other. M. Jacqui Alexander writes to women of color that to "*become* women of color we need to become fluent in each other's histories" (*Pedagogies of Crossing*, 269). White women could exercise their white privilege to assume they cannot build connections with women of color; however, Aimee Carillo Rowe calls white feminists, too, to account to Alexander's call to women of color: "This becoming is both a function of taking responsibility for doing our 'homework' so that we can arrive with some capacity for fluency, and also a relational practice of enacting bridge work within our communication practices" (*Power Lines*, 89).

13. The women in the screened-in room understood this session as part of a larger feminist conversation about racial justice; earlier that year in Seattle the National Black Feminist Organization and the white feminist Sagaris Collective had worked together to hold a session on racism and sexism. Womanbooks, spiral notebook (cofounders' notes), 1975–1976, Womanbooks Papers, Lesbian Herstory Archives.

14. "Native American Women," *Feminist Bookstores Newsletter* 1.2 (November 1976): 5; "Black Women," *Feminist Bookstores Newsletter* 1.2 (November 1976): 5; "Young Women & Youth Liberation Booklist," *Feminist Bookstores Newsletter* 1.2 (November 1976): 6.

15. "Native American Women," *Feminist Bookstores Newsletter* 1.2 (November 1976): 5.

16. Carol Seajay, "Opening Celebration," *Feminist Bookstores Newsletter* 1.1 (October 1976): 5.

17. In the spiral notebook they brought to the Women in Print Conference, the women from Womanbooks documented the gathered bookwomen's "commitment to increase effectiveness of femt media esp. support distr.," that is, their commitment to increase the effectiveness of feminist media, especially by supporting distribution.

Womanbooks, spiral notebook (cofounders' notes), 1975–1976, Womanbooks Papers, Lesbian Herstory Archives.

18. "New Titles," *Feminist Bookstores Newsletter* 1.2 (November 1976): 7–8, 8.

19. "Distributors," *Feminist Bookstores Newsletter* 1.2 (November 1976): 6–7.

20. Nina Wouk and Susan Post, interview with author, 4 June 2002.

21. Kay Turner, interview with author, 3 July 2003.

22. Much later, Andrew Laites describes this challenge for independent bookstores in general (*Rebel Bookseller*, 164–165); Laites's discussion about the unnecessary and skewed nature of returns, already earlier laid out by the feminist bookwomen, indicates the role of grassroots movement institutions in pushing more mainstream activism. Here, feminist bookwomen laid the groundwork for general independent bookstore activism.

23. "Things You Always Wanted to Know," *Feminist Bookstores Newsletter* 1.3 (January 1977): 11–12.

24. "Things You Always Wanted to Know," 11–12.

25. "Things You Always Wanted to Know," 12.

26. Feminist bookwomen here were traveling a well-worn path of feminist literary activists. Describing the work of Black clubwomen as a counterpublic preparing to influence and then influencing a larger public sphere, Elizabeth McHenry answers the question "How did black women become literary activists?" Her book offers a thorough and revelatory account of this process, in brief: "In the face of tremendous challenges, clubwomen depended on one another to provide the constructive feedback that would help them to develop and strengthen their literary talents and sustain their confidence in themselves and enthusiasm for their work" (*Forgotten Readers*, 202).

27. New Words, "Dear Publisher," *Feminist Bookstores Newsletter* 1.3 (January 1977): 3.

28. Jean MacRae and Gilda Bruckman, "Dear Carol [Seajay] and Andre," *Feminist Bookstores Newsletter* 1.3 (January 1977): 2.

29. André and Carol Seajay, "Dear Everybody," *Feminist Bookstores Newsletter* 1.2 (November 1976): 4.

30. "Questionnaire," *Feminist Bookstores Newsletter* 1.4 (1977): 1.

31. "Questionnaire," 1.

32. Rosalie Nichols, "Dear FBN," *Feminist Bookstores Newsletter* 1.4 (1977): 2–3, 2.

33. Feminist or women's sections in chain bookstores serve as the (often sparse) remnants of attempts to contain movements with capital. In her discussion of the development of a white gay male travel industry during the same time as the rise of the feminist bookstores, M. Jacqui Alexander describes legitimation by capital as cooptation: "It is indeed a paradox that more than three decades after the gay movement deployed pride in identity to destabilize the internalized shame of heterosexism, heterosexual capital now moves to redeploy gay identity in the service of legitimizing its own heterosexual pride" (*Pedagogies of Crossing*, 76). That is, by limiting "visibility" to "the lesbian and gay press" and by using advertisements to "effectively [seal] a relationship between white gay citizenship and white gay consumption," capitalism racializes, genders, and restricts gay identity as it engages in "wooing an audience of which it is

contemptuous" (76, 75). When corporations claim a piece of activist or community-based identity, Miranda Joseph explains, "that corporate deployment of the given form or style makes it at least in part alien to and against those who generated it" (*Against the Romance of Community*, 44). So, too, are the "women's studies" sections in chain stores and the rise of a mainstream women's literature in part alien to and against the feminist movement that fought for them. Joseph also offers us a way out: "The diversity of groups useful as niche market consumers can turn around and understand themselves, assert themselves, as producers" (53). Feminist bookwomen enacted this practice Joseph describes as interrupting capital: "I have shown not that there are no sites of potential resistance but a great proliferation of sites of weakness, of contradiction and crisis, in the circuits of capital and that those sites are us, in our desires and discontents" (174). Appropriately for my work here, Joseph finds some of those articulations of desires and discontents in feminist books: "The publication of works such as Cherríe Moraga and Gloria Anzaldúa's *This Bridge Called My Back*, Audre Lorde's collected essays *Sister Outsider*, Anzaldúa's *Borderlands*, and bell hooks's *Ain't I a Woman*, among many others, raised doubts about singular identity categories as an organizing principle for social change. These works make it very clear that to imagine that women are a community is to elide and repress differences among women, to enact racism and heterosexism within a women's movement" (xxii). In this list of books, Joseph gathers a collection of women's literature as a way of understanding the relationships among different feminisms. Where feminist bookwomen assembled together Joseph's listed feminist books, I argue that a place of "weakness, of contradiction and crisis, in the circuits of capital" occurred and produced a feminist literary public sphere.

34. André, "An Update," *Feminist Bookstores Newsletter* 1.2 (November 1976): 4.

35. Pamela and Leslie, for the Emma Collective, "Good Sisters," *Feminist Bookstores Newsletter* 1.4 (1977): 5–6, 6.

36. Kit Quan, interview with author, 11 August 2007.

37. Kit Yuen Quan, "Alliances in Question."

38. In this very statement, Kit Quan is simultaneously participating in and critiquing feminist rhetoric. This practice enacts what Chela Sandoval called "differential consciousness," women of color using different strategies in different situations to create change (*Methodology of the Oppressed*, 146). For example, while women of color use and remake feminist rhetoric as a useful tool for change in the academy, in politics, and in other central public spheres, within the bookstore feminists of color could, Quan argued, acknowledge that the pressure on everyone to use the tool in the same way prioritized some feminists' experiences and identities over others. Patricia Hill Collins saw this tension as well. She valued Black feminist thought as a tool to respond to new and old forms of oppression, and she also pointed out, as Quan explains here, that historically marginalized groups themselves had different levels of power: "Black women's knowledge or collective voice interconnects with many others. Some remain dominant to Black feminist thought in some sense, whereas others are subordinate to it." For Collins, acknowledging this complexity that Quan describes allows deeper

work toward justice and alliances: "The climate of multiple 'voices' greatly shifts the terms of the debate. Dialogues among the formerly silenced and their silencers seem simplistic" (*Fighting Words*, 53–4). Indeed, the dialogues and meaningful silences Quan describes within the bookstore suggest the power of reflexive feminist print-based institutions that would acknowledge different types of literacies; while bookwomen did not achieve this vision, Quan attempts the imagining. Quan's work at the bookstore documents some of the complex conversations and relationships that feminist bookstores made possible, and her reflections and analysis gesture toward new futures. Quan, "The Girl Who Wouldn't Sing," 215.

39. Emily Shweber's line drawing appeared first on issue 1.5 (April 1977), and last appeared on issue 3.2 (February 1979).

40. "This Is What We Like about FBN," *Feminist Bookstores Newsletter* 2.1 (1978): 3.

41. Carol Seajay, "Dear Friends," *Feminist Bookstores Newsletter* 1.8 (1977): 1–2, 1.

42. "The List of Feminist Bookstores and Distributors in the U.S. and Canada," *Feminist Bookstores Newsletter* 1.5 (April 1977): 4–5.

43. "Bookstores," *Feminist Bookstores Newsletter* 2.2 (1978): 3–5.

44. "This Is What We Like about FBN," *Feminist Bookstores Newsletter* 2.1 (1978): 3.

45. Isabel Santos, "Dear Sisters," *Feminist Bookstores Newsletter* 1.9/10 (December 1977): 11.

46. Carol Seajay, "State of the Newsletter Letter," *Feminist Bookstores Newsletter* 1.9/10 (December 1977): 1–2, 1.

47. "We Want More Of," *Feminist Bookstores Newsletter* 2.1 (1978): 5–6, 5.

48. "More Rumors," *Feminist Bookstores Newsletter* 1.5 (April 1977): 8.

49. Carol Seajay, "Fate of the Newsletter/Advertising?," *Feminist Bookstores Newsletter* 2.1 (1978): 7–8, 8.

50. Anne Enke sees this revolutionary, capitalist-interrupting work in feminist spaces, including Amazon Bookstore in Minneapolis. By 1975, the fifth year the bookstore was open, "Amazon Bookstore began to turn profits"; Enke narrates this shift by claiming that "a market niche had developed alongside the activist niche" (*Finding the Movement*, 70). In fact, bookwomen argued for and were at pains to create this "market niche" and, simultaneously, to resist being confined by it.

51. Seajay, "Fate of the Newsletter/Advertising?," 8.

52. "This Is an Advertisement," *Feminist Bookstores Newsletter* 2.4 (August 1978): 7.

53. "Strategy Session: Getting Books Re-Issued," *Feminist Bookstores Newsletter* 1.9/10 (December 1977): 13–14, 13.

54. Seajay, interview with author.

55. "Strategy Session," 13.

56. "Strategy Session," 13.

57. Seajay, interview with author.

58. "Strategy Session," 13.

59. George J. Sullivan, "Dear Ms. Wallace," *Feminist Bookstores Newsletter* 2.1 (1978): 9.

60. "Write Now," *Feminist Bookstores Newsletter* 5.1 (June 1981): 7.

61. Joanna Russ, letter to the author, 8 August 2004.

62. Joanna Russ, *The Female Man*.

63. "Blitz," *Feminist Bookstores Newsletter* 3.2 (1979): 11.

64. Esther Broner, letter to Carol Seajay, 2 November 1979, Feminist Bookstore News Records, James C. Hormel Gay and Lesbian Center, San Francisco Public Library.

65. Darlene Pagano, "Going to the ABA Convention?," *Feminist Bookstores Newsletter* 2.2 (1978): 1.

66. Susan Post, interview with author, 29 January 2004.

67. Gilda Bruckman, interview with author, 23 July 2003.

68. Among others, Ntozake Shange's *For Colored Girls Who Have Considered Suicide When the Rainbow Is Enuf*, published by Shameless Hussy in 1975 and the Women's Press Collective in 1976, was picked up by its current publisher, Macmillan (now Scribner's), in 1977. Sandra Cisneros's *My Wicked Wicked Ways*, first published by Third Woman press in 1987, was picked up by Knopf in 1995. Rita Mae Brown's classic lesbian coming-of-age novel *Rubyfruit Jungle* was published by Daughters Press from 1973 until 1977, when Brown signed on with Bantam. Dorothy Allison published *Trash* in 1988 and *The Women Who Hate Me* in 1991 with the lesbian-feminist Firebrand Press before signing on with Dutton to publish *Bastard Out of Carolina* in 1992.

69. Karyn London, "Doing Remainders," *Feminist Bookstores Newsletter* 1.9/10 (December 1977) 14–16, 14.

70. London, "Doing Remainders," 15.

71. Old Wives' Tales, "Royalties on Remainders?????," *Feminist Bookstores Newsletter* 5.1 (June 1981): 6.

72. Karyn London, interview with author, 11 December 2003.

73. The field of book history has generated versions of a cycle of communication; starting with Robert Darnton's "Communications Circuit," Simone Murray describes a revised version for a "feminist 'communications circuit.'" Movement scholar Maylei Blackwell offers an exciting connection between these models and the work of Chicana "movement print culture." In Darnton's chart of the communications circuit, he connects the work of authors, publishers, printers, shippers, booksellers, and readers, along with the external economic, social, and political influences along the way ("What Is the History of Books?," 31). To map a feminist communications circuit, Murray inserts references to "the hiatuses, disruptions, and silences in the process" as well as to "the subterfuge and tension characterizing much feminist interaction with the publishing process" (*Mixed Media*, 16, 17). Though framed in negative language, Murray's revisions point to the political work of feminist publishing; the high stakes of social change result in both interpersonal and interinstitutional challenges and growth. In the places where Murray sees hiatuses, disruptions, and tension, I suggest we read again for movement-based education and learning that looks unproductive to a market framework but is essential for a movement. In a watershed essay, Blackwell offers a model for this reading when she traces the short but vital life of the publication *Hijas de Cuauhtémoc* from 1971 to 1973. Describing the publication's formation of a Chicana counterpublic, Blackwell reads these "publication practices and circuits of distribution"

as they form "part of a Chicana feminist strategy to rework modes of print communication already operating in the Chicano movement as well as to create new ones, thus multiplying the spaces of participation for women" ("Contested Histories," 70). This reworking creates within a publishing process a theory of Chicana feminist activism and suggests a way to read and understand, as well, the work of feminist bookwomen as theorizing an approach in movement information.

74. Karyn London, interview with author.

75. Eleanor Olds Batchelder, interview with author, 3 July 2003.

76. Seajay, interview with author.

77. Here bookwomen are in conversation with a long history of ongoing feminist literary activism by women of color. Elizabeth Maguire and Elizabeth McHenry examine, respectively, the late and early twentieth-century advocacy by women of color that required white-male-led mainstream publishing to acknowledge, if briefly, a readership for Black women authors. Maguire, "University Presses and the Black Reader"; McHenry, *Forgotten Readers*.

78. "Scream Quietly," *Feminist Bookstores Newsletter* 1.8 (1977): 4.

79. "Marion Zimmer Bradley's," *Feminist Bookstores Newsletter* 1.5 (April 1977): 8.

80. Batchelder, interview with author.

81. Carol Seajay, "State of the Newsletter Letter," *Feminist Bookstores Newsletter* 1.9/10 (December 1977): 1–2, 2.

82. "More from Feminist Literary Agency," *Feminist Bookstores Newsletter* 1.9/10 (December 1977): 6.

83. Carol Seajay, "Dear Bookstore Women," *Feminist Bookstores Newsletter* 2.5/6 (1978): 1–2, 2. For more information on Celeste West as a feminist publisher, see Samek, "Unbossed and Unbought"; Samek, Roberto, and Lang, *She Was a Booklegger*.

84. Carol Seajay, "Dear Bookstore Women," *Feminist Bookstores Newsletter*, 1.

85. Seajay, "Dear Bookstore Women," 1.

86. "Should We Accept Subscriptions from Individual Women," *Feminist Bookstores Newsletter* 2.1 (1978): 2.

87. "Questionnaire Responses," *Feminist Bookstores Newsletter* 3.1 (1979): 1–2, 1.

88. Significantly, *Face the Music* (distributed by Olivia Records, the record company Christian helped to found) featured a range of guest artists making it a collective force of the multiracial womyn's music scene: Holly Near, Sweet Honey in the Rock, Teresa Trull, Linda Tillery, and others. Annie Dinerman authored the lyrics for "Face the Music." Meg Christian, *Face the Music* (Los Angeles: Olivia Records, 1977).

89. "Basis of Unity: Developing a Coalition Policy, Success and Process at A Woman's Place—Portland," *Feminist Bookstores Newsletter* 2.2 (1978): 9–12, 9.

90. "Basis of Unity," 9.

91. "Basis of Unity," 10.

92. "Basis of Unity," 12.

93. "Basis of Unity," 11.

94. Carol Seajay connected the A Woman's Place documents to Old Wives' Tales collective discussions about committing bookstore endorsement as a political statement:

"We (OWT) have been in the process of trying to figure out some basis for who to 'endorse' & who not to endorse, and how to make that endorsement mean something, or should it (continue?) to be almost a rubber stamp action." "Basis of Unity," 9.

95. "Response to the Bookstore's Coalition Policy—reprinted from A Woman's Place Newsletter," *Feminist Bookstores Newsletter* 2.2 (1978): 13–14, 13.

96. "More from A Woman's Place—Portland," *Feminist Bookstores Newsletter* 2.3 (June 1978): 2–3, 2.

97. "More from A Woman's Place—Portland," 3.

98. "More from A Woman's Place—Portland," 3.

99. Niobe Erebor, "Dear Sisters," *Feminist Bookstores Newsletter* 3.2 (1979): 1.

100. Carol Seajay, "WIND Ended," *Feminist Bookstores Newsletter* 3.3 (1979): 1–2, 1.

101. "At the 1976 Women in Print Conference," *Feminist Bookstores Newsletter*.

102. For international bookwomen, this budgeting was not possible; the end of WIND meant, in the case of SisterWrite in London, that they "simply won't be able to stock some of the small press titles, as we have to pay so much for bank drafts, etc., as to price them out of the market." For the bookstore that imported "a large part of our stock from the US," this newly limited ordering resulted in a mainstreaming of their shelves. Lynn Alderson, for the SisterWrite collective, "Feminist Bookshops in England: A Letter from SisterWrite," *Feminist Bookstores Newsletter* 4.1 (June 1980): 3.

103. Seajay, "WIND Ended," 1–2, 1.

104. Seajay, "WIND Ended," 2; Judy Grahn, *Edward the Dyke and Other Poems* (Oakland: Women's Press Collective, 1971).

105. "The Feminist Bookstores Newsletter List of Bookstores," *Feminist Bookstores Newsletter* 3.4 (1979): insert after 4.

106. Seajay, "WIND Ended," 1.

107. Carol Seajay, "FBN Turns into a List Distribution Center (and more)," *Feminist Bookstores Newsletter* 3.5 (October 1979): 1.

108. Minnie Bruce Pratt, letter to Carol Seajay (on *Feminary* stationery), 24 August 1979, Feminist Bookstore News Records, James C. Hormel Gay and Lesbian Center, San Francisco Public Library.

109. "And, No, Sister, You're Not Crazy," *Feminist Bookstores Newsletter* 3.5 (October 1979): 12.

110. "And, No, Sister, You're Not Crazy," 12.

111. Old Wives' Tales, "Fourth Annual Old Wives' Tales State of the (feminist publishing) World and Third Birthday Statement," November 1979, Old Wives' Tales Bookstore Records, James C. Hormel Gay and Lesbian Center, San Francisco Public Library.

112. Old Wives' Tales, "Old Wives' Tales' Fourth Birthday Halloween 1976–Halloween 1980," 1980, Old Wives' Tales Bookstore Records, James C. Hormel Gay and Lesbian Center, San Francisco Public Library, 3.

113. Old Wives' Tales, "Old Wives' Tales' Fourth Birthday Halloween 1976–Halloween 1980," 2.

114. Old Wives' Tales, "Old Wives' Tales' Fourth Birthday Halloween 1976–Halloween 1980," 4.

115. Womanbooks, "Agreement made this day of January, 1981," January 1981, Womanbooks Papers, Lesbian Herstory Archives.

116. Old Wives' Tales, "Fourth Annual Old Wives' Tales State of the (feminist publishing) World and Third Birthday Statement."

117. "They Went That-a-Way!," *Feminist Bookstores Newsletter* 4.1 (June 1980): 9.

118. "Hot Flash," *Feminist Bookstores Newsletter* 3.6 (February 1980): 5.

3. Accountable to Each Other, 1980–1983

1. Loraine Hutchins, "Trouble and Mediation at Yosemite," *off our backs* 11.10 (30 November 1981): 12.

2. Reagon, "Coalition Politics," 356.

3. This call is more than metaphor, emphasizes feminist disability studies scholar Alison Kafer: "Reagon is theorizing from the disabled body, using her embodied experience of disability—having a physical limitation in a sociopolitical setting that acts as if that limitation were nonexistent, or at least irrelevant—as a springboard for thinking about difference, relation, and politics" (*Feminist, Queer, Crip*, 152). Through queer feminist disability studies, the future becomes, rather than a fantasy of perfection, an extension of the present work in generative alliance building. Kafer offers, with her formulation of "crip time," a call to examine prevalent ideas about the "future" (27). Social constructions of the future, she argues, interweaving disability studies with queer theory, render judgments about whose lives society values in the present. Rather than reflecting on the present from a fantastic and eugenic future, Kafer asks, how can we instead use the present to redefine socially just futures? Looking to Reagon's talk, she poses the question: "How accessible—financially, culturally, intellectually, physically—are feminist spaces, spaces in and through which feminist futures are imagined?" (152). Alison Kafer, *Feminist, Queer, Crip*.

4. Reagon, "Coalition Politics," 360.

5. This connection, built on decades of analysis by women of color, had been legendarily made by the members of the Combahee River Collective, who started meeting in 1974 and wrote in 1977 that they "find it difficult to separate race from class from sex oppression because in our lives they are most often experienced simultaneously." Combahee River Collective, "A Black Feminist Statement," 237.

6. Reagon, "Coalition Politics," 361.

7. Reagon, "Coalition Politics," 368.

8. At the 1976 Women in Print Conference, feminist bookwomen mapped out seven visions for "Future Plans" of feminist bookstores. In the second of these, bookwomen claimed "feminist bookstores as a network of 'woman's places' and information centers across the country." Significantly, the possible homogeneity of "woman's places" would be productively undermined by the role of bookstores as "information centers"

intentionally full of living pages of antiracist feminist thought meant to inform practice. "At the 1976 Women in Print Conference," *Feminist Bookstores Newsletter* 1.1 (October 1976): 2.

9. Feminist bookwomen opened bookstores named A Woman's Place in cities including Oakland, California; Phoenix, Arizona (Womansplace); Portland, Oregon; Toronto; and Vancouver, British Columbia.

10. Throughout this chapter, I seek to unsettle a sense of the bookstores as sites of feminist "home." Andrea Smith connects feminist critiques of "home" as safe—since home is also a site of pervasive intimate partner violence—with racial justice critiques of the nation as "home"—since the nation is also a site of violence against all people of color, indigenous people, and queer people. Smith refigures these emotional relationships (whose home?) to imagine alliances across movements. Rather than envision feminist bookstores as a nonexistent feminist "home" space, I read the bookstores as vital spaces of negotiation. The space of a bookstore changed according to who was in the collective or working the desk, what event was taking place, or what the recent issue of FBN had challenged the collective to do next. In mapping these negotiations, I look to Chandra Talpade Mohanty and Biddy Martin's warning against "reproducing the most conventional articulations" of "home and family" ("What's Home Got to Do with It?," 85). Their essay, significantly, takes place across the shelves of this chapter as they dialogue with Bernice Johnson Reagon on coalition and with Minnie Bruce Pratt in her "Identity: Skin, Blood, Heart." Mohanty and Martin offer a specific reading of Pratt's essay: "What we have tried to draw out of this text is the way in which it unsettles not only any notion of feminism as an all-encompassing home but also the assumption that there are discrete, coherent, and absolutely separate identities—homes within feminism, so to speak—based on absolute divisions between various sexual, racial, or ethnic identities" (86). Ultimately, Mohanty and Martin "open up the question of how political community might be reconceptualized within feminist practice" (105). Bookwomen in this chapter offer approaches to this dialogue. Andrea Smith, "Beyond the Politics of Inclusion."

11. Tiana Arruda, Carol Seajay, Pell, and Sherry Thomas, "From the Old Wives' Tales Collective," [unknown journal], September 1982, [unknown page numbers], Old Wives' Tales Bookstore Records, James C. Hormel Gay and Lesbian Center, San Francisco Public Library.

12. West Coast Women's Music Festival Staff, "The West Coast Women's Music Festival," [unknown journal], September 1982, [unknown page numbers] , Old Wives' Tales Bookstore Records, James C. Hormel Gay and Lesbian Center, San Francisco Public Library.

13. "At the 1976 Women in Print Conference," 2.

14. Feminist theorists have used the term "feminist accountability" to describe feminists' responsibilities to each other and, at times, a practice of alliance building across differences between feminists. Here I name feminist accountability as a more formal and framing practice for feminism, the ethical framework feminism itself works to define and evolve, the map for the world in which we want to live. This ethic in the 1980s documents an instance of Caren Kaplan's sense of "accountability" that

she sees missing in much of 1980s Euro-American feminism. Kaplan points out that "accountability can begin to shift the ground of feminist practice . . . to the complex interpretive practices that acknowledge the historical roles of mediation, betrayal, and alliance in the relationships between women in diverse locations" (*Questions of Travel*, 169). Here, Kaplan is thinking toward transnational feminisms as well; in this chapter and in chapter 4, I see bookwomen enacting this shift and creating an infrastructure that models how to sustain it.

15. Among authors who analyze the ways lesbian identity commits lesbians to antiracist work are Aimee Carillo Rowe, Mab Segrest, and the Combahee River Collective. Rowe suggests, "Lesbian desire poses a troubled relationship to family for queer women, which may provide a point of entry for such women to cultivate *transracial* identifications" (*Power Lines*, 108). Segrest shows how this might work when she describes her movement from white family to antiracist organizing: "my culture raised me to compete: for grades, for jobs, for money, for self-esteem. As my lungs breathed in competition, they breathed out the stale air of individualism, delivering the toxic message to cells and corpuscles: *You are on your own*. Being 'queer' only amplified the problem. Traveling across race and class and cultural boundaries, my ear eventually became tuned to different vibrations so that I began to hear, first as a murmur, then as clearly articulated sound: *We . . . are . . . in . . . this . . . together*. My lungs relaxed some, my cells gasped the clearer air" (*Memoir of a Race Traitor*, 174). And the Black lesbian feminists of the Combahee River Collective identified their lesbianism as informing a particular antiracist practice: "A combined antiracist and antisexist position drew us together initially, and as we developed politically we addressed ourselves to heterosexism and economic oppression under capitalism" ("A Black Feminist Statement," 237). I see the origins of this work in specifically *lesbian* antiracism because of political lesbian connections to feminism; this legacy provides a history directly connected to today's queer antiracist feminisms, which continue and deepen the lesbian antiracist feminist project of taking apart racism, sexism, and heterosexism. I include these histories and this term, lesbian antiracism, as an invitation to use our queerness as a call to antiracist practice.

16. Anjula Gogia, interview with author, 21 January 2007.

17. Toronto Women's Bookstore, Written in Colour Program, 2006.

18. Carol Seajay, interview with author, 17 July 2003.

19. Sherry Thomas, Old Wives' Tales, "ABA Conference," *Feminist Bookstores Newsletter* 5.1 (June 1981): 4–5, 5.

20. Carol Seajay, André, and Jesse Meredith, "Changes, Changes," *Feminist Bookstores Newsletter* 4.1 (June 1980): 1.

21. Jesse Meredith, "Dear Folks," *Feminist Bookstores Newsletter* 4.5 (marked V.5) (February 1981): 1–2, 2.

22. Jesse Meredith, "Dear Folks," 2.

23. "Some of You Just," *Feminist Bookstores Newsletter* 4.6 (April 1981): 2.

24. Kate Rushin and Laura Zimmerman, interview with author, 2 April 2006.

25. Kate Rushin, "The Bridge Poem," lvii–lviii, lvii.

26. Rushin and Zimmerman, interview with author.

27. Rushin, "The Bridge Poem," lviii.

28. Pell, interview with author, 26 March 2008.

29. Pell, interview with author.

30. Kit Quan, interview with author, 11 August 2007.

31. Pell, interview with author.

32. "The last decades of the 19th century until the 1940s saw Sixth Street become home to 17 trades and professions practiced by African Americans. The Carver Center of African-American History produced an exhibition in 1981 entitled The Black Entrepreneurs of East Sixth Street." Some of the businesses remained through the 1970s. Allen Childs, *Sixth Street*, 45.

33. Susan Post, interview with author, 29 January 2004.

34. Post and Nina Wouk also relate another impetus to change the name: Judy Grahn was unhappy at the use of her poem. "She came to read at the bookstore on Sixth Street," Post remembers, and she asked to be paid for the use of her title. In naming the Common Woman Bookstore, early collective members had tried to grasp and hold what Judy Grahn in her Common Woman poems had worked to develop, a redefinition of the word "common" as a connected group capable of allying to create change. Wouk explains, "I don't think it occurred to any of us at the time, that it was anybody's intellectual property. . . . We thought we were honoring her." At that point, according to Post, "when we had to change the name, it seemed not as bad because she was unhappy that we had chosen that [name]." Nina Wouk and Susan Post, interview with author, 4 June 2002.

35. Post, interview with author.

36. Yoko Ono, *Grapefruit*. Yoko Ono initially created Wunternaum Press and published *Grapefruit* herself.

37. Kay Turner, interview with author, 11 December 2003.

38. Ono offers this exercise in "LET'S PIECE I." Ono, *Grapefruit*.

39. "The Feminist Bookstores Newsletter List of Bookstores," *Feminist Bookstores Newsletter* 3.4 (1979): insert after 4.

40. Pell, interview with author.

41. Jesse Meredith, "Organizing for Survival," *Feminist Bookstores Newsletter* 4.3 (October 1980): 1–3, 1.

42. Meredith, "Organizing for Survival," 2.

43. Meredith, "Organizing for Survival," 2.

44. Meredith, "Organizing for Survival," 3.

45. Sonya Wetstone, Wetstone Books & Cheese, "Dear Friends," *Feminist Bookstores Newsletter* 4.4 (December 1980): 2.

46. Ellen, New Earth, "Jesse," *Feminist Bookstores Newsletter* 4.4 (December 1980): 3.

47. Meredith, "Dear Folks," 2.

48. Holt, "Creative Merchandising, Attention to Detail Help a Feminist Bookshop to Flourish," 37.

49. Holt, "Creative Merchandising, Attention to Detail Help a Feminist Bookshop to Flourish," 37.

50. Holt, "Creative Merchandising, Attention to Detail Help a Feminist Bookshop to Flourish," 38.

51. Carol Seajay, "Publishers Weekly Covers a Feminist Bookstore in Bookselling and Marketing Column," *Feminist Bookstores Newsletter* 4.6 (April 1981): 4–5, 5.

52. Holt, "Creative Merchandising, Attention to Detail Help a Feminist Bookshop to Flourish," 39.

53. Thomas, "ABA Conference," *Feminist Bookstores Newsletter*, 5.

54. Carol Seajay, "The Women-in-Print Conference Is Coming," *Feminist Bookstores Newsletter* 5.1 (June 1981): 3.

55. Old Wives' Tales, "Five Solid Years," 1981, Old Wives' Tales Bookstore Records, James C. Hormel Gay and Lesbian Center, San Francisco Public Library.

56. Keiko Kubo, "Dear Carol, Darlene, Jesse, and Natalie," 1981, ICI: A Woman's Place Papers, Lesbian Herstory Archives.

57. Here Kubo identifies white collective members refusing to understand the experience of women of color in the women-in-print movement; in this theory building, Kubo is in conversation with other antiracist feminist writers. With savvy satire, Aída Hurtado has described this refusal to understand as "The Pendejo Game," in which white women attempt to maintain white privilege by exhaustingly failing to understand—while at the same time requiring women of color to repeatedly explain—race and racism: "I will ask you to educate me and spend your energies in finding ways of saying things so that I can understand. I will *not* do the same for you" (*The Color of Privilege*, 135). Aimee Carillo Rowe recognizes the refusal to speak as a claim to agency as well, and urges allies to take responsibility "for shared meaning" (*Power Lines*, 184).

58. Seajay, "Women—in—Print. . . . . . . Extravaganza Issue #1," *Feminist Bookstores Newsletter* 5.3 (October 1981): 2, 5, 5.

59. Pell, interview with author.

60. Seajay, "Women—in—Print. . . . . . . Extravaganza Issue #1," 2.

61. Old Wives' Tales, "Summary Other Years," 1986, Old Wives' Tales Bookstore Records, James C. Hormel Gay and Lesbian Center, San Francisco Public Library.

62. Quan, interview with author.

63. Seajay, "Women—in—Print. . . . . . . Extravaganza Issue #1," 2.

64. Seajay, "Women—in—Print. . . . . . . Extravaganza Issue #1," 5.

65. Seajay, "Women—in—Print. . . . . . . Extravaganza Issue #1," 2.

66. Celeste West (unsigned), "Medea Media's Hotterline," *Feminist Bookstores Newsletter* 5.3 (October 1981): 15.

67. Mary Farmer and Susanna Sturgis, "Dear Carol and ♀♀," 25 December 1981, *Feminist Bookstores Newsletter* 5.4 (February 1982): 13.

68. A 1984 collection published by Firebrand Press documents ongoing conversations on the interrelationships and differences between feminist work against anti-Semitism and against racism. In her essay in this three-part collection, Barbara Smith summarizes this tension: "Jewish women's perception of Black and other women of color's indifference to . . . anti-Semitism and Third World women's sense that major segments of the Jewish feminist movement have failed to acknowledge the weight of

their white-skin privilege and capacity for racism, have inevitably escalated suspicion and anger between us" ("Between a Rock and a Hard Place," 67–68). Smith emphasizes that the two kinds of oppression are distinct but related (80). Elly Bulkin's essay follows Smith's, and she raises Celeste West's column in the FBN as an example of anti-Semitism's circulation in US feminism ("Breaking a Cycle," 145). (Bulkin did not cover the conversation that followed in the FBN, though her mention of West's original piece indicates the volume of discussion around this FBN article.) The relationship between antiracism and work against anti-Semitism remains complex and related. In her introduction to the third edition of *This Bridge Called My Back*, Gloria Anzaldúa draws on both to describe the publication history of the collection: "Persephone, a 'white'/Jewish press, and later Kitchen Table Press, a woman of color press, put to use all their resources to produce the book" ("Foreword, 2001," xxxvi). Anzaldúa's inclusion of "white" in quotation marks here emphasizes both her resistance of that totalizing identity and its attendant power as well as her claiming of solidarity between women of color and Jewish women. I connect the two threads here because feminist bookwomen built activist skills around each that are useful for both vital efforts.

69. Adrienne Rich, "Dear Carol," 8 December 1981, *Feminist Bookstores Newsletter* 5.4 (February 1982): 16–17, 16.

70. Irene Klepfisz, "Anti-Semitism in the Lesbian Feminist Movement," from *Womanews*, *Feminist Bookstores Newsletter* 5.4 (February 1982): 18.

71. Farmer and Sturgis, "Dear Carol and ♀♀."

72. Celeste West, "Medea Media (a.k.a. Celeste West) Replies," *Feminist Bookstores Newsletter* 5.4 (February 1982): 25.

73. Carol Seajay, "Carol's Response," *Feminist Bookstores Newsletter* 5.4 (February 1982): 26–28, 26–27.

74. Seajay, "Carol's Response," 26.

75. Susanna Sturgis, "Dear Carol," 18 February 1982, *Feminist Bookstores Newsletter* 6.1 (1982): 3–4, 4.

76. Maureen Brady and Judith McDaniel, "Dear Sister," *Feminist Bookstores Newsletter* 4.3 (October 1980): 7.

77. Maureen Brady, Spinsters, Ink, "Dear Carol," *Feminist Bookstores Newsletter* 5.1 (June 1981): 2.

78. Barbara Smith, "Dear Women," 13 September 1982, *Feminist Bookstores Newsletter* 6.3 (October 1983): 5.

79. Lynn Alderson, SisterWrite Collective, letter to Carol Seajay, *Feminist Bookstores Newsletter* 4.1 (June 1980): 3; Sigrid Nielson, "Dear Carol and FBN," 9 September 1982, *Feminist Bookstores Newsletter* 6.3 (October 1983): 1.

80. Alderson, SisterWrite Collective, letter to Carol Seajay.

81. Laura Memurry, letter to New Words, 9 March 1984, Schlesinger Library, Radcliffe Institute for Advanced Study, Harvard University, 2002-M173, New Words Records.

82. Coindesfemmes Collective, letter to New Words, 7 January 1980, Schlesinger Library, Radcliffe Institute for Advanced Study, Harvard University, 2002-M173, New Words Records.

83. Vivienne Crawford, letter to New Words, 15 March n.d., Schlesinger Library, Radcliffe Institute for Advanced Study, Harvard University, 2002-M173, New Words Records.

84. Gilda Bruckman, interview with author, 23 July 2003.

85. "Arson Destroys Toronto Women's Bookstore," *Feminist Bookstore News* 7.1 (September 1983): 7–8, 8.

86. Carol Seajay, "Northern California Booksellers Association Sues Avon Books," *Feminist Bookstores Newsletter* 6.1 (1982): 15.

87. Old Wives' Tales: Carol Seajay, Sherry Thomas, Pell, Tiana Arruda, and Lydia Bigsby-Hermida, "Six Years Old, Old Wives' Tales Annual Birthday Statement," 1982, Old Wives' Tales Bookstore Records, James C. Hormel Gay and Lesbian Center, San Francisco Public Library.

88. Seajay, "Northern California Booksellers Association Sues Avon Books."

89. Carol Seajay, "The Chains and Us," *Feminist Bookstores Newsletter* 6.1 (1982): 19.

90. Seajay, "The Chains and Us," 19.

91. Seajay, "The Chains and Us," 19.

92. Carol Wilson and Alice Molloy, "This collective," 12 September 1982, ICI: A Woman's Place Papers, Lesbian Herstory Archives.

93. The open letter documents the use within movement organizations of the term "hegemonic feminism" to describe a white feminist ideology that resisted multiple priorities. In her analysis of 1980s feminisms in the United States, Chela Sandoval explained that, in opposition to hegemonic feminism, "U.S. third world feminism functioned as a central locus of possibility, an insurgent social movement that shattered the construction of any one ideology as the single most correct site where truth can be represented" (*Methodology of the Oppressed*, 58.9). That is, the Locked Out Four pointed out, by holding on to a singular feminism Wilson, Molloy, and Lando unraveled their own capacity to resist patriarchal authority rather than replicate it. Darlene Pagano, Elizabeth Summers, Jesse Meredith, and Keiko Kubo, "An Open Letter Regarding the LOCK-OUT AT A WOMAN'S PLACE BOOKSTORE," 18 September 1982, ICI: A Woman's Place Papers, Lesbian Herstory Archives.

94. Carol Seajay referred FBN readers to this coverage. "Collective Crisis and Legal Struggles at ICI-A Woman's Place," *Feminist Bookstores Newsletter* 6.3 (1982): 13.

95. Carol Seajay, "The Struggle for A Woman's Place—Oakland," *Feminist Bookstore News* 6.4/5 (winter 1983): 19.

96. Alice Molloy, Carol Wilson, and Natalie Lando, "One Side," *Feminist Bookstore News* 6.4/5 (winter 1983): 20–22, 21.

97. Darlene Pagano, Elizabeth Summers, Jesse Meredith, and Keiko Kubo, "The Other Side," *Feminist Bookstore News* 6.4/5 (winter 1983): 23–26, 24.

98. Pagano et al., "The Other Side," 24.

99. Pagano et al., "The Other Side," 24.

100. Pagano et al., "The Other Side," 23.

101. Pagano et al., "The Other Side," 23.

102. Teresa Carey, Helen Stewart, and Roma Guy, "The Arbitrators Decision," *Feminist Bookstore News* 6.4/5 (winter 1983): 27–28, 27.

103. Kit Yuen Quan, "Alliances in Question," *Sinister Wisdom*, 34.

104. Such breaks, Aimee Carillo Rowe suggests, seem necessary to transracial feminist alliances: "Recognizing that women-of-color allies may 'tell you what you don't want to hear,' for instance, may allow white women to reframe the critiques women of color share with them—to understand them not as personal attacks, but as *alliance practices*" (*Power Lines*, 175). Kubo, Summers, Meredith, and Pagano's practice of alliance offers a model for using feminist texts (the cassette of Reagon's talk, in this case) to connect across difference and then, in turn, to create new texts (here the articles in the FBN) to add tools to feminist practice. These texts should activate a sense of longing for each other, as Cherríe Moraga enacts in her writing: "so often the women seem to feel no loss, no lack, no absence when women of color are not involved; therefore, there is little desire to change the situation. This has hurt me deeply" ("La Guerra," 33). Valuing the story of the Locked Out Four opens a constant longing in me as a white feminist antiracist ally to read, learn, and talk with women of color and antiracist allies.

105. Quan, "Alliances in Question," 34.

106. Carol Seajay, "Dear SisterBookWomen," *Feminist Bookstores Newsletter* 6.1 (1982): 2.

107. The September 1982 journal came out as the *Feminist Bookstores News*, changing just *Newsletter* to *News*. In November 1982 the journal briefly returned to the *Feminist Bookstores Newsletter*.

108. The style first changed with the September 1982 issue, which appeared booklet style with a yellow paper cover.

109. "The Feminist Bookstore News," *Feminist Bookstore News* 6.4/5 (winter 1983): 2.

110. "New FBN List of Bookstores Available," *Feminist Bookstore News* 6.4/5 (winter 1983): 18.

111. Old Wives' Tales, Collective Meeting Minutes, 30 November 1982, Old Wives' Tales Bookstore Records, James C. Hormel Gay and Lesbian Center, San Francisco Public Library.

112. "Gloria Evangelina Anzaldúa: September 26, 1942–May 15, 2004," memorial booklet, Austin, Texas, 2004, personal collection of the author.

113. Kit Quan, letter to Gloria Anzaldúa, 13 October 1982, box 18, folder 10, Gloria Evangelina Anzaldúa Papers, Benson Latin American Collection, University of Texas Libraries, University of Texas at Austin.

114. Quan, letter to Gloria Anzaldúa, 13 October 1982.

115. Kit Quan and Yumi, letter to Gloria Anzaldúa, 28 July 1983, box 18, folder 10, Gloria Evangelina Anzaldúa Papers, Benson Latin American Collection, University of Texas Libraries, University of Texas at Austin.

116. Carol Seajay, "How FBN Is Compiled," *Feminist Bookstores Newsletter* 5.4 (February 1982): 29.

117. Old Wives' Tales (Carol Seajay, Tiana Arruda, Pell, Lydia Bigsby-Hermida), Collective Meeting Minutes, 11 May 1983, Old Wives' Tales Bookstore Records, James C. Hormel Gay and Lesbian Center, San Francisco Public Library.

118. Old Wives' Tales (Carol Seajay, Tiana Arruda, Pell, Lydia Bigsby-Hermida), Collective Meeting Minutes, 11 May 1983, Old Wives' Tales Bookstore Records, James C. Hormel Gay and Lesbian Center, San Francisco Public Library.

119. Seajay, interview with author.

120. Carol Seajay, "Dear Feminist Publisher, Small Press, Corporation, Sisters, Friends, and Co-Workers in the book-world, and other creditors," letter, 17 June 1983, Feminist Bookstore News Records, James C. Hormel Gay and Lesbian Center, San Francisco Public Library.

121. "Women's Bookstore Publishes a Magazine," *Media Report to Women: What Women Are Thinking and Doing to Change the Communications Media*, Women's Institute for Freedom of the Press 11.5 (September–October 1983): 19.

4. The Feminist Shelf, 1984–1993

1. Kate Rushin and Laura Zimmerman, interview with author, 2 April 2006.

2. Milan Women's Bookstore Collective/Libreria delle Donne, *Sexual Difference*, 92.

3. Womanbooks, Newsletter, spring 1976, Womanbooks Papers, Lesbian Herstory Archives.

4. Common Woman Bookstore Collective, brochure, 1976, BookWoman Papers, Susan Post.

5. Feminist writers have framed and contested the naming and conceptualization of transnational feminisms. I use "transnational" throughout this book to indicate dialogue and relationship building across national borders and within contested nations and to resist the potentially more totalizing sense of "international" or "global," terms that can connote an impossibly homogeneous worldview and reify nation-state borders. For example, Inderpal Grewal assesses the term "global feminism" as carrying a faulty assumption of "common agendas for all women." Instead, she advises, "this global feminism is, however, not global; rather it is transnational, moving through particular connectivities through which communities of feminists are produced" (*Transnational America*, 130). This sense of transnational connectivities builds on her earlier work with Caren Kaplan in which they "use the term 'transnational' to problematize a purely locational politics of global-local or center-periphery" and to acknowledge that "transnational linkages influence every level of social existence" (*Scattered Hegemonies*, 13). Throughout this book I gesture toward transnational connectivities through feminist bookstores that challenged feminist bookwomen in multiple geographies to see their lives, work, and learning as both interconnected and distinct. Chandra Talpade Mohanty and Kathy Davis both offer strategies for transnational feminist dialogue in their approaches to related feminist projects of anticapitalist activism or sharing and reclaiming health information, respectively. This engagement in dialogue without appropriation or exoticization, as I examine toward the end of this chapter, defines my sense of the transnational throughout this book. Chandra Talpade Mohanty, *Feminism without Borders*; Kathy Davis, *The Making of "Our Bodies, Ourselves."*

6. Carol Seajay, interview with author, 17 July 2003; Pell, interview with author, 26 March 2008; May Lui, interview with author, 6 April 2007.

7. Rita Arditti, interview with author, 19 June 2004.

8. Feminist bookstores influenced the development of women's studies on a national level. Kristen Hogan, "Women's Studies in Feminist Bookstores."

9. Janet Romero, interview with author, 26 July 2005.

10. Rather than looking to theorists to validate or explain what bookwomen are doing, I offer bookwomen as theorists in their own right who were codeveloping this explanation of how reading works. In the 1970s the field of reader response theory began to challenge the new critics. New critics claimed that the meaning of a text was located solely within that text, to the exclusion of historical or biographical context. Minnie Bruce Pratt remembers her time as a student at the University of Alabama, a center of new criticism: "We bent ourselves to a closer and closer examination of words, making of writing a world in itself, applying what we understood of the New Criticism by escaping into art, into the story, into the poem. We shut out the feelings, thoughts, and histories of people who lived in another dimension of the world than ours" (*Rebellion*, 157). Reader response critics, many of them feminists, claimed that the context of other readings influenced the meaning readers make of a text and, in the process, of themselves. A feminist ethic of connection and sharing experiences laid the foundation for this textual interconnection. "I began to live as myself," Pratt explains, "because I knew I was not alone. I knew that there were other women to talk to, and there was more than one book to read" (161). Feminist bookwomen had, as evidenced by those opening brochures, understood that "works by women" could "define their context by being brought together in one place" and, in turn, make new reading practices and new readers possible. Bookwomen were reader response theorists.

11. ICI: A Woman's Place, Mail Order Guide, 1973, ICI: A Woman's Place Papers, Lesbian Herstory Archives.

12. New Words Collective, Open letter, 1986, Schlesinger Library, Radcliffe Institute for Advanced Study, Harvard University, 2002-M173, New Words Records.

13. Joni Seager, "New Words Directory," 1986, Schlesinger Library, Radcliffe Institute for Advanced Study, Harvard University, 2002-M173, New Words Records.

14. Joni Seager and Ann Olson, *Women in the World*.

15. Kate Rushin and Laura Zimmerman, interview with author, 2 April 2006.

16. The change from "Dear Third World Women" to "Dear Women of Color" addressed the differences in power among women of color and the reflection on a collective identity within the United States and in transnational alliance. In an open letter in dialogue with Barbara Smith and published in *Bridge*, Mirtha Quintanales reflected on naming in the movement: "Not all Third World women are 'women of color'—if by this concept we mean exclusively 'non-white.' . . . And not all women of color are really Third World—if this term is only used in reference to underdeveloped or developing societies (especially those not allied with any superpower)." Of women of color in the United States naming themselves Third World Women, Quintanales cautioned, "if we extend the concept of Third World to include internally 'colonized' racial and

ethnic minority groups in this country . . . the crucial issue of social and institutional racism and its historic tie to slavery in the U.S. could get diluted, lost in the shuffle" ("I Paid Very Hard for My Immigrant Ignorance," 168). And this new naming meant working against such potential erasures. Gloria Anzaldúa and Cherríe Moraga, Call for submissions, Correspondence, 43.9, Gloria Evangelina Anzaldúa Papers, Benson Latin American Collection, University of Texas Libraries, University of Texas at Austin.

17. Laura Zimmerman, "New Words Collective Changes," *Feminist Bookstore News* 15.2 (July/August 1992): 39–40, 40.

18. Karen L. Kilcup comes just short of offering up bookstore space as a kind of subversive anthology: "If we were able to resist or evade the economic pressures of publishers, perhaps we could envision anthologizing in a comprehensive as well as individual sense, that is, to consider press series (or even the publishing landscape in individual areas) as another form of this activity" ("The Poetry and Prose of Recovery Work," 118).

19. Linda Tuhiwai Smith, "Creating Anthologies and Other Dangerous Practices," 532, 524.

20. Gloria Anzaldúa, "Haciendo caras, una entrada," xvi–xvii.

21. Juana Maria Paz, "Paz Press: Odyssey of a Small Publisher," *Feminist Bookstore News* 7.2 (July 1984): 27–29, 27.

22. Linda Tuhiwai Smith, "Creating Anthologies and Other Dangerous Practices," 521.

23. I want to build on my previous note about bookwomen as reader response theorists. Bookwomen understood not only that books gathered together would change readers' understandings of books, they also knew that this change could transform readers into activists. For example, Rushin knew that a women of color section would make space for women of color in the bookstore and would change how the bookwomen themselves talked with each other. These skills were essential to feminism's larger project of working toward a more just society. Feminist reader response theorists also made such claims. Jane P. Tompkins pointed out that the point of engaging with literature was not necessarily, as the New Critics had argued, "to specify meaning" of the text itself ("The Reader in History," 200). Rather, she reaches back to Greek rhetoricians "for whom mastery of language meant mastery of the state" (226). Put this way, critical engagement with literature could prepare readers to redefine language and influence the structure of society. Feminist scholars, including Minrose Gwin and Katherine McKittrick, trace in literature particularly by women of color a map for a relational future, so literature becomes a tool of learning and connection. Feminist bookwomen shared this sense of the power of interpretation and wielded that power as feminist literary activism. Similarly, in this book I seek to use interpretation of bookwomen's work as a reminder and enactment of their work. For other examples of reader-response-based criticism linking reading practices with social change, see Amy Erdman Farrell, *Yours in Sisterhood*; Maylei Blackwell, "Contested Histories"; and Patrocinio P. Schweickart and Elizabeth A. Flynn, eds., *Reading Sites*. Minrose Gwin, "Space Travel"; Katherine McKittrick, *Demonic Grounds*.

24. M. Jacqui Alexander, *Pedagogies of Crossing*, 258.

25. Alexander, *Pedagogies of Crossing*, 261.

26. M. Jacqui Alexander and Chandra Talpade Mohanty write of the construction of this political solidarity born of racialization: "None of the racial, religious, or class/caste fractures we had previously experienced could have prepared us for the painful racial terrain we encountered here. We were not born women of color, but became women of color here. From African American and U.S. women of color, we learned the peculiar brand of U.S. North American racism and its constricted boundaries of race" ("Introduction: Genealogies, Legacies, Movements," xiv). A few years later, Alexander formulated a practice of becoming women of color as alliance building: "to become women of color we would need to become fluent in each other's histories, to resist and unlearn an impulse to claim most-devastating, one-of-a-kind, defying-comparison oppression" ("Remembering *This Bridge*, Remembering Ourselves," 91).

27. Alexander, *Pedagogies of Crossing*, 259.

28. Alexander, *Pedagogies of Crossing*, 283.

29. Thank you to Ann Cvetkovich for sharing news of *On the Shelf* with me, and to Sara Zia Ebrahimi for generously sending me a copy of her and Naomi Skoglund's film.

30. Founded as a feminist bookstore, Bluestockings shifted to identify as "a radical bookstore" including a focus on feminism. Bluestockings, 19 March 2015, Web.

31. Sara Zia Ebrahimi and Naomi Skoglund, *On the Shelf*.

32. bell hooks, *All about Love*, 11.

33. Chela Sandoval, *Methodology of the Oppressed*, 136.

34. Sandoval, *Methodology of the Oppressed*, 170.

35. Rowe, *Power Lines*, 3.

36. Audre Lorde, *Sister Outsider*.

37. Womanbooks, Newsletter, spring 1976, Womanbooks Papers, Lesbian Herstory Archives.

38. Love, *Feminists Who Changed America, 1963–1975*, 193.

39. ICI: A Woman's Place, flyer, August (1980s), ICI: A Woman's Place Papers, Lesbian Herstory Archives.

40. Laura Zimmerman and Kate Rushin, New Words Bookstore/Cambridge, "A Booksellers Report from Montreal," *Feminist Bookstore News* 11.3 (September 1988): 11–12, 11.

41. Zimmerman and Rushin, "A Booksellers Report from Montreal," 12.

42. Zimmerman and Rushin, "A Booksellers Report from Montreal."

43. Program for the Third International Feminist Book Fair, Montreal, 1988, Feminist Bookstore News Records, James C. Hormel Gay and Lesbian Center, San Francisco Public Library.

44. Ann David, "Belgium," 100.

45. Roberto Doveris, interview with Ximena Pizarro and Paulina Pizarro, "Librería Lila, Literatura Género desde 1984," *Tapiz*, 2 May 2014, 14 November 2014, Web.

46. Streelekha, "Some Aspects of the Feminist Book Trade in India," speech delivered at the 3rd International Feminist Book Fair, Montreal, Schlesinger Library,

Radcliffe Institute for Advanced Study, Harvard University, 2002-M173, New Words Records, 12. The fact of the bookstore itself seemed to provide evidence of more than "fledgling" movements, though certainly the neoliberalism that made a thriving export of North American publishing fed on the economic difference it created between the global North and the global South. For more on this system and feminist interventions, see Urvashi Butalia and Kali for Women founder Ritu Menon, *Making a Difference*.

47. "Quise abrir un espacio para las mujeres, en un momento en que la represión estaba muy presente. Santiago estaba en estado de sitio, y quise instalarme con una librería de género, por mujeres y para mujeres. Era muy estricta y muy acotada al tema mujer, mucho feminismo y teoría de género, así como también escritoras o libros con temáticas de mujeres." Doveris. Translation by the author and Janet Romero.

48. "Entonces también era un centro de distribución de material para las marchas, reuniones para que las mujeres se pudieran reunir y organizer."

49. Streelekha, "Some Aspects of the Feminist Book Trade in India," 13.

50. Zimmerman and Rushin, "A Booksellers Report from Montreal," 11–12.

51. Zimmerman and Rushin, "A Booksellers Report from Montreal," 11.

52. Joni Seager, interview with author, 28 April 2004.

53. New Words, Newsletter, summer 1989, Schlesinger Library, Radcliffe Institute for Advanced Study, Harvard University, 2002-M173, New Words Records.

54. Gilda Bruckman, Mary Lowry, Kate Rushin, Joni Seager, Laura Zimmerman, "Book Donations Wanted, or, from your library to theirs," New Words Newsletter, fall 1988, Schlesinger Library, Radcliffe Institute for Advanced Study, Harvard University, 2002-M173, New Words Records.

55. Seager, interview with author; Sharon Fernandez, interview with author, 31 July 2007.

56. Fernandez, interview with author.

57. For a history of the political forces involved in publishing authors of the global South in the global North and selling these texts back at a high price, see Butalia and Menon, *Making a Difference*. Streelekha, "Some Aspects of the Feminist Book Trade in India," 4.

58. Streelekha, "Some Aspects of the Feminist Book Trade in India," 6. The speech also outlined projects for translating books into the Kannada language of their region (8), publishing literature in Kannada (8), and recording and distributing tapes of women's oral histories (9).

59. Linda Alcoff, "The Problem of Speaking for Others," 5.

60. Later republished as *Bobbi Lee: Indian Rebel* (Toronto: Women's Press, 1990).

61. Susanne de Lotbinière-Harwood, interview of Lee Maracle, 31.

62. The larger geography of the conference in Quebec was also contentious between Quebecois feminists, who supported Quebec separatism, and Indigenous feminists, who supported Indigenous sovereignty, including land rights in and across the borders of the province called Quebec. Kate Rushin and Laura Zimmerman, interview with author.

63. Esther Vise, interview with author, 6 April 2007.

64. Vise, interview with author.

65. Butalia and Menon, *Making a Difference*, 8.

66. Patti Kirk, interview with author, 28 May 2007.

67. Fernandez, interview with author.

68. Vise, interview with author.

69. Fernandez, interview with author.

70. Toronto Women's Bookstore, *Mail-Order Catalogue*, 1970s, accessed at the Toronto Women's Bookstore, 3–4.

71. See Kimberly Springer and Anna Enke for additional corrections to such histories. Reflecting on the devastating erasures of ancestry perpetrated by enslavement, Patricia J. Williams makes a larger argument for why it is important to prioritize the writings by and for women of color and Indigenous women: "I, like so many blacks, have been trying to pin myself down in history, place myself in the stream of time as significant, evolved, present in the past, continuing into the future. To be without documentation is too unsustaining, too spontaneously ahistorical, too dangerously malleable in the hands of those who would rewrite not merely the past but my future as well" ("On Being the Object of Property," 5). Kimberly Springer, *Living for the Revolution*; Anna Enke, *Finding the Movement*.

72. Sharon Fernandez, in collaboration with Cindy Beggs and the Toronto Women's Bookstore Collective, *Women of Colour Bibliography*, cover.

73. Alexander, "Remembering *This Bridge*, Remembering Ourselves," 91.

74. Fernandez, in collaboration with Cindy Beggs and the Toronto Women's Bookstore Collective, *Women of Colour Bibliography*, 10–15.

75. Fernandez et al., *Women of Colour Bibliography*, 41.

76. Fernandez et al., *Women of Colour Bibliography*, 49.

77. Fernandez et al., *Women of Colour Bibliography*, 40.

78. Fernandez et al., *Women of Colour Bibliography*, 75.

79. Fernandez et al., *Women of Colour Bibliography*, 74.

80. Fernandez et al., *Women of Colour Bibliography*, 73.

81. Vise, interview with author.

82. Lynn McClory, interview with author, 29 May 2007.

83. Lorde, *Sister Outsider*, 41.

84. Fernandez, interview with author.

85. Anjula Gogia, interview with author, 21 January 2007.

86. May Lui, interview with author.

87. Carol Seajay, "IV International Feminist Bookfair Barcelona June 19–23, 1990," *Feminist Bookstore News* 13.2 (August 1990): 22.

88. Streelekha, "Some Aspects of the Feminist Book Trade in India," 12.

89. "New Zealand Feminist Bookshops," reprinted from *Herstory* 1988, *Feminist Bookstore News* 11.3 (September 1988): 29–32, 29, 31.

90. Carol Seajay, interview of Susana Sommer, SAGA cofounder, "SAGA: Librería de la Mujer," "The Periodicals Issue," *Feminist Bookstore News* 12.5 (January/February 1990): 39–45, 42.

91. Jean MacRae, "Ms. Crayonhouse the Tokyo Feminist Bookstore," *Feminist Bookstore News* 19.5 (January/February 1997): 19–22, 20.

92. Fembooks, homepage, accessed 15 November 2014, Web.

93. Morgan, "Fem Books: The First Chinese-Language Feminist Bookstore," *Feminist Bookstore News* 18.5 (January/February 1996): 19.

94. Chandra Talpade Mohanty specifically critiques the blanket assumption of economic development policy advocates that "all Third World women have similar problems and needs. Thus, they must have similar interests and goals." Instead, Mohanty points out, "women are constituted as women through the complex interaction between class, culture, religion, and other ideological institutions and frameworks. They are not 'women'—a coherent group—solely on the basis of a particular economic system or policy. Such reductive cross-cultural comparisons result in the colonization of the specifics of daily existence and the complexities of political interests that women of different social classes and cultures represent and mobilize" (*Feminism without Borders,* 30). This call to acknowledge and build dialogue with women across difference echoes Bernice Johnson Reagon's call for taking apart the category of women to enact effective coalition building; in chapter 3 I have documented US feminist bookwomen grappling with this accountability. Reagon, "Coalition Politics: Turning the Century."

95. Carol Seajay, "IV International Feminist Bookfair Barcelona June 19–23, 1990," 22.

96. Carol Seajay, "The Feminist Bookstores Day: ABA Las Vegas," *Feminist Bookstore News* 13.2 (August 1990): 27–33, 27.

97. Carol Seajay, "News from the Bookstores," *Feminist Bookstore News* 13.2 (August 1990): 11–13, 11.

98. Carol Seajay, "Notes from the Computer Table," *Feminist Bookstore News* 13.2 (August 1990): 1.

99. Carol Seajay, "Publisher's Service Award," *Feminist Bookstore News* 13.2 (August 1990): 52, 64, 64.

100. Ruthann Robson, "'The Envelope, Please . . .'"

101. Seajay, "Publisher's Service Award," 52.

102. Audre Lorde, "What Is at Stake in Lesbian and Gay Publishing Today?" *Feminist Bookstore News* 13.2 (August 1990): 45–46. Lorde's speech was republished by *Callaloo* in 1991 and again in 2009.

103. In 2014, Mariame Kaba and Andrea Smith, reflecting on backlash against online conversations among and by women of color, pointed out that learning to be held accountable is essential to a just future: "In an ideal world, women of color's critiques of a feminist future would be welcomed as gifts. . . . Because we know that organizing means failing more often than not, new voices and ideas would be embraced as helping to end global oppression." Kaba and Smith's words here also speak to recently renewed refutations of Smith's claim to Cherokee identity. Indigenous activist scholars in this conversation disagree about how to identify indigeneity and why it matters; certainly the volume of this conversation indicates the depth of the stakes. Our identities (including Smith's identity) still matter since each of us, depending on our racialized

histories, has experienced different realities shaped by the benefits of unearned privilege and the violence of systems of oppression. Smith calls critiques against her "violent identity-policing" ("My Statement on the Current Media Controversy"), and Klee Benally questions the motives and "implications of tearing down such a fierce force in Indigenous feminism at such a critical time in struggle against heteropatriarchy, white supremacy, capitalism, and colonialism" ("Statement from Klee Benally"). Alternatively, Carol Patton Cornsilk emphasizes the violence wrought by cultural appropriation, and Pamela Jumper Thurman cautions that if Smith had "written as an ally, honesty would be woven into the thread" (Thurman et al., "Cherokee Women Scholars' and Activists' Statement on Andrea Smith"). Indigenous feminist scholars Lisa Kahaleole Hall, LeAnne Howe, J. Kēhaulani Kauanui, Jean O'Brien, Kathryn W. Shanley, Noenoe K. Silva, Shannon Speed, Kim Tallbear, and Jacki Thompson Rand point out that, as some writers "express fear that the power of indigenous feminist critique might be undermined by raising these concerns" about Smith's identity, this fear is a reminder that feminists should know the work of many Indigenous feminists, not only one. They call on readers to "extend their reading and citational practices" in order to "strengthen ethical indigenous scholarship," and they claim this ethical reading practice as "one of the core guiding values of indigenous feminisms." Practicing the feminist shelf, they demonstrate the power of listing in their article: "Looking at the US and Canada alone, work by Paula Gunn Allen, Kim Anderson, Beth Brant, Chrystos, Sarah Deer, Ella Deloria, Jennifer Denetdale, Mishuana Goeman, Joy Harjo, Sarah Hunt, E. Pauline Johnson, Winona LaDuke, Emma LaRoque, Lee Maracle, Bea Medicine, Dian Millon, Deborah Miranda, Dory Nason, Melissa K. Nelson, Jessica Bissett-Perea, Kimberly Robertson, Luana Ross, Priscilla Settee, Audra Simpson, Leanne Simpson, Lina Sunseri, Elle-Maija Tailfeathers, and Melanie Yazzie to name only some, demonstrates the vitality and richness of indigenous women's voices that speak against the racial, gendered, and sexualized violences of colonialism" (Hall et al., "Open Letter from Indigenous Women Scholars"). The importance and power of moving beyond tokenism and building dialogue across movements is at the heart of this book. Cornsilk points out, "Too often, a fake Cherokee voice is substituted for an authentic one in academic and public discourse" (Thurman et al., "Cherokee Women Scholars"). This chapter seeks to lay out some of this history to help today's feminists interrupt the appropriation of identities and histories and to build more constructive feminist ethics from here.

104. Carol Seajay, "Indian Spiritual Abuse in Books and Bookstores," *Feminist Bookstore News* 13.2 (August 1990): 35, 38–39, 35.

105. I draw on Craig Womack's definition of literary sovereignty and Robert Allen Warrior's intellectual sovereignty. Craig S. Womack, *Red on Red*; Robert Allen Warrior, *Tribal Secrets*.

106. Andrea Smith, NWSA Indigenous and Native American Task Force, NWSA Women of Color Caucus, "A Position Paper on Indian Spiritual Abuse," *Feminist Bookstore News* 13.2 (August 1990): 36–38, 37.

107. Smith, "A Position Paper on Indian Spiritual Abuse," 37.

108. Smith, "A Position Paper on Indian Spiritual Abuse," 38.

109. Seajay, "Indian Spiritual Abuse," 35.

110. Seajay, "Indian Spiritual Abuse," 38.

111. Seajay, "Indian Spiritual Abuse," 38.

112. Carol Seajay, "Last Minute Flash!," *Feminist Bookstore News* 13.2 (August 1990): 39.

113. Seajay, "Feminist Bookstores Day," 30.

114. Seajay, "Indian Spiritual Abuse," 39.

115. Seajay, "Indian Spiritual Abuse," 38. A year later Alcoff would publish her theory on speaking *with* rather than *for* "others"; her theory built on vibrant ongoing conversations in the women in print movement, including among feminist bookwomen. Alcoff, "The Problem of Speaking for Others."

116. Press Gang printed twenty-five hundred copies of the broadside in 1990. The poem was published in the FBN in 1990 and a year later in Chrystos's collection *Dream On*. Chrystos, "Shame On!," *Feminist Bookstore News* 13.3 (September/October 1990): 22–23.

117. Seajay, "Indian Spiritual Abuse," 39.

118. Seajay, "Indian Spiritual Abuse," 39.

119. "The Toronto Women's Bookstore was the only store present with a formal policy. Their policy was developed with input from a number of sources in the Native communities including the council of elders in their area, various reading lists and an article about 'plastic shamans' published in *Akwesasne Notes*. They don't carry Lynn Andrews' books but recommend other titles to their customers. TWB is quite specific about kinds of titles they *do* carry and the books they *don't* carry and have working (though not written up in a form that's publishable) guidelines to use in evaluating new titles. They brought information that the Aboriginal people in Australia have 'banned' *The Crystal Woman*, the Lynn Andrews title that purports to portray aboriginal spirituality and heritage. TWB's position reflects their clarity that the issue is genocide." Seajay, "Indian Spiritual Abuse," 35, 38.

5. Economics and Antiracist Alliances, 1993–2003

1. Matt Richardson, interview with author, 1 November 2013.

2. I discussed Niobe Erebor's work in chapter 2 and Sharon Fernandez's work in chapter 4. For documentation of Sisterspace, see Gwendolyn Osborne, "A Black Women's Oasis for Reading Empowerment."

3. Carol Seajay, "Notes from the Computer Table," *Feminist Bookstore News* 16.1 (May/June 1993): 1–2, 1.

4. Rowe, *Power Lines*, 175.

5. An invitation to recognize that any feminist success depends on racial justice asks feminists to become critically conscious in a systemic sense, to build methodological thinking. Chela Sandoval offered a vision of such methodological thinking and practice, grounded in the work of US Third World feminism, in what she called a differential consciousness (*Methodology of the Oppressed*, 15), describing the ways feminists of color have created "a tactical subjectivity" with the ability to use different strategies appropriate to the goal (58). She points out that this methodology prioritizes alliances: "the

differential occurs when the affinities inside of difference attract, combine, and relate new constituencies into coalitions of resistance" (63). Many have pointed to Sandoval, as Sandoval pointed to Hurtado, to emphasize that white feminist histories overlook the feminism of women of color, and these white feminist histories have become hegemonic. This book is in conversation with many others working toward a rewriting of feminist remembering for a feminist future of racial justice. Aída Hurtado, "Reflections on White Feminism."

6. Seajay, "Notes from the Computer Table" (1993): 1–2, 1.

7. Anjula Gogia, interview with author, 21 January 2007.

8. Richardson, interview with author.

9. Dawn Lundy Martin, interview with author, 20 October 2013.

10. "ABA Hires PR Firm to Promote Independent Bookstores," Feminist Bookstore News 17.2 (July/August 1994): 22.

11. In 1996, FBN reported on the ABA's sale of the trade show: "In a move that took its membership by surprise, the American Booksellers Association sold its remaining 51% of the ABA Trade Show & Convention to Association Expositions & Services (AE&S), the division of Reed Exhibition Companies that purchased 49% of the show in 1993. The show will be renamed BookExpo America" ("ABA Sells Trade Show—Book Expo America—," Feminist Bookstore News 19.4 [November/December 1996], 7). The issue goes on to point out the growing monopoly held by Reed Exhibition Companies: "Reed Exhibition also produces the London Book Fair, Salon du Livre, and the Tokyo Book Fair. The global parent company, Reed Elsevier also owns Cahners (PW, Library Journal, and School Library Journal), R. R. Bowker (Books in Print and Literary Market Place), as well as book publishing concerns" (8). The ABA used revenue from this sale in part to create BookSense, what the ABA calls an "integrated marketing campaign," a series of services provided to independent booksellers in an attempt to compensate for the chain bookstores' competitive advantages (7–8). "About ABA," BookWeb.org, 2005, American Booksellers Association, 11 August 2004, Web.

12. John Mutter, "ABA Begins to Move on Miami Resolutions."

13. Martin, interview with author.

14. "C's Notes, FBDays 1995," Feminist Bookstore News Records, James C. Hormel Gay and Lesbian Center, San Francisco Public Library.

15. While feminist bookwomen were meeting for the Feminist Bookstore Days before the ABA Convention, feminist publishers also met together. The day after the feminist publishers gathering in 1993, Martha Ayim and Deborah Baretto of the Women's Press in Toronto, Jamie Lee Evans of Aunt Lute Books in San Francisco, and Barbara Smith, Matt Richardson, and Lillien Waller of Kitchen Table: Women of Color Press in Albany met together to talk about their analysis of professionalism as racism in feminist publishing and the vital work of feminists of color in publishing. Martha Ayim, Deborah Baretto, Jamie Lee Evans, Barbara Smith, Matt Richardson, and Lillien Waller, "Packing Boxes and Editing Manuscripts: Women of Color in Feminist Publishing."

16. I attended the Canadian Book Expo in Toronto in 2006, where Mark Avin Domnitz was a featured speaker. Remembering that he had been ABA president during

some of the 1990s, I asked him about his perception of feminist bookwomen's activism in the ABA during that time. He remembered their work vividly and said they had advocated for change "very effectively."

17. Carol Seajay, "ABA 93," *Feminist Bookstore News* 16.2 (August 1993): 37–45, 39.

18. John Mutter and Jim Milliot, "ABA Members," *ABA Newswire*, 7 June 1993, back page, Feminist Bookstore News Records, James C. Hormel Gay and Lesbian Center, San Francisco Public Library.

19. Martin, interview with author.

20. John Mutter, "A Bigger, More Open ABA Convention Seen This Year," 17.

21. Martin, interview with author.

22. John F. Baker with reporting by John Mutter, Daisy Maryles, Paul Hilts, and Sybil Steinberg, "ABA '94: Big, Busy—and a Bit Tense," 14.

23. Arnie Levin, cartoon.

24. Jim Milliot, "The Suit."

25. John Mutter, "Show Time in Los Angeles," 37.

26. Carol Seajay, "What a Scene!," *Feminist Bookstore News* 17.2 (July/August 1994): 17–21, 20.

27. Carol Seajay, comp., "The Feminist Bookstore Network Conference," *Feminist Bookstore News* 17.2 (July/August 1994): 27–30, 30.

28. Feminist bookwomen at the 1994 Feminist Bookstore Days included: Mev Miller and Johanna der Boer of Amazon Bookstore, Minneapolis; Karen Axness and Sandi Torkildson of A Room of One's Own, Madison, Wisconsin; Simone Wallace and Julie Mitchell of Sisterhood Bookstore, Los Angeles; Louise Hager of Women in Print, Vancouver; Jennie Boyd Bull of 31st Street Bookstore, Baltimore; Barb Tatum and Lynn Gigy of Gualala Books, Gualala, CA; Kasha Songer and Dorothy Holland of The Book Garden, Denver; Denise Sallee and Lara Sallee of Raven in the Grove, Pacific Grove, CA; Theresa Corrigan and Ann Corrigan of Lioness Books, Sacramento; Colleen Ernst of Crazy Ladies Bookstore, Cincinnati; Susan Post of BookWoman, Austin, TX; Catherine Sameh and Catherine Tetrick of In Other Words, Portland, OR; Audrey May of Meristem, Memphis; Izzie Harbough of Mother Kali's Books, Eugene, OR; Margie Struble and Gale Kuehling of Sisterspirit Bookstore, San Jose, CA; Kayla Rose of Herland Book-Café, Santa Cruz, CA; Loretta Staub and Debbie Staub of Different Drummer Books, Laguna Beach, CA; River Artz and Diana Iffland of Pandora's Books for Open Minds, Kalamazoo, MI; Carol Walker and Jacki Hampton of Page One, Pasadena, CA; Jane Troxell and Rose Fennel of Lammas Women's Bookstore, Washington, DC; Darlene Pagano and Tricia Lambie of Old Wives' Tales, San Francisco; Evelyn Nellum and Melinda Fayette of Crone's Harvest, Jamaica Plain, MA; Lee Boojaura of Womankind Books, Huntington Station, New York; Genevieve Beenen of Wild Iris Bookstore, Claremont, CA; and representatives from Women and Children First, Chicago. List of Feminist Bookwomen at Feminist Bookstore Days, 1994, Old Wives' Tales Bookstore Records, James C. Hormel Gay and Lesbian Center, San Francisco Public Library.

29. Carol Seajay, "Notes from the Computer Table," *Feminist Bookstore News* 17.2 (July/August 1994): 1.

30. Martin, interview with author.

31. Carol Seajay, comp., "ABA Stands Up for Independents, Fights Unfair/Illegal Discounts in Court," *Feminist Bookstore News* 17.2 (July/August 1994): 23–25, 100, 23–24.

32. Seajay, "ABA Stands Up for Independents," 24.

33. In July 1994, the five defendant publishers requested that the suit be dismissed, claiming in part that the Federal Trade Commission (FTC) had already undertaken a case that addressed the same issues. In 1979 the FTC had filed an investigation of a number of publishers and renewed its investigation at the request of the ABA in 1987 (Baker, "Penguin to Court on ABA Suit"). The investigation of Random House, Simon and Schuster, the Hearst Group, Putnam Berkley, HarperCollins, and Macmillan (none listed in the ABA suit) charged that "through discriminatory pricing practices, the respondent publishers sold or distributed books at lower prices to some retailers than to others. . . . Favored retailer purchasers included the nation's [then] three largest bookstore chains—Waldenbooks, B. Dalton, and Crown Books—and . . . the disfavored purchasers included most, if not all, of the nation's independent booksellers" (Clark, "The Robinson-Patman Act"). In 1992, according to Donald S. Clark, former secretary of the FTC, "the six matters were withdrawn from adjudication so that the Commission could evaluate nonpublic proposed consent agreements signed by complaint counsel and each of the respondents" (Clark, "The Robinson-Patman Act"). When by 1996 the proposed consent agreements had not yet been made public, the FTC dismissed the agreements and the complaints against the publishers, making vague references to the ways it considered the complaints outdated but offering no assurance that this meant illegal practices had ceased. Clark quotes the FTC: "The industry has changed appreciably since the consent agreements were signed. . . . Moreover, it appears that major book publishers generally have modified pricing and promotional practices. Finally, the respondents generally have replaced the principal forms of alleged price discrimination that prompted the complaints—unjustified quantity discounts on trade books and secret discounts on mass market books—with other pricing strategies." In 1994 this dismissal was still in the future, but the ABA noted that the book market had been waiting for an FTC decision since 1987 and alternative action needed to be taken to protect literature. The request to dismiss the suit was denied (Milliot, "Judge Denies Publishers' Motions to Dismiss ABA Suit"). Carol Seajay, "ABA Suit Ready to Go," *Feminist Bookstore News* 18.1 (May/June 1995): 16.

34. Dawn L. Martin, comp., "Women of Color Booklist, Part I," *Feminist Bookstore News* 17.1 (May/June 1994): 41–50, 41.

35. Dawn L. Martin, comp., "Women of Color Booklist, Part II," *Feminist Bookstore News* 17.2 (July/August 1994): 43–51, 58.

36. Carol Seajay and Dawn L. Martin, Introduction, "Women of Color Booklist, Part I," *Feminist Bookstore News* 17.1 (May/June 1994): 41–50, 41.

37. Richardson, interview with author.

38. Ayim et al., "Packing Boxes and Editing Manuscripts," 10.

39. Martin, interview with author.

40. Old Wives' Tales, "Old Wives' Tales Proposed Principles of Unity, Consultant: Susan Colson," August 1992, Old Wives' Tales Bookstore Records, James C. Hormel Gay and Lesbian Center, San Francisco Public Library.

41. Here the San Francisco bookwomen's document echoes a transnational ethic of feminist bookwomen creating bookstores as sites of a relational practice of feminist accountability, as I described in chapter 4. At the 1988 International Feminist Book Fair, Bangalore feminist bookwoman Donna Fernandez explained, on behalf of the feminist Streelekha bookstore, "We would see a special role for the feminist book shops, of endeavoring the widest possible circulation of feminist values through literature." Streelekha, "Some Aspects of the Feminist Book Trade in India," speech delivered at the 1988 Feminist International Book Fair, Montreal, Schlesinger Library, Radcliffe Institute for Advanced Study, Harvard University, 2002-M173, New Words Records, 13.

42. Old Wives' Tales, "Old Wives' Tales Principles of Unity," November 1992, Old Wives' Tales Bookstore Records, James C. Hormel Gay and Lesbian Center, San Francisco Public Library.

43. Old Wives' Tales, "Women's Voices/Old Wives' Tales Presents," 1994, Old Wives' Tales Bookstore Records, James C. Hormel Gay and Lesbian Center, San Francisco Public Library.

44. Old Wives' Tales and the Women's Buildings, "Women's Voices: Readings, Cultural Events, Announcements," 1995, Old Wives' Tales Bookstore Records, James C. Hormel Gay and Lesbian Center, San Francisco Public Library.

45. One of the collective members noted, "I ordered Stone Butch Blues but the only place we could get it was Avon, Kentucky (not too many stone butches there I guess) so . . . it will be a while before we get it." Old Wives' Tales, spiral notebook (collective members' notes to each other), 22 March 1994, Old Wives' Tales Bookstore Records, James C. Hormel Gay and Lesbian Center, San Francisco Public Library.

46. Old Wives' Tales and the Women's Voices events series received city-wide recognition with "a Certificate of Honour by the City of San Francisco through Assemblyperson Carole Migden and the San Francisco Board of Supervisors: The Board salutes OWT Bookstore for 'continuing their commitment to the feminist movement; for the inspirational Women's Voices Series which includes the "Celebration of Children," "Open Michelle Night," and the Thursday Night Reading Series. And finally, for 19 years of providing a safe meeting place for women to share their thoughts, dreams and inspirations. This Board is proud to honour Old Wives' Tales for their outstanding service to the women of San Francisco.'" Old Wives' Tales and the Women's Buildings, "Women's Voices: Readings, Cultural Events, Announcements," 1995, Old Wives' Tales Bookstore Records, James C. Hormel Gay and Lesbian Center, San Francisco Public Library.

47. Victoria Alegría Rosales, letter to Old Wives' Tales, 17 August 1995, Old Wives' Tales Bookstore Records, James C. Hormel Gay and Lesbian Center, San Francisco Public Library.

48. Old Wives' Tales, letter to Victoria Alegría Rosales, 1 September 1995, Old Wives' Tales Bookstore Records, James C. Hormel Gay and Lesbian Center, San Francisco Public Library.

49. Esther Vise, interview with author, 6 April 2007.

50. Gogia, interview with author.

51. For more on the radical work of Desh Pardesh, see Sharon Fernandez, "More Than Just an Arts Festival."

52. Gogia, interview with author.

53. Karen Angel and John F. Baker, "ABA Settles with Hugh Lauter Levin in Price Suit."

54. John F. Baker, "ABA Sues Random on Pricing."

55. Jim Milliot, "Random House and ABA Settle Antitrust Lawsuit."

56. Jim Milliot, "St. Martin's Settles with ABA."

57. Carol Seajay, "ABA Settles with Rutledge Hill & St. Martin's Press," Feminist Bookstore News 19.3 (September/October 1996): 11–12, 11.

58. Carol Seajay, "As We Go to Press . . . ," Feminist Bookstore News 20.4 (November/December 1997): 1; Jim Milliot, "Penguin in Multi-Million Dollar Settlement with ABA."

59. Seajay, "As We Go to Press . . . ," 1.

60. Seajay, "As We Go to Press . . . ," 1.

61. Carol Seajay, "As We Go to Press," Feminist Bookstore News 21.1 (spring 1998): 1–2, 1. For more on Barnes & Noble website collaborations, see Carol Seajay, "Selling Their $ouls: The High Cost of Posting B&N Web Site Banners," Feminist Bookstore News 21.5 (January/February 1999): 55–58.

62. Karla Jay, "Is Lesbian Literature Going Mainstream?," 73.

63. Carol Seajay, "ABA Sues Borders, Barnes & Noble!," Feminist Bookstore News 21.1 (spring 1998): 9–13, 9.

64. Seajay, "ABA Sues Borders," 13.

65. May Lui, interview with author, 6 April 2007.

66. Joseph Barbato, "Chain Superstores," 57.

67. John Mutter, "Altruda."

68. Nora Rawlinson, "Who, Me?"

69. Carol Seajay, "Returns: Too Much Wallpaper on a No-Growth Industry," Feminist Bookstore News 19.4 (November/December 1996): 39–41, 41; Jim Milliot, "Books as Wallpaper? An Explanation for Returns."

70. Gogia, interview with author.

71. Feminist Bookstores' Catalog, Feminist Bookstore Network, 1990s. Thank you to Lynn Makau for gifting me this copy of the Feminist Bookstores' Catalog from Wild Iris Bookstore in Claremont, California.

72. Feminist Bookstores Questionnaire, Feminist Bookstore Network, 1993–2000, Feminist Bookstore News Records, James C. Hormel Gay and Lesbian Center, San Francisco Public Library.

73. Feminist Bookstores' Catalog, Feminist Bookstore Network, 1996, Feminist Bookstore News Records, James C. Hormel Gay and Lesbian Center, San Francisco Public Library.

74. *Feminist Bookstores' Catalog*, Feminist Bookstore Network, 1996, 35.

75. Carol Seajay, "Dear FB-Net Members," Feminist Bookstore Network, 5 December 1997, Feminist Bookstore News Records, James C. Hormel Gay and Lesbian Center, San Francisco Public Library.

76. "ABA Announces Settlement—Industry Abuses Revealed; Association to Continue Struggle"; "A Lawsuit Q&A With ABA President Neal Coonerty."

77. May Lui, interview with author. May Lui had taken her analysis to the Canadian mainstream publishing journal *Quill and Quire* to urge, "It is essential that all publishing houses and booksellers, particularly those based in Toronto and Vancouver, strive to actively promote the hiring of people of colour." May Lui, "Racism in Canadian Publishing Does Exist."

78. Claire Kirch, "The Struggle Continues," 21.

79. Carol Seajay, "Amazon.com Settles with Amazon after Dyke-Baiting Fails," *Feminist Bookstore News* 22.6 (spring 2000): 16–17, 25, 17. (Brackets in FBN.)

80. Lambda Literary Foundation, "Writers Retreat for Emerging LGBTQ Voices," Lambda Literary Foundation, Web, 3 January 2015.

81. Use of "community" as an economic unit drives Miranda Joseph to caution against the uncritical development of community, since capitalism "[depends] on and [generates] community" (*Against the Romance of Community*, xxxi). As a result of this dependence, "The corporate embrace of multiculturalism and diversity is a strategy for the production of subjects for capitalism" (22). For Amazon.com, then, "virtual community" draws on no political commitment or commonality, just the simulation of such. Membership is generated by purchasing a product on their website, which assigned a purchaser her own "gold box" (as in "Kristen's Gold Box"), and the website thereafter welcomed each member by name (as in, "Hello, Kristen Hogan"), followed by the simulated bookstore clerk's "We have recommendations for you." The subsequent disclaimer reveals the system's inability, ultimately, to distinguish one customer from another: "If you're not Kristen Hogan, click here." Carol Seajay explains how web-based bookstores fail women: "I think people still need the connection. You can hardly go to a website and get a good book recommendation. People just don't make that connection; there's 'If you read this, you'll also like that,' but that doesn't help the woman who's going in and really needs specific information about abortion access or AIDS or any health issues, or all the rest of the things that women's bookstores do. So the need, the need is there, the finances are much harder." Seajay, interview with author, 17 July 2003.

82. Gloria Anzaldúa, *Borderlands/La Frontera*, 109.

83. Elizabeth Bernstein, "Amazon.com's Amazing Allure," 24.

84. Seajay, "As We Go to Press," *Feminist Bookstore News* 21.1 (spring 1998): 1–2.

85. Phyllis Tickle and Lynn Garrett, "Amazon Drops Ingram for Religion."

86. Jim Milliot, "Amazon Co-op Riles Independent Houses," 5. Emphasis mine.

87. Milliot, "Amazon Co-op Riles Independent Houses," 8.

88. Sharon Bridgforth, interview with author, 22 July 2005.

89. Carol Seajay, "Amazon.com Settles with Amazon after Dyke-Baiting Fails," 16–17, 25, 17.

90. Melissa Kesler Gilbert and Catherine Sameh, "Building Feminist Educational Alliances in an Urban Community," 191.

91. "Mission Statement," *Otherwise: News from In Other Words Women's Books and Resources* (holiday 2002): 4, In Other Words Bookstore Records, Portland, Oregon.

92. Johanna Brenner, interview with author, 25 February 2004.

93. Lui, interview with author.

94. Alexander, "Remembering *This Bridge*."

95. Kirch, "The Struggle Continues," 21.

96. The last print issue was the "Spring Announcements Issue," 27.6 (2000), and Seajay put out the last email issue that summer.

97. Seajay, interview with author.

98. In the conclusion of her discussion of activism in the marketplace, Anne Enke addresses the frequent misunderstanding of movement-based businesses as strictly businesses. Enke quotes one woman voicing a frequently heard refrain, here about Poor Woman's Paradise coffeehouse: "If it wasn't supported, then maybe it wasn't needed." Enke sees this woman reading "the success or failure of feminist businesses as a reflection of the coherence and relevance of the movement," but Enke reminds us, "Feminist activism was not a commercial venture, however. Nor should the longest-lasting, most explicitly feminist commercial ventures define the historic parameters of the movement" (*Finding the Movement*, 100). In fact, when revolutionaries in capitalist systems close their shop doors, what "wasn't needed" by capital might indeed be this heterogeneous, contentious site of feminist meaning. In this rich history of feminist bookwomen, then, the sites of contention are places where they make meaning and shape a complex identity that could not survive as a capitalist slogan. This is not to wax nostalgic (following Miranda Joseph's titular caution against the romance of community) but rather to suggest, with Enke, that readers not use capitalist measures of success to evaluate the functions of the feminist bookstores. Joseph, *Against the Romance of Community*.

99. Barbara Smith, interview with author, 17 May 2002.

100. Richardson, interview with author.

Epilogue

1. Audre Lorde, *The Black Unicorn*.

2. The last time I met Mill at Pearson airport and made our way back to Roxton Road by bus and subway, the last time to Kensington Market for cheese and fruit, the last time to High Park for a farewell picnic for Zahra and me by our coworkers, the last time to Noah's for dried mango, the last time to Ruthann and Anne-Marie's for dinner, the last time to Zahra's aunt's place near where Janet grew up, the last time bicycling on the elevated pedestrian bridge over the Queen's Quay and up the shore of Lake Ontario, the last time to the bookstore as a recent comanager.

3. Throughout the epilogue I refer to my friends and colleagues at TWB by their first names, immersed in my connection with them. The TWB-related people I men-

tion by first name in this epilogue are, in order of appearance: Zahra Jacobs, Ruthann Lee, Anne-Marie Estrada, Janet Romero, T——, Rose Kazi, OmiSoore Dryden, Alex MacFadyen, and Reena Katz. I am grateful to have been, to be, in relationship with each of you.

4. Zahra Jacobs, interview with author, 7 May 2007.

5. May Lui, interview with author, 6 April 2007.

6. Sharon Fernandez, interview with author, 31 July 2007.

7. Esther Vise, interview with author, 6 April 2007.

8. Carol Seajay, interview with author, 17 July 2003.

9. While I worked on this book, Megan Alrutz finished her book, infused with theories in dialogue around alliances for racial, gender, and youth justice, *Digital Storytelling, Applied Theatre, and Youth: Performing Possibility* (London: Routledge, 2014).

BIBLIOGRAPHY

Interviews

FEMINIST BOOKSTORE NEWS

Martin, Dawn Lundy. Interview with the author. 20 October 2013.
Seajay, Carol. Interview with the author. 17 July 2003.

COMMON WOMAN/BOOKWOMAN, AUSTIN, TEXAS

Post, Susan. Interview with the author. 29 January 2004.
Wouk, Nina, and Susan Post. Interview with the author. 4 June 2002.

IN OTHER WORDS, PORTLAND, OREGON

Brenner, Johanna. Interview with the author. 25 February 2004.

NEW WORDS, CAMBRIDGE, MASSACHUSETTS

Arditti, Rita. Interview with the author. 19 June 2004.
Bruckman, Gilda. Interview with the author. 23 July 2003.
Rushin, Kate, and Laura Zimmerman. Interview with the author. 2 April 2006.
Seager, Joni. Interview with the author. 28 April 2004.

OLD WIVES' TALES, SAN FRANCISCO

Pell. Interview with the author. 26 March 2008.
Quan, Kit. Interview with the author. 11 August 2007.
Seajay, Carol. Interview with the author. 17 July 2003.

TORONTO WOMEN'S BOOKSTORE, TORONTO

Fernandez, Sharon. Interview with the author. 31 July 2007
Gogia, Anjula. Interview with the author. 21 January 2007.
Jacobs, Zahra. Interview with the author. 7 May 2007.
Kirk, Patti. Interview with the author. 28 May 2007.
Lui, May. Interview with the author. 6 April 2007.
McClory, Lynn. Interview with the author. 29 May 2007.
Romero, Janet. Interview with the author. 26 July 2005.
Vise, Esther. Interview with the author. 6 April 2007.

WOMANBOOKS, NEW YORK

Batchelder, Eleanor Olds. Interview with the author. 3 July 2003.
London, Karyn. Interview with the author. 11 December 2003.

AUTHORS

Bridgforth, Sharon. Interview with the author. 22 July 2005.
Turner, Kay. Interview with the author. 3 July 2003.
Turner, Kay. Interview with the author. 11 December 2003.

KITCHEN TABLE: WOMEN OF COLOR PRESS

Richardson, Matt. Interview with the author. 1 November 2013.
Smith, Barbara. Interview with the author. 17 May 2002.

Archival Sources

"C's Notes, FBDays 1995." Feminist Bookstore News Records, James C. Hormel Gay and Lesbian Center, San Francisco Public Library.
"Gloria Evangelina Anzaldúa: September 26, 1942–May 15, 2004." Memorial booklet. Austin, Texas, 2004. Personal collection of the author.
"Mission Statement." *Otherwise: News from In Other Words Women's Books and Resources* (Holiday 2002): 4. In Other Words Bookstore Records, Portland, Oregon.
"Women Acting on Austin." *The Rag.* n.d. BookWoman Papers, Susan Post, Austin, Texas.
Anzaldúa, Gloria, and Cherríe Moraga. Call for submissions. Correspondence, 43.9. Gloria Evangelina Anzaldúa Papers, Benson Latin American Collection, University of Texas Libraries, University of Texas at Austin.
Arditti, Rita, Gilda Bruckman, Mary Lowry, and Jean MacRae. "Statement from New Words on Our Fourth Birthday, April, 1978." Schlesinger Library, Radcliffe Institute for Advanced Study, Harvard University, 2002-M173, New Words Records.

Arruda, Tiana, Carol Seajay, Pell, and Sherry Thomas. "From the Old Wives' Tales Collective." Unknown publication. September 1982. N.p. Old Wives' Tales Bookstore Records, James C. Hormel Gay and Lesbian Center, San Francisco Public Library.

Bluh, Bonnie. "Empty Shelves at Labyris." *Majority Report: The Women's Newspaper.* April 5, 1975. Womanbooks Papers, Lesbian Herstory Archives.

Broner, Esther. Letter to Carol Seajay. 2 November 1979. The Feminist Bookstore News Records, James C. Hormel Gay and Lesbian Center, San Francisco Public Library.

Bruckman, Gilda, Mary Lowry, Kate Rushin, Joni Seager, and Laura Zimmerman. "Book Donations Wanted, or, from your library to theirs." *New Words Newsletter,* fall 1988. Schlesinger Library, Radcliffe Institute for Advanced Study, Harvard University, 2002-M173, New Words Records.

Cablao, Elena. "Feminist Mission de Guadalupe: A Hystory of 2004 Guadalupe, Austin," *Our Lady's Mission* 3.2 (March/April 1983), 1, 14. BookWoman Papers, Susan Post, Austin, Texas.

Coindesfemmes Collective. Letter to New Words, 7 January 1980. Schlesinger Library, Radcliffe Institute for Advanced Study, Harvard University, 2002-M173, New Words Records.

Common Woman Bookstore Collective. Brochure. 1976. BookWoman Papers, Susan Post, Austin, Texas.

Crawford, Vivienne. Letter to New Words, 15 March [n.d.], Schlesinger Library, Radcliffe Institute for Advanced Study, Harvard University, 2002-M173, New Words Records.

Feminist Bookstores' Catalog. Feminist Bookstore Network, 1996. The Feminist Bookstore News Records, James C. Hormel Gay and Lesbian Center, San Francisco Public Library.

Feminist Bookstores' Catalog. Feminist Bookstore Network. 1990s. The Feminist Bookstore News Records, James C. Hormel Gay and Lesbian Center, San Francisco Public Library.

Feminist Bookstores Questionnaire. Feminist Bookstore Network, 1993–2000. The Feminist Bookstore News Records, James C. Hormel Gay and Lesbian Center, San Francisco Public Library.

Fernandez, Sharon, in collaboration with Cindy Beggs and the Toronto Women's Bookstore Collective. *Women of Colour Bibliography.* Toronto: Toronto Women's Bookstore, 1989. Personal collection of the author; copied from original accessed at the Toronto Women's Bookstore.

ICI: A Woman's Place. Flyer. August [1980s]. ICI: A Woman's Place Papers, Lesbian Herstory Archives.

ICI: A Woman's Place. Letter. 1970. ICI: A Woman's Place Papers, Lesbian Herstory Archives.

ICI: A Woman's Place. Mail Order Guide. 1973. ICI: A Woman's Place Papers, Lesbian Herstory Archives.

Kubo, Keiko. "Dear Carol, Darlene, Jesse, and Natalie." 1981. ICI: A Woman's Place Papers, Lesbian Herstory Archives.

Labyris. "Poetry Reading." N.d. Womanbooks Papers, Lesbian Herstory Archives.

List of Feminist Bookwomen at Feminist Bookstore Days. 1994. Old Wives' Tales Bookstore Records, James C. Hormel Gay and Lesbian Center, San Francisco Public Library.

Memurry, Laura. Letter to New Words, 9 March 1984. Schlesinger Library, Radcliffe Institute for Advanced Study, Harvard University, 2002-M173, New Words Records.

Mutter, John, and Jim Milliot. "ABA Members." ABA Newswire, 7 June 1993, back page. Feminist Bookstore News Records, James C. Hormel Gay and Lesbian Center, San Francisco Public Library.

New Words. Newsletter, summer 1989. Schlesinger Library, Radcliffe Institute for Advanced Study, Harvard University, 2002-M173, New Words Records.

New Words. Order form for Paperback Booksmith. 12 March 1974. Schlesinger Library, Radcliffe Institute for Advanced Study, Harvard University, 2002-M173, New Words Records.

New Words Collective. Open letter, 1986. Schlesinger Library, Radcliffe Institute for Advanced Study, Harvard University, 2002-M173, New Words Records.

Old Wives' Tales. "Birthday Statement #2." November 1978. The Feminist Bookstore News Records, James C. Hormel Gay and Lesbian Center, San Francisco Public Library.

Old Wives' Tales. "Birthday Statement." 1976. The Feminist Bookstore News Records, James C. Hormel Gay and Lesbian Center, San Francisco Public Library.

Old Wives' Tales. Collective Meeting Minutes. 30 November 1982. Old Wives' Tales Bookstore Records, James C. Hormel Gay and Lesbian Center, San Francisco Public Library.

Old Wives' Tales (Carol Seajay, Tiana Arruda, Pell, and Lydia Bigsby-Hermida). Collective Meeting Minutes. 11 May 1983. Old Wives' Tales Bookstore Records, James C. Hormel Gay and Lesbian Center, San Francisco Public Library.

Old Wives' Tales. "Five Solid Years." 1981. Old Wives' Tales Bookstore Records, James C. Hormel Gay and Lesbian Center, San Francisco Public Library.

Old Wives' Tales. "Fourth Annual Old Wives' Tales State of the (feminist publishing) World and Third Birthday Statement." November 1979. Old Wives' Tales Bookstore Records, James C. Hormel Gay and Lesbian Center, San Francisco Public Library.

Old Wives' Tales. Letter to Victoria Alegría Rosales, 1 September 1995. Old Wives' Tales Bookstore Records, James C. Hormel Gay and Lesbian Center, San Francisco Public Library.

Old Wives' Tales. "Old Wives' Tales' Fourth Birthday Halloween 1976–Halloween 1980." 1980. Old Wives' Tales Bookstore Records, James C. Hormel Gay and Lesbian Center, San Francisco Public Library.

Old Wives' Tales. "Old Wives' Tales Principles of Unity." November 1992. Old Wives' Tales Bookstore Records, James C. Hormel Gay and Lesbian Center, San Francisco Public Library.

Old Wives' Tales. "Old Wives' Tales Proposed Principles of Unity, Consultant: Susan Colson." August 1992. Old Wives' Tales Bookstore Records, James C. Hormel Gay and Lesbian Center, San Francisco Public Library.

Old Wives' Tales: Carol Seajay, Sherry Thomas, Pell, Tiana Arruda, and Lydia Bigsby-Hermida. "Six Years Old, Old Wives' Tales Annual Birthday Statement." 1982. Old Wives' Tales Bookstore Records, James C. Hormel Gay and Lesbian Center, San Francisco Public Library.

Old Wives' Tales. Spiral notebook (collective members' notes to each other). 22 March 1994. Old Wives' Tales Bookstore Records, James C. Hormel Gay and Lesbian Center, San Francisco Public Library.

Old Wives' Tales. "Summary other years." 1986. Old Wives' Tales Bookstore Records, James C. Hormel Gay and Lesbian Center, San Francisco Public Library.

Old Wives' Tales. "Women's Voices/Old Wives' Tales Presents." 1994. Old Wives' Tales Bookstore Records, James C. Hormel Gay and Lesbian Center, San Francisco Public Library.

Old Wives' Tales and the Women's Buildings. "Women's Voices: Readings, Cultural Events, Announcements." 1995. Old Wives' Tales Bookstore Records, James C. Hormel Gay and Lesbian Center, San Francisco Public Library.

Pagano, Darlene, Elizabeth Summers, Jesse Meredith, and Keiko Kubo. "An open letter regarding the LOCK-OUT AT A WOMAN'S PLACE BOOKSTORE." 18 September 1982. ICI: A Woman's Place Papers, Lesbian Herstory Archives.

Pratt, Minnie Bruce. Letter to Carol Seajay (on *Feminary* stationery). 24 August 1979. The Feminist Bookstore News Records, James C. Hormel Gay and Lesbian Center, San Francisco Public Library.

Program for the 3rd International Feminist Book Fair, Montreal. 14–19 June 1988. Feminist Bookstore News Records, James C. Hormel Gay and Lesbian Center, San Francisco Public Library.

Quan, Kit. Letter to Gloria Anzaldúa. 13 October 1982. Box 18, folder 10. Gloria Evangelina Anzaldúa Papers, Benson Latin American Collection, University of Texas Libraries, University of Texas at Austin.

Quan, Kit, and Yumi. Letter to Gloria Anzaldúa. 28 July 1983. Box 18, folder 10. Gloria Evangelina Anzaldúa Papers, Benson Latin American Collection, University of Texas Libraries, University of Texas at Austin.

Rosales, Victoria Alegría. Letter to Old Wives' Tales. 17 August 1995. Old Wives' Tales Bookstore Records, James C. Hormel Gay and Lesbian Center, San Francisco Public Library.

Russ, Joanna. Letter to the author. 8 August 2004. Personal collection of the author.

Seager, Joni. "New Words Directory." 1986. Schlesinger Library, Radcliffe Institute for Advanced Study, Harvard University, 2002-M173, New Words Records.

Seajay, Carol. "Dear FB-Net Members." Feminist Bookstore Network. 5 December 1997. Feminist Bookstore News Records, James C. Hormel Gay and Lesbian Center, San Francisco Public Library.

Seajay, Carol. "Dear Feminist Publisher, Small Press, Corporation, Sisters, Friends, and Co-Workers in the book-world, and other creditors." Letter. 17 June 1983. Feminist Bookstore News Records, James C. Hormel Gay and Lesbian Center, San Francisco Public Library.

Streelekha. "Some Aspects of the Feminist Book Trade in India." Speech delivered at the 3rd International Feminist Book Fair, Montreal, 14–19 June 1988. Schlesinger Library, Radcliffe Institute for Advanced Study, Harvard University, 2002-M173, New Words Records.

Toronto Women's Bookstore. *Mail-Order Catalogue.* 1970s. Personal collection of the author; copied from original accessed at the Toronto Women's Bookstore.

Toronto Women's Bookstore. Written in Colour Program. 2006. Personal collection of the author.

West Coast Women's Music Festival Staff. "The West Coast Women's Music Festival." Unknown publication. September 1982. N.p. Old Wives' Tales Bookstore Records, James C. Hormel Gay and Lesbian Center, San Francisco Public Library.

Wilson, Carol, and Alice Molloy. "This collective." 12 September 1982. ICI: A Woman's Place Papers, Lesbian Herstory Archives.

Womanbooks. "Agreement made this day of January, 1981." January 1981. Womanbooks Papers, Lesbian Herstory Archives.

Womanbooks. Founding Charter. Womanbooks Papers, Lesbian Herstory Archives.

Womanbooks. Newsletter. Spring 1976. Womanbooks Papers, Lesbian Herstory Archives.

Womanbooks. Newsletter. Summer 1976. Womanbooks Papers, Lesbian Herstory Archives.

Womanbooks. Opening flyer. March 1974. Womanbooks Papers, Lesbian Herstory Archives.

Womanbooks. Spiral notebook (cofounders' notes). 1975. Womanbooks Papers, Lesbian Herstory Archives.

Articles in the Feminist Bookstores Newsletter / Feminist Bookstore News

"ABA Hires PR Firm to Promote Independent Bookstores." *Feminist Bookstore News* 17.2 (July/August 1994): 22.

"ABA Sells Trade Show—Book Expo America—." *Feminist Bookstore News* 19.4 (November/December 1996): 7–8.

"And, No, Sister, You're Not Crazy." *Feminist Bookstores Newsletter* 3.5 (October 1979): 12.

"Arson Destroys Toronto Women's Bookstore." *Feminist Bookstore News* 7.1 (September 1983): 7–8.

"At the 1976 Women in Print Conference." *Feminist Bookstores Newsletter* 1.1 (October 1976): 2.

"Basis of Unity: Developing a Coalition Policy, Success and Process at A Woman's Place—Portland." *Feminist Bookstores Newsletter* 2.2 (1978): 9–12.

"Black Women." *Feminist Bookstores Newsletter* 1.2 (November 1976): 5.

"Blitz." *Feminist Bookstores Newsletter* 3.2 (1979): 11.

"Bookstores." *Feminist Bookstores Newsletter* 2.2 (1978): 3–5.

"Collective Crisis and Legal Struggles at ICI-A Woman's Place." *Feminist Bookstores Newsletter* 6.3 (1982): 13.

"Distributors." *Feminist Bookstores Newsletter* 1.2 (November 1976): 6–7.

"The Feminist Bookstore News." *Feminist Bookstore News* 6.4/5 (winter 1983): 2.

"The Feminist Bookstores Newsletter List of Bookstores." *Feminist Bookstores Newsletter* 3.4 (1979): insert after 4.

"Hot Flash." *Feminist Bookstores Newsletter* 3.6 (February 1980): 5.

"List of Feminist Bookstores and Distributors in the U.S. and Canada." *Feminist Bookstores Newsletter* 1.5 (April 1977): 4–5.

"Marion Zimmer Bradley's." *Feminist Bookstores Newsletter* 1.5 (April 1977): 8.

Masthead. *Feminist Bookstore News* 11.2 (August 1988): 3.

"More from A Woman's Place—Portland." *Feminist Bookstores Newsletter* 2.3 (June 1978): 2–3.

"More from Feminist Literary Agency." *Feminist Bookstores Newsletter* 1.9/10 (December 1977): 6.

"More Rumors." *Feminist Bookstores Newsletter* 1.5 (April 1977): 8.

"Native American Women." *Feminist Bookstores Newsletter* 1.2 (November 1976): 5.

"New FBN List of Bookstores Available." *Feminist Bookstore News* 6.4/5 (winter 1983): 18.

"New Titles." *Feminist Bookstores Newsletter* 1.2 (November 1976): 7–8.

"New Zealand Feminist Bookshops." Reprinted from *Herstory* 1988. *Feminist Bookstore News* 11.3 (September 1988): 29–32.

"Questionnaire." *Feminist Bookstores Newsletter* 1.4 (1977): 1.

"Questionnaire Responses." *Feminist Bookstores Newsletter* 3.1 (1979): 1–2.

"Response to the Bookstore's Coalition Policy—reprinted from A Woman's Place Newsletter." *Feminist Bookstores Newsletter* 2.2 (1978): 13–14.

"Scream Quietly." *Feminist Bookstores Newsletter* 1.8 (1977): 4.

"Should We Accept Subscriptions from Individual Women." *Feminist Bookstores Newsletter* 2.1 (1978): 2.

"Some of You Just." *Feminist Bookstores Newsletter* 4.6 (April 1981): 2.

"Strategy Session: Getting Books Re-Issued." *Feminist Bookstores Newsletter* 1.9/10 (December 1977): 13–14.

"They Went That-a-Way!" *Feminist Bookstores Newsletter* 4.1 (June 1980): 9.

"Things You Always Wanted to Know." *Feminist Bookstores Newsletter* 1.3 (January 1977): 11–12.

"This Is an Advertisement." *Feminist Bookstores Newsletter* 2.4 (August 1978): 7.

"This Is What We Like about FBN." *Feminist Bookstores Newsletter* 2.1 (1978): 3.

"We Want More Of." *Feminist Bookstores Newsletter* 2.1 (1978): 5–6.

"Write Now." *Feminist Bookstores Newsletter* 5.1 (June 1981): 7.

"Young Women & Youth Liberation Booklist." *Feminist Bookstores Newsletter* 1.2 (November 1976): 6.

Alderson, Lynn, for the SisterWrite collective. "Feminist Bookshops in England: A Letter from SisterWrite." *Feminist Bookstores Newsletter* 4.1 (June 1980): 3.

Alderson, Lynn, SisterWrite Collective. Letter to Carol Seajay. *Feminist Bookstores Newsletter* 4.1 (June 1980): 3.

André and Carol Seajay. "Dear Everybody." *Feminist Bookstores Newsletter* 1.2 (November 1976): 4.

André. "An Update." *Feminist Bookstores Newsletter* 1.2 (November 1976): 4.

Brady, Maureen, Spinsters Ink. "Dear Carol." *Feminist Bookstores Newsletter* 5.1 (June 1981): 2.

Brady, Maureen, and Judith McDaniel. "Dear Sister." *Feminist Bookstores Newsletter* 4.3 (October 1980): 7.

Braun, Heide, Sal de Casa/Valencia, interview by Carol Seajay and Rose Katz. "Past and Present: Running the Feminist Bookstores in Spain." *Feminist Bookstore News* 13.4 (November/December 1990): 57–65.

Carey, Teresa, Helen Stewart, and Roma Guy. "The Arbitrators Decision." *Feminist Bookstore News* 6.4/5 (winter 1983): 27–28.

Ellen, New Earth. "Jesse." *Feminist Bookstores Newsletter* 4.4 (December 1980): 3.

Erebor, Niobe. "Dear Sisters." *Feminist Bookstores Newsletter* 3.2 (1979): 1.

Farmer, Mary, and Susanna Sturgis. "Dear Carol and ♀♀." 25 December 1981. *Feminist Bookstores Newsletter* 5.4 (February 1982): 13.

Klepfisz, Irene. "Anti-Semitism in the Lesbian Feminist Movement." Reprinted from *Womanews*. *Feminist Bookstores Newsletter* 5.4 (February 1982): 18.

Lens, Marian, Artemys. "Artemys: Running the Feminist Bookstore in Belgium: Presented by Marian Lens at the Third International Feminist Bookfair." *Feminist Bookstore News* 11.5 (January 1989): 9–10.

London, Karyn. "Books in Spanish." *Feminist Bookstores Newsletter* 1.1 (October 1976): 3–4.

London, Karyn. "Doing Remainders." *Feminist Bookstores Newsletter* 1.9/10 (December 1977): 14–16.

Lorde, Audre. "What Is at Stake in Lesbian and Gay Publishing Today?" *Feminist Bookstore News* 13.2 (August 1990): 45–46.

MacRae, Jean. "Ms. Crayonhouse the Tokyo Feminist Bookstore." *Feminist Bookstore News* 19.5 (January/February 1997): 19–22.

MacRae, Jean, and Gilda Bruckman. "Dear Carol [Seajay] and Andre." *Feminist Bookstores Newsletter* 1.3 (January 1977): 2.

Martin, Dawn L., comp. "Women of Color Booklist, Part I." *Feminist Bookstore News* 17.1 (May/June 1994): 41–50.

Martin, Dawn L., comp. "Women of Color Booklist, Part II." *Feminist Bookstore News* 17.2 (July/August 1994): 43–51, 58.

Meredith, Jesse. "Dear Folks." *Feminist Bookstores Newsletter* 4.5 (marked V.5) (February 1981): 1–2.

Meredith, Jesse. "Organizing for Survival." *Feminist Bookstores Newsletter* 4.3 (October 1980): 1–3.

Molloy, Alice, Carol Wilson, and Natalie Lando. "One Side." *Feminist Bookstore News* 6.4/5 (winter 1983): 20–22.

Morgan, Beth. "Fem Books: The First Chinese-Language Feminist Bookstore." *Feminist Bookstore News* 18.5 (January/February 1996): 17–22.

New Words. "Dear Publisher." *Feminist Bookstores Newsletter* 1.3 (January 1977): 3.

Nichols, Rosalie. "Dear FBN." *Feminist Bookstores Newsletter* 1.4 (1977): 2–3.

Nielson, Sigrid. "Dear Carol and FBN." 9 September 1982. *Feminist Bookstores Newsletter* 6.3 (October 1983): 1.

Old Wives' Tales. "Royalties on Remainders?????" *Feminist Bookstores Newsletter* 5.1 (June 1981): 6.

Pagano, Darlene. "Going to the ABA Convention?" *Feminist Bookstores Newsletter* 2.2 (1978): 1.

Pagano, Darlene, Elizabeth Summers, Jesse Meredith, and Keiko Kubo. "The Other Side." *Feminist Bookstore News* 6.4/5 (winter 1983): 23–26.

Pamela and Leslie, for the Emma Collective. "Good Sisters." *Feminist Bookstores Newsletter* 1.4 (1977): 5–6.

Paz, Juana Maria. "Paz Press: Odyssey of a Small Publisher." *Feminist Bookstore News* 7.2 (July 1984): 27–29.

Rich, Adrienne. "Dear Carol." 8 December 1981. *Feminist Bookstores Newsletter* 5.4 (February 1982): 16–17.

Santos, Isabel. "Dear Sisters." *Feminist Bookstores Newsletter* 1.9/10 (December 1977): 11.

Seajay, Carol, comp. "ABA Stands up for Independents, Fights Unfair/Illegal Discounts in Court." *Feminist Bookstore News* 17.2 (July/August 1994): 23–25, 100.

Seajay, Carol, comp. "The Feminist Bookstore Network Conference." *Feminist Bookstore News* 17.2 (July/August 1994): 27–30.

Seajay, Carol. Interview of Susana Sommer, SAGA cofounder. "SAGA: Librería de la Mujer." "The Periodicals Issue," *Feminist Bookstore News* 12.5 (January/February 1990): 39–45.

Seajay, Carol. "IV International Feminist Bookfair Barcelona June 19–23, 1990." *Feminist Bookstore News* 13.2 (August 1990): 19–23.

Seajay, Carol. "5th International Feminist Book Fair: Amsterdam." *Feminist Bookstore News* 15.2 (July/August 1992): 27–34.

Seajay, Carol. "ABA 93." *Feminist Bookstore News* 16.2 (August 1993): 37–45.

Seajay, Carol. "ABA Settles with Rutledge Hill & St. Martin's Press." *Feminist Bookstore News* 19.3 (September/October 1996): 11–12.

Seajay, Carol. "ABA Sues Borders, Barnes & Noble! Unprecedented Legal Action Alleges Illegal Practices and Seeks Compensation." *Feminist Bookstore News* 21.1 (Spring 1998): 9–13.

Seajay, Carol. "ABA Suit Ready to Go." *Feminist Bookstore News* 18.1 (May/June 1995): 16.

Seajay, Carol. "Africa's First Feminist Bookstore: Binti Legacy." *Feminist Bookstore News* 19.4 (November/December 1996): 15–17.

Seajay, Carol. "Amazon.com Settles with Amazon after Dyke-Baiting Fails." *Feminist Bookstore News* 22.6 (spring 2000): 16–17, 25.

Seajay, Carol. "As We Go to Press . . ." *Feminist Bookstore News* 20.4 (November/December 1997): 1.

Seajay, Carol. "As We Go to Press." *Feminist Bookstore News* 21.1 (spring 1998): 1–2.

Seajay, Carol. "Carol's Response." *Feminist Bookstores Newsletter* 5.4 (February 1982): 26–28.

Seajay, Carol. "The Chains and Us." *Feminist Bookstores Newsletter* 6.1 (1982): 19.

Seajay, Carol. "Dear Bookstore Women." *Feminist Bookstores Newsletter* 2.5/6 (1978): 1–2.

Seajay, Carol. "Dear Friends." *Feminist Bookstores Newsletter* 1.8 (1977): 1–2.

Seajay, Carol. "Dear SisterBookWomen." *Feminist Bookstores Newsletter* 6.1 (1982): 2.

Seajay, Carol. "Dear Sisters." *Feminist Bookstores Newsletter* 1.1 (October 1976): 1.

Seajay, Carol. "Fate of the Newsletter/Advertising?" *Feminist Bookstores Newsletter* 2.1 (1978): 7–8.

Seajay, Carol. "FBN Turns into a List Distribution Center (and More)." *Feminist Bookstores Newsletter* 3.5 (October 1979): 1.

Seajay, Carol. "The Feminist Bookstores Day: ABA Las Vegas." *Feminist Bookstore News* 13.2 (August 1990): 27–33.

Seajay, Carol. "How FBN Is Compiled." *Feminist Bookstores Newsletter* 5.4 (February 1982): 29.

Seajay, Carol. "Indian Spiritual Abuse in Books and Bookstores." *Feminist Bookstore News* 13.2 (August 1990): 35, 38–39.

Seajay, Carol. "Last Minute Flash!" *Feminist Bookstore News* 13.2 (August 1990): 39.

Seajay, Carol. "News from the Bookstores." *Feminist Bookstore News* 13.2 (August 1990): 11–13.

Seajay, Carol. "News from the Bookstores." *Feminist Bookstore News* 18.1 (May/June 1995): 27–29.

Seajay, Carol. "News from the Bookstores." *Feminist Bookstore News* 18.4 (November/December 1995): 15–19.

Seajay, Carol. "Northern California Booksellers Association Sues Avon Books." *Feminist Bookstores Newsletter* 6.1 (1982): 15.

Seajay, Carol. "Notes from the Computer Table." *Feminist Bookstore News* 13.2 (August 1990): 1–2.

Seajay, Carol. "Notes from the Computer Table." *Feminist Bookstore News* 15.2 (July/August 1992): 1.

Seajay, Carol. "Notes from the Computer Table." *Feminist Bookstore News* 16.1 (May/June 1993): 1–2.

Seajay, Carol. "Notes from the Computer Table." *Feminist Bookstore News* 17.2 (July/August 1994): 1.

Seajay, Carol. "Opening Celebration." *Feminist Bookstores Newsletter* 1.1 (October 1976): 5.

Seajay, Carol. "Publisher's Service Award." *Feminist Bookstore News* 13.2 (August 1990): 52, 64.

Seajay, Carol. "Publishers Weekly Covers a Feminist Bookstore in Bookselling and Marketing Column." *Feminist Bookstores Newsletter* 4.6 (April 1981): 4–5.

Seajay, Carol. "Returns: Too Much Wallpaper on a No-Growth Industry." *Feminist Bookstore News* 19.4 (November/December 1996): 39–41.

Seajay, Carol. "Selling Their $ouls: The High Cost of Posting B&N Web Site Banners." *Feminist Bookstore News* 21.5 (January/February 1999): 55–58.

Seajay, Carol. "State of the Newsletter Letter." *Feminist Bookstores Newsletter* 1.9/10 (December 1977): 1–2.

Seajay, Carol. "The Struggle for A Woman's Place—Oakland." *Feminist Bookstore News* 6.4/5 (winter 1983): 19.

Seajay, Carol. "What a Scene!" *Feminist Bookstore News* 17.2 (July/August 1994): 17–21.

Seajay, Carol. "WIND Ended." *Feminist Bookstores Newsletter* 3.3 (1979): 1–2.

Seajay, Carol. "Women—in—Print. . . . . Extravaganza Issue #1." *Feminist Book-stores Newsletter* 5.3 (October 1981): 2, 5.

Seajay, Carol. "The Women-in-Print Conference Is Coming." *Feminist Bookstores Newsletter* 5.1 (June 1981): 3.

Seajay, Carol, André, and Jesse Meredith. "Changes, Changes." *Feminist Bookstores Newsletter* 4.1 (June 1980): 1.

Seajay, Carol, and Judy Grahn. "Some Beginnings: An Interview with Judy Grahn." *Feminist Bookstore News*. 13.1 (May/June 1990): 19–25.

Seajay, Carol, and Dawn L. Martin. Introduction. "Women of Color Booklist, Part I." *Feminist Bookstore News* 17.1 (May/June 1994): 41–50.

Smith, Andrea, NWSA Indigenous and Native American Task Force, NWSA Women of Color Caucus. "A Position Paper on Indian Spiritual Abuse." *Feminist Bookstore News* 13.2 (August 1990): 36–38.

Smith, Barbara. "Dear Women." 13 September 1982. *Feminist Bookstores Newsletter* 6.3 (November 1983): 5.

Sturgis, Susanna. "Dear Carol." 18 February 1982. *Feminist Bookstores Newsletter* 6.1 (1982): 3–4.

Sullivan, George J. "Dear Ms. Wallace." *Feminist Bookstores Newsletter* 2.1 (1978): 9.

Thomas, Sherry, Old Wives' Tales. "ABA Conference." *Feminist Bookstores Newsletter* 5.1 (June 1981): 4–5.

Toronto Women's Bookstore Collective. "Toronto Women's Bookstore Celebrates 15 Years!" *Feminist Bookstore News* 11.5 (January 1989): 24.

West, Celeste (unsigned). "Medea Media's Hotterline." *Feminist Bookstores Newsletter* 5.3 (October 1981): 15.

West, Celeste. "Medea Media (a.k.a. Celeste West) Replies." *Feminist Bookstores Newsletter* 5.4 (February 1982): 25.

Wetstone, Sonya, Wetstone Books & Cheese. "Dear Friends." *Feminist Bookstores Newsletter* 4.4 (December 1980): 2.

Zimmerman, Laura. "New Words Collective Changes." *Feminist Bookstore News* 15.2 (July/August 1992): 39–40.

Zimmerman, Laura, and Kate Rushin, New Words Bookstore/Cambridge. "A Booksellers Report from Montreal." *Feminist Bookstore News* 11.3 (September 1988): 11–12.

Other Published Sources

"ABA Announces Settlement—Industry Abuses Revealed; Association to Continue Struggle." BookWeb.org. 19 April 2001. American Booksellers Association. Web. 13 July 2004.

"About ABA." BookWeb.org. 2005. American Booksellers Association. Web. 11 August 2004.

"A Lawsuit Q&A with ABA President Neal Coonerty." BookWeb.org. 4 May 2001. American Booksellers Association. Web. 13 July 2004.

"Women's Bookstore Publishes a Magazine." *Media Report to Women: What Women Are Thinking and Doing to Change the Communications Media*, Women's Institute for Freedom of the Press 11.5 (September–October 1983): 19.

Alcoff, Linda Martín. "The Problem of Speaking for Others." *Cultural Critique* 20 (winter 1991–92): 5–32.

Alexander, M. Jacqui. *Pedagogies of Crossing: Meditations on Feminism, Sexual Politics, Memory, and the Sacred*. Durham, NC: Duke University Press, 2005.

Alexander, M. Jacqui. "Remembering *This Bridge*, Remembering Ourselves: Yearning, Memory, and Desire." *This Bridge We Call Home: Radical Visions for Transformation*. Ed. Gloria Andzaldúa and AnaLouise Keating. New York: Routledge, 2002. 81–103.

Alexander, M. Jacqui, and Chandra Talpade Mohanty. "Introduction: Genealogies, Legacies, Movements." *Feminist Geneaologies, Colonial Legacies, Democratic Futures*. Ed. M. Jacqui Alexander and Chandra Talpade Mohanty. New York: Routledge, 1997. xiii–xlii.

Allison, Dorothy. *Two or Three Things I Know for Sure*. New York: Dutton, 1995.

Alrutz, Megan. *Digital Storytelling, Applied Theatre, and Youth: Performing Possibility*. London: Routledge, 2014.

Angel, Karen, and John F. Baker. "ABA Settles with Hugh Lauter Levin in Price Suit." *Publishers Weekly*, 13 February 1995: 10.

Anzaldúa, Gloria E. *Borderlands/La Frontera*. San Francisco: Aunt Lute Books, 1987.

Anzaldúa, Gloria E. "Foreword, 2001." *This Bridge Called My Back: Writings by Radical Women of Color*. Ed. Cherríe L. Moraga and Gloria E. Anzaldúa. 3rd ed. Berkeley: Third Woman Press, 2002. xxxiv–xxxix. (Originally published Watertown, MA: Persephone, 1981; reprint, New York: Kitchen Table: Women of Color Press, 1983.)

Anzaldúa, Gloria E. "Haciendo caras, una entrada." *Making Face, Making Soul/Haciendo Caras: Creative and Critical Perspectives by Feminists of Color*. Ed. Gloria Anzaldúa. San Francisco: Aunt Lute, 1990. xv–xxviii.

Anzaldúa, Gloria E., ed. *Making Face, Making Soul/Haciendo Caras: Creative and Critical Perspectives by Feminists of Color*. San Francisco: Aunt Lute, 1990.

Atwood, Margaret. *Robber Bride*. Toronto: McLelland & Stewart, 1993.

Ayim, Martha, Deborah Baretto, Jamie Lee Evans, Barbara Smith, Matt Richardson, and Lillien Waller. "Packing Boxes and Editing Manuscripts: Women of Color in Feminist Publishing." *Sojourner* 18.12 (June 1993): 10–11.

Baker, John F. "ABA Sues Random on Pricing." *Publishers Weekly*, 8 January 1996: 10.

Baker, John F. "Penguin to Court on ABA Suit: Wait for FTC Ruling." *Publishers Weekly*, 11 July 1994: 10.

Baker, John F., with reporting by John Mutter, Daisy Maryles, Paul Hilts, and Sybil Steinberg. "ABA '94: Big, Busy—and a Bit Tense." *Publishers Weekly*, 6 June 1994: 14–15.

Barbato, Joseph. "Chain Superstores: Good Business for Small Presses?" *Publishers Weekly*, 9 November 1992: 56–59.

Batchelder, Eleanor Olds. Email to the author. 15 October 2005.

Benally, Klee. "Statement from Klee Benally (Diné/Russian-Polish)." *Against a Politics of Disposability*. 4 July 2015. Web. (Accessed 23 July 2015.)

Bernstein, Elizabeth. "Amazon.com's Amazing Allure: Word-of-Mouth Publicity and Astute Marketing Make Amazon.com the Most-Talked-About Online Bookseller." *Publishers Weekly*, 4 November 1996: 24–26.

Blackwell, Maylei. *¡Chicana Power! Contested Histories of Feminism in the Chicano Movement*. Austin: University of Texas Press, 2011.

Blackwell, Maylei. "Contested Histories: *Las Hijas de Cuauhtémoc*, Chicana Feminisms, and Print Culture in the Chicano Movement, 1968–1973." In *Chicana Feminisms: A Critical Reader*. Ed. Gabriela F. Arredondo, Aída Hurtado, Norma Klahn, Olga Najera-Ramirez, and Patricia Zavella. Durham, NC: Duke University Press, 2003. 59–89.

Bluestockings. Web. (Accessed 22 April 2014.)

Brand, Dionne. *Love Enough*. Toronto: Knopf Canada, 2014.

Brand, Dionne. *Sans Souci and Other Stories*. Toronto: Williams-Wallace, 1988; Ithaca, NY: Firebrand, 1989.

Bulkin, Elly. "Breaking a Cycle." *Yours in Struggle: Three Feminist Perspectives on Anti-Semitism and Racism*. By Elly Bulkin, Minnie Bruce Pratt, and Barbara Smith. Ithaca, NY: Firebrand Books, 1984. 139–153.

Butalia, Urvashi, and Ritu Menon. *Making a Difference: Feminist Publishing in the South*. Chestnut Hill, MA: Bellagio, 1995.

Chant, Ian. "Lack of Diversity at BEA BookCon Criticized." *Library Journal* 139.10 (1 June 2014): 24.

Childs, Allen. *Sixth Street: Images of America*. Charleston, SC: Arcadia, 2010.

Christian, Meg. *Face the Music*. Los Angeles: Olivia Records, 1977.

Chrystos. *Dream On*. Vancouver: Press Gang, 1991.

Chrystos. "Shame On!" *Feminist Bookstore News* 13.3 (September/October 1990): 22–23.

Clark, Donald S. "The Robinson-Patman Act: Annual Update." Before the Robinson-Patman Act Committee Section of Antitrust Law, Forty-Sixth Annual Spring Meeting, Washington, DC, 2 April 1998. Federal Trade Commission. Web. (Accessed 8 January 2005.)

Collins, Patricia Hill. *Fighting Words: Black Women and the Search for Justice*. Minneapolis: University of Minnesota Press, 1998.

Combahee River Collective. "A Black Feminist Statement." April 1977. *This Bridge Called My Back: Writings by Radical Women of Color*. Ed. Cherríe L. Moraga and Gloria E. Anzaldúa. 3rd ed. Berkeley: Third Woman Press, 2002. 234–244. (Originally published Watertown, MA: Persephone, 1981; reprint, New York: Kitchen Table: Women of Color Press, 1983.)

Córdova, Jeanne. *When We Were Outlaws: A Memoir of Love and Revolution in the 70s*. Midway, FL: Spinsters Ink, 2011.

Cowan, Liza, and Penny House. "California Diary." *Dyke Quarterly* 1 (1975): 70–74.

Cvetkovich, Ann. *An Archive of Feelings: Trauma, Sexuality, and Lesbian Public Cultures*. Durham, NC: Duke University Press, 2003.

Cvetkovich, Ann. *Depression: A Public Feeling*. Durham, NC: Duke University Press, 2012.

Daly, Mary. *Beyond God the Father: Toward a Philosophy of Women's Liberation*. Boston: Beacon Press, 1973.

Daly, Mary. *Gyn/Ecology: The Metaethics of Radical Feminism*. 1978. Boston: Beacon Press, 1990.

Darnton, Robert. "What Is the History of Books?" *Reading in America: Literature and Social History*. Ed. Cathy N. Davidson. Baltimore: Johns Hopkins University Press, 1989. 27–52.

David, Ann. "Belgium." *Lesbian Histories and Cultures: An Encyclopedia*. Vol. 1. Ed. Bonnie Zimmerman. New York: Routledge, 1999. 100–101.

Davis, Kathy. *The Making of Our Bodies, Ourselves: How Feminism Travels across Borders*. Durham, NC: Duke University Press, 2007.

DeVeaux, Alexis. *Warrior Poet: A Biography of Audre Lorde*. New York: Norton, 2004.

Dever, Carolyn. *Skeptical Feminism: Activist Theory, Activist Practice*. Minneapolis: University of Minnesota Press, 2004.

Doveris, Roberto. Interview with Ximena Pizarro and Paulina Pizarro. "Librería Lila, Literatura Género desde 1984." *Tapiz*. 2 May 2014. Web. (Accessed 14 November 2014.)

Ebrahimi, Sara Zia, and Naomi Skoglund. *On the Shelf*. Spark to Fire Productions, 2003.

Enke, Anna. *Finding the Movement: Sexuality, Contested Space, and Feminist Activism*. Durham, NC: Duke University Press, 2007.

Enszer, Julie R. "Have Fun So We Do Not Go Mad in Male Supremacist Heterosexual Amerika: Lesbian-Feminist Poetry in *The Furies*." *Poetry Quarterly* 11.2 (spring 2010). Web.

Faderman, Lillian. *To Believe in Women: What Lesbians Have Done for America, a History*. Boston: Houghton Mifflin, 1999.

Faderman, Lillian, and Stuart Timmons. *Gay L.A.: A History of Sexual Outlaws, Power Politics, and Lipstick Lesbians*. New York: Basic Books, 2006.

Farrell, Amy Erdman. *Yours in Sisterhood: Ms. Magazine and the Promise of Popular Feminism*. Chapel Hill: University of North Carolina Press, 1998.

Felski, Rita. *Beyond Feminist Aesthetics: Feminist Literature and Social Change*. Cambridge, MA: Harvard University Press, 1989.

Fembooks. Homepage. Web. (Accessed 15 November 2014.)

Fenkl, Heinz Insu, and Walter K. Lew, eds. *Kori: The Beacon Anthology of Korean American Fiction*. Boston: Beacon Press, 2001.

Fernandez, Sharon. "More Than Just an Arts Festival: Communities, Resistance, and the Story of Desh Pardesh." *Canadian Journal of Communication* 31.1 (2006): Web.

Flannery, Kathryn Thoms. *Feminist Literacies 1968–1975*. Urbana: University of Illinois Press, 2005.

Fraser, Nancy. "Rethinking the Public Sphere: A Contribution to the Critique of Actually Existing Democracy." *Habermas and the Public Sphere*. Ed. Craig Calhoun. Cambridge, MA: MIT Press, 1999. 109–142. (Originally published 1992.)

Gallo, Marcia M. *Different Daughters: A History of the Daughters of Bilitis and the Rise of the Lesbian Rights Movement*. New York: Carroll and Graf, 2006.

Garber, Linda. "Lesbian Identity Politics: Judy Grahn, Pat Parker, and the Rise of Queer Theory." PhD diss., Stanford University, 1995.

Garza, Alicia. "A Herstory of the #BlackLivesMatter Movement." *Feminist Wire*, 7 October 2014. Web. (Accessed 15 March 2015.)

Gilbert, Melissa Kesler, and Catherine Sameh. "Building Feminist Educational Alliances in an Urban Community." *Teaching Feminist Activism: Strategies for the Field*. Ed. Nancy A. Naples and Karen Bojar. New York: Routledge, 2002. 185–206.

Grahn, Judy. *Edward the Dyke and Other Poems*. Oakland: Women's Press Collective, 1971.

Grahn, Judy. *The Highest Apple: Sappho and the Lesbian Poetic Tradition*. San Francisco: Spinsters Ink, 1985.

Grewal, Inderpal. *Transnational America: Feminisms, Diasporas, Neoliberalisms*. Durham, NC: Duke University Press, 2005.

Grewal, Inderpal, and Caren Kaplan, eds. *Scattered Hegemonies: Postmodernity and Transnational Feminist Practices*. Minneapolis: University of Minnesota Press, 1994.

Gwin, Minrose. "Space Travel: The Connective Politics of Feminist Reading." *Signs* 21.4 (July 1996): 870–905.

Hall, Lisa Kahaleole, LeAnne Howe, J. Kēhaulani Kauanui, Jean O'Brien, Kathryn W. Shanley, Noenoe K. Silva, Shannon Speed, Kim Tallbear, and Jacki Thompson Rand. "Open Letter from Indigenous Women Scholars Regarding Discussions of Andrea Smith." *Indian Country Today*, 7 July 2015. Web. (Accessed 2 August 2015.)

Harris, Bertha. *Lover*. Plainfield, VT: Daughters Press, 1976. Reprint, New York: New York University Press, 1993.

Hitomi, Sawabe. "Yuriko, Da Svidanya." Trans. Eleanor Batchelder and Fumiko Ohno. *Conditions* 17 (1990): 20–29.

Hogan, Kristen. "Women's Studies in Feminist Bookstores: 'All the Women's Studies Women Would Come In.'" *Signs* 33.3 (spring 2008): 595–621.

Holt, Patricia. "Creative Merchandising, Attention to Detail Help a Feminist Bookshop to Flourish." *Publishers Weekly*, 27 March 1981. 36–39.

hooks, bell. *All about Love: New Visions*. New York: Perennial, 2001.

Howe, Florence, ed. *Female Studies II*. Pittsburgh: KNOW Press, 1970.

Hurtado, Aída. *The Color of Privilege: Three Blasphemies on Race and Feminism*. Ann Arbor: University of Michigan Press, 1996.

Hurtado, Aída. "Reflections on White Feminism: A Perspective from a Woman of Color." *Social and Gender Boundaries in the United States*. Ed. Sucheng Chan. New York: Edwin Mellen Press, 1989. 155–186.

Hutchins, Loraine. "Trouble and Mediation at Yosemite." *off our backs* 11.10 (30 November 1981): 12.

Jay, Karla. "Is Lesbian Literature Going Mainstream?" *Ms.*, July/August 1993: 70–73.

Johnson, Barbara. *The Feminist Difference: Literature, Psychoanalysis, Race, and Gender*. Cambridge, MA: Harvard University Press, 1998.

Joseph, Miranda. *Against the Romance of Community*. Minneapolis: University of Minnesota Press, 2002.

Kaba, Mariame, and Andrea Smith. "Interlopers on Social Media: Feminism, Women of Color and Oppression." *truthout*, 1 February 2014. Web. (Accessed 9 October 2014.)

Kafer, Alison. *Feminist, Queer, Crip*. Bloomington: Indiana University Press, 2013.

Kaplan, Caren. *Questions of Travel: Postmodern Discourses of Displacement*. Durham, NC: Duke University Press, 1998.

Kendall, Mikki. "On Feminist Solidarity and Community: Where Do We Go from Here?" *Ebony*, 19 August 2013. Web. (Accessed 15 March 2015.)

Kilcup, Karen L. "The Poetry and Prose of Recovery Work." *On Anthologies: Politics and Pedagogy*. Ed. Jeffrey R. Di Leo. Lincoln: University of Nebraska Press, 2004. 112–141.

Kirch, Claire. "The Struggle Continues: Amazon Bookstore Cooperative's Financial and Psychological Turnaround through Grassroots Support." *Publishers Weekly*, 13 October 2003: 20–21.

Laites, Andrew. *Rebel Bookseller: Why Indie Businesses Represent Everything You Want to Fight For: From Free Speech to Buying Local to Building Communities*. 2nd ed. New York: Seven Stories Press, 2011.

Lambda Literary Foundation. "Writers Retreat for Emerging LGBTQ Voices: Our Sponsors." Lambda Literary Foundation. Web. (Accessed 3 January 2015.)

Lawrence, Bonita, and Enakshi Dua. "Decolonizing Antiracism." *Social Justice* 32.4 (2005): 120–143.

Le Guin, Ursula K. *Dancing at the Edge of the World: Thoughts on Words, Women, Places*. New York: Grove Press, 1989.

Lee, Rachel. "Notes from the (Non)Field: Teaching and Theorizing Women of Color." *Women's Studies on Its Own: A Next Wave Reader in Institutional Change*. Ed. Robyn Wiegman. Durham, NC: Duke University Press, 2002. 82–105.

Lee, Ruthann. "The Production of Racialized Masculinities in Contemporary North American Popular Culture." Ph.D. diss., York University, 2011.

Lesbian Herstory Archives. "History and Mission." Web. (Accessed 9 March 2014.)

Levin, Arnie. Cartoon. *Publishers Weekly*, 6 June 1994: 15.

Liddle, Kathleen. "More Than a Bookstore: The Continuing Relevance of Feminist Bookstores for the Lesbian Community." *Journal of Lesbian Studies* 9.1/2 (2005): 145–159.

Lorde, Audre. *The Black Unicorn: Poems*. New York: Norton, 1978.

Lorde, Audre. "An Open Letter to Mary Daly." *This Bridge Called My Back: Writings by Radical Women of Color*. Ed. Cherríe L. Moraga and Gloria E. Anzaldúa. 3rd ed. Berkeley: Third Woman Press, 2002. 101–105. (Originally published Watertown, MA: Persephone, 1981; reprint, New York: Kitchen Table: Women of Color Press, 1983.)

Lorde, Audre. *Sister Outsider: Essays and Speeches*. New York: Crossing Press, 1984.

de Lotbinière-Harwood, Susanne. Interview of Lee Maracle. "Conversations at the Book Fair: Susanne de Lotbinière-Harwood Interviews Gloria Anzaldúa and Lee Maracle." *Trivia: A Journal of Ideas* 14 (spring 1989): 24–36.

Love, Barbara J., ed. *Feminists Who Changed America*. Champaign: University of Illinois Press, 2006.

Loza, Susana. "Hashtag Feminism, #SolidarityIsForWhiteWomen, and the Other #FemFuture." *Ada: A Journal of Gender, New Media, and Technology* 5 (2014). Web. (Accessed 9 October 2014.)

Lui, May. "Racism in Canadian Publishing Does Exist: Acknowledging It and Understanding It Are the First Steps toward Fighting It." *Quill and Quire* 66.6 (June 2000): 13.

Maguire, Elizabeth. "University Presses and the Black Reader." *The Black Public Sphere: A Public Culture Book*. Ed. The Black Public Sphere Collective. Chicago: University of Chicago Press, 1995. 317–324.

McCormick, Dale. *Against the Grain: A Carpentry Manual for Women*. Iowa City: Iowa City Women's Press, 1977.

McHenry, Elizabeth. *Forgotten Readers: Recovering the Lost History of African American Literary Societies*. Durham, NC: Duke University Press, 2002.

McKittrick, Katherine. *Demonic Grounds: Black Women and the Cartographies of Struggle*. Minneapolis: University of Minnesota Press, 2006.

Messer-Davidow, Ellen. *Disciplining Feminism: From Social Activism to Academic Discourse*. Durham, NC: Duke University Press, 2002.

Milan Women's Bookstore Collective/Libreria delle Donne. *Sexual Difference: A Theory of Social-Symbolic Practice*. Bloomington: Indiana University Press, 1987.

Miller, Laura J. *Reluctant Capitalists: Bookselling and the Culture of Consumption*. Chicago: University of Chicago Press, 2006.

Milliot, Jim. "Amazon Co-op Riles Independent Houses: Publishers View Proposals as Ultimatums." *Publishers Weekly*, 31 May 2004: 5, 8.

Milliot, Jim. "Books as Wallpaper? An Explanation for Returns." *Publishers Weekly*, 11 November 1996: 28.

Milliot, Jim. "Judge Denies Publishers' Motions to Dismiss ABA Suit." *Publishers Weekly*, 13 March 1995: 8.

Milliot, Jim. "Penguin in Multi-Million Dollar Settlement with ABA." *Publishers Weekly*, 6 October 1997: 10.

Milliot, Jim. "Random House and ABA Settle Antitrust Lawsuit." *Publishers Weekly*, 25 November 1996: 10.

Milliot, Jim. "St. Martin's Settles with ABA." *Publishers Weekly*, 19 August 1996: 11.

Milliot, Jim. "The Suit: What It Means—and How the Book People on Both Sides Reacted." *Publishers Weekly*, 6 June 1994: 15.

Mohanty, Chandra Talpade. *Feminism without Borders: Decolonizing Theory, Practicing Solidarity*. Durham, NC: Duke University Press, 2003.

Mohanty, Chandra Talpade, with Biddy Martin. "What's Home Got to Do with It?" *Feminism without Borders: Decolonizing Theory, Practicing Solidarity*. Durham, NC: Duke University Press, 2003. 85–105.

Moraga, Cherríe. "La Guerra." *This Bridge Called My Back: Writings by Radical Women of Color*. Ed. Cherríe L. Moraga and Gloria E. Anzaldúa. 3rd ed. Berkeley: Third Woman Press, 2002. 24–33. (Originally published Watertown, MA: Persephone, 1981; reprint, New York: Kitchen Table: Women of Color Press, 1983.)

Moraga, Cherríe L., and Gloria E. Anzaldúa, eds. *This Bridge Called My Back: Writings by Radical Women of Color*. 3rd ed. Berkeley: Third Woman Press, 2002. (Originally published Watertown, MA: Persephone, 1981; reprint, New York: Kitchen Table: Women of Color Press, 1983.)

Murray, Simone. *Mixed Media: Feminist Presses and Publishing Politics*. London: Pluto Press, 2004.

Mutter, John. "ABA Begins to Move on Miami Resolutions." *Publishers Weekly*, 2 August 1993: 18.

Mutter, John. "Altruda: Books Will Drive Borders Growth." *Publishers Weekly*, 28 June 2004: 13.

Mutter, John. "A Bigger, More Open ABA Convention Seen This Year." *Publishers Weekly*, 9 May 1994: 17, 18.

Mutter, John. "Show Time in Los Angeles." *Publishers Weekly*, 20 June 1994: 36–38.

Ono, Yoko. *Grapefruit: A Book of Instructions + Drawings*. 3rd ed. New York: Simon and Schuster, 2000. (Originally published Tokyo and Bellport, NY: Wunternaum Press, 1964.)

Osborne, Gwendolyn. "A Black Women's Oasis for Reading Empowerment." *Black Issues Book Review* 3.2 (March/April 2001): 28.

Pelligrini, Ann. *Performance Anxieties: Staging Psychoanalysis, Staging Race*. New York: Routledge, 1996.

Pratt, Minnie Bruce. *Rebellion: Essays 1980–1991*. Ithaca, NY: Firebrand Books, 1991.

Puar, Jasbir. *Terrorist Assemblages: Homonationalism in Queer Times*. Durham, NC: Duke University Press, 2007.

Quan, Kit Yuen. "Alliances in Question." *Sinister Wisdom* 52 (spring/summer 1994): 30–37.

Quan, Kit Yuen. "The Girl Who Wouldn't Sing." *Making Face, Making Soul/Haciendo Caras: Creative and Critical Perspectives by Feminists of Color*. Ed. Gloria Anzaldúa. San Francisco: Aunt Lute, 1990. 212–220.

Quintanales, Mirtha. "I Paid Very Hard for My Immigrant Ignorance." *This Bridge Called My Back: Writings by Radical Women of Color*. Ed. Cherríe L. Moraga and Gloria E. Anzaldúa. 3rd ed. Berkeley: Third Woman Press, 2002. 167–174. (Originally published Watertown, MA: Persephone, 1981; reprint, New York: Kitchen Table: Women of Color Press, 1983.)

Raff, Daniel. "Superstores and the Evolution of Firm Capabilities in American Bookselling." *Strategic Management Journal* 21 (2000): 1043–1059.

Ratcliffe, Krista. *Rhetorical Listening: Identification, Gender, Whiteness*. Carbondale: Southern Illinois University Press, 2005.

Rawlinson, Nora. "Who, Me? Afraid of Chain Superstores?" *Publishers Weekly*, 23 November 1992: 8.

Reagon, Bernice Johnson. "Coalition Politics: Turning the Century." *Homegirls: A Black Feminist Anthology*. Ed. Barbara Smith. New York: Kitchen Table: Women of Color Press, 1983. 356–368.

Rich, Adrienne. "Compulsory Heterosexuality and Lesbian Existence." 1980. *Lesbian and Gay Studies Reader*. Ed. Henry Abelove, Michèle Aina Barale, and David M. Halperin. New York: Routledge, 1993. 227–254.

Richardson, Matt. "No More Secrets, No More Lies: African American History and Compulsory Heterosexuality." *Journal of Women's History* 15.3 (autumn 2003): 63–76.

Richardson, Matt. *The Queer Limit of Black Memory: Black Lesbian Literature and Irresolution*. Columbus: Ohio State University Press, 2013.

Robson, Ruthann. "'The Envelope, Please . . .' Winning and Losing in Las Vegas: The Politics of Lesbian and Gay Literary Awards." *Gay Community News* 18.3 (28 July 1990): 7.

Rowe, Aimee Carillo. *Power Lines: On the Subject of Feminist Alliances.* Durham, NC: Duke University Press, 2008.

Rushin, Kate. "The Bridge Poem." *This Bridge Called My Back: Writings by Radical Women of Color.* Ed. Cherríe L. Moraga and Gloria E. Anzaldúa. 3rd ed. Berkeley: Third Woman Press, 2002. lvii–lviii. (Originally published Watertown, MA: Persephone, 1981; reprint, New York: Kitchen Table: Women of Color Press, 1983.)

Russ, Joanna. *The Female Man.* Boston: Bluestreak-Beacon Press, 2000.

Samek, Toni. "Unbossed and Unbought: Booklegger Press, the First Women-Owned American Library Publisher." *Women in Print: Essays on the Print Culture of American Women from the Nineteenth and Twentieth Centuries.* Ed. James P. Danky and Wayne A. Wiegand. Madison: University of Wisconsin Press, 2006. 126–158.

Samek, Toni, K. R. Roberto, and Moyra Lang, eds. *She Was a Booklegger: Remembering Celeste West.* Duluth, MN: Library Juice Press, 2010.

Sandoval, Chela. *Methodology of the Oppressed.* Minneapolis: University of Minnesota Press, 2000.

Sasseen, Rhian. "Unsteady Shelf: The Endangered Landscape of Feminist Bookstores." *Bitch Magazine* 62 (spring 2014): 8–9.

Schweickart, Patrocinio P., and Elizabeth A. Flynn, eds. *Reading Sites: Social Difference and Reader Response.* New York: Modern Language Association of America, 2004.

Seager, Joni, and Ann Olson. *Women in the World: An International Atlas.* New York: Simon and Schuster, 1986.

Segrest, Mab. *Memoir of a Race Traitor.* Cambridge, MA: South End Press, 1994.

Shange, Ntozake. *For Colored Girls Who Have Considered Suicide When the Rainbow Is Enuf.* New York: Scribner, Simon and Schuster, 1997.

Shantz, J. "Pat Parker." In *Writing African American Women: An Encyclopedia of Literature by and about Women of Color.* Ed. Elizabeth Ann Beaulieu. Westport, CT: Greenwood Press, 2006. 692–694.

Short, Kayann. "Publishing Feminism in the Feminist Press Movement, 1969–1994." Ph.D. diss., University of Colorado at Boulder, 1994.

Shub, Ellen. "Wonder Woman." Image, 1976. Postcard, Syracuse Cultural Workers.

Smith, Andrea. "Beyond the Politics of Inclusion: Violence against Women of Color and Human Rights." *Meridians: Feminism, Race, Transnationalism* 4.2 (2004): 120–124.

Smith, Andrea. "My Statement on the Current Media Controversy." *Andrea Smith's Blog.* 9 July 2015. Web. (Accessed 23 July 2015.)

Smith, Barbara. "Between a Rock and a Hard Place: Relationships between Black and Jewish Women." *Yours in Struggle: Three Feminist Perspectives on Anti-Semitism and Racism.* By Elly Bulkin, Minnie Bruce Pratt, and Barbara Smith. Ithaca, NY: Firebrand Books, 1984. 67–87.

Smith, Linda Tuhiwai. "Creating Anthologies and Other Dangerous Practices." *Educational Theory* 50.4 (fall 2000): 521–533.

Sojwal, Senti. "These Are the Last of America's Dying Feminist Bookstores." Mic.com. 5 June 2014. Web. (Accessed 2 November 2014.)

Springer, Kimberly. *Living for the Revolution: Black Feminist Organizations, 1968–1980*. Durham, NC: Duke University Press, 2005.

Taylor, Verta, and Leila J. Rupp. "Women's Culture and Lesbian Feminist Activism: A Reconsideration of Cultural Feminism." *Signs* 19.1 (autumn 1993): 32–61.

Thurman, Pamela Jumper, Ellen Guttillo Whitehouse, Pamela Kingfisher, Carol Patton Cornsilk, and Patti Jo King. "Cherokee Women Scholars' and Activists' Statement on Andrea Smith." *Indian Country Today Media Network*. 17 July 2015. Web. (Accessed 23 July 2015.)

Tickle, Phyllis, and Lynn Garrett. "Amazon Drops Ingram for Religion." *Publishers Weekly*, 14 June 2004: 15.

Tolentino, Jia. "A Chat with Mikki Kendall and Flavia Dzodan about #SolidarityIsFor WhiteWomen." *Hairpin*. 16 August 2013. Web. (Accessed 10 October 2014.)

Tompkins, Jane P. "The Reader in History: The Changing Shape of Literary Response." *Reader-Response Criticism: From Formalism to Post-Structuralism*. Ed. Jane P. Tompkins. Baltimore: Johns Hopkins University Press, 1980. 201–232.

Warrior, Robert Allen. *Tribal Secrets: Recovering American Indian Intellectual Traditions*. Minneapolis: University of Minnesota Press, 1995.

We Need Diverse Books. We Need Diverse Books: Official Campaign Site. Web. (Accessed 10 October 2014.)

Williams, Patricia J. "On Being the Object of Property." *Signs: Journal of Women in Culture and Society* 14.1 (1998): 5–24.

Womack, Craig S. *Red on Red: Native American Literary Separatism*. Minneapolis: University of Minnesota Press, 1999.

Woolf, Virginia. *Three Guineas*. New York: Harcourt, 1966. (Originally published 1938.)

Wouk, Nina. "Dear Tide Collective." Letter. *Lesbian Tide* 5.4 (March/April 1976): 24.

Zavitz, Carol. "The Toronto Women's Bookstore: An Interview with Patti Kirk and Marie Prins." *Canadian Woman Studies* 1.3 (1979): 113–114.

INDEX

Chicana print community, xxii, 199n26,
212–13n73
Christophersen, Ann, 163
Chrystos, 143, 158, 192, 230n103, 231n116
Cliff, Michelle, 90–91
Collins, Patricia Hill, 210–11n38
Combahee River Collective, 76, 215n5,
217n15
Common Woman Bookstore. *See*
BookWoman
Córdova, Jeanne, 1–2
Cornsilk, Carol Patton, 230n103
Cortez, Jayne, 121
Cotera, Martha, 40
Cowan, Liza, 201n19
Crown Books, 96–97, 234
Cullors, Patrisse, xvi
Culpepper, Emily, 23
Cvetkovich, Ann, 200n7, 205n71, 226n29

Daly, Mary, 23–25, 54, 85, 205n63
Darnton, Robert, 212–13n73
Daughters of Bilitis, 1, 99, 206n79
Daughters Press, 29–30, 63, 212
Davis, Kathy, 223n5
Dever, Carolyn, 202–3n37
Diana Press, 2, 10, 63, 206n79
differential consciousness, 12, 202n28,
210–11n38, 231–32n5
Djuna Books (bookstore, New York), 32
Dryden, OmiSoore, 186–87, 239n3
Dua, Enakshi, xvi–xvii
Dyke Quarterly, 10, 201n19

Ebrahimi, Sara Zia, 116–19, 226n29
Edel, Deborah, 5, 65
Editora Das Mulheres (Lisbon), 47
El Salvador Sanctuary Movement, 121
Emma (bookstore, Buffalo), 45
Enke, Anne, 211n50, 228n71, 238n98
Erebor, Niobe, 59–60, 145
Estrada, Anne-Marie, 180–81, 188–89,
238n2, 238–39n3

Faderman, Lillian, xx
Farmer, Mary, 86, 90
FBI, 30, 206n79
Felski, Rita, 200–201n11
Fembooks (bookstore, Taiwan), 137, 196n4
Feminary, 63, 91
feminisms: across identity movements,
xx, 197n18, 215n3, 215n5; Asian North
American feminisms, 5, 73, 88, 103–4,
180–81; Black feminisms, xx, 93,
197n18, 208n13, 210–11n38, 217n15,
228n71; hashtag, xvi–xvii, 196–97n13;
hegemonic, 12, 98, 221n93; Indigenous
feminisms, xix, 73–74, 109–110, 126,
142, 150, 192, 216n10, 227n62,
229–30n103; intersectional, 98–102,
103–4, 221n93; Latina and Chicana feminisms, xix–xxii, 94, 111, 181, 199n26,
212–13n73; South Asian feminisms,
134, 137–38, 159; trans people excluded
from, 2; trans-positive, xiii, 73–74, 164,
182–83, 190, 192; transnational, 15,
122–25, 138, 223n5, 229n94; US Third
World, 221n93, 224–25n16, 231–32n5;
waves analogy for, xx. *See also* Indigenous feminists, lesbian antiracism
feminist accountability: bookwomen
prioritizing economic survival over,
xviii, xxv, 105, 110, 146–50, 153, 168–69,
174, 176; bookwomen's shaping of, xxiii,
72–73, 178, 216–17n14; breaks as indications of attempts at, xviii, 14, 98–102,
185, 202–3n37, 222n104; and collective
accountability, xiv, 34, 125; definition of,
xxiv, 71; as embodied work, xxii, xxvii;
feminist remembering as, xxvi, 188–89,
191–93; home, as making, 192–93;
home, as unsafe for, 216n10; silence
and, 183–84; and solidarity, xvi–xvii; and
white privilege, 24–25, 58–60, 69–70,
87–88, 98–102, 142–43, 182, 186–87, 191,
205n63, 219n57. *See also* feminist love;
feminist shelf; lesbian antiracism

Feminist Bookshop (bookstore, Sydney, Australia), 32

Feminist Bookstore Network: *Feminist Bookstores' Catalog*, 167–69; members' advocacy within ABA, 52–53, 149–50, 152–54; naming of, 83–84, 149; publicity campaigns of, xviii, 197n15

Feminist Bookstore News: ABA coverage in, 147–48; book lists in, xx, 38–40, 112, 115; circulation of, 86, 103, 195n4; closure of, xviii, 177; editorship of, 47–48, 75, 102, 104–5; as feminist accountability mechanism, xiv, 3, 34, 57–60, 89–92, 144; feminist bookwomen's activism, coordinated through, 48–55, 71, 74–75, 83–84; founding of, xxiii, 34–35, 37–38; industry practices revealed in, 42–43, 49, 55–56, 66–67, 95–98; Lambda Literary Awards and, 139; layout changes of, 61, 102–3; lesbian antiracism, as tool for, 98–100, 222n104; mailing lists of, 62–63, 103; market influence of, 48–49, 105, 138; naming of, 102–3, 222n107; subscription policy of, 43–44, 55–56, 75; transnational network through, xxiv, 47, 93, 95, 103, 136–38; "Woman of Color Booklist" in, 156. *See also* Carol Seajay

Feminist Bookstores Newsletter. See Feminist Bookstore News

feminist bookstores: capitalism and movement in conflict in, 4, 15–16, 19–20, 30–32, 61–64, 72–73, 158–59, 161, 164–68; collective meetings in, xix–xx, 3, 6–7, 44–45, 57–60, 70–74, 86–87, 90, 99–105, 133, 182–83; ethical frameworks for, xxiii, 25–26, 71, 103, 184, 205n68, 216–17n14; internal space of, 7, 18, 203n45; as lesbian workspaces, 31, 41–42, 45–46, 206–7n82; love, finding in, 116–20, 184; media coverage of, recent, xix, 197n17; as a movement, 4, 29–33, 36–37, 45, 47, 109,

137, 144, 200n11; as movement sites, 13–14, 17–18, 25–27, 30–32, 57–60, 71–72; and NGOs, 137–38; numbers of, xv, 30, 37–38, 47, 62, 82, 97–98, 103, 195n4; pilgrimages to, 2, 26, 205n66; Principles of Unity documents of, 57–58, 147, 157–58, 169, 213–14n94; in public memory (erased), xiv, xviii, 174, 178, 181; sales numbers of, 73, 97–98, 103, 238; success of, redefined, xxv, 101–2, 138, 147, 177, 178, 184, 191, 238n98; transnational feminist movements sustained by, 15, 93–95, 122–23; and women carpenters, 27–28; as women's studies sites, 4, 16–17, 22–23, 175; as validating intersectional identities, 125, 135, 159, 166, 173. *See also names of individual bookstores*

feminist bookstores, locations mentioned: in Arizona, *see* Womansplace; in California, *see* ICI: A Woman's Place, Mama Bears, Ms. Atlas, Old Wives' Tales, Oracle, Rising Woman, Sisterhood; in Connecticut, *see* Bloodroot, Sonya Wetstone Books; in Florida, *see* Wild Iris; in Georgia, *see* Charis; in Illinois, *see* Women & Children First; in Massachusetts, *see* New Words; in Michigan, *see* Her Shelf; in Minnesota, *see* Amazon Bookstore; in Missouri, *see* New Earth; in New Mexico, *see* Full Circle; in New Zealand, 195n4, *see also* Broadsheet; in New York, *see* Djuna Books, Emma, Labyris, Womanbooks, Women's Works; in Ohio, *see* Crazy Ladies, People Called Women; in Oklahoma, *see* Herland; in Oregon, *see* In Other Words, A Woman's Place; in Pennsylvania, *see* Alternative Booksellers; in Tennessee, *see* Meristem; in Texas, *see* BookWoman, Resistencia; in Utah, *see* Open Book; in Washington, DC, *see* Lammas, Sisterspace; in

Wisconsin, see Room of One's Own,
Sister Moon; in Argentina, see Libreria
de Mujeres, SAGA; in Australia,
see Feminist Bookshop; in Bangladesh, see Narigrantha Prabartana; in
Belgium, see Artemys; in Canada,
see Mother Tongue/Femmes des Paroles, Northern Woman's Bookstore,
Toronto Women's Bookstore, Vancou-
ver Women's Bookstore, Women's
Bookstop; in Chile, see Librería Lila; in
England, 195n4, see also SisterWrite; in
Germany, 196n4, see also Lilith Frauenbuchladen; in India, see Streelekha;
in Italy, see Libreria delle Donne; in
Japan, 195n4, see also Ms. Crayonhouse; in Kenya, see Binti Legacy; in
the Netherlands, see Savannah Bay,
Xantippe; in Pakistan, 195n4; in
Peru, 195n4; in Scotland, see Lavender
Menace; in Spain, 195n4, see also Sal de
Casa; in Taiwan, see Fembooks; in the
Philippines, 195n4
feminist bookwomen: buying practices
as activism, 49, 53–55, 143, 173–74; and
capitalism, interrupting, xxiii–xxiv, 45,
63–65, 84–85, 209–10n33; chain bookstores influenced by, 82, 95–96, 110,
209–10n33; educating readers about,
63–65; feminist books supported by,
xviii, 12–13, 39–40, 48–55, 61–64, 92–
93, 166–67, 172–73, 212n68; feminist
literature, proving market for, 48–49,
54–55, 74–75, 82–85, 110, 139, 163, 166;
industry influence of, xviii, 146, 177;
as lesbians, xix–xx, 3–4, 8–9, 13–14,
27–28, 31, 41, 80–81, 85, 199–200n6;
letter writing campaigns of, 36–37,
49–52, 86; literary advocacy of, erased,
xviii, xix, 162–63, 167, 197n17; professionalization and, 151, 174; publishers,
influence on, 42–43, 48–51, 53, 143,
212n68; as reader response theorists,

111–12, 224n10, 225n23; theoretical
interventions of, xv, xxii, 4–10, 22,
57–60, 98–102, 114–15, 122, 125–26,
133–35, 175, 185, 188, 219n57; transnational alliances among, 47, 121–25,
136–38; as women of color, xix–xx,
xxiv, xxv, 3, 5, 135, 59–60, 71, 73, 78–79,
101–2, 145–46, 178, 183–84. See also
names of individual bookwomen
feminist crafting, 26–27, 29, 64, 81, 205n71
Feminist Federal Credit Union, 30–31,
64, 206n80
feminist futures: accountability in,
72–73, 81, 110, 153; antiracist alliances
for, xxv, 70–73, 178; feminist of color
critiques for, 46, 87–88, 147, 150–51,
222n104, 229–30n103; and queer feminist disability studies, 215n3; this book
as a tool for, xix, xv–xvii, xxvii, 189,
231–32n5; vocabulary and relationship
building for, xxi–xxiii, 25, 71, 101–2,
107, 120, 129–30, 134
feminist literary agents, 48–49
feminist literary counterpublic, 7, 30–31,
43–44, 47, 51, 63, 86, 91, 200–201n11
feminist love, 109–10, 116–20, 136,
185–87; ethic of, xxi, xxv. See also alliance building; feminist accountability
Feminist Press, 63–64, 92–93
feminist publishers: distribution of,
61–64; professionalism as racism
and, 232n15; women of color as, 88,
130–31, 156–57. See also names of feminist
publishers
feminist remembering. See feminist
accountability
feminist shelf: as activist creation, 6, 82,
103–4; as alliance building practice,
133–34; bookstore events as context
for, 80–81, 96, 120–21; definition of,
xxiv, 109; as feminist accountability
practice, 109–10, 135, 142; and feminist
books, understanding of, 50–51; and